D0899336

THE CARIBBEAN SLAVE

STUDIES IN ENVIRONMENT AND HISTORY

Editors

Donald Worster   *Brandeis University*
Alfred Crosby   *University of Texas at Austin*

Advisory Board

Reid Bryson   *Institute for Environmental Studies, University of Wisconsin*
Raymond Dasmann   *College Eight, University of California, Santa Cruz*
E. Le Roy Ladurie   *College de France*
William McNeill   *Department of History, University of Chicago*
Carolyn Merchant   *College of Natural Resources, University of California, Berkeley*
Thad Tate   *Institute of Early American History and Culture, College of William and Mary*

Other Books in the Series

Donald Worster   *Nature's Economy: A History of Ecological Ideas*

THE CARIBBEAN SLAVE

A BIOLOGICAL HISTORY

KENNETH F. KIPLE

Department of History, Bowling Green State University

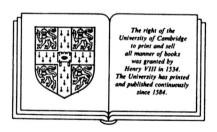

The right of the
University of Cambridge
to print and sell
all manner of books
was granted by
Henry VIII in 1534.
The University has printed
and published continuously
since 1584.

CAMBRIDGE UNIVERSITY PRESS

Cambridge
London   New York   New Rochelle
Melbourne   Sydney

PUBLISHED BY THE PRESS SYNDICATE OF THE UNIVERSITY OF CAMBRIDGE
The Pitt Building, Trumpington Street, Cambridge, United Kingdom

CAMBRIDGE UNIVERSITY PRESS
The Edinburgh Building, Cambridge CB2 2RU, UK
40 West 20th Street, New York NY 10011–4211, USA
477 Williamstown Road, Port Melbourne, VIC 3207, Australia
Ruiz de Alarcón 13, 28014 Madrid, Spain
Dock House, The Waterfront, Cape Town 8001, South Africa

http://www.cambridge.org

© Cambridge University Press 1984

First published 1984
First paperback edition 2002

Library of Congress Cataloguing in Publication data
Kiple, Kenneth F., 1939–
The Caribbean slave.
(Studies in environment and history)
Continues: Another dimension to the Black diaspora.
1981.
Bibliography: p.
Includes index.
1. Blacks – Diseases – West Indies – History. 2. Blacks –
Diseases – Caribbean Area – History. 3. Blacks – West
Indies – Nutrition – History. 4. Blacks – Caribbean Area –
Nutrition – History. 5. Slavery – West Indies – Condition
of slaves. 6. Slavery – Caribbean Area – Condition of
slaves. 7. West Indies – History. 8. Caribbean Area –
History. I. Kiple, Kenneth F., 1939– . Another
dimension to the Black diaspora. II. Title. III. Series.
RA455.K56 1984 616'.008960729 84–19865

ISBN 0 521 26874 5 hardback
ISBN 0 521 52470 9 paperback

For My Parents
JANE AND FRANK KIPLE

God hath made of one blood all nations to dwell
on the face of the earth.

St. Paul, Acts 17:26

CONTENTS

TABLES

PREFACE

This book is the second in a projected trilogy of studies on the biological history of the black in the Americas. In its predecessor, *Another Dimension to the Black Diaspora*, coauthored with Virginia Himmelsteib King, the reader will find a preface containing an apologia of sorts for attempting to unite the research of the biological and social sciences on the one hand, and to bring the findings to bear on black history on the other. Given the historical record of mistreatment of blacks by scientific and pseudoscientific racists, an initial statement of this nature was rightly *de rigueur*. A second would be redundant, and quite possibly presumptuous, for the reception of *Another Dimension* has made clear the existence of a methodologically sophisticated audience of scholars that needs no lecturing from me on either the obscurantism of old nature–nurture arguments or the value of cross-disciplinary research.

If, however, no one spied evil intent in *Another Dimension*, a few were disquieted by the speculative or conjectural nature of some of its arguments, and because portions of the book that follow are similarly vulnerable to such criticism, I feel compelled at this point to say a few words in defense of conjecture.

Broadly defined, the term means to infer from insufficient evidence. Thus, historians in particular, but social scientists as well, who are invariably faced with insufficient evidence are by definition conjecturers every time they assign meaning to a phenomenon or link two or more phenomena into an inferential chain of reasoning. Most historians, however, would not respond kindly if their works were tagged with the label "conjecture" and would respond (perhaps with some heat) that because their inferences were based on the best evidence available, only the reasonability of the inferences should be at issue. And, indeed, at bottom this is all that historians whose data have traditionally been mostly soft and impressionistic can seriously demand of one another – that their inferences be reasonable and derived from the best evidence available.

The plight of those working in what is sometimes called "biohistory" is that much of the data generated by ongoing research in the medical and biological sciences is also soft and many hypotheses are tentative; moreover, there are countless obscure corners and contours in man's recent biological pathway, let alone his distant evolutionary journey. Consequently, like their more traditional counterparts, biological historians find themselves having to make inferences from the best available, often incomplete evidence, which is to say that they are conjecturing. Surely when this occurs they too might ask to be judged on the reasonability of their inferences rather than on the fact that they are making those inferences in the first place.

One of the more useful methods of generating inferences to illuminate man's biological past is to shine the light of modern medical, biological, nutritional, and demographic knowledge upon it. This method is used frequently in the study that follows; that it is laden with some danger should be noted at the outset for in nature little remains static, and certainly not the relationship of a people with their nutritional and epidemiological environment. A related danger is that today's knowledge can easily distort the lenses through which the past is scrutinized.

I have tried to keep these pitfalls in mind and to sidestep them as they came to my attention, but in a work of this nature, covering unfamiliar terrain, I must have inevitably missed a few. For this reason, I have done my best throughout the text, notes, and introductions to indicate clearly what is conjecture and what is fact. Readers will also note that I have taken great pains (which are sometimes unorthodox ones, such as presenting factual information in introductory sections) to add new information as it is needed, while reminding them of numerous old threads of fact and inference that tie together with the new. This inevitably means some repetition here and there, which I hope will prove more helpful than annoying.

If I have done all of this correctly, however, the reader will be able to follow arguments smoothly in both the conjectural and factual realms, and will perhaps come to believe, as I do, that both have important places in cross-disciplinary research and that both can be powerful tools in generating new insights as well as evaluating old tenets.

São João do Estoril,   K.F.K.
Portugal

ACKNOWLEDGMENTS

I wish to thank the *Journal of Interdisciplinary History* for permission to use material from "Deficiency Diseases in the Caribbean," which appeared in volume XI (Autumn, 1980), 197–215 and the University of Sevilla, Spain, for permission to reprint portions of "Dimensión epidemiológica de la esclavitud negra en el Caribe," which originally appeared in *La influencia de España en el Caribe, la Florida y la Luisiana 1500–1800* (Madrid, 1983).

I am enormously indebted to the Joint Committee on Latin American Studies of the Social Science Research Council and the American Council of Learned Societies for a research grant that made possible several research visits to the Caribbean during the years 1977 through 1979. I have an indebtedness of like magnitude to the Bowling Green Faculty Research Committee for research fellowships and travel grants, which have both supported research and permitted full attention to writing for extended periods of time. Indeed Thomas Barry Cobb, Carol L. Davis, and Ronald J. Etzel of Bowling Green's Research Services office have all made so many contributions to my research efforts over the years that it is impossible to express my appreciation adequately. Thanks go as well to the Rockefeller Archive Center for a grant to visit its fine collection in Pocantico Hills, New York, and to the Committee on Research of the American Philosophical Society, whose partial support of an ongoing Brazilian project enabled me to add important materials to this study.

The staffs of many libraries and archives also contributed to this study with their helpfulness and graciousness. I am particulary grateful to those individuals at the National Library of Medicine who always make my visits so pleasant. I have also frequented the libraries of the University of Michigan and the University of Florida in the writing of this study and am most grateful to the staffs of these fine institutions. The staffs of the Rockefeller Archive Center in North Tarrytown, New York, the Archives of Barbados in Bridgetown, the Archives of Jamaica at Spanish Town, the Archivo General and Biblioteca Nacional of the Dominican Republic at Santo Domingo, and the Archivo General and

Biblioteca Nacional of Puerto Rico maintained by the Instituto de Cultura in San Juan were also exceedingly courteous and helpful.

As usual, despite the help of all these fine people, I managed to overlook many volumes and, as usual, Kausalya Padmajaran of the Bowling Green State University Inter-Library Loan Department cheerfully processed literally hundreds of requests to remedy my oversights.

I am indebted to numerous colleagues and friends who read parts of the manuscript, among them David Brion Davis, Robert Dirks, David L. Eltis, August Meier, Joseph C. Miller, Todd L. Savitt, and Bowling Green colleagues James Q. Graham, Donald K. Rowney, and Antonio Buron. My debt to Stanley L. Engerman, who read the entire manuscript, grows larger by the year because (unfortunately for him) I have become so accustomed to his exhaustive and penetrating comments and criticisms that I now regard them as indispensable. Thanks go also to Virginia King for her efforts in *Another Dimension*, which helped to elaborate many of the methodological techniques employed in this study as well. Finally, I would like to express my very considerable gratitude to Frank Smith, my editor at Cambridge University Press, who had the patience and took the time to help make this a much better book than it was when it first reached his desk. The fact that I was not in the United States during the editorial and publication process did not make his task any easier.

Certainly the most pleasant aspect of academic research is that each project brings new friends. It was during the course of writing this study that I entered into a lengthy and richly rewarding correspondence with Joseph C. Miller concerning various aspects of biology and black history, and Chapter 4 in particular reflects many of his splendid suggestions and insights. This study also brought me together with Antonio Buron, whose marvelous patience and sense of humor must have been tried countless times, despite his interest in "cosas del Caribe," by late-night sessions during which he was forced to listen as the book grew. It was also Antonio who helped enormously with the translation of Chapter 1, much of which was originally presented at the Congress of la Rabida in September 1981.

To Connie Willis, I offer a wary thank you for typing the numerous drafts of this study, as well as an apology for all of the "extra" drafts and a promise to do better next time. I am also grateful to Judy Gilbert, who typed the tables and did much of the photocopying, and to Phyllis Wulff, who exerts herself in my behalf in so many thoughtful ways.

When she was still Dalila de Fatima Assis de Sousa, Lila helped to research a part of this project. As Dalila Kiple she more or less graciously permitted our honeymoon in Portugal to be interrupted while I presented the results of that research at a conference in Spain. Subsequently, despite the rigors of her own Ph.D. studies, Lila has read and criticized the study, translated German and French materials, and proved to be an enthusiastic partner in scholarship as well as in marriage.

I am also indebted to Thomas Wilson, a Ph.D. candidate at Bowling Green, who not only read and criticized the manuscript and offered valuable advice based on his own research on black hypertension, but also mobilized both the history department's graduate students and the university's computers to check citations and footnotes.

Special thanks go to Margaret Willard, copy editor, who labored long hours on the manuscript and in so doing saved me much embarrassment.

Finally, my mother, Jane D. Kiple, who always "itches" to lay editorial hands on convoluted sentences and careless reasoning, got perhaps more than she bargained for with this study. The graceless sentences that remain are most assuredly not her fault, and it is to her and to my father who have given me so much over the years that I dedicate this book.

Kenneth F. Kiple

PART I

BACKGROUND AND BIOLOGY

INTRODUCTION

I have called this principle, by which each slight variation, if useful, is preserved, by the term of natural selection.

Charles Darwin (1859)[1]

The islands of the Caribbean have a disjointed history. Politically and economically their past has been written largely from the perspective of their European colonizers and, more recently owing to proximity, from the viewpoint of the United States. Socially and intellectually, their story has been European in orientation uneasily superimposed on a vibrant African culture. That Caribbean history is seen as part of a European or an African past, or even a North American past is unfortunate, but no accident, for the islands are truly artificial. Only the limestone, coral, volcanic rock, and underlying mountain ranges upon which they rest are really of this hemisphere, while most of the flora that adorn them and the fauna that inhabit them are imported. So are the men who dominate them. The original inhabitants, the Arawak and Carib Indians, passed into oblivion long ago, to be replaced manyfold by Africans, Europeans, and, in some places, Asians.

The most important reason for the disappearance of the Indians has to do with still more transients – microorganisms that traveled with the Europeans and the Africans in their hair, on their breath, in their blood, saliva, and bowels. Indeed the newcomers fairly bristled with parasites with whom they had long before worked out a kind of life-preserving compromise. As William McNeill has portrayed the process, man by his migrations, changing habits and altered lifestyle frequently created new conditions for himself, which in turn created new and virulent diseases.[2] He paid for this with the quick demise of many of his numbers, especially the weakest and the most susceptible. The parasites, too, paid a price for, in killing off their hosts, they killed themselves as well. Gradually, therefore, the most virulent strains of a disease died out, along with the most susceptible humans. The survivors – those who had successfully resisted a disease – bred others with resistance, and the result after a number of generations was a relatively mild disease hosted by humans well able to withstand it – usually a childhood disease that a youngster could expect to endure as a kind of rite of passage.

3

Without this immunological initiation, however, one people's child-hood illness became another people's plague and so it was for the American Indians, whose portion of the globe, previously insulated from this interaction of human carriers and pathogens, was suddenly invaded by both. But the Navaho or Sioux or Aztec all ultimately survived the invasion, while Arawak and Carib did not; for only the Caribbean Indians were caught in the vise of both European and African diseases.

Yet the Europeans proved as susceptible to African pathogens as the Indians, while, by contrast, the Africans had long before developed tolerance for most of the diseases that the Europeans were accustomed to. Thus a major theme of Chapter 1 is that disease inexorably selected the black for labor in the tropics and the "myth" that the black was singularly suited for such a role had a sound immunological foundation.

Had the Caribbean Indians not proved so susceptible to foreign pathogens, and had the Europeans not proved so susceptible to African pathogens, it is doubtful that anywhere near the estimated 4.5 million, mostly West African, blacks[3] would have been wrenched from their homeland and delivered to the islands of the Caribbean – all of which serves to illustrate the profound role that disease has played in the history of the West Indies.

Perhaps the extraordinary magnitude of that role can be discerned by recourse to the counterfactual. Suppose for a moment that, instead of discovering a benign disease environment in this hemisphere, the Europeans had sailed into one alive with hostile, virulent microorganisms – but microorganisms to which the Indians had developed resistance. How then might the history of the Americas have been different? A good portion of the answer may lie in the experience of the Europeans in West Africa. There, yellow fever and falciparum malaria formed a deadly barricade just beyond the beaches which Europeans were not really able to penetrate until medical advances of the late nineteenth and early twentieth centuries made it possible.[4]

Had these diseases protected the West Indies instead of West Africa, had the Indians been relatively immune to them, and had West Africa provided a largely disease-free environment, then today we would probably be studying the phenomenon of Europeans moving into West Africa, of black Africans dying in wholesale lots from European and Indian pathogens, and of Indian slave cargoes transferred eastward to till the soils of Africa.[5]

The West Africans' migration to the West Indies marked the beginning of one black odyssey to which the remaining parts of this book are devoted. But (relative to man's time on earth) this odyssey has lasted for only a brief but painful instant, and Part I lingers to consider another black odyssey – their evolutionary journey within West Africa

that molded them genetically and biochemically. Out of this consideration emerges another theme of this study, which is that the ecological
system of West Africa in all its epidemiological and nutritional dimensions wrought a human product that would naturally differ biologically
from the product of, say, a European ecological system.

The portrait of West Africa is not pleasant. Rather the region is starkly
viewed as the home of man's most dangerous diseases and one of the
world's most nutritionally impoverished areas, both yesterday and today. Indeed one of the methods employed in Part I is to scrutinize the
findings of modern studies on West African nutrition, disease, and demography in an effort to assess the health and nutritional status of those
who embarked from West Africa via the slave trade. Many of these
studies were conducted during the first decade or so after World War II
as colonial governments suddenly woke up to the fact that nutrition was
an important component in the health of subject peoples; these surveys
(done before much of an ameliorative effort was made) leave no doubt of
massive malnutrition among a disease-ridden people.

Nor are West African disease and malnutrition recent phenomena,
but rather seem to have been omnipresent facts of life in the region for
millenia. However, just as West Africans developed defenses to survive the diseases of their homeland, they also seem to have developed
an ability to live with malnutrition in a way that few people can. Yet
there is a price for these defenses against both diet and disease, and
that price has been a fearful rate of infant and child mortality, as nature
ensured that only the strongest survived to face the rigors of adult life
in West Africa.

As products of this cruel selection process, the West Africans
destined for the West Indies were incredibly well suited to survive the
nutritional and epidemiological rigors awaiting them from capture,
through the middle passage to the plantations of the New World. That
many did not survive merely underscores the devastating quality of
those rigors.

CHAPTER 1

THE PEOPLES AND THEIR PATHOGENS

Medical statistics have shown, in treating on the different races of mankind the dangers of changing one's position on the globe. . .

G. Pouchet (1864)[1]

Wherever the European has trod, death seems to pursue the aboriginal.

Charles Darwin (1836)[2]

The European

Since the time of Hippocrates weather and climate have been viewed as important determinants of man's state of health. Consequently when western Europeans began their expansion in the fifteenth century, those bold enough to venture into strange and exotic climates did so conscious of considerable risk to their health from illness as well as from the elements. When Europeans died of new diseases, as they frequently did in tropical regions, they first blamed the sun for throwing their "humors" out of balance, then noxious air became the culprit, and finally they found the climate itself at fault by declaring themselves "unacclimated" and therefore susceptible. Yet in newly discovered temperate zones there was little need to blaspheme the sun or the air or the climate, for there the Europeans seemed truly "acclimated" and in fact tended to enjoy a level of health and a longevity superior even to that of those they had left behind in the mother country.[3]

The Europeans have not prospered in the tropics, however, and in the Caribbean, despite long residence, they still constitute only a tiny minority of 5 percent or less on most of the islands they have dominated for so long.[4] Interestingly, the exceptions are found in areas settled by the Iberians, such as the islands of Cuba and Puerto Rico. Thus, in modern Cuba and even more so in Puerto Rico, European phenotypical characteristics prevail, whereas islands such as Jamaica or Barbados are overwhelmingly black.[5]

7

To a great extent the phenomenon of black-English and white-Spanish islands speaks to questions of settlement patterns, imperial philosophies, and an English enthusiasm for the slave trade, not matched by the Spaniards. But to some extent the phenomenon may also speak to questions of disease resistance, and may even hint at a heretofore unexplored reason as to why the Iberians so successfully led the expansion of Europe.

Indeed it might be speculated that history had long been preparing the Iberians immunologically for that adventure. From the time of the Roman conquest they had been exposed sooner rather than later to most of the world's diseases. Iberian soldiers marched on foreign soils, and returned with foreign parasites.[6] The invasion of wave after wave of Germanic tribes would have made a substantial contribution to Iberia's pathogenic environment, as well as to its genetic pool. Then in 711 A.D., with the invasion of the Moors, the Peninsula was put in touch with African diseases, as well as those from as far away as Persia and India. Later, Lisbon became a regular port of call for vessels bound for or returning from the Crusades, while the Catalans exposed themselves to new microorganisms via a newly established Mediterranean empire.

From the fourteenth century on, the Portuguese enjoyed a brisk seaborne commerce with northern Europe and then, following the Portuguese leap to Ceuta on Africa's north coast, came the movement down Africa's west coast which ultimately resulted in an African as well as an East Indian empire. This activity was financed in part by a brisk traffic in black African slaves – so brisk in fact that a few parts of Portugal may have been more black than white by the close of the fifteenth century, and blacks were certainly not unfamiliar sights in Spain.[7]

With this epidemiological background, there should have been few diseases in the European and Mediterranean worlds with which the Iberians had not had some intimate contact, and consequently they should have been reasonably well equipped biologically to survive them.

Certainly it meant that the Iberians were better equipped to ward off many Old World diseases than most other Europeans, which would have spared them casualties during the pestilential invasion accidentally unleashed on New World Indians. However, in the absence of a full-scale medical study of fifteenth-century Iberia, the extent to which the Iberians may have been able to resist African pathogens can only be guessed.[8] There is no question that strains of African malaria reached Iberia in black bodies prior to the Columbian voyages and in fact falciparum malaria was, at least according to one authority, responsible for the depopulation of the Tagus Valley. Yellow fever could also have paid pre-Columbian visits to peninsular coastal cities, while some authorities believe that African treponemas must have reached Spain and Portugal prior even to the Portuguese expansion into Africa.[9]

That the Spaniards may have had immune systems better prepared to ward off African diseases than other Europeans is suggested by the observation of the Abbé Raynal, who wrote in the latter part of the eighteenth century when falciparum malaria and yellow fever were rife in the Caribbean, that "of ten men that go into the Islands, [by nationality] four English die; three French; three Dutch; three Danes; and one Spaniard."[10]

Yet while it may be true that the Spaniards fared better demographically than other Europeans in the West Indies, it is doubtful that they ever lost as few as 10 percent of a group of newcomers to the region prior to the twentieth century. Rather, they too suffered greatly from African pathogens and a host of other illnesses, including many European diseases during the early years of exploration and conquest. These were diseases that overwhelmed bodies weakened considerably by malnutrition and outright starvation – both conditions endemic to the New World's exploration and conquest, and conditions that invite intercurrent infections, weaken the body's ability to resist, and can turn a mild infection into a fatal illness.

Yet, with the establishment of settled government, the Spanish seem to have done well demographically, despite smallpox epidemics and the periodic raids of European privateers, while the Indians of the Caribbean region, by contrast, simply melted away.[11] Thus it is clear that the Spaniards who arrived in the New World were biologically equipped for the biological warfare that accidentally ensued. As far as the Indians were concerned, the Spaniards had much to give and very little to receive.[12]

The Indian

By 1570, only eight decades after Columbus had united the New World with the Old, most of the original inhabitants of the Antilles had disappeared. Indeed only a few short years after Cuba was conquered (1511), the Spanish historian López de Gómara could write that this island "was once heavily populated by Indians; today there are only Spaniards."[13] It has been just fairly recently that scholars have come to understand that it was not so much the impact of a foreign culture that killed the Indians, but rather the impact of foreign disease.

In most of the Americas, however, the result was not obliteration. Rather as Alfred Crosby has pointed out in his splendid study, *The Columbian Exchange: Biological and Social Consequences of 1492*, the pattern for most Indian populations was not to die out completely, but rather to suffer a "sharp diminution of numbers, which was then followed by renewed population growth. . . ." Diminution occurred as immunologically defenseless peoples suddenly found themselves the target of a bewildering blitzkrieg of European diseases with smallpox, which apparently reached the Americas in 1507, leading what P.M. Ashburn has called *The Ranks of Death.*[14]

Much of the reason for the Indian susceptibility is that they had lived for millennia little troubled by pathogens that were tormenting most of the world's peoples. In part this epidemiological exemption occurred because most Indian populations had not attained a sufficient density to sustain many of the diseases in question. In part too the Indians had few large domesticated animals (with whom man shares so many illnesses) to infect them.[15] The major reason, however, stemmed from the isolation of America from a world that in establishing higher and higher levels of civilization (and consequently dense urban populations) had inadvertently stimulated higher and higher levels of parasite activity as well.[16]

Thus, speaking in general terms, the Indians succumbed in huge numbers to the onslaught of epidemic disease because of immunological "virginity" as it were. The faces of many a conqueror bore the scars of smallpox. As youngsters they had entertained the usual European childhood illnesses, as had their parents and grandparents before them, and out of this had emerged a tolerance of sorts for their pathogens – a tolerance that the Indians most certainly did not enjoy.[17]

Yet under this general umbrella there were also very specific reasons for the devastation of the Indian populations. One had to do with the age of the victims. Many diseases run a relatively mild course in children, but deal much more harshly with adults, especially young adults. Because they had no opportunity to earn their immunities during childhood, Indians of all ages – but especially those of reproductive age – fell prey to the new pathogens.[18]

A second reason for the demographic disaster stemmed from the variety of new pathogens which arrived with the Europeans. Had each of the new diseases descended on the Indians in orderly fashion, spacing themselves to give their hosts time to recover strength for the next onslaught, the initial diminution would not have been so severe. But instead the illnesses fell pell-mell upon the Indians, one after another, and often simultaneously, pulverizing populations as they did so.

From these two reasons there emerges a third, for in epidemic circumstances disease receives plenty of lethal assistance from filth, malnutrition, and outright starvation. With almost everyone ill, especially the young adults, there were few to plant and harvest, hunt and fish, and also to cook for and tend the sick and keep their surroundings clean. Consequently the ill were further weakened by a lack of food and by intercurrent diseases such as dysentery springing from unclean conditions.[19]

Finally, individuals who survived this initial gauntlet of pathogenic terror were still not safe from European diseases. For after weathering the initial encounter with epidemic disease they still had to deal with long-run, less spectacular (but not necessarily less destructive) sicknesses such as tuberculosis and venereal diseases.[20]

At this point, however, individuals who lived through acute viral infections such as measles would not normally have to face them again. Females, by surviving diseases, developed immunities that they were able to pass along to their offspring before birth across the placenta and after birth through their milk. Many of these immunities of course were only effective for a short time, but at least they permitted tiny bodies to gain some strength before disease began to test their defenses. Infants, along with adults too weak or too susceptible to survive the onslaught, would have been weeded out, while stronger and less susceptible survivors remained alive to produce others more likely to survive.[21]

The result of this marshaling of immunological defenses would have been new generations better able to live in some harmony with their new disease environment. Meanwhile the pathogens too would have been accomplishing some harmony. The more virulent strains of disease would have been eradicating themselves by eliminating their hosts and an ideal approached whereby host and parasite were both able to survive their encounter, with the host obligingly passing the parasite along to a new human being.

This ideal was ultimately achieved by most mainland Indian peoples and, after a few generations, population growth resumed. It was not, however, achieved by the Caribbean Indians, nor by many of those occupying the low-lying mainland areas of the Caribbean basin, because of still another wave of new pathogens, and herein lay the real tragedy. For scarcely had the Indians begun to weather the storm created by microorganisms from Europe, when they were suddenly confronted with African parasites as well, and they found themselves quite literally victims of biological warfare on two fronts.

The Caribbean has been appropriately likened to a corridor, its waterways linking Europe with Latin America and the Pacific beyond. Because pathogens as well as men passed incessantly through that corridor, the Caribbean Indians received little respite from disease, while by contrast mainland populations were exposed at a more gradual rate. But what probably made the difference between diminution and obliteration for the mainland Indians was that they were located sufficiently inland, and on terrain sufficiently elevated that the wave of insect-borne African pathogens did not reach them. Thus they survived as a people while the Caribbean Indians did not.[22]

Fernando Ortiz Fernandez pronounced them victims of a hurricane of culture which swept their islands, and to some extent this older view of the Indians' demise still holds true. The Spanish "culture" was militaristic and imperialistic, neither trait notable for promoting salu-

brity among subject peoples and the Spanish conquistadores have seldom been credited with humane qualities. But neither, for that matter,
have most imperial powers, and the Spanish in the West Indies were
the first to confront the problem that would bedevil all other European
nations trailing in their wake – a lack of labor for colonizing the region.
Their initial solution was to put the Indians to work, which meant the
use of force and this, coupled with the shock of social dislocation,
surely did the Indians no good.[23]

Yet the Africans, soon to arrive to perform the labor the Indians
could not, endured the same use of force and social dislocation, in
addition to forced migration. As a people they not only survived the
pottage of pathogens that the Caribbean basin was to become, but
centuries of slavery as well. And in the end they not only survived but
attained an overwhelming demographic majority throughout the region. Clearly their biological past had differed considerably from that
of both the American Indians and the Europeans.

The African

Black Africans were present in the New World from the very beginning
of its discovery and conquest. Two individuals on the first voyage of
Columbus were probably black, and as early as 1501 Governor Nicolas
de Ovando of Hispaniola received permission from the Spanish Crown
to import *ladinos* (peninsular born, christianized slaves).[24] Black slavery,
as we have already noted, was a familiar institution in Iberia and it was
natural enough that some of these servants would be sent to the
Americas to perform those chores that their masters found either too
odious or too arduous. Nonetheless, had the Indians not proved themselves to be such poor slave material by dying in wholesale lots, it is
doubtful that the Atlantic slave trade would have attained anything
approaching the magnitude that it did.

But the Indians did die, while those who survived labored so poorly
that King Ferdinand was informed, ". . . one Black could do the work
of four Indians." In addition to the blacks' ability as laborers, the Spanish quickly noticed how durable they were in the face of illnesses that
were felling Indians. Indeed Father Las Casas observed that the feeling
existed among the whites that the only way a black would die would
be if they hanged him.[25] By 1518 the clamor for black slaves on Hispaniola had persuaded Charles I and his advisors to grant permission
for the importation of slaves directly from Africa, and the transatlantic
slave trade had begun; so too had the transatlantic flow of African
pathogens.

It is a widely held view that those African immigrants who survived
the slave coffles in Africa, the middle passage, and seasoning in the
New World constituted something of an elite.[26] Unquestionably there is

much truth in the assertion, but not simply because they survived the trauma of capture, the rigors of the march to the sea, and the middle passage. For those reaching the plantations of the Caribbean were an immunological elite as survivors of one of the most formidable disease environments in the world.

In West Africa leprosy, scabies, yaws, and septic skin afflictions were all common illnesses worn externally, while amebiasis, bilharziasis, roundworm, and guinea worm and hookworm infection gnawed away within. Diarrhea and dysenteries were signals of helminthic infections as well as a host of other maladies including nutritional disorders, as evidenced by such symptoms as edema, dirt eating, the bleeding gums of scurvy, and the convulsions of tetany. Death was also omnipresent in the air, borne by insects in the form of all of man's malarial types, yellow fever, and sleeping sickness. That air also bore a host of Eurasian illnesses that had reached West Africa with the Moslems. Tuberculosis and bacterial pneumonia apparently were fairly new to the region when the first Europeans arrived – and in fact those Europeans probably brought the diseases to many. From their reports we know that the Africans had mustered little tolerance for them. The West Africans' experience with smallpox, diphtheria, whooping cough, measles, mumps, and influenza seems to have been a longer one, for their tolerance for these diseases was much like that of the European.[27]

In terms of immunities, it was the blacks' ability to resist "fevers" which most bemused the Europeans. The fevers in question were mostly falciparum malaria and yellow fever, a pair of tropical killers which together ringed West Africa with a pathogenic barricade more deadly to outsiders than any army and effective against European efforts to penetrate the region for over 400 years. Indeed Europeans learned quickly to confine their activities to the coastal perimeter (they spoke of going to the African coast or the Guinea coast rather than to Africa or Guinea), yet even this slight contact with the continent was so deadly that they bestowed upon it the sobriquet of "the white man's grave."[28]

According to late eighteenth-century records of the Royal African Company, about half of the Europeans sent to West Africa died within one year, while only one in ten ever returned to England. The Dutch on the Gold Coast apparently fared somewhat better, losing an average of only 20 percent of their numbers annually to disease during the first half of that century. During the early nineteenth century, the British Army in parts of West Africa lost somewhere between 500 and 700 men per thousand mean strength annually. Independent observers also confirmed this fearful mortality of Europeans in Africa by reporting death rates upwards of 80 percent annually and pronouncing regions such as the Bight of Biafra "healthy" because only a quarter or less of the whites there died annually of fevers.[29]

Yet the mortality of whites in West Africa, terrific though it was, appears even more dreadful when contrasted with its dramatic absence among individuals of West African origin. Perhaps the most vivid example can be found in nineteenth-century data on black and white troop mortality in the region. Whites serving the British Crown perished at a rate that fluctuated between 483 and 668 per thousand mean strength per annum, while their black counterparts died at a rate of only 31 per thousand mean strength per annum. The reason for the differential is not hard to discern. Almost all of the white deaths were attributed to "fevers," while very few blacks died from this cause.[30]

Other examples of an African tolerance for African fevers can be found in the early efforts of the British to reach the interior of the continent by traversing rivers that, to borrow a phrase from Michael Gelfand, became for white men "Africa's Rivers of Death." The great Niger expedition of 1841 is illustrative of all such efforts in that of the 145 Europeans in the expedition, 42 individuals, or 30 percent, died of fevers. Yet all of the 158 "Africans and coloured men" returned safely.[31]

Thus for the Europeans in Africa the tables were turned and it was the invader, not the native, who was doing the dying. A few decades ago this differential experience with disease would not have demanded nor would it have received much in the way of an explanation, save perhaps the observation that Africans had indeed developed a tolerance for illnesses which Europeans certainly did not possess. But in the last quarter of a century or so, medical researchers and geneticists have begun to uncover some of the reasons for this tolerance, especially in the case of malaria.[32]

African Diseases

Malaria

There are four types of malaria in the world which affect man, three of which are of interest to us. The first, *Plasmodium vivax*, is the most widespread across the globe while the second, *Plasmodium malariae*, although no stranger to many parts of the world, remains most prevalent in Africa. Both of these malarial types are relatively benign, meaning that as a rule the victim shakes and aches while alternating between chills and fever, but infrequently dies. The third type, *Plasmodium falciparum*, however, is definitely not benign and even today is a front-runner as the major cause of death in parts of Africa as well as other tropical regions.

The reason that *P. falciparum* is considerably more deadly than its cousins is, on the surface at least, a fairly simple one. After the malarial parasites (protozoa) are injected into the human body by an infected mosquito (usually of the anopheline variety), they head for the liver to multiply and then break out into the bloodstream where they begin to feed on red blood cells. In the case of *P. vivax*, young erythrocytes are the preferred prey, while *P. malariae* normally invades only mature cells. In either case the level of infection or parasitization is self-limiting. But *P. falciparum* is not so finicky and invades both young and old cells indiscriminately. The result is that *P. falciparum* achieves a much higher and consequently a much more life-threatening level of parasite activity. In addition, cells invaded by *P. falciparum* have a tendency to become sticky and clump together, and these clumps are deadly when they cause hemorrhage by blocking blood vessels leading to internal organs or to the brain.

Because *P. falciparum* is not self-limiting, people with a long history of experience with the disease have evolved blood characteristics to impose the restraint that the parasite does not exercise. Sickle-shaped blood cells, for example, perform this function and greatly reduce mortality, although exactly why and how the cells of individuals with sickle trait discourage parasite proliferation is not known. Hypotheses range from the thought that the shape itself denies easy access to the parasite, to the notion that the sickle cell may be more efficient in eliminating itself and the parasites from the bloodstream once it has been invaded. But, for whatever reason, individuals with sickle trait seldom reveal the high parasite counts typical of those without this protection.

Unfortunately nature charges dearly for this form of malaria resistance. For when both parents of a child possess sickle trait, then the odds are one in four that the child will develop sickle cell anemia – a disease that shortens life considerably for its victims.[33] Perhaps for this reason, other less expensive forms of protection have also evolved, the best known of these being a blood enzyme deficiency called glucose-6-phosphate dehydrogenase deficiency, understandably, better known simply as G6PD deficiency. Again the reasons that this blood anomaly resists parasitic prosperity in the bloodstream are not known.[34] But as with sickle trait its geographic distribution correlates well with those areas where falciparum malaria was or still is endemic. Nor have all the possible consequences to the health of those who possess G6PD deficiency been determined. Some studies have shown that susceptibility to anemia and illnesses generally may be a price for this protection. It is known that those with some variants of G6PD deficiency are in danger of hemolysis (the destruction of red cells) in the presence of diseases such as chicken pox and infectious hepatitis along with certain drugs and vegetables, most especially the fava bean.[35]

In addition there are also variations of both sickle trait and G6PD deficiency which seem to protect against falciparum malaria. Hemoglobin C is one, thalassemia traits alone and in combination with sickle traits constitute another, and there are over 100 variants of G6PD deficiency. In West African regions where falciparum malaria is prevalent, the frequency of sickle trait averages between 20 and 25 percent (although frequencies as high as 40 percent have been discovered), while the frequency of G6PD deficiency averages between 8 and 24 percent.[36]

In the Caribbean the frequency of these blood anomalies varies considerably. Sickle trait, for example, has been found in about 11 percent of the blacks tested in Jamaica. In Haiti-Tortuga the trait was discovered in a bit over 12 percent of the population, and in St. Lucia, about 14 percent. On the other hand, in Barbados only about 7 percent of the population carry the trait.[37] Since malaria either vanished early or never took root on a few islands such as Barbados where ecological circumstances made life impossible for its mosquito vector, we seem to be witnessing the natural elimination of a trait not needed for malaria protection for centuries by Barbadian blacks.[38] By contrast, in British Honduras, where falciparum malaria continues to be a problem to this day (and where the population tested had retained the African genotype with very little race mixing), sickle trait occurs among 23 percent of the Black Carib population.[39]

These seem to be the Caribbean extremes however, while an average frequency of sickle trait in the region approximates that found among blacks in the United States – about 10 percent. From the few tests which have come to our attention, it would also seem that Caribbean blacks possess hemoglobin C and thalassemia traits at about the same rate (something over 3 percent) as well as G6PD deficiency (7 to 9 percent).[40]

It bears repeating that the defenses discovered thus far against falciparum malaria are not racial in the sense that they only occur in blacks. Rather, they are found in all peoples who have been exposed to the disease over a long period of time. It is only because West African peoples have had the longest and most intensive relationship with the disease, that they, along with their American cousins, reveal higher frequencies of traits that protect against the disease than other racial groups.[41]

On the other hand, individuals of West African ancestry do appear to have what might be fairly termed a racial resistance to *Plasmodium vivax*. A black refractoriness to this malarial type has long been observed, but only recently explained. The mechanism here is also connected with the blood, for it seems that a majority of blacks lack the Duffy blood group determinants Fy^a and Fy^b – a condition "extremely rare in groups without Black admixture."[42] The frequency of this condition approaches 100 percent in parts of West Africa, which may well explain why vivax malaria is so rare in the region today. Certainly the trait has served the black well in the western hemisphere where the disease has generally been the most prevalent malaria type.[43]

West Africans, then, reached the Americas well prepared to tolerate those protozoa that were rapidly becoming the chief ingredient in the New World's pathogenic pottage with perhaps 25 percent carrying the sickle trait, another 25 percent with G6PD deficiency, and most lacking the Duffy blood group determinants.[44] But peoples tolerant of a disease are frequently its carriers and freshly imported slaves served as a steady reservoir for *P. falciparum* throughout the whole of the slave trade period.

By contrast, the carriers of *P. vivax* were almost certainly Europeans who were all too familiar with this particular "ague," which made them shake and burn and occasionally die.[45] Neither falciparum nor vivax malaria would have had any particular difficulty in establishing endemicity in the Americas, for the New World seems to have abounded with anopheline mosquitos (the usual malaria vector) that would have sucked up the protozoa and begun the cycle of disease propagation from man to mosquito to man.[46]

Endemic malaria has long been one of man's most implacable enemies and less than a half century ago was blamed for some half of the world's deaths annually. However, because malaria for the most part quietly winnows the population, its lethal behavior has often gone unremarked, while epidemic diseases dramatic in their onset, and terrible in their ferocity, have received most of the attention of observers. Certainly this has been the story with yellow fever.

Yellow Fever

As a general rule, man suffers most from those diseases for which he is not the primary target. In the case of bubonic plague, for example, the disease is one of rodents. But on notable occasions the disease has incidentally infected man, with devastating consequences. Yellow fever is another example of the same kind of phenomenon. It is primarily a disease of monkeys, who act as a reservoir of the virus, which is transmitted among them by mosquito vectors – but vectors that do not usually prey on man. This normal form of the disease is called sylvan, or jungle yellow fever, and at this point it is "enzootic," meaning a pattern of transmission from nonhuman primate to mosquito to nonhuman primate. The endemic form of the disease occurs when the disease leaves the treetops, and the cycle becomes one of nonhuman primate to mosquito to man, while the epidemic form of yellow fever – with the disease far removed from its original hosts and haunts – is a man to mosquito to man pattern of transmission, with man the place where the virus changes mosquitoes.[47]

For the man-mosquito-man pattern to take place, a number of conditions must be met, most of them dictated by the *Aëdes aegypti* mosquito, the usual vector of the disease for man. First, the range of the

Aëdes is very short, normally a few hundred yards at most. This means that the virus must be brought to the mosquitoes since they cannot transport it over long distances. It also means a closely packed population to support the mosquitoes with blood meals and provide a constant source of fresh infection – for this reason the disease as it affects man is frequently called "urban" yellow fever.

Second, the urban area must be enjoying warm weather, because the *Aëdes* will not bite at temperatures less than 62 degrees. In the Caribbean, although weather was seldom a problem for the mosquito, only a few islands such as Trinidad had the requisite monkey population and not many met the urban requirements for a sustained yellow fever siege. Thus, it is not really accurate to speak of yellow fever as being "endemic" to the Caribbean, unless, of course, one defines the region to encompass the jungles of Central America.

Third, the urban areas with the potential for hosting yellow fever epidemics had to have plenty of standing water about, because the *Aëdes* cannot survive for more than a few days without water. Finally, the population at risk had to contain a sufficient number of nonimmune individuals to sustain an epidemic.

Acquired immunity to yellow fever comes about as it does with many diseases, especially virulent viruses, by the individual hosting the disease and surviving it. Historically, however, adults have had difficulty in accomplishing the second step – that of survival – while children have shrugged off the illness as just one more in the inevitable train of childhood illnesses which spoil their play for a few days.[48] Thus individuals born in regions frequently visited by yellow fever, as for example the Creoles of the West Indies, normally earned their yellow fever immunity early in life, and came to look upon yellow fever as strictly a disease of newcomers or, as many called it, "stranger's fever."

Unfortunately the Islands did not lack in the fresh blood of "strangers" to support the yellow plague. Immigrants, indentured servants, soldiers, and sailors all obliged the virus, often at the expense of their lives. Blacks, however, although they were by far the most numerically important of the newcomers to the Caribbean, were seldom yellow fever casualties. In part this was because they had hosted the disease either in Africa or the Caribbean and consequently were immune. But for the most part the reason was that blacks have a tolerance for the disease, once they do contract it, which permits them to entertain the illness in a very mild form, while their white counterparts retch and hemorrhage their way to a yellow fever grave.

Epidemiologists have long suspected a racial immunity of a kind not yet understood. Many laymen, however, have mistakenly explained black yellow fever refractoriness in terms of acquired immunity alone. But, as we have shown in other studies, large populations of blacks who could not possibly have acquired immunities to yellow fever nonetheless, when suddenly confronted with the illness, have demonstrated a remarkable resistance to it, while their white neighbors died in droves.[49]

The question of the origin of this ability to resist yellow fever links with the intriguing epidemiological question of the origin of yellow fever. Again, because we have expressed our views elsewhere, we will only summarize them here.[50] It is true that today yellow fever is well established in enzootic form in the jungles of both South America and West Africa. It is also true that yellow fever was recognized and described as a separate disease in the West Indies long before this occurred in West Africa, and finally it is true that the records of pre-Columbian Indian populations reveal epidemics of what *could* have been yellow fever. On the basis of these facts some have concluded that yellow fever was American in origin.

On the other hand, entomological evidence indicates that the *Aëdes* is very likely an import from Africa, and certainly today Africa has many more species of the *Aëdes* than America. But more telling is the demonstrated ability of the blacks to resist the disease – an ability that the native Americans simply did not have. Indeed the blacks' refractoriness to yellow fever alone indicates a long experience with it during which tolerance was developed. That this experience apparently was denied the New World Indians implies little or no previous contact with the illness.

Moreover, West African humans are not the only primates with this ability. West African monkeys are also refractory to the disease, whereas American monkeys are much more susceptible.[51] Thus immunological evidence seems to point an emphatic finger at West Africa as the cradle of yellow fever. Of course it is always possible that the ancient Indian texts are describing yellow fever, but they could also be describing a score of other epidemic ailments. Finally an argument for an American origin of the disease based on the fact that yellow fever epidemics were not reported among the natives of West Africa is, given their relative immunities, no argument at all.

The nature of the immunities with which West Africans were gifted is not known. It does not seem to be racial, for black Africans in non-yellow fever regions of Africa have reportedly suffered from the disease much as whites have.[52] On the other hand, the ability to resist yellow fever does seem to be genetically transferable. Blacks in the New World, for example, with little or no white admixture remained so refractory to the ravages of the disease that when they did contract it, the illness passed practically unnoticed. Mulattos by contrast proved much more susceptible to the yellow plague although not to the same extent that whites did.[53]

Yet apparently for the first century and a half of Europe's presence in the Caribbean no one had to worry much about yellow fever. Both the virus and the *Aëdes* vector had to be imported from Africa, and equally important, during this early period there were few closely packed urban populations to support them after they were imported. Thus while the disease probably did make a number of unrecorded visits to the Americas, it was not until the middle of the seventeenth century that conditions permitted the yellow plague to launch a full-scale invasion of the West Indies.[54]

By 1647 the population of Barbados had reached a density of some 200 individuals to the square mile, and it was in that year that yellow fever made the first of a long series of unwelcome visits to that island, which earned it the nickname "Barbados distemper." The following year it spread to Guadeloupe, St. Kitts, Cuba, and the Yucatan Peninsula, killing whites and Indians but sparing blacks in its sweep across the Caribbean basin.[55]

Thereafter, the yellow plague became an increasingly regular visitor to the West Indies, but invariably those visits were associated with ships newly arrived from Africa. Thus even after the disease had presumably established itself in New World jungles, it continued to reach out to batter the Caribbean from an African reservoir, unleashing such pestilence on whites that in the terse words of a Spanish witness to a 1695 epidemic in Santiago, Cuba, "of those attacked, few escaped with their lives."[56] It was as if Africa were punishing the Europeans for her rape by sending with her sons and daughters plagues specifically aimed at their captors. Yet ironically, by punishing the whites, yellow fever and malaria also eliminated the possibility that white labor in the form of indentured servants might help to colonize the vastness of the Americas, which left the black the sole candidate quite literally by the process of elimination.[57]

Other African Pathogens and Disease Susceptibilities

This concludes for now the look at West African disease immunities. Because their susceptibilities constitute the subject matter of much of the remainder of this volume, only a few, to provide background for ensuing chapters, will be dealt with here in cursory fashion. First let us glance at an insect-borne disease, which, although transported to the Americas, fortunately did not take root there. The illness in question is African trypanosomiasis, or sleeping sickness, so deadly to both man and animal in much of the tropical regions of that continent. The reason it failed to establish itself in the American tropics is that this hemisphere is free of the tsetse fly (genus *Glossina*), the vector of trypanosomiasis; and the *Glossina*, unlike the *Aëdes* mosquito, was not able to make a successful ocean crossing. Therefore, although telltale enlarged neck glands were sometimes noted among West Indian slaves, they were invariably slaves newly introduced from Africa and not blacks born in the islands.[58]

The rule that a long and intimate association with a pathogen produces tolerance to that pathogen holds true for man's tiny parasites, but not always for his larger ones. Indeed with the larger parasites the rule is often turned upside down, with the larger parasites being more dangerous to their accustomed hosts than to new ones.[59] Thus Africans have proven much more liable than whites to the guinea worm and the filariasis that they brought to the New World. However, there are exceptions. Hookworm was also an African import, yet blacks in the Americas have demonstrated an ability to resist the ravages of hookworm disease, which whites do not possess.[60]

Yaws, another African affliction, for some reason seldom affected whites, yet spared few of the West Indian slave young until the slave trade itself ceased to bring fresh sources of infection. At that point better living conditions and a better diet combined to begin elimination of the disease from most of the West Indies. However, in Haiti today, where there has been little improvement in the quality of life for many since the days of slavery, the disease affects about one half of the population, which apparently gives that country the unwanted distinction of having the highest incidence of yaws in the world.[61]

Leprosy, called "one of the most horrible of Negro diseases," was often confused with yaws.[62] Yet blacks in both Africa and the Americas have proven much more susceptible to the illness than whites, at least for the past 500 years or so, and it quickly became known in the islands of the Caribbean as another black man's disease.[63]

So, for that matter, did tetanus. Blacks cannot be blamed for importing the tetanus bacillus to the hemisphere, but it is nonetheless an acute infectious illness to which they have been enormously susceptible.[64] There are, of course, many reasons of an environmental nature why blacks in the West Indies should have contracted the disease at a higher rate than whites, just as there may be good reasons to account for the fact that blacks in the United States today experience a rate of mortality from the disease fourteen times greater than that suffered by whites.[65] But it may also turn out that the judgment of West Indian physicians was correct and that blacks do harbor some sort of extraordinary susceptibility to the illness.

Certainly they were correct in their assessment of the slaves as being especially susceptible to lung ailments. Pneumonia has been one of the biggest killers of blacks historically and blacks have also proved enormously vulnerable to other respiratory illnesses such as whooping cough. Part of the reason, in the case of pneumonia at least, may be found in the now familiar concept of "unfamiliarity" with a disease, for bacterial pneumonia was unknown in West Africa until introduced by the Europeans.[66] Part, too, must be blamed on the crowded living conditions often forced upon blacks, but there are also genetic factors that may bear upon the question of black susceptibility to pneumonia and other respiratory ailments.

The most tenuous linkage has to do with the lungs themselves, for blacks (especially males) tend to have a smaller lung volume (vital capacity) than whites of the same age, height, and weight.[67] Another factor entails heat and cold tolerance. Experiments conducted during and after the Korean war on blacks and whites left no doubt that, while the black has a greater adaptive capacity than whites to the stresses of heat, he is much more susceptible to cold, with his metabolic rate lagging substantially behind whites similarly exposed, and his cold hemagglutinin titers are higher.[68] As will be seen, cold nights punished blacks severely even in the tropical Caribbean – so much so that white observers came to believe that cold was a significant source of disease for the slaves.

Perhaps lung capacity and cold intolerance by themselves predisposed slaves to respiratory diseases, or perhaps they combined with the anemias already discussed and a nutritional heritage along with an unbalanced diet, which will be explored throughout much of the rest of the study.

Indeed this is a problem that we will confront again and again as we examine the etiologies of black-related diseases in the Caribbean – that problem being the extent to which blacks were innately susceptible to a particular illness, and the extent to which environmental factors such as poor shelter and food created the susceptibilities. Certainly nutrition is frequently an overlooked factor in studies of how a particular people fared with disease, yet bodies are often rendered susceptible to disease simply because they lack the nutrients necessary to mount a proper immune response. Moreover a deficiency of specific nutrients can also produce diseases that kill all by themselves. Thus a people's disease environment cannot properly be studied apart from their nutritional heritage, which in turn is linked to genetic heritage. Clearly a holistic understanding of the blacks' demographic experience in the Caribbean must give careful attention to all three of these factors. Therefore, having seen how West African pathogens in the Caribbean helped to create a demand for black laborers in the region, we should proceed next to an examination of the nutritional health of those laborers prior to their embarkation from West African shores.

CHAPTER 2

WEST AFRICAN DIET AND DISEASE

And [man] has favored disease-selection by developing dietaries that are themselves growth limiting, and inimical to the maintenance of an optimum immunochemical [defense] system.

S.M. Garn (1963)[1]

In Africa malnutrition lurks like an evil spirit in the homes of the majority and exerts its most devastating effect on the very young.

R.G. Hendrickse (1966)[2]

It has been observed that "if we compare the heights and weights of African children with those of their age mates in Europe and America, we find that the vast majority of African children are well below the expected norm for their ages."[3] This observer we have just quoted, as others, had no difficulty in explaining the variance in heights, for studies have made it clear that the reason a people fail to achieve their genetic potential for height is generally a function of malnutrition,[4] and sub-Saharan children are, as a rule, considerably less well nourished than European or North American counterparts.

Thanks to a number of recent examinations of slave height data, we can discern similar evidence of West African malnutrition for the early nineteenth century. These ongoing studies have revealed that slaves born in the West Indies (Creoles) were significantly taller (one to three inches) than counterparts born in Africa.[5] Because the phenomenon of a rapid increase in the height of a people (such as second- and third-generation Japanese and Chinese in the United States) is linked tightly to nutrition, the conclusion seems inescapable that even the miserable diet of slaves in the Americas was superior to (or at least more protein laden than) that of their African cousins.[6]

West African Nutrition

Protein

Unfortunately, it may also be true that the diet of a nineteenth-century slave in America was superior nutritionally to that consumed by the average West African of the mid-twentieth century. Certainly malnutrition remains the region's most important and pressing problem of health, and a look at the problem today may help to shed some light on the nutritional status of those who yesterday were put aboard the slave ships.

A comparison of the diets of an American (Creole)-born slave and a modern-day West African was not intended to be gratuitous for the slave's diet probably contained more high-quality protein. And protein was almost certainly responsible for the superior height of Creole-born slaves in the West Indies, while its lack lay at the root of the West-African-born slaves' failure to achieve his potential physical stature.[7] Protein deficiency also constitutes a major reason why most present-day West Africans are malnourished. For, on the one hand, proteins are the building materials of the muscles, blood, and internal organs of the human body while, on the other, by forming enzymes and antibodies, they help to sustain health and fight foreign substances that threaten the body's health.[8]

Protein deficiency is a confusing concept, largely because there are high-quality proteins and proteins of a substantially lesser quality, depending on a protein's amino acid content, which is the state to which proteins decompose during the digestion process. The body can and does manufacture all but eight of the twenty-two or so amino acids required to make human protein. The eight it cannot manufacture are called "essential" amino acids, and hence the quality of proteins humans consume is scored on the number of essential amino acids they deliver.

The scores are high for proteins derived from meat and dairy products and, in fact, these are usually "complete" proteins, meaning they contain all the essential amino acids. Much lower, however, are the scores for proteins yielded by vegetables and fruits, because at least one (and usually more) of the essential amino acids is lacking. When this occurs – when just one of the essential amino acids is either missing from the protein intake or forthcoming hours later than the others – "human protein synthesis will either cease or decrease to a very low level."[9]

Unfortunately protein synthesis is inhibited throughout much of West Africa because the bulk of the protein intake is of the incomplete kind with very little of the complete variety from animal foods. In part this is due to the tsetse fly, which, by discouraging the raising of large animals, hindered the development of meat production and dairying. Thus, excepting a minority of hunting tribes, the majority of West Africans only taste meat on special occasions when a goat, pig, or a few chickens might be slaughtered.[10]

But culture as well as nature plays an active role in denying West Africans an adequate intake of complete protein. For example, in the North, outside the area of forty-inch rainfall, cattle can be raised, yet meat is still not widely available because the cattle are treasured as signs of wealth and hoarded as more modern men might hoard money. Elsewhere in West Africa the consumption of meat is generally "thought to reflect an extravagant and wasteful disposition."[11] Thus it is wasteful to kill a chicken that lays eggs, but it is also wasteful to consume eggs because they could become chickens. Moreover there are taboos against egg consumption because of a conviction that they interfere with childbirth, precipitate sterility, or cause a young consumer to become a thief in later life. As a consequence, many West Africans do not take advantage of even these readily available sources of protein.[12]

Finally the West African soils that support the vegetation consumed by grazing animals are so poor that where cattle can be raised their milk and meat yield is extremely low. By comparison, European cattle provide on the average of eight to ten times more milk and three times more beef than their West African equivalents.[13]

Thus even West African soils must bear blame for the region's malnutrition. Some are heavily acidic, most are nitrogen deficient, and almost all are leached of their mineral content (especially phosphorus and calcium) by heavy tropical rains. Among the consequences is that crops grown on this soil will have a low protein and mineral content.[14]

Until a few hundred years ago those crops consisted of relatively low-yielding vegetables and cereals, notably taro, the small African yam, and millet. However, beginning in the sixteenth century, a momentous change began to take place in West African agriculture as these crops were largely displaced by the introduction of much higher-yielding American crops such as maize, cassava (manioc), larger yams, and sweet potatoes. The American crops in turn stimulated the growth of West African populations, many of which, unhappily and ironically, were drained off by the African diaspora to the hemisphere that had supplied the plants to begin with.[15]

Yet the contribution of American plants to West African nutrition was more one of quantity than of quality. The higher-yield crops made more food available during good times, while roots such as cassava and New World yams may have ensured against total famine during those years unfavorable to grains, although as recent studies have shown, famine in West Central and Southwest Africa (and thus perhaps in parts of West Africa as well) has played an important historical role in shaping the African's nutritional status.[16]

But while the arrival of the American vegetables may have rendered problems of undernutrition less pressing, those of malnutrition remained, for the new plants did little to correct the widespread protein deficiency that plagues the region.[17] They could have done much, however, if two or three or more vegetable crops had been cultivated and consumed by a people. The likelihood of that people consuming a complete protein would have been increased enormously, as one vegetable source would have had the opportunity to supply amino acids that another lacked (such as beans and rice, which together provide a complete protein). But, unfortunately, cultivation, and therefore diets, tended to focus on a single crop such as maize, or rice, or cassava, or millet, or yams, and the diets, as a rule, were not sufficiently supplemented with beans, peas, groundnuts, and sorghum, let alone animal protein sources to deliver enough high quality protein for even minimal good health by Western standards.

Vitamin B Complex

A shortage of animal protein in the diet does not automatically condemn a people to B vitamin deficiencies, but it does make their situation precarious, for the B vitamins are somewhat like amino acids in that they too must be in balance; if the diet is low in a particular B vitamin, such as niacin, then the body's ability to utilize the remainder of its B vitamin intake is substantially impaired. Thus, once again, if a variety of cereals and vegetables is consumed, the odds of receiving a sufficient amount of all the B vitamins are considerably enhanced. By contrast, if the diet centers too closely on a single cereal, then the consumers will most likely experience serious B vitamin deficiencies. Historically, those with maize as their principal cereal have proved to be niacin deficient; those whose diet centered closely on rice have been thiamine deficient; and those whose diets revolved around cassava or millet have inevitably shown signs of severe riboflavin deficiency.[18] In West Africa, all these deficiencies are widespread, with multiple deficiencies of the B complex being the rule rather than the exception.[19]

Vitamin C

A well-known authority on West African nutrition commented during the early 1950s that widespread vitamin C deficiency would "be hard to understand in the tropics if one were not aware that African children are discouraged from eating fruit for fear that it will give them worms."[20] Another investigator was amazed to discover that 36 percent of the Africans he examined in Portuguese Guinea were vitamin C deficient despite the many types of fruit close at hand.[21] Yet other workers made similar discoveries throughout West Africa, as they too discovered West Africans to be vitamin C deficient to a greater or lesser degree.[22]

Vitamin A

Superficially, it would seem that vitamin A deficiency should not be a significant problem because of the high intake of carotene by many in the form of palm oil, red peppers, and depending on the type, corn and sweet potatoes (white corn, many sweet potatoes, and almost all of the varieties of yams consumed in West Africa contain no carotene). Unfortunately, despite high intakes of carotene, many West Africans receive an insufficient amount of vitamin A because of the chemistry involved in its utilization. Vitamin A is one of the fat-soluble vitamins, meaning that dietary fat is crucial for its utilization. The West African diet, however, is extraordinarily low in fats save for palm oil, which, although viewed as the major source of vitamin A for West Africans, may be of no help, for when a fat is rancid it destroys vitamin A and it has been reported that palm oil in West Africa "is, as a rule, rancid." Thus, the substance that has been credited with delivering much vitamin A to West Africans not infrequently also destroys the vitamin, which doubtless goes far toward explaining why deficiency signs have been reported throughout the region.[23]

Calcium

The tsetse fly, by discouraging the raising of large animals in much of West Africa, has also discouraged the development of milk-drinking cultures. Yet the tsetse fly is not completely to blame, because even among many peoples who are rich in cattle outside the areas frequented by the tsetse fly, milk is seldom consumed. In part, this is because of the poor milk yield of the cattle, in part because of lactose intolerance (see Chapter 3) and in part because of culture. Butter, for example, is seldom consumed, but rather is employed by the women as a cosmetic, while goats, where kept, are not milked because goats' milk is not regarded as fit for human consumption.[24] Thus, in addition to losing the high-quality protein in milk, West Africans also are denied an important source of calcium, which would certainly help to alleviate the calcium deficiency chronic among them.[25]

Iron

Although the cereals consumed by West Africans contain iron in some abundance, iron is poorly absorbed by bodies lacking a sufficient intake of ascorbic acid, lactose, and animal protein. Moreover its absorption is also hindered by phosphorus, with which the West African diet bristles, because of competition for metal-binding sites in the intestinal mucosa. For these reasons the West African must have been extremely iron deficient prior to the introduction of iron cooking pots, for even with their usage, iron deficiency anemia has been pinpointed by many as among the most serious nutritional problems of the region.[26] Yet iron intake and absorption are only parts of the difficulty, for with iron, as with most West African nutritional deficiencies, the problem is intertwined with parasitic disease.

West African Nutritional Diseases

Protein and Disease

A poverty of high-quality protein in their diet must predispose almost all West Africans to infectious disease. This poverty also plays a vital role in the etiology of West African diseases, including one that is devastating to the very young. For it is the children who bear the burden of the most serious nutritional disease in the region called protein energy malnutrition, or PEM. PEM is a disease designation that encompasses a number of disorders, with two of these, kwashiorkor and marasmus occupying opposite symptomatic poles.

It usually strikes children during their first four to five years of life, frequently right after the weaning process, which deprives them suddenly of milk – a major protein source that the new diet invariably does not replace. If it is kwashiorkor, the major symptom is the distended stomach with which any visitor to the world's poverty-stricken regions is all too familiar. The edema, along with other complications such as anorexia, diarrhea, fatty liver, skin lesions, and changes in hair pigmentation, are caused principally by a protein shortage in the diet, both absolutely and relative to calorie intake. Marasmus, by contrast, is a wasting disease typified by the "skin and bones" appearance of a child. This is produced by a lack of sufficient proteins and calories and is quite simply starvation.[27]

Kwashiorkor occurs in the more humid portions of West Africa where low-protein-yielding root crops are the chief dietary staple, whereas marasmus is a problem in the wet–dry zones where crops can fail, or are used up too quickly, with seasonal hunger the result.[28] Unfortunately, in West Africa these are not diseases confined to a handful of children. Rather, this is the region where kwashiorkor was first recognized and described as a disease, and where some experts feel that a majority of youngsters suffer PEM in some form ranging from mild to severe. Certainly PEM is a major cause of Africa's tragically high mortality rates among the young,[29] and it frequently curses even those who survive it with impaired mental abilities or crippling or fatal liver disease in later life.[30]

Vitamin B Deficiency Diseases

The prevalence of PEM in West Africa is melancholy proof of the low protein quality of the diet in the region. As noted previously, diets lacking in animal protein make it difficult for the consumer to maintain an adequate intake of the vitamin B complex and, unfortunately, proof of severe vitamin B deficiencies in West Africa abounds. Many West Africans, for example, "live on the brink of pellagrous developments," which not infrequently burst forth into full-blown cases.[31] Pellagra is usually associated with niacin deficiency, characteristic of peoples whose diets are low in animal protein and center too closely on corn. But the human body can manufacture its own niacin from tryptophan, niacin's precursor and one of the essential amino acids. The real difficulty with corn seems to be that it contains leucine in abundance and leucine frustrates the conversion of tryptophan to niacin. These twin factors, then, leave very pellagra prone those whose diets center too closely on corn.

Beriberi, caused by thiamine deficiency and usually associated with diets that bulk large with polished rice, has also been reported with some regularity in West and West Central Africa.[32] Indeed a survey of Kongo found 41 percent of a population sampled to be afflicted with the disease.[33] On the other hand, the most widespread of all the B vitamin deficiencies is riboflavin deficiency, with symptoms in the form of eye and skin lesions, which have been reported to affect as many as 65 percent of some populations.[34]

Vitamin A Deficiency Signs

Perhaps the most obvious sign of vitamin A deficiency is night blindness, which some have reported as "common" throughout much of West Africa. Yet most surveys that have come to our attention have tended to assume the deficiency was common because of eye ailments generally, and as we just saw, eye ailments can be as symptomatic of riboflavin deficiency as of vitamin A deficiency. They can also be symptomatic of parasitic activity, and indeed, eye complaints from both nutritional and parasitic causes are appallingly common in West Africa. Thus, where night blindness is reported as common, we can be assured that vitamin A deficiency is the culprit, as was suggested by our brief nutritional analysis. But evidence that night blindness is widespread over all of West Africa, if it exists, is buried in generalized eye disease.[35]

Vitamin C Deficiency Disease

Perhaps because they are seldom life threatening, symptoms of vitamin C deficiency have received less comment from observers than other nutritional ailments. Nonetheless enough has been reported to confirm that the problem is widespread. In Nigeria swollen and bleeding gums of populations of schoolchildren have spelled borderline scurvy to observers, while others have commented on the prevalence of subclinical scurvy throughout West Africa.[36]

Iron and Anemia

Proof of iron deficiency anemia among West Africans is overwhelmingly abundant because of the countless studies that have been conducted on women and children in an effort to combat the region's fearfully high rates of infant and child mortality. Thus, in Nigeria a study found a third of all women examined to have a "clinical degree" of anemia, while another in Portuguese Guinea found fully 82 percent of the pregnant women in its sample to be seriously anemic.[37] Other surveys have revealed anemia rates ranging from 87 percent to 95 percent of school-aged populations.[38] These and other studies leave no doubt that most West African women and children are anemic to a greater or lesser extent, and for this reason some have branded anemia as the region's most important and common disease.[39] However, the problem, as indicated previously, is not only one of inadequate iron intake but also one of parasitic activity.[40]

Calcium

Just as one is startled to discover vitamin C deficiency in the tropics, one is also surprised to encounter rickets. Yet during the early 1950s rickets was reported as "not uncommon" in West Africa.[41] Rickets is a disease of children characterized by defective bone growth and usually results from an insufficient intake of vitamin D or not enough exposure to the sun, which stimulates vitamin D production in the body. Vitamin D, of course, is essential to the absorption of calcium; hence its deficiency can cause inadequate amounts of calcium for bone growth, even when there is enough calcium intake. It is also the case, however, that youngsters enjoying plenty of vitamin D can and do develop rickets if their diet is seriously deficient in calcium.[42] This seems to be the primary reason for rickets in West Africa. Indeed even those on the breast sometimes become calcium deficient, either because their mothers are so lacking in the mineral that their milk is also depleted, or more frequently because malnutrition greatly reduces the quantity of their milk. In the case of children who have been weaned the problem is more obvious – the diet to which they are weaned generally contains little or no calcium.[43]

Summary

A look at West African diets suggested that, despite variations, those diets have tended to center on a single starchy staple and are insufficiently supplemented with other vegetable and animal food sources. Protein deficiencies of a widespread nature have been confirmed by the prevalence of PEM in the region and serious vitamin B deficiencies have been documented by the presence of pellagra, beriberi, and hyporiboflavinosis symptoms. Vitamin C deficiency seems to be endemic in much of West Africa in view of the reports of borderline and subclinical scurvy, and possibly vitamin A deficiency as well, although symptoms of eye difficulties caused by vitamin A deficiency are blurred by the myriad eye problems of the region. Calcium deficiency also seems endemic, as pointed up by the not "uncommon" appearance of rickets, while iron deficiency anemia affects the majority of West African women and children for reasons that have to do with iron intake, but also with parasitic disease.

Parasitic Diseases

Parasitic diseases both cause and complicate enormously the nutritional problems of West Africa, for it is with the parasites that the West African must share what we have seen to be a very meager intake of nutrients to begin with.

Intestinal Parasites

A survey of "healthy" villagers in the Gold Coast found that 76 percent was infested with the roundworm, *Ascaris*, and 52 percent with hookworm, while another survey in Nigeria discovered that 73 percent of a student population of about 5,000 individuals was infected by *Ascaris*, 39 percent by *Trichuris*, and 15 percent with hookworm.[44] These data reflect the multiple worm infections that plague the West African, although the "mix" varies from region to region. In Portuguese Guinea, for example, it was discovered that in some areas 100 percent of the population carried a load of hookworms and the average for the country was an infection rate of 63 percent. By contrast, only 2 percent of the population carried *Ascaris* and 4 percent carried *Trichuris*.[45] On the other hand, in Nigeria *Ascaris* is the most common intestinal parasite, with heavy loads reported.[46]

It has been pointed out frequently that where standards of living, and consequently nutritional intake, are good, intestinal parasites tend to be less harmful to one's health.[47] But when the intake of nutrients is poor, the results can be devastating as the worms rob the body of much needed protein and iron. Certainly heavy worm loads carried by many West Africans are an important cause of anemia in the region.

Malaria

Despite the protective mechanisms with which many West Africans have been endowed to resist malaria, their immunity is relatively rather than absolutely protective, particularly with falciparum malaria, where blood anomalies seem to limit the extent to which the body can be infected with protozoa. Thus prior to the antimalaria measures taken in the region from the 1950s onward, malaria parasitism was widespread among West Africans.[48] It was estimated in the Gold Coast, for example, that between 86 percent and 90 percent of all youngsters aged one to three years were stricken with the disease, with falciparum malaria the predominant form.[49] In Accra, where birth and death registration data are fairly complete, it has been estimated that 50 of every 1,000 children born die of malaria before age five, while in Nigeria postmortems performed on over 3,000 infants and children revealed malaria to be the cause of death in 10 percent of the cases.[50]

After age five, deaths from malaria in West Africa tend to fall off dramatically as youngsters gain some tolerance for the parasites. Many, however, remained parasitized. According to a report published in 1954, a group of schoolchildren aged nine to thirteen in the Gold Coast, for example, still harbored malaria parasites in 41 percent of the cases, while another Gold Coast group of all ages tested revealed an infection rate of 32 percent.[51] Clearly then, malaria parasites, at least until recently, were responsible for a significant portion of West African infant and child mortality, as well as aggravating the health problems, particularly the anemias, of those that they did not kill.

Other Parasites

In addition to intestinal worms and malarial parasites, West Africans, depending on location, also host a wide variety of more exotic ailments. Where the tsetse fly is numerous, there are pockets of sleeping sickness to be found.[52] Elephantiasis, schistosomiasis (bilharziasis), leishmaniasis, and onchocerciasis all exhibit high frequencies in certain regions, and very often combine with each other and with other parasites, including the protozoa of malaria to further ravage bodies that are malnourished to begin with.

West African Selection: The Twentieth Century

An African nutritionist looking at the Gold Coast has reported that "a normal family consists of a father and a number of wives. The children are not considered as important as the parents and their needs are not normally catered for in the way that British parents, for example, cater for their children . . . the idea that the child is the central point around which the family revolves is foreign to us . . . that the child grows to manhood is due to the scientific fact of 'the survival of the fittest. . .[in] the struggle for existence.' "[53]

Whether or not the Gold Coast is atypical in West Africa in its perception of the child, it is nonetheless true that the West African infant faces dismal odds of survival and, if he does survive, has passed through a rigorous selection process. For, as we have seen in our survey of West African diet and disease, although all ages suffer from malnutrition and parasitism, the heaviest burden by far is born by the children. It is the children who are killed and crippled by PEM and by calcium deficiency, and whose bodies are anemic and most vulnerable to the myriad ailments of a very hostile disease environment, including malaria and a host of intestinal parasites.

Actually the selection, or weeding out process, begins even before the child is born, and although rates of stillbirths and miscarriage are hard to locate in a region with very imperfect demographic data, what few data have come to our attention place the rate of loss at around 14 percent of all pregnancies.[54] As for the infants born live, records from the Gold Coast indicate that from 23 percent to about 35 percent die within their first year of life, while surveys of Nigeria indicate a loss of some 30 percent within the first year.[55] Other surveys put the range at a low of one hundred per thousand for parts of the Congo to over four hundred per thousand in Sierra Leone, with the average for the region guessed to be somewhere around three hundred per thousand live births.[56]

The causes for these staggering rates of child loss from the womb forward are varied, but they cluster around the malnourished state of the West African. Malaria in a mother can aggravate an anemic state and easily cause her to abort a fetus, while infants born of heavily parasitized, and therefore, anemic, mothers are often born prematurely with reduced iron stores that leave them unable to ward off even mild infections. Gross maternal malnutrition affects the infant in other ways as well. Indeed it has been reported that some West African infants have actually been born with the kind of liver damage that physicians are accustomed to seeing only in an older child suffering from severe kwashiorkor. Malnutrition, as we mentioned previously, can also cause a mother's milk production to fail, which generally spells death, for it is commonplace that in West Africa, at least until recently, babies whose mothers died during childbirth, or whose mothers could not provide them with milk, stood little chance of survival.[57]

More often, however, the problem is not one of complete failure of milk production, but rather of reduced quantity due to malnutrition, in which case the infant slowly starves to death, for among West African peoples it is generally customary not to introduce supplementary foods to the child's diet until he has reached about one year of age.[58]

Even after solid foods have been introduced, however, breast feeding continues for an extended period of time. The Yoruba of Nigeria who breast feed between two and three years, and tribes in Guinea-Bissau who continue the practice for four years or more probably serve to represent the lower and upper limits.[59]

Studies on mother's milk in West Africa have revealed that generally the quantity declines after six months or so; that the calcium content is low; that the milk is very low in fat, and in protein by United States standards. Nonetheless, prolonged breast feeding has been seen by experts as the best chance of survival for the West African child, for despite the quality of the mother's milk, it at least contains a high-quality protein that the child will be without when he is finally weaned.[60]

Indeed it is after weaning that the West African child is most vulnerable to PEM. Infant and child feeding patterns are said to be fairly uniform throughout sub-Saharan Africa and, to the extent that this is true, the following generalizations about that feeding apply: Children begin their careers with solid foods in the form of a pap made from cornmeal, cassava, rice or millet, or yams depending on the principal crop of their parents' group. Sometimes groundnuts, green vegetables, and other supplements are added to the pap, but nothing with any high protein content is given the child until at least age two. Meat is believed to cause worms if consumed prior to that age, eggs are frowned upon for reasons already given, while bovine or goat's milk is, as a rule, simply not available.[61]

After the age of two the African toddler is usually given a share of the family stew. Unhappily this seldom contains animal protein, but at least it generally represents an improvement over pap alone. Yet there are sometimes serious obstacles to getting a share of that stew. Often the African toddler is expected to feed himself and many lack sufficient dexterity to manage this task. Moreover, in parts of West Africa the family "soup" is well laced with red peppers, which can quickly discourage a palate accustomed to the blandness of breast milk and pap. Finally, African children, and especially female children, sometimes get only leftovers that the adults do not eat and thus their portions are often scanty. How frequently this occurs among West Africans is a matter of conjecture. In the Gold Coast it has been alleged that children only get the "scraps" after the adults have finished eating. In Nigeria it has been said a bit more cautiously that "the children of peasant farmers, artisans and petty traders do not receive a fair share of the family rations," while still another report has denounced a priority for eating in the region, which for female children is "just before the household dog."[62]

Certainly wherever eating priorities such as these do exist, they are bound to help perpetuate a dreadful cycle of nutritionally impoverished females giving birth to nutritionally impoverished children, who grow to adulthood in this condition to repeat the process. But that is in the future. More immediately, it is at about this time that the youngsters experience another round of heavy mortality because of malnutrition. For it is now that they are acquiring malarial and intestinal parasites, and very often it is this added stress that triggers the onset of PEM. And PEM, if it does not kill directly, frequently predisposes the child to pneumonia, or tuberculosis, or other intercurrent diseases that do kill him.[63]

Indeed it is this round of mortality that sets West Africa apart from most other underdeveloped regions of the world. Generally, in these areas, mortality peaks shortly after birth and then subsides. In West Africa, however, the mortality continues after this first peak to peak again at eighteen months, or twenty-four months, or thirty-six months, depending on the region.[64] The result of this continuation of mortality and the second peak is at least another one hundred children per thousand born who die before the age of five.[65] Moreover, some believe that, as with infant mortality, the mortality of young children is also seriously underreported, and that the combined totals of infant and child mortality would, if accurate records were kept, indicate that more than half of all children born in West Africa die before the age of four or five.[66]

Following the age of five, the death rate drops off sharply. In part this is because of a tolerance developed for the region's pathogens. But, in large part, one suspects it is because those who have survived the life-threatening gauntlet, as those reaching this age have managed to do, are indeed survivors and well tempered biologically to live with, not just the pathological, but also the nutritional hardships that West Africa holds in store for them.

Not all children born face such a bleak future in the region; there are many variations in the health of West Africans. PEM, for example, is not found among those people of Senegal who live between the Gambia and Guinea-Bissau and whose diets include plenty of protein in the form of fish, crabs, and oysters. Nor is it found among those relatively rare West African peoples who do use bovine milk. However, PEM is extremely prevalent in the children of groups whose diets center heavily on cassava flour. Another example of diversity in disease may be found in Nigeria. Skin lesions due to vitamin deficiencies are widespread among northern Nigerians because of droughts that create outright food shortages. While these symptoms are not so widespread in wet, humid eastern Nigeria, the climate there encourages the proliferation of those bloodsucking insects that contribute heavily to denying a high-quality protein to the people of the area.[67]

In addition, there is much seasonal variation in West African diets. It was found that most of the people of old Portuguese Guinea ate a fairly well-balanced diet between December and mid-June or July when fruits and vegetables were maturing, but for the remainder of the year consumed a nutritionally precarious diet. Similarly, a survey carried out in Nigeria revealed that a supposedly vitamin C-deficient people did in fact take in sufficient vitamin C during the rainy season when plenty of leafy vegetables were available.[68]

Yet despite variation, there are enough similarities to permit generalizations about the West Africans' nutritional status. As we have noted, most diets center closely on a single vegetable source for most of the nutrients, most diets are practically devoid of animal protein, and experts tell us that "there is a considerable degree of uniformity" in infant and child feeding.[69] And finally there exists the awful similarities of infant and child mortality within West Africa, which means that today infant mortality rates in the area are three to ten times higher than those of North America or Europe, while the death rates of those aged one to four years are an incredible thirty to fifty times higher.[70]

West African Selection in the Slave Days

The question now becomes one of the extent to which the nutritional status of West Africans today reflects that of the West Africans yesterday who embarked on slave ships for the West Indies. A student of historical nutrition has wisely cautioned that "one of the most perilous assumptions to make is that diet, as such a fundamental part of culture, experienced very few changes in the past."[71] We have already taken note of one momentous change for the better with the introduction of American plants. On the other hand, it could be argued that the beginning of colonial agriculture signaled a decided change for the worse, which has continued until the present day to adversely affect nutrition in the region.

The advent of cash crops in West Africa doubtless did lead in many instances to the decline of both traditional diets and well-rounded food production, and indeed the problem of cash crops diverting resources from local food production remains chronic. Moreover monoculture has led to soil exhaustion; the clearing of forests created favorable breeding grounds for *Anopheles gambiae*, another of malaria's vectors; while irrigation projects provided ideal habitats for the snails that carry schistosomiasis, and more exposure to the guinea worm and other parasites.[72]

Thus colonial agriculture, by militating against local food crops and encouraging the proliferation of local parasites, did West African nutrition no good. Yet it is also true that these evils were balanced to a greater or lesser extent by the introduction of preventive as well as curative medicine and of animal husbandry, which may have made a bit more protein available for many. In addition it could be argued that colonial agriculture did provide some hedges against famine, and gave to a number of West Africans a greater ability to purchase a wider variety of foods.[73]

For these reasons it seems likely that despite the damage that colonial agriculture and its modern-day outgrowth did to West African nutrition, the West African who became a West Indian slave was no better off, and in fact probably even more poorly nourished, than present-day inhabitants. Cultural taboos against nutritionally important foods and priorities in eating, which may frequently have discriminated against females and children, were even more widespread in the past than they are today. Prolonged lactation was prevalent then as now, which suggests a longstanding awareness of the dangers of weaning a West African child to West African foods.[74] The tsetse fly discouraged animal husbandry and thus encourged low intakes of complete protein and calcium long before the advent of colonial agriculture.

Genetic traits such as those that confer malaria protection speak of a struggle with protozoa that began thousands of years before lands were cleared and irrigation systems built for and by the Europeans, and those lands were being leached of their nitrogen and calcium content by tropical rains eons prior to the first cash crops.

That yesterday's West African suffered severely from nutritional ailments also seems confirmed by literature that provides glimpses of skin afflictions of a pellagra-like nature, "dropsies" in children, which modern physicians would very likely have diagnosed as PEM, and even the swellings of beriberi and the bleeding gums of scurvy.[75] Finally, the abrupt increase in height of Creole-born Caribbean slaves, on what was hardly a regimen of either nutritional plenty or nutritional balance, serves only as a last piece of evidence to confirm what the nutritional status of today's West African implies: that slaves destined for the Americas left behind them a land that had molded them with massive malnutrition on the one hand, and a host of man's most dangerous diseases on the other.

As we observed in Chapter 1, the slaves reaching the West Indies were an immunological elite. But they were something more as well. Somehow they had also succeeded in meeting the challenge of African malnutrition and in view of their ability to overcome both poor nutrition and disease, they might better be viewed as a biological elite – an elite that had survived a rigorous weeding-out process even before their ordeal of slavery began. The following chapter will delve briefly into ways in which the West African may have been equipped to deal with malnutrition.

CHAPTER 3

THE PARAMETERS OF WEST
AFRICAN SURVIVAL

It would be foolish to proceed on the assumption of biochemical similarity between widely separated peoples, when archaeology, palaeoanthropology, and history have given us every reason to expect otherwise.

Norman Kretchmer (1977)[1]

There are indeed important differences between blacks and whites with respect to the manifestations of disease, and. . .these differences need to be further documented and investigated so that we might handle them more intelligently.

Richard Allen Williams (1974)[2]

If nature gave West Africans the ability to live with malnutrition in a manner that most peoples cannot, then biological evidence of such an ability must exist. This chapter is devoted to exploring the hypothesis that such evidence is extant and may be found in the ways in which the nutritional requirements of West Africans and people of West African ancestry seem to differ from people of European ancestry whose nutritional requirements, at the moment, constitute the world's "standards."

Iron

We saw in the previous chapter that iron deficiency anemia was widespread among heavily parasitized West Africans. Yet numerous studies have revealed that Americans of West African origin, without heavy parasite loads, also experience a high frequency of iron deficiency anemia – a frequency much higher than that of white Americans. Put more technically, studies on blacks and whites, especially children, have determined that white children have much higher red blood cell volumes and higher hematocrit readings than black children.[3] Moreover, this important difference does not appear to be a function of immediate environmental circumstances as has often been argued[4] (e.g., a less nutritious black diet owing to socioeconomic status), for the condition does not seem to be altered by iron supplementation. In light of this, some researchers have concluded either that blacks require less iron than whites or that anemia is "normal" for blacks.[5]

It is tempting to speculate that perhaps after millennia of parasites gnawing away at their iron supply, West Africans developed the ability to make do with less iron. Alternatively, it may be that an anemic body does not provide a favorable habitat for the proliferation of certain kinds of parasites. Certainly more research is needed on the question of black iron requirements, although it may turn out that much of the research will simply entail fitting together pieces already unearthed. For example a consideration of the etiology of black iron deficiency anemia does not normally include blood anomalies developed for malaria protection. Doubtless this is because while iron deficiency anemia does appear to confer protection against some bacterial infections, it does not seem to discourage malarial parasites.[6] On the other hand, all the West African blood anomalies so far discovered ranging from sickle trait to glucose-6-phosphate dehydrogenase (G6PD) deficiency to the tendency to lack the Duffy blood group determinants, perhaps combined with others still awaiting discovery, may possibly have produced a genetic "additive" effect, which is responsible for the lower hematocrit readings.

Today we know that about 25 percent of black North Americans (and, owing to a common West African heritage, about the same percentage of black West Indians) are born with a blood anomaly, which protects against falciparum malaria, and most are born lacking the Duffy blood group determinants, which protect against vivax malaria.[7] In modern West Africa the frequency of these traits is much higher, and so is the prevalence of iron deficiency anemia – so high in fact that the condition has been described as "nearly universal" in many regions.[8] Yet, at present, although nutritional and medical investigators are inclined to concede that the answer to black iron deficiency anemia is probably genetic, geneticists have not been inclined to take up a problem that they seem to see as one of a nutritional nature.

This in turn leaves us with the knowledge that Caribbean slaves were undoubtedly experiencing much iron deficiency anemia (as measured by white standards), probably due to the fact that they were of West African origin. But when we begin to consider the slaves' nutritional status, we can only speculate on how anemia might have affected that status.

Calcium and Vitamin D

Recently a nutritionist concerned with the problem of iron deficiency anemia in black youngsters proposed that milk be fortified with iron.[9]

Superficially this seemed a fine suggestion, for a mother with depleted iron stores will produce an iron-deficient infant, and because mothers' milk contains very little iron, the problem in the youngster would not have been corrected by the time of weaning. But as a rule, after weaning, milk has never figured prominently in the diet of those of West African descent for the very good reason that they exhibit a high frequency of lactose intolerance.[10]

Since 1958, science (much to the dismay of the dairy industry) has been discovering what most of the world's peoples already knew[11] – that they cannot drink much milk without suffering from cramps, abdominal bloating, and diarrhea.[12] Indeed the ability to consume milk after infancy is limited largely to those of European ancestry, who manage to maintain high levels of an enzyme (lactase) that breaks down the milk sugars (which cause the bloating, cramps, etc.) so they can be absorbed by the body. Lactase levels are normally high in infants, but with most peoples the levels begin to fall following infancy, so that in the case of those of West African ancestry, by the time adulthood is reached almost 80 percent exhibit some degree of lactose intolerance.[13]

Hypotheses are numerous to explain why some peoples maintain high lactase levels throughout life while others do not. A logical one to account for lactose tolerance centers on a northern climate with its long winters and overcast skies during much of the year, signifying numerous days without sunshine for the inhabitants. One consequence may have been insufficient ultraviolet irradiation and hence an insufficient stimulation of vitamin D production. For many females late rickets, deformed pelves, and difficult or impossible births would have been the result, with the latter acting as a selective device for the lactase enzyme. Those with the enzyme who could drink milk consumed both a rickets preventative (calcium) and a substitute for vitamin D (lactose), avoided the deformed pelves, and produced babies who in turn were more likely to maintain the lactase enzyme into adulthood and consequently more likely to reproduce.[14]

By contrast, a hypothesis to explain low levels of the lactase enzyme in the West African might merely reverse the European experience by suggesting that with adequate year-round sunshine in West Africa there were no vitamin D deficiency problems to summon the mechanics of genetic selection. Yet it is not that simple because other black Africans, Kenyans for example, seem to be mostly lactose tolerant.[15] Thus the determining factor for West Africa may well have been the tsetse fly, which stood ready in much of the region to discourage a milk-drinking culture even had there been environmental pressure to develop one. For as discussed in Chapter 2, the raising of cattle and other large domesticated animals has long been unprofitable, if not impossible, throughout much of the area. As a result, some have argued, a milk-drinking culture did not develop and consequently the majority of those of West African descent are lactose intolerant today.[16]

Indeed, in all probability a large proportion of the 20 percent or so of the "blacks" in the Caribbean and North America who are lactose tolerant maintain high levels of the lactase enzyme as a result of racial mixing, which provided them with the genetic ability for this maintenance.[17] There is an "adaptive" theory, which minimizes genetics by suggesting that for those who continue to drink milk after infancy, lactase enzyme levels will of necessity remain high or at least not fall so abruptly. But against this is evidence that lactase levels in the newborn of lactose-intolerant African peoples often begin to fall even during breast-feeding, causing severe problems of malnutrition during the first year of life.[18]

Thus as with the suggestion of the nutritionist who wanted milk fortified with iron, the adaptive theory could prove dangerous. For despite carefully cultivated notions of milk as a near "perfect food," its inclusion in the diet of the lactose intolerant can be positively harmful. It frequently induces diarrhea, causing the loss of many other nutrients besides the lactose the body is ridding itself of, while certain disease states, in which even the mildly lactose intolerant find themselves, can be substantially exacerbated by milk.[19]

Fortunately those without the lactase enzyme quickly learn to be wary of milk. As early as 1913, for example, attempts were made to supply free condensed milk to children in Barbados. Researchers, however, puzzled that few took advantage of it. A decade or so later an investigator for the International Health Board who visited St. Kitts discovered that "milk is hardly ever used among the colored people, even for baby feeding." More recently, in Puerto Rico, a surplus food program distributed canned powdered milk and many complained that they could not "stomach" it.[20]

Unfortunately, the lactose intolerant who cannot use milk frequently have a significant nutritional problem with inadequate calcium intakes, and many blacks in the Americas of West African origin, especially children and women who are pregnant and lactating, have been found to be calcium deficient, just like their West African counterparts.

How significant this is for blacks in North America and the Caribbean remains open to debate, as do so many nutritional questions. While some researchers feel that there is no evidence to indicate that calcium deficiency by itself is harmful, others point to populations who live in very sunny areas but who nonetheless have high frequencies of rickets precipitated by calcium (and phosphorus) deficiency.[21]

We touched briefly on vitamin D and sunshine when discussing hypotheses bearing on the development of the lactase enzyme. At this point we might delve into the subject a bit more deeply within the murky context of evidence which indicates that persons of West African descent may have different calcium requirements than Europeans.[22] Man's major source of vitamin D, so essential to metabolizing calcium (and magnesium), is his own body, which is stimulated to manufacture the vitamin by the reflection of ultraviolet radiation from his skin. Darker skins reflect considerably less and absorb considerably more of the sun's rays than lighter skins, with the result that while the skin of the average white reflects 43 percent and absorbs 57 percent of the sun's rays, the average black will reflect only 16 percent of those rays while absorbing 84 percent.[23]

In other words a white skin will receive almost three times more stimulation to produce vitamin D than a black skin, which is a major reason why rickets has historically been a severe health problem for blacks living in temperate climates.[24] The chief symptom of rickets is the inability of bones to retain calcium owing to a deficiency of calcium, or phosphorus or vitamin D, which facilitate calcium absorption. Thus while it is true that in tropical West Africa or the tropical West Indies, sunlight has meant that rickets has been much less of a problem than in the temperate zones,[25] it has nonetheless caused difficulties for numerous West African children. Nor is the disease unknown in the Caribbean, for it has been reported in rural Jamaica where children are often kept indoors too much.[26] Significantly the victims have all been "dark negroid children," leaving no doubt as to the ability of pigment to affect calcium absorption.[27]

Thus a black skin can, by limiting vitamin D production, negatively affect the absorption of what for many is an apparently insufficient intake of calcium to begin with. Moreover there are still other problems of calcium absorption to consider. Populations such as those of West Africa whose diet has centered closely on cereals consume much phytic acid, which inhibits calcium absorption.[28] Another culprit where calcium is concerned is oxalic acid, which tends to combine with calcium (and magnesium) to form highly insoluble compounds. Oxalic acid occurs in relatively few foods, but many of those few such as yams, okra, peanuts, cassava, and wild greens figured more or less prominently in the West African (and the Caribbean slave) diet.[29] Finally in this connection the suggestion has been offered (but not to our knowledge pursued) that, if a diet is low in vitamin A (as were many West African and Caribbean slave diets), then the consumer may not be able to manufacture sufficient vitamin D, despite adequate sunlight.[30]

There are also both normal and abnormal calcium losses to debit in any accounting of intake adequacy, with both occurring through the natural body processes of perspiration and elimination, while unnatural problems such as chronic diarrhea and dysentery (which it will be seen plagued both West Africans and West Indian slaves) greatly accelerate calcium as well as other important nutrient losses. Moreover, excessive perspiration from hard labor under a tropical sun would tend to place even more pressure on the individual's calcium supply – so much in fact that some authorities believe heavy exercise in the tropics precipitates enough of a calcium (and iron) loss through perspiration to elevate calcium requirements significantly.[31]

Curiously, however, blacks as a general rule perspire less than whites, which brings us to a number of black physiological differences that seem to bear on calcium as well as other apparent nutritional deficiencies.[32] For pigment, lactose intolerance, and a high intake of phytic and oxalic acids should have combined to create a severe problem of health for West Africans in the form of calcium deficiencies. However, researchers report that despite these factors, despite heavy rains, which leach West African soils (and consequently plants) of calcium, and despite a very low calcium intake on the part of the inhabitants, most adults, at any rate, have normal plasma calcium.[33]

Moreover, in the western hemisphere, black *adults* also seem to have fewer dental caries and less osteoporosis than whites, although one would expect the opposite in a supposedly calcium-deficient people.[34] However, we have carefully stressed the word *adult*, for while black adults seem extraordinarily well suited to cope with the harsh West African environment, infants and children are not. We have already taken note of their susceptibility to rickets, even though as adults they are unlikely to endure osteoporosis. And while it is true that adult blacks have fewer dental caries than whites, their children have significantly more.[35] Thus the young unquestionably suffer most from the nutritional and biological circumstances of West African ancestry, whereas adults, by surviving, seem to have made the necessary adjustments to these circumstances.

Low Birthweights and Growth Patterns

Many of the problems of the young seem to stem from a different pattern of development that nature has elaborated for blacks beginning in the womb, which means that on the average their babies weigh less at birth than white babies, both in Africa and in the Americas.[36] In part this is a function of a black rate of premature births about 60 percent greater than the white rate.[37] But even when duration of gestation is held constant, black infants weigh less than white infants and in fact in the United States are twice as heavily represented (by percent) as whites in every low-birthweight category.[38]

Until recently the weight differential at birth was viewed as a function of a lower socioeconomic status for blacks and it was assumed that, as this status began to rise so too would black birthweights. That this has not turned out to be the case suggests strongly that genetic or biochemical factors may be important variables in determining black birthweights.[39]

Certainly there seems to be something of a genetic or biochemical nature at work throughout the period of fetal development. During all of the first and much of the second trimester of pregnancy the black fetus is heavier than a white, and it is only during the last trimester that the white fetus becomes the heavier of the two.[40]

Thus it could be argued that lower black birthweights (in the United States the average is 200 grams less) are "normal" given the curtailment of black fetal growth during the third trimester of pregnancy.[41] However, it has also been hypothesized that the phenomenon is a response to centuries of black nutritional deprivation within a hostile disease environment, which so impoverished female bodies that they could not withstand the rigors of giving birth to large babies. The response was a selection for smaller babies.[42]

Another less speculative genetic reason for a lower average black than white birthweight has to do with sickle trait. It seems that mothers who possess the trait will produce infants weighing some 5 to 15 percent less than nonsickling mothers, perhaps owing to a lack of oxygenation for the fetus.[43] Since about 10 percent of the Afro-American females carry sickle trait and about 13 percent of the black births in the United States are low-birthweight babies, one can see that sickle trait alone may be responsible for much of the black birthweight problem. And it is a problem, for of the 50,000 infants born annually in the United States who do not survive a year of life, fully 75 percent are low birthweight babies.[44]

For Caribbean blacks the situation would seem comparatively worse than for blacks living in the United States, or at least it seems so based on the handful of available Caribbean information. Studies conducted on the birthweight of babies born in Barbados during the late 1950s and 1960s revealed their average birthweight to be almost 200 grams less than the average black birthweight in the United States, while other surveys have shown West Indian children to be somewhat shorter (and weigh less) than U.S. counterparts. Thus there seems no question that a combination of low black birthweights and severe malnutrition (or a combination of genetic and environmental factors) are to blame for infant and child mortality rates in much of the region[45] that soar far above those of Afro-Americans in the United States, in spite of the fact that North American blacks have between an 80 and 90 percent greater chance than whites of dying during their first year of life.[46]

For those who survive malnutrition there is evidence of an ability to "catch up" in terms of physical growth,[47] and most blacks, it has been reported, seem to have this ability built right into their growth pattern. Although initially smaller than white infants, they are much more developed physically, which gives them a better chance of survival than a white baby of identical birthweight.[48] Moreover this mature development seems to be the reason for the precociousness of the black young, relative to Caucasian age-mates, for the first two years or so of life.[49]

Following these first two years, black youngsters begin to grow more rapidly than white children all the way into early adolescence.[50]

However, this early developmental maturity, with its subsequent growth surge, has serious nutritional implications, for it means that both the first and second sets of teeth will appear earlier, skeletal development will be more advanced, and the skeletal mass will be greater and will be composed of a larger mineral mass and higher bone density.[51] Thus the black youngster's nutritional demands are also greater, especially for protein, calories, phosphorus, vitamin D, and of course calcium.[52]

It may be, however, that in the different developmental pattern of blacks lies the answer to the riddle of a seemingly calcium-deficient people who as adults do not seem to suffer from calcium deficiency. For just as it has been hypothesized that African groups such as Hottentot women developed the ability to store calories in their buttocks as a defense against famine, it seems also that West Africans may have evolved a method of storing calcium early in life against the rigors of a lifetime of deprivation.

West Africans have traditionally breast-fed infants for a prolonged period of time, ranging upwards of three years and longer. During the first two years the advanced skeletal maturation of the black infant seems to be able to store the calcium derived, while a final few months of breast-feeding beyond the two years gives him added calcium as he begins his period of accelerated growth.[53]

Evidence that this may be the case – that blacks do store calcium and then draw largely from their own skeletal structure for most of their lifetime calcium needs – can be found in the much heavier bone structure of young blacks. Indeed it is so heavy that historically many blacks have had great difficulty in learning to swim because they cannot float.[54] However, as they age their bone density decreases, suggesting, of course, a steady release of calcium over time. Thus even though they are on a calcium-deficient diet, persons of West African origin will generally have normal serum calcium levels, except females during pregnancy and lactation when the demands of the fetus frequently overwhelm their bodies' ability to release enough calcium to satisfy the needs of both mother and child.[55]

Hence, as with iron, blacks may have evolved a different pattern of supplying calcium needs which adapted them for making optimal use of some of West Africa's meager nutritional offerings. However, as we continue to emphasize, it seems that the cost for these adaptations is levied mostly on the young. Infants of iron-deficient mothers will themselves be iron deficient and consequently less able to grapple successfully with illness, while multiparous mothers after a few cycles of pregnancy and lactation will be unable to satisfy the calcium needs of the fetus from their own depleted stores. Therefore while adults seem to have the ability to function even with quite serious mineral deficiencies, many infants born with these deficiencies do not, and consequently their chances of survival are impaired.

Hypertension

There is one important black health problem, however, that does not spare adults, but rather is often their biggest killer. This is hypertension, which seems also to be a condition spawned by the circumstances of African ancestry.[56] Again there is much debate over the etiology of black hypertension and a body of literature has accumulated on the problem in the United States which lays the blame on stress stemming from the economic, social, and political circumstances of second-class citizenship in a color-conscious society. Yet because black hypertension is also known to be an acute problem of health in the Bahamas, Jamaica, the Virgin Islands, and in West Africa where presumably this sort of stress would be less, the probability is that the problem is more genetic than environmental in origin.[57]

Sodium of course has also been implicated in the etiology of essential hypertension. Indeed, because the ancient West African environment offered little of this mineral (a minimal amount of which is crucial for the maintenance of life itself), West Africans may have evolved mechanisms for making maximum use of small salt intakes by retaining much of it within their systems. Furthermore, because blacks generally perspire less than whites, they lose less salt, although even in a situation where a black and a white are sweating at similar rates, the black loses far less salt than the white. This and their apparently inherent ability to discharge less salt in the urine suggests a bodily knack for salt retention.[58]

Logically the reason for this "knack" should lie in a somewhat different kidney system adapted to the rigors of the West African environment. But it may also have to do with calcium and magnesium (and hence also with vitamin D), for this pair of minerals have important assignments in regulating body salts, as well as a soothing effect on the central nervous system.[59]

Clearly if West Africans had developed mechanisms for salt retention, then their transfer from a low-salt West African regimen to a New World diet of salt pork, beef, and fish should inevitably have created problems with hypertension. Moreover, because the hypertensive individual often craves salt, it seems significant that in the Caribbean there is much evidence that slaves were fond of and consumed a great deal of salt.[60]

Yet even this adult killer leads back to the young. For black women, who are even more hypertensive than men, suffer far more than white women from the phenomenon of the "toxemia" of pregnancy, which has been blamed for some 30,000 neonatal deaths and stillbirths annu-

ally in the United States.[61] The affliction is characterized by fluid retention, elevated blood pressure, and the convulsions of eclampsia, symptoms which suggest strongly to researchers that the etiology of the
toxemia of pregnancy for black women may include the same unknown factors that precipitate essential black hypertension.[62] But whatever medical research may ultimately reveal on the subject, we may be
reasonably assured that black hypertension is not just a problem of the
last few decades and consequently that it was a problem of health on
the plantations of the West Indies just as it is in the Islands today. This
being the case, we may also be assured that some percentage of slave
mothers suffered from the toxemia of pregnancy, and therefore, that
this disease made something of a contribution to the stillbirth and
infant mortality toll.

Implications of West African Survival

The foregoing has covered some genetic and biochemical characteristics
of West Africans and their descendents that should have affected their
nutritional status in the West Indies, and consequently, often their
very lives. Sometimes the influence of these characteristics will be
plainly, even painfully, obvious through the mist of the past. At other
times we will only be able to speculate on their possible significance in
affecting those lives.

   Indeed, we are speculating that many of the characteristics did
evolve as mechanisms of survival. Certainly the notion that blacks have
lower requirements for minerals such as iron and calcium has the virtue of making a certain amount of sense. It seems reasonable that
survivors would develop lower requirements for crucial minerals after
eons of deprivation, just as it seems logical that they would develop
ways of conserving a mineral crucial to life itself, such as sodium. In
fact, even the view that blacks have a genetic tendency to produce
smaller babies than whites cannot be dismissed out of hand, for
smaller babies must have spared malnourished mothers much mortality both in West Africa and in this hemisphere as well.

   But in this century these traits have not proved so beneficial, and
many are downright destructive of black health. Hypertension has become their biggest adult killer, low birthweights predispose many infants to disease and in some cases to mental retardation, and sickle
trait has doomed others to the tragedy of sickle cell anemia. Skin color
has meant problems of calcium absorption for innumerable black
youngsters, and severe iron deficiency has left them vulnerable to innumerable diseases, while even traits such as G6PD deficiency may not
be as benign as was previously believed.

   During slavery, however, the West Indies became in many ways a
duplicate of the West African environment, both in terms of nutrition

and disease, and therefore all of the traits, save that of an apparent ability to retain sodium, would have continued to enhance the blacks' ability to survive in the West Indies as they had in West Africa.

Selection for the Slave Trade

A final set of circumstances might be examined at this point, which, as an outgrowth of West African nutritional circumstances, may have helped to shape the West Africans' demographic experience on both sides of the Atlantic ocean.

Most peoples who left Old Worlds for the New did so because they were forced to by economic, social, political, or religious circumstances. In this sense they were outcasts from societies that had little use for them, and this applies to Africans as well as to Europeans and Asians. The black slaves who reached the Caribbean were the displaced of West Africa, victims of expanding imperial states that, it has fairly recently been demonstrated, used slavery and a slave trade to strengthen their own political and economic development even prior to the beginning of the transatlantic slave trade.[63]

In tandem with this understanding that West African natives did in fact have substantial control over the slave trade comes the question of why the percentage of men sold into that trade was so much higher than that of women. Generally this has been viewed as an African response to West Indian planter demand. But expanding imperial nations with a tight grip on supply were in a position to do more than simply respond to West Indian planter demand; they must also have influenced the supply side of the equation.

The question is complicated even further by the realization that males would have constituted a significant minority in West Africa, even without the slave trade, partly because of an as yet inexplicably lower black than white sex ratio at birth. Among whites, 106 males for every 100 females are born. Among blacks the ratio is only 103 and it has been hypothesized that this significant differential is a function of malnourished mothers on the one hand and a more fragile male than female fetus on the other—a fetus not so able to withstand the stress imposed by maternal malnutrition.[64]

This lower sex ratio at birth has probably contributed to the phenomenon of today's black population in West Africa and the West Indies containing far more females than males. Contributing also is the fact that the male disadvantage in terms of longevity, which begins even before birth, continues throughout a lifetime. Thus black sex ratios as low as 75 or 80 for modern populations are not unusual, and this tendency toward the West African female demographic preponderance may have been even more pronounced yesterday.[65]

This phenomenon of the male disadvantage will be treated in more detail later in the study because it has important implications for slave demography. But at this point we might speculate that the imbalance of males and females has had much to do with the practice of polygamy, which although certainly not the only form of family organization in West Africa, has nonetheless historically been the usual form of family structure in the region. Perhaps, too, the excess of females has had something to do with the West African division of labor, which appointed them the agriculturalists rather than the males. Certainly they were employed equally with men, or even used proportionally more than men for basic agricultural activities in the West Indies. Yet, curiously, though West African females were familiar with agriculture and constituted a demographic majority, it was mostly males who were sold off to the New World.[66]

This may not have been entirely without design. It has been discovered that at least by the seventeenth century in West African slave markets, women brought as much as men. Their agricultural skills and potential for serving as wives and concubines made them highly prized within West Africa where frequently, in the words of Herbert Klein, "They were the cheapest way to acquire status, kinship, and family."[67]

Thus, given the internal demand for slaves in West Africa, Klein has argued persuasively that the "least indispensable" slaves made up the cargoes bound for the New World, and given the internal demand for females the "least indispensable" slaves were most often males.[68] If there is some truth in the hypothesis then pursued to its logical end, it would also seem that those females who were sold into the transatlantic slave trade were among the "least indispensable" of that gender.

Doubtless one criterion of dispensability was an impaired ability to bear children, which would have come to light in many cases during the usual "time lag between capture and the moment when a buyer presented himself," and that lag was sometimes considerable. In the words of one investigator, although "Africans were captured with a view to being sold to European slavers. . .they remained for greater or lesser periods (or sometimes forever) in the service of their African captors."[69]

Evidence that fertility might have been a variable in selection for the slave trade may exist in the fact that females born in West Africa were not, within Caribbean slave populations, quite so fertile as their West Indian-born sisters, and, according to West India physicians, they had a much higher frequency of female-related health problems.[70]

Thus it could be argued that the supply side of the Atlantic slave trade not only restricted the number of women sent to the West Indies, but also saw to it that on the whole the fertility of those who did make the middle passage would be lower than the norm for West African women. If true it seems that epidemiological, nutritional, and black biological and cultural circumstances all intertwined to influence the slave trade and slavery in a number of heretofore unappreciated ways.

Black disease immunities, as we have seen, played a crucial role in stimulating West Indian planter demand. West African supply, which weighted cargoes lightly with females, and very possibly females with diminished ability to reproduce, increased the possibility that demand would not be diminished by naturally growing West Indian slave populations. Rather demand increased and was met by a swelling West African population encouraged by the introduction of American cultivated plants on the one hand and the retention of females in West Africa on the other. The sum of these parts that meshed so insidiously was that West Africa and the West Indies were locked together in a system that encouraged a kind of perpetual motion of the slave trade.

Yet this is only one sum in a differential equation. It may help to explain why first-generation Africans in the Americas failed to reproduce themselves, but it sheds no light on the problem of why Creole-born slaves also failed to do so. That answer of course must lie in the biological history of the black in the West Indies, which the following chapter begins to examine first by considering the pathological consequences of the middle passage, and then by an initial consideration of slave nutrition and a new disease environment.

Those making the middle passage and entering this environment, were, as we have seen, survivors of nutritional hardship and a disease environment that rigorously eliminated the weak. That they carried immunities against disease we know. That they may also have carried "immunities" against nutritional deprivation, can only be guessed at, although it would seem that, to some extent at least, this was the case. Many more men than women were put aboard the slave ships for reasons, we have speculated, that had much more to do with West African biology, demography, political economy, and culture, than they did with West Indian planter demand.

One more selective factor for a place beneath the decks of a slave ship was age. They were mostly young men and women who were chosen, the vast majority still in their teens or early twenties, for it was understood that the young were more durable as well as flexible. But despite this youth and despite abilities to resist pathogens and malnutrition, many would die during the voyage and during the seasoning process that followed.

PART II

DIET, DISEASE, AND DEMOGRAPHY

INTRODUCTION

Reproduction is a fundamental nutritional task of women.
United Nations (1977)[1]

Part I explored some of the West Africans' evolutionary odyssey. Part II takes up their second odyssey in the West Indies. The first and second odysseys were inextricably linked for, as we noted, the immunological experience gained in the first was pivotal in bringing about the second. Yet crucial in determining that enormous numbers would make that odyssey was the failure of the slaves to perpetuate their numbers in the West Indies.

It is true that there was enormous wastage of black lives during life in the West African barracoons and during the middle passage; Chapter 4 examines the causes of many of these deaths during this transitional period between enslavement and plantation labor. It is also true that plantation labor was not structured with the longevity of the slave uppermost in mind. But the thrust of Part II is that the most significant wastage of black lives, and the major reason for their failure to increase their numbers in the West Indies during slavery, was an incredibly high rate of infant and child mortality, as the weeding out process that we witnessed in West Africa continued in the West Indies.

That such a process was perpetuated in the Caribbean is unfortunate, but not surprising, because the West Indies became practically a duplicate of the West African disease and nutritional environment. One says practically, for it was not completely a duplicate. The tsetse fly, for example, did not take up New World residence and consequently was not on hand to discourage the production of animal protein. Thus there was more potential animal protein available to the slaves, even though most of this type of protein that reached slave stomachs was imported by the planters. But at least the slaves' diet in the Caribbean contained enough good quality protein to increase slave heights significantly.

On the other hand, the diets of the slaves, like those of the West Africans, continued to center on a single cereal, with too little in the way of supplementation, while the parasites that had traveled with them to the New World continued to increase nutritional requirements

53

that the diet could not meet in the first place, with the result that severe malnutrition continued to plague the West African.

Because, to reword slightly the opening quote to this introduction, reproduction is fundamentally a nutritional task for women, perpetuation of malnutrition would, as it had in Africa, fall with heaviest weight on the very young, and Part II argues that its weight was too heavy to bear for more than half of the slave young who perished before the age of five.

The argument is advanced in step-by-step fashion beginning in Chapter 4 with a look at the kinds and quantities of foods available to slaves in the Caribbean. Chapter 5 constructs slave diets based on this information and then subjects those diets to analysis with a close eye on the nutritional chemistry of the utilization of the nutriments and nutrients in question. Chapter 6 begins an effort to verify serious nutritional deficiencies in the slave diet pointed up by nutritional analysis, by searching the historical record for those nutritional diseases that such deficiencies would have surely produced in the adult consumer. For in the case of thiamine, in particular, a deficiency suffered by the slave mothers would have automatically meant a tremendous rate of infant mortality. Chapter 7 pauses in the search for nutritional diseases to discuss West Indian slave birth and death records, and then returns briefly to West Africa in search of a demographic model to make plausible the possibility that the slaves' infant and child mortality rates embraced over half of those born, while Chapter 8 proceeds to examine the diseases that would have contributed most to this slaughter. Finally, Chapter 9, while it touches upon slave genetic diseases and slave medical care, is primarily concerned with a number of infectious diseases that also winnowed the slave population. Yet even here malnutrition receives much of the blame, in part because some cases of these so-called infectious diseases turn out to be nutritional diseases in disguise, and in part because, as a rule, the malnourished are less able to fight off infections than the healthy individual.

It is true that there are enormous risks in attempting to diagnose yesterday's diseases on the basis of often vaguely described symptoms, but it is hoped that our procedure has minimized that risk; first, a nutritional deficiency revealed by analysis has to be a serious one in order to be vigorously pursued and, second, a serious disease with symptoms known to be the result of that deficiency has to be widespread among the slaves before a possible "match" between deficiency and disease is claimed. Third, an attempt is made to examine and eliminate other possible causes of the illness besides nutrition, and finally the disease must be one peculiar to slaves.

The latter is a criterion because the whites in the Islands serve as a control group of sorts. For while the slaves were malnourished, the whites (save soldiers, sailors, and the racially mixed lower classes of

Puerto Rico and Cuba) were not. Rather there is abundant evidence that they consumed prodigious quantities of both fresh and imported meats, which suggests that they had little difficulty with B vitamin deficiencies or iron for that matter, and surely no problem of a low protein or fat intake. Whites were also lavish in their use of citrus fruits, including juices for various punch drinks, which meant that they had a more than adequate vitamin C intake, while the large quantities of imported butter and cheese alone probably would have kept vitamin A deficiency at bay (not to mention calcium deficiency) even had they consumed no corn, eggs, cream, or vegetables, which they did.[2]

In short then, if the slave diet was severely deficient in a vitamin or mineral and if slaves suffered in large numbers from the symptoms produced by this deficiency while whites did not, and if other explanations for the etiology of the disease can be discounted or minimized, then it is felt that the risk of claiming the existence of a nutritional disease among the slaves has also been minimized.

CHAPTER 4

THE MIDDLE PASSAGE AND MALNUTRITION

. . .and it will still continue true, that never can so much misery be found condensed into so small a space as in a slave ship during the middle passage.

William Wilberforce (1807)[1]

I think it could be plausibly argued that changes of diet are more important than changes of dynasty or even of religion. . .yet it is curious how seldom the all-importance of food is recognized.

George Orwell (1937)[2]

The "scramble" was held soon after a slave ship entered port – the captain anxious to be rid of his cargo with its ever-present danger of revolt, particularly now that the slaves knew they were no longer at sea. But despite this anxiety blacks were first "made up" by experts among the crew; skins were rubbed with oil to make them shine, rum was administered to clear the eyes and brighten the countenance, sores were covered with iron rust and gunpowder, lesions closed, and even anuses corked to prevent the telltale leakage of the flux.[3]

Thus, during the scramble, defects often escaped detection as prospective buyers rushed about claiming slaves. Only later might the owner discover that his new acquisitions were plagued with yaws or severe worm infestation or dysentery or all three. Yet the spectacle of the scramble, with all its haste and attendant financial risk highlighted the eagerness of West Indian planters for black slaves. They had become convinced that only the black man could labor and survive in warm climates.

Many, however, did not survive and as the early "scramble" method of slave purchasing gave way to the auction, buyers had more of an opportunity to study prospective acquisitions, with an eye to potential longevity. Youth brought a premium, for the young were more resilient. Those with smallpox scars commanded a higher price than those without. Emaciation demanded keen judgment. Was it evidence of the flux, which killed so many during seasoning, or was it merely debilitation, which a few weeks of good diet would cure? Eyes met eyes as buyers studied corneas for signs of fever and jaundice. Teeth, gums, and tongue were checked, muscles probed, skin inspected. The classic marks of good health were "a glossy sleekness of unblemished skin, clear eyes, red tongue, open chest [and] small belly," but all too frequently buyers saw only the small belly.[4] Tribal scars worn by many on their faces were also of interest. Those with homelands on the Gold and Windward Coasts were believed, by the British at least, to make the most durable, although not necessarily the most docile, slaves and prior to 1790 or so Jamaican planters bought around 80 percent of the Gold Coast slaves shipped to the Caribbean by the English slave trade.[5]

Interestingly slaves from the Gold Coast were about an inch taller than the average Africans entering the West Indies.[6] The principal cereal on the Gold Coast was corn, which popular wisdom of the day held made consumers healthier than those from yam- or cassava-eating cultures – a popular wisdom with which modern nutritionists would agree as yams and cassava are notoriously low in their protein yield.[7] Interestingly, too, those regions such as the Bight of Biafra and Central Africa, where the diet centered on yams or cassava, produced the shortest slaves introduced to the West Indies.[8] By contrast, the tallest Africans were recorded as originating from the northern portions of West Africa – Sierra Leone, and especially Senegambia – where today many are herdsmen, others are farmers, and high-quality protein plays a fairly prominent role in the diet.[9]

Women posed another kind of problem for slave buyers. Although their muscle would be employed as a man's in the fields, their notoriously high frequency of gynecological problems could incapacitate them as well as diminish their ability to reproduce.[10] Of the African-born women, Ibos, who were reportedly the least healthy and least well nourished, were also allegedly the most subject to "obstructions of the menstrua" or amenorrhea, a phenomenon often linked to malnutrition.[11]

Slave height data may also suggest that women generally were more malnourished than men, which might buttress observations about West African eating priorities. For while one study showed that the average height of African males (5 feet, 3½ inches) was an inch less than Creole-born counterparts (5 feet, 4½ inches), African-born females were an inch and a-half shorter (5 feet) than Creole-born females (5 feet, 1½ inches).[12]

The scrutiny slaves received at West Indian auctions was not the first time they had been critically evaluated by whites. A physical examination of sorts had previously been administered by a slaving captain or ship's physician at the time of purchase on the African Coast, with shrewd eyes attempting to determine whether or not bodies were strong enough to withstand the normal rigors of the middle passage.

Eyes also searched for signs of hidden disease, which could multiply those rigors many times.[13] But the normal rigors alone would produce an in-transit mortality rate of between 5 and 15 percent,[14] in an experience that could scarcely have been more nutritionally devastating for the slaves.

First, of course, West Africans boarding a slaving vessel shared a history of general malnutrition, although some were more malnourished than others. Recent research has revealed that many slaves destined for Brazil were put into the trade during times of famine to relieve pressure on the food supply, and this may have been true, at times, for slaves shipped to the Caribbean as well.[15] But, as we have seen, even those nurtured by a normal West African nutritional regimen were far from well nourished. And from capture to sale into the slave trade, malnutrition must have often worsened considerably. The forced march to the coast demanded much caloric output that could easily exceed nutritional intake, while life in the barracoons on the coast was, doubtless, often characterized by poor treatment, including scanty rations.

However, despite their poor nutritional state, the slaves (at least those not held in dungeons) had received adequate stimulation from the sun to facilitate vitamin D production. But after boarding a slaving ship to be chained beneath decks in the darkness, even this was denied them, save for those lucky enough to be given daily exercise periods on deck. Unfortunately, however, even lucky individuals with black skin would not have been able to take full advantage of a brief time in the sun for purposes of vitamin D production and a vitamin D deficit would have impaired calcium absorption and forced bodies to draw heavily on stores in the bones.

This would probably not have been damaging for slaves whose vessel immediately set sail for the New World where abundant sunshine awaited them some forty to ninety days hence.[16] For many, however, departure was not immediate, because slavers – at least until the nineteenth century – rarely filled their holds at a single place, but rather ranged up and down the coast picking up a few slaves here and a few more there. Usually securing a full cargo was a matter of long weeks or months so that some slaves actually endured up to a year without adequate sunlight before they stepped ashore in the West Indies.[17]

A lack of vitamin C was another health problem for slaves on board for extended periods of time because scurvy breaks out after about four to six months of vitamin C deprivation. Its dietary absence, however, would have impaired the slaves' ability to ward off other illnesses much sooner. Some slaving captains were aware of scurvy prevention practices and had lemon or lime juice regularly issued to the slaves. Yet these were the exception. As late as the early nineteenth century, most seamen of the world's navies were still suffering from this ancient curse and certainly it was an important cause of death on slaving voyages.[18]

Diets aboard ship varied over time and from ship to ship. But generally rice and yams made up the core diet, boiled into a kind of soup to which was often added a sauce made of boiled fish, shrimp, or beef. Other additions and sometimes mainstays were corn and European horsebeans. Palm oil, red peppers, and perhaps flour for thickening are also mentioned as soup ingredients.[19]

Had slaving vessels offered all of the above items (including the citrus juice) for the whole of the voyage, the unwilling passengers would have at least consumed a reasonably well-balanced diet. But most did not and, at the opposite extreme, there were slaving ships that served only boiled rice and yams. Slaves fed this meager fare would have been severely deficient in almost all nutrients and their bodies would actually have been starving, although their stomachs were full. That this happened all too frequently, at least in the latter stages of a voyage, seems confirmed by the expectation that slaves reaching the West Indies would in fact be badly malnourished. During the early eighteenth century when the English held the *Asiento* (right to supply slaves to Spanish America), the British South Sea Company used the island of Jamaica to "refresh" newly arriving slaves by feeding them well before sending them on to Spanish ports, while French slavers used Martinique for much the same purpose. Elsewhere planters fully expected to have to do this sort of "refreshing" after purchase with plenty of fresh meat and vegetables, for a description of slaves reaching the ports of the New World as "thin and weake" was a normal one.[20]

Klein and Engerman have shown that the cost of food bought on the African Coast along with water and water casks was a negligible portion (less than 5 percent) of the total cost of outfitting a slaver and consequently slave ship masters were not likely to skimp on provisions for financial reasons.[21] On the other hand storage space was a problem. It has been estimated that some ten tons of food were required for every 100 slaves, while the space required for water casks was enormous.[22] Live animals such as goats and chickens if taken aboard would therefore have been consumed first; salted and dried meats and fish next, so that by mid-voyage most of the complete protein available probably would have been consumed leaving yams and rice as the staples. Yams of course could rot and rice could become rancid, so doubtless toward the end of even a normal voyage problems of food spoilage led to reduced rations of the vegetable and cereal stores. Extended voyages obviously would have produced sharply increasing mortality rates, as food supplies dwindled in both quality and quantity, while ships that ran short of water would have quickly witnessed astronomically high mortality rates.

There was more at work, however, than simply an inadequate intake of nutrients to produce a slave's "thin and weake" appearance upon arrival in the New World. Joseph Miller has indicated that mortality aboard slaving vessels peaked at the time of embarkation and the first few days at sea and then declined sharply, only to rise again if the voyage was substantially prolonged.[23] One logical conclusion offered by Miller is that the U-shaped or declining mortality curve indicates that slave treatment aboard ship was not nearly so bad as it had been during the preembarkation experience.

This, of course, conforms with our arguments that the generally malnourished state of West Africans may have been exacerbated considerably by the march to the sea and, as noted, the extended stay in holding areas prior to embarkation could have been nutritionally devastating. This coupled with the shock of being moved into a dank, dark hold, and the despair of knowing that one had seen the last of his homeland and family must surely account for some of the high mortality throughout the initial stage of the voyage.[24] But another factor normally overlooked is seasickness. Klein, Stein, and Postma have all shown that the "tight packing" of slaves in vessels had no significant impact on mortality.[25] But whether slaves were packed tightly or not, they were nonetheless crowded together in a hot, airless hold fetid with the stench of perspiration and excrement.

These were not, for the most part, a seafaring people, but even if they were, the stink and the fear would have helped to produce seasickness soon after the ship glided past the channel entrance and plowed through the first of the breakers rolling in from the South Atlantic to begin its characteristic plunging, yawing, and rising motion.[26] At this point the odor of vomit would have joined the "normal" stench of mucus and feces and sweat and the seasickness would have "spread" as if contagious. Doubtless for some this was the breaking point and madness or death overtook them. For others, however, seasickness would have brought death in a more insidious fashion.

Slaving captains knew that as they began the middle passage their vessel was now a bomb with the fuse lit. The trick was to make the middle passage quickly enough to defuse the bomb, which would otherwise explode in the form of scurvy, amebic dysentery, and a food and water shortage. Many, therefore, must have been of the hard-driving variety who crowded on every inch of sail in a pell mell dash across the Atlantic. If so, this tactic would have tended to perpetuate an initial slave seasickness for days, which in turn would have deprived individuals of almost all nutrients, for whether they managed to eat or not, they would not have retained the food.

This lack of nutrients alone would have been serious. For those already nutritionally depleted by their preembarkation experience, it could easily have become life threatening, particularly when the heavy load of helminthic parasites that the slaves carried is taken into consideration.[27] In the words of Josué de Castro, "with good nutrition . . . worms become quite inoffensive, sharing the regime of abundance like peaceful fellow boarders . . . all that is necessary is to furnish enough food for both men and worms."[28]

When sufficient food is not forthcoming worms get restless, and when it is almost totally absent, they become downright dangerous. Symptoms include abdominal pain and swelling and diarrhea. Diarrhea in turn could only have resulted in further nutritional depletion and dehydration, while the deterioration in hygiene from diarrhea would most likely have precipitated bacillary dysentery in epidemic form early in the voyage. The reduced vitality in turn could easily have activated latent amebiasis that would explode into epidemic proportions later on.[29]

There is no question that these diseases, then called the "white and bloody fluxes," were the major killers of slaves aboard ships,[30] and with our step-by-step review of the onset of these illnesses it can easily be understood why this was the case. Nutritional deprivation prior to embarkation, and dysentery, which has been reported as "prevalent" in the barracoons on the coast, joined with seasickness shortly after sailing and the ever-present parasites to kill the least hardy among the black cargoes early in the middle passage. In addition the generally weakened condition of slaves produced by this syndrome would also have rendered them especially susceptible to contagious diseases such as smallpox, the most dreaded of shipboard illnesses, while measles, influenza, and the like could and did also take a heavy toll in cramped quarters.

But assuming the vessel was spared these epidemics, slaves would have gradually recovered from their seasickness and assuming that, at this point in the voyage at least, salted pork or fish were included in their regimen, they would have taken in enough nutrients to allay the dysentery and quiet the parasites, thereby beginning to regain lost nutritional ground. Yet during the final stages of the voyage they would once more begin to lose that ground. Lengthy vitamin C deprivation would finally be producing the debilitating signals of at least subclinical scurvy, vitamin A deficiency would be creating the night blindness so characteristic of slaves aboard ships, and bodies would have become progressively weaker owing to vitamin D deprivation and calcium depletion. Moreover it was during the latter stages that the ship was most likely to run short of water along with foods supplying animal protein, and a shortage of the B complex (particularly riboflavin) would have once again precipitated diarrhea. The sum of these factors in the latter stages of the voyage would have produced the "thin and weake" appearance of those who arrived in West Indian ports – so weak in fact that Baron von Humboldt reported that in Cuba during the "hot months" slave mortality during the sale alone was sometimes as high as 4 percent.[31]

The factors also probably account for other kinds of mortality among those aboard ship and newly arrived in the West Indies including "fixed melancholy," a mysterious form of death in which slaves seemed to withdraw into themselves, refused food, and apparently willed themselves to die, which they did quite suddenly. Doubtless this very process did occur and will someday be explained as modern medicine broadens and deepens its knowledge of the interrelationship between the psyche, bodily functions, and disease. But somatic causes could also contribute to the appearance of "fixed melancholy." Chronic dysentery, for example, combined with the vomiting of seasickness and the perspiration produced by overcrowding in the heat below decks would have quickly undermined the ability of slave bodies to maintain water balance by disrupting osmotic pressure. Kidneys, in an effort to retrieve water, would have worked to retain sodium and in the process would actually have pulled even more water out of the cells, with dehydration the result, and a dehydration that may have been even more serious for West Africans than most peoples given their ability to retain sodium (see Chapter 3). Among the symptoms of dehydration are sunken features and eyes that are particularly notice-able because they tend to recede into their orbits (giving the impression of withdrawing into oneself). Moreover a sudden, as opposed to a lingering death, is likely because in dehydration potassium is pulled out of the cells and excreted. As this occurs the brain cells are affected to the point where the victim becomes unaware of thirst and his need for water, and as potassium losses continue the victim dies of heart failure caused by potassium loss. This sudden onset of death shortly after the initial symptoms of sunken eyes must have seemed mysteri-ous indeed to slaving crews.[32]

A diagnosis of "fixed melancholy" at other times may have cloaked cases of outright starvation. Slaves who were semistarved upon em-barking for the New World, and then robbed of their nutrient intake during the voyage by seasickness and dysentery could easily have developed those signs of personality derangement that accompany starvation including a refusal to eat, with which slaving crews were frequently confronted, and were prepared to deal with by forced feed-ing. The refusal to eat, which also occurred among slaves newly ar-rived in the Caribbean, was interpreted as an attempt at suicide. But in fact it is "normal" behavior after a certain point in the starvation pro-cess. Significantly, "fixed melancholy" was claimed to have been a condition more prevalent among the Ibos than other African peoples – significant because the Ibos were reputed to be the most poorly nour-ished of the major West African groupings.[33]

Another piece of evidence which indicates that newly arrived slaves

did indeed suffer starvation has to do with the superior ability of females to endure both the middle passage and the seasoning process. In
the words of Orlando Patterson, "a fact of some significance regarding
the mortality of newly arrived Africans was that far more women
tended to survive than men."[34] At sea, Patterson attributed this to
better treatment on the slaving vessel because females posed less threat
of mutiny and because they were sexually exploited by the seamen.
During seasoning Patterson again feels that a female's chances of survival were greater because they were in such demand sexually by male
slaves that they were once again assured better treatment.

Doubtless all of this is true, but it is also a fact that females have
significantly more body fat than males and therefore have historically
proved themselves better able to withstand conditions of starvation
than males, who die from the condition much earlier.[35] Thus a combination of better treatment for females coupled with a greater ability to
withstand nutritional hardship seems to have accelerated the process
of the African males' actuarial disadvantage, even though the males
may have been better nourished than females in West Africa. This, in
turn, acted from the middle passage onward to begin closing the male
heavy sex ratio of West Indian slave populations.

Interestingly, like the slave buyers who scrutinized the new arrivals,
physicians and ship captains too believed that slaves from the Gold
Coast and Whydah (where the principal foodstuff was corn) were more
durable, and insisted that they "showed the least mortality" during the
middle passage. The "next best in health" were those from the Windward Coast, whose diet centered on rice and corn, while those from
the Bight of Guinea, who consumed mostly yams, were "subject to the
greatest mortality."[36]

Thus once again we have evidence that the traders and buyers of
human bodies to some extent based financial judgments of those
bodies on whatever had nourished them in Africa. Not only is corn a
superior food to yams, but cultures that grow corn are also more likely
to have some animal protein in the diet and slaves from the Gold Coast
did raise goats and hogs according to a physician in the slave trade.[37]

In short, the nutritional background of slaves does seem to have
been a very important parameter in middle passage survival. It also
appears to have played a role in survival following arrival in the West
Indies, for a greater challenge to the slaves' survival than the middle
passage still lay ahead of them in the form of that period of psychological and physiological adjustment to West Indian plantation life euphe-
mistically called "seasoning."

It was a time during which newly arrived slaves died at a much
higher rate than others on the plantation. But the length of that period
and the rates at which slaves died form questions that have received
vague or contradictory answers. For example, a nineteenth-century ob-

server of Cuban slavery discussed seasoning in terms of a single year and placed the mortality rate at between 7 and 12 percent.[38] A student of Jamaican slavery, however, has defined the period as lasting from one to three years during which between 25 and 33 percent of the new arrivals died,[39] while for Brazil it is claimed that "seasoning" was a four-year process with a mortality rate upwards of 50 percent, a rate it is acknowledged that was probably higher than Caribbean rates.[40]

Others have offered seasoning mortality rates without specifying the time elapsed. For example Fogel and Engerman have placed the seasoning rate for the West Indies generally as high as one-third of the new arrivals "during their first few years," while for Cuba a recent estimate has 25 percent of the new imports perishing sometime during their early careers on the island.[41]

These are but a few of many such estimates, but a representative few, which when haphazardly synthesized yield a seasoning period of about three years during which one quarter or so of the new slaves died, with half of this mortality occurring during their initial year in the Islands.

There are good reasons why mortality should have been at its highest during this first year and at least one very good reason why this mortality should have peaked during the very first days and weeks of that year. The reason is amebic dysentery. Certainly slaving captains did not knowingly take slaves aboard suffering from the disease. But it came aboard nonetheless, often in a latent form with an incubation period of between twenty and ninety days. As noted earlier, malnutrition on board would have activated latent amebiasis, if the preembarkation diet had not already done so, and the lack of hygenic conditions aboard ship would have quickly abetted its invasion of heretofore uninfected bodies.[42] Hence, although some slaves would suffer from the illness during the voyage, particularly during the latter stages, while others would be stricken just as the voyage ended (certainly slave buyers had learned to be on the lookout for the "bloody flux"), it very often did not explode among the slaves until after they had reached their new plantation homes.

Michael Craton, for example, reports that on Jamaican plantations the bloody flux was the chief cause of seasoning deaths, which occasionally killed as many as one-third of all new arrivals.[43] Others too report dysentery a major killer of newly imported slaves which suggests that many slaves were weakened twice by dysentery connected with the middle passage – bacillary dysentery early and the amebic type late in the voyage or shortly after arrival in the West Indies.[44]

The virulence of amebic dysentery has a good deal to do with nutrition and the disease in modern times is treated with a diet "high in protein, low in carbohydrates and supplemented by ample sources of vitamins, especially the B complex."[45] Unfortunately the diet confronting the newly arrived slave was frequently the opposite – low in protein and the B complex and high in carbohydrates.

In part this was by design for West Indian physicians urged that slaves upon reaching the plantation should be placed under an older person from the same West African region, who would be responsible for his diet. That diet, said Dr. James Grainger in 1764, should be as close as possible to that of the new slave's homeland.[46] Had this consideration been generally given to slaves, they would have at least derived some psychological comfort in their misery if not nutritional help. But another physician writing decades later lamented, "It is little considered what they [the slaves] are accustomed to eat before they came among us. We give them what we have, and, frequently we may not have the means of getting that which may be most proper for them."[47]

One familiar with West Indian foodstuffs might easily linger with some puzzlement over these statements for the slave diet would seem in most ways to have been a duplicate of that of West Africa. Cornmeal or rice were generally the core cereals, cassava and plantains were other mainstays, while yams, bananas, sweet potatoes, eddoes, coconuts, red peppers, and catalue (a kind of spinach) also figured to a greater or lesser extent into the diets of slaves across the Caribbean.[48] The only apparent important difference from the West African regimen seems to have been the more or less regular injection of a little animal protein in the form of salt fish, beef, or pork, which presumably was a major factor in the height increase of Creole-born slaves.

The problem facing the new arrivals, however, was that although the nutriments available in the West Indies did duplicate those of West Africa, the foods from their particular regions were not always those featured in the diets of a plantation or island. Thus some were so unaccustomed to animal protein that they became ill upon ingesting it, while others, particularly those few imported from East Africa, reportedly sometimes died because of a lack of animal protein. Slaves whose core diets had previously consisted of plantains, yams, and cassava were often suddenly confronted with corn or rice, while others arriving at islands like Puerto Rico found plantains and yams to subsist on instead of the corn or rice they were accustomed to.[49] Those of course whose bodies had difficulty in adjusting to new dietary regimens (and many doubtless did, for such changes often produce a lengthy bout with diarrhea) faced reduced odds of surviving, for in the face of amebic dysentery as well as other nutritionally draining diseases, they needed all the nutrients they could get.

Other factors with nutritional implications at this stage that militated against slave survival included cool West Indian evenings and chilly mornings, particularly in the winter months. Here the West African's relative intolerance for cold would have exacerbated his weakened condition were he unfortunate enough to arrive in the cold season while his malnourished state would probably have contributed to low blood sugar leaving him even more susceptible to the cold. In this state the slave would have been a near helpless prey to the "fevers," particularly pneumonia from which the newly arrived suffered so severely.[50]

Finally of course were a slave put to work immediately the requisite caloric output could only worsen his already nutritionally depleted condition. Thus in one form or another malnutrition becomes a lethal constant in any explanation of why slaves died "wholesale" upon arrival.[51] Moreover survivors of the initial stages of the seasoning process were still not free from the specter of starvation. For assuming that they had made the adjustments to their new diet and renewed their strength they, along with the others, now became subject to the capricious manner in which West Indian economics, politics, and weather could and did trifle with their very lives, by depriving them of the nutriments essential to those lives.

There were two major methods of providing for slave comestibles in the Islands. The first, common to Barbados and the Leewards, was to devote almost all the land to sugar cultivation and import the bulk of the slave provisions. The second, common to Jamaica and some of the Windwards, was to plant lands not suitable for sugar with maize and other crops for slave consumption.[52] In the case of the Spanish Islands, Puerto Rico falls firmly into the latter category and Cuba more or less into the former.

Yet neither system was mutually exclusive, for all Islands imported the slaves' major source of animal protein in the form of salted fish, pork, and beef. Moreover the system(s) changed over time. For example, early in the history of slavery in Barbados, "planters strove to make quick fortunes, then to return to Great Britain as wealthy squires."[53] This aim meant that on the one hand planters were unwilling to give slaves land and the free time to grow provisions, and on the other that they refused to spend much of their profits on imported provisions.[54] Yet, by the latter part of the eighteenth century, economic circumstances had so increased the value of slaves, and wars by cutting off supplies and creating famine had been so destructive of the slaves, that Barbadian planters began a policy of "amelioration," which included an effort to raise slave provisions locally. As a result, by 1815 or so many estates were devoting as much as two-thirds of their land for slave provisions, and not incidentally at this point the island's slaves were reputed to be the healthiest in the region.[55]

Home-grown crops, however, did not necessarily guarantee healthy slaves. For one thing it was the slaves' responsibility to tend these provision grounds and there is much evidence that they did so indifferently.[56] For another, there was a basic conflict between slaves and planters over what should be planted. According to Bryan Edwards, slaves tended to prefer cultivating plantains, corn, and other above-ground crops at risk of wind damage, as opposed to "ground" provisions such as yams, eddoes, potatoes, and cassava, which were not.[57] Thus when hurricanes did strike the result was near famine unless the planter was prudent enough to have stored provisions against such an eventuality.[58] Droughts, if severe, spared neither above-ground nor below-ground crops while those crops could also fail for any one of a dozen reasons.

Perhaps at least in part for this reason, even Jamaica, which is usually singled out as the foremost example of a "self-feeding" island, seems to have relied on both methods. The Jamaica Slave Act(s) required that one acre be planted with provisions for every ten slaves on the plantation and this "exclusive" of the slaves' own gardens.[59] The slaves then by cultivating both provision grounds and gardens were "expected to maintain themselves (except in times of scarcity arising from hurricanes and droughts). . ."[60] and thus Jamaica was intended to become "less dependent on outside supplies," and allegedly imported little for the slaves save for salted fish.[61]

Yet investigators of Worthy Park Plantation have discovered that "little of the staple diet. . .was grown on the fertile lands of the estate itself because the slaves were too fully occupied working the sugar land to be diverted to food cultivation and most of the Jamaican food was bought not grown."[62] Thus even with much land theoretically available for provision crops Jamaican planters could elect, like their Barbadian counterparts, to concentrate slave labor on sugar and purchase outside supplies. Moreover the tendency to appropriate the best and closest land to the plantation for sugar cultivation meant that slave provision grounds were frequently located some distance from the plantation. Indeed after 1760 or so in Jamaica the practice was to assign slaves marginal lands for cultivation often up in the hills.[63] It is easy to speculate that distance militated against the proper cultivation of those provision grounds by weary slaves.

Jamaica's system then was a mixed method of feeding slaves, and many planters doubtless bought large quantities of cereals for their slaves off the plantation, although not necessarily outside of the Island. Whether the grain was purchased or grown, however, it was rationed to the slaves along with animal protein much as it was in Barbados, and elsewhere in the Caribbean.[64]

If one is to believe planter claims of openhandedness[65] and that laws were obeyed regarding slave rations,[66] then most slaves would have had no difficulty at least with undernutrition. There were critical travelers in Puerto Rico[67] and Cuba[68] during the early nineteenth century who felt that planters did obey the law by issuing at least a half pound of salted meat or fish daily, and some modern authorities also believe that this was the normal ration.[69]

Cornmeal and rice were the principal cereals allotted, with slaves receiving one or the other at the rate of about a pint daily, which seems to have been somewhat standard across the Caribbean. In Barbados corn was the cereal issued, whereas in Jamaica, Puerto Rico, and Cuba both corn and rice are mentioned as staples with cost and availability doubtless the determining factors.[70]

In addition to the cereal and fish or meat allowance, plantains, cassava, and yams were grown on many plantations and issued as supplements when they were in season.[71] Slaves also grew seasonal items, including those just mentioned, along with greens and fruit. Moreover many apparently raised hogs and chickens, but studies stress that these, along with much of the produce, were usually more important to the slaves economically than they were nutritionally, since slaves sold both produce and animals, using the earnings for clothing, liquor, tobacco and other extras.[72]

Nevertheless, the picture that appears to emerge is one of meat or fish and cereal allotments coupled with some produce from slave gardens providing a diet that, if a bit monotonous, was at least nutritionally adequate. Yet the picture can be misleading. For example, although some contemporary accounts and modern studies alike suggest that Cuban slaves were well provided for in terms of protein, early nineteenth-century height data have identified Cuban Creole-born slaves along with counterparts in Guiana and Trinidad as among the shortest of Caribbean slaves.[73] Moreover, and more to the point, Creole-born slaves in the Caribbean as a group were significantly shorter than those of the United States.[74] Since the protein allotment for slaves in the southern United States was about three pounds of salt pork weekly, this suggests that most Caribbean slaves did not receive the generous allotment of animal protein that has been claimed.[75] This appears to be confirmed by checks of salt fish imports to Jamaica and Barbados, which, along with plantation allotment records, point to a pound of salt fish weekly as closer to the norm.[76]

Higman has also discovered that the shorter Creole slaves lived on islands devoted to intense sugar cultivation, whereas the taller slaves lived in the Bahamas, the Grenadines, and Bermuda where sugar was not extensively cultivated and presumably slaves had more time to fish, garden, and generally take care of their own nutritional needs.[77] One implication of these findings that deserves serious consideration is that sugar slaves on planter allotments did not have the time, opportunity, or energy to supplement their diets to any great extent and Higman for one believes that "differences in nutrition may account for a large part of the observed differences in growth."[78]

It would seem, then, that even though the height data suggest that the Caribbean slave diet was superior to what they ate in West Africa, it was nonetheless a miserably limited regimen for many sugar slaves whose diet was apparently more or less confined to a little animal protein and lots of carbohydrates.[79] Confirmation of a lack of variety in slave comestibles may be found in numerous sources. It has been reported for example that some slaves in Cuba received only two meals daily consisting solely of corn and salt fish. Slave diets in Puerto Rico and Santo Domingo have been described as so low in quality that they barely sustained life, while those in St. Domingue and other French islands have been characterized as poor because of a heavy carbohydrate concentration relative to protein and an absolute lack of variety.[80]

More variety in slave comestibles was a regular theme of physicians; many visitors deplored the lack of animal protein given to slaves, and government officials frequently expressed concern about the quality of slave diets.[81]

Finally it has been alleged that some planters regularly stinted on rations, which surely meant hunger for those who could not or did not tend gardens. Hence Orlando Patterson has observed that even in Jamaica where provisions were supposed to be home grown "there were still enough loop-holes in the system to lead many slaves to beg and steal for their daily sustenance."[82] Based on this sort of evidence, some modern authorities have concluded that the slave diet was at best rich in starches and poor in proteins.[83]

Thus it would seem that the slave diet of the late eighteenth and early nineteenth century, which produced a significant height increase in first-generation Creoles, is nonetheless nutritionally suspect. How much worse must the diet have been for, say, British slaves a few decades before when wars with the Dutch and with the French disrupted shipping and brought famine and death to many. The Caribbean naval conflict during the American Revolution did the same, and in its aftermath as the price of slaves rose planters began to concern themselves with improving the material conditions of slave life. Hence it was only during the late eighteenth and in the early nineteenth century that a conscious policy of "amelioration" was implemented that resulted in improved nutritional circumstances for the slaves.[84]

Yet improved does not mean good, just better, for climatic, economic, and political considerations continued to affect slave diets. Six hurricanes in seven years (1780–1786) coupled with a greater cost in supplies after 1783 brought nutritional hardship to many Jamaican slaves and economic ruin to many planters.[85] For late eighteenth-century Cuba, the sugar revolution was just beginning and while a contraband slave trade would make slaves plentiful, its contraband nature made the political and economic future uncertain for a new group of planters who were as eager to become wealthy as their British and French predecessors had been.[86]

Moreover, in all slave islands, hunger of a seasonal nature stalked many plantations. During the dry season (December to June) most provision crops were harvested, fruits were available, and money too, as the sugar cane was cut and processed. During the wet season, however, slaves too often went hungry.[87]

Consequently even during "amelioration" concern was voiced about slave hunger and the possibility of famine.[88] Unquestionably malnutrition was a cruel fact of life for the whole of the period of Caribbean slavery, which was mitigated somewhat only towards the end of the eighteenth century. One therefore might legitimately suspect that were slave heights to become available for the early part of that century there would have been little difference between those of the African and Creole born.

A final problem with slave nutrition is that their meager intake had to be shared. We have already observed that West Africans carry a large load of worms and noted the damage that worms becoming hungry may have done to slaves aboard ship. These worms of course were also migrants and, along with their hosts, took up residence in the New World. Slaves then are credited with importing a number of helminthic infections from Africa including the misnamed *Necator americanus*, better known as hookworm.[89]

Yet contrary to popular belief the hookworm was probably not a major factor in damaging black health. Ever since the Rockefeller-funded hookworm eradication program was launched early in this century, researchers have been aware of a relative resistance to the ravages of hookworm infection on the part of Afro-Americans.[90] However, that researchers continue to report widespread hookworm infection among them has seemed a contradiction, which has misled students of black health.[91]

The problem is that one must distinguish between hookworm infection and hookworm disease. Clinically the distinction is usually based on the presence or absence of iron deficiency anemia, and as a rule a good diet containing large amounts of iron, vitamins, and protein will provide a partial immunity to hookworm disease, whereas a bad diet can predispose an individual to the worst of its consequences.[92]

This of course explains why hookworm disease has been so devastating to poor whites throughout the hemisphere, but sheds absolutely no light on the nature of the blacks' ability to consistently maintain a lighter level of hookworm infection and reveal fewer symptoms of hookworm disease than whites similarly infected.[93] One observer has called it an "example of acquired resistance," which "the experts refuse to describe as racial immunity,"[94] while one of the first to report on the phenomenon in the American South commented that for some unknown reason blacks were resistant to the effects of hookworm infection (anemia) although not to invasion by the hookworm.[95]

The reason is still not known, although similar findings have been reported throughout the hemisphere. In Barbados, for example, the inspector of health dismissed hookworm disease as a serious problem of health because among the blacks the hookworm "does not produce any serious symptoms." A year later Rockefeller researchers confirmed this allegation by discovering the highest incidence of hookworm infection on the Island among poor whites, reaching a rate of 60 to 90 percent in the Scotland district. By contrast, only 36 percent of the blacks were similarly infected.[96] More important, the researchers also reported that the effects of hookworm infection were "less marked" in blacks than whites. A similar situation was found on St. Kitts where a pocket of lower class French inhabitants was discovered to be "heavily infected," while still another existed on Dominica where the disease produced pronounced clinical symptoms among "the descendants of old French settlers who still show a preponderance of white blood." The blacks on both islands, by contrast, revealed few or no symptoms of infection. That the black immunity was racial seemed obvious to investigators after they discovered that not only whites but East Indians as well suffered significantly more than the black from hookworm infection. In St. Lucia, in Jamaica, and in Trinidad it was observed that although blacks and East Indians "live in the same conditions, in adjoining villages and follow similar occupations," only the East Indians suffered the ravages of hookworm disease. Thus among the Rockefeller physicians it became a "well known fact that the Negro is less affected by hookworm infection than is the white, brown or yellow race. This has been borne out by our work in the West Indies. It has been especially noted in British Guiana and Trinidad in which places very many West Indians have come under our observation. The incidence of the infection among Negroes *may be greater* [italics mine] but the effect as shown by clinical symptoms is not as marked. In fact, most of them do not suspect that they are infected until so informed [as] the symptoms are so light as not to attract attention."[97]

Additional evidence that the resistance of blacks was innate came from Puerto Rico where the residents were "brown" as opposed to black. For of all the Caribbean Islands, Puerto Rico was the one most troubled by severe hookworm disease with, according to a 1914 estimate, over half the population infected, while 30 percent of the island's deaths were also blamed on the disease.[98]

Thus blacks for the most part were "carriers" of hookworm rather than sufferers of hookworm disease, and again ironically their resistance to the disease was one more relative immunity that made them so valuable as slaves. Indeed without this immunity they could scarcely have survived, let alone labored well in the West Indies, for coffee and banana groves along with cane fields provide an ideal habitat for the hookworm larvae, which as a rule enter the human body through the skin of bare feet.[99]

On the other hand there are other worms that infect blacks more severely than whites – worms that so troubled and killed slaves that Spanish officials on Hispaniola speculated that perhaps somehow "the blood of the black favored the production of worms."[100] Foremost among these helminthic invaders were the *Ascaris* and *Trichuris*, the former a long roundworm, the latter a long threadworm, with both discovered to be still abundant in black bodies by Rockefeller surveys in the early twentieth-century Caribbean.[101]

Heavy burdens of *Trichuris* frequently cause diarrhea, as well as anemia; neither condition likely to aid the malnourished.[102] *Ascaris*, by contrast, can create intestinal obstructions with constipation the result and swollen abdomens the outward symptom.[103] Its larvae, moreover, when passing through the lungs produce symptoms that simulate pneumonia – coughing, bronchial rales, and so forth.[104] Thus on Caribbean plantations these worms were active in creating a fair share of the bowel and lung complaints so frequently registered by the slaves. In fact one West Indian slave physician went so far as to brand worms a major killer of slaves, although most saw them as merely "a great source of disease" for the slaves.[105]

Yet widespread worm infection in tandem with malnutrition does cast worms in the role of major killers (or at least major accomplices). The human body, which can usually tolerate one or the other, is placed under enormous stress in the presence of both. Low intakes of protein, iron, and the vitamin B complex – too low to be shared – are nonetheless shared, bodily resistance to intercurrent infections dwindles, and sooner rather than later some illness, which a healthy immune system could easily overcome, instead overcomes its host.[106]

Another worm notorious for infesting West Indian slaves was *Dracunculus medinensis*, better known as the guinea worm, which can grow as long as four feet in the connective tissue of man. Many visitors to the region reported with morbid fascination having observed slaves extracting them from their bodies, using the time-honored African method of winding the worm's head around a stick and then twisting the stick at regular intervals until the entire worm had been removed.[107]

A final worm that tormented the slaves and often produced hideous symptoms in the process was the filarial roundworm *Wucheria bancrofti*, which causes elephantiasis. The disease was (and is) widespread in parts of West Africa and according to an expert on West African illnesses "it is certain that many slaves with microfilariae in their blood but without clinical symptoms were shipped to the western hemisphere."[108]

In the West Indies that blood was imbibed by one of the culex mosquito family and the disease began to spread from man to man, but not as easily as yellow fever or malaria were spread, for it requires a number of bites from infected mosquitoes to induce a long-lasting filarial infection.[109] Immunology also plays an important if not understood role in determining victims. Males, for example, are more susceptible than females, suggesting that hormones may have something to do with infection, while those in the fifteen- to twenty-year-old category are most likely to become infected.[110]

Following infection, symptoms are delayed while the worms mature. As this occurs those worms living in the lymphatics and lymph nodes of the victim grow large enough to close off lymphatic circulation, whereupon swellings occur – sometimes the hideous swelling of the scrotum, feet, and especially legs, which makes the disease so terrible to behold and which prompted the colloquial Caribbean cognomen of "Barbados leg" for the illness. West India physicians were aware that the disease had arrived on slave ships, but Barbados got the dubious honor of lending its name to the illness nonetheless because the island became an early endemic focus of filarial infection in the region.[111]

However, the disease was soon a familiar one to physicians throughout the Caribbean, with Cuba becoming a late endemic focus as its slave trade intensified during the early decades of the nineteenth century. Ironically by this time Barbados, whose slave trade had ended, was less troubled by "Barbados leg,"[112] suggesting that as with other African diseases such as yellow fever or yaws, Old World reservoirs of disease remained reponsible for much infection even after New World endemicity was established. The latter, however, has meant that elephantiasis has continued to be something of a Caribbean health problem into this century and one that, now as then, seems peculiarly drawn to the black.[113]

To summarize then, it was suggested earlier that West Africans bound for the West Indies may well have possessed the ability to endure long-run nutritional hardship in a way that most people could not. Yet no amount of ability could have saved many of the slaves from deaths caused by the enormous short-run nutritional stress placed on them by capture, the march to the sea, life in the barracoons, the middle passage and seasoning.

This chapter has tried to show how dysentery, seasickness, and parasites would have formed a deadly coalition to ravage poorly nourished slaves and precipitate the mortality patterns common during the middle passage in the absence of epidemic disease; high levels of mortality early in the voyage, and then again late in the voyage, if the voyage were prolonged. If, however, the voyage was of normal duration, then deaths caused by amebic dysentery would probably have been delayed until after the slaves had landed in the West Indies.

Yet amebas were not the only cause of dysentery during seasoning. For it is very possible that a change of diet also produced intestinal disruptions. It is true that the nutriments available to slaves in the West Indies were mostly those that they had become accustomed to in

West Africa. But, as in West Africa, they were not uniformly available, and as a result, slaves often found themselves with a new diet of mostly strange foods. And finally, dysentery was also often the work of other parasites the slaves had carried with them during the middle passage, who settled into the New World.

Thus the West Indies became almost a copy of the West African nutritional and disease environment, with the result that malnutrition continued to be the norm for the survivors of the middle passage. The following chapter represents an effort to isolate specific deficiencies of the chief nutrients in the diets of the slaves by means of nutritional analysis.

CHAPTER 5

PLANTATION NUTRITION

The plantation, as a segmented social microcosm, may be regarded as the dominant social and economic unit of the Caribbean.

H. Hoetink (1967)[1]

Precise knowledge of what happens to the food entering the organism must be the subject of ideal physiology, the physiology of the future.

I.P. Pavlov (1904)[2]

Food reached slave cooking pots in the basic ways discussed in Chapter 4. Only in fringe areas of Caribbean slavery such as the Bahamas did slaves have the free time to fish or raise animals and thus add complete protein to the yams, taro, plantains, and perhaps corn or millet that they grew. That this was the best method nutritionally seems confirmed by height data, which showed Bahamian slaves to be among the tallest in the Caribbean.

At the opposite extreme, slaves were expected to feed themselves without receiving much in the way of free time to do so. Presumably planters stood ready with emergency rations in case of real shortages of slave-grown provisions occasioned by physical or political disasters. But generally the slave diet was a product of their own efforts and consequently was almost totally vegetable in nature, containing little or no animal protein. This diet seems characteristic of many Cuban plantations as well as those of Trinidad and Guiana, which produced the shortest Creole-born slaves – all regions where intense sugar slavery was a fairly recent phenomenon during the early nineteenth century when the height data were amassed.[3]

The third method, that of slaves supplementing a basic allotment of meat or fish and cereal with foods such as plantains and yams, seems to have been the most widespread method for most of the islands most of the time. However, it is important to stress again that none of these methods was mutually exclusive nor so clearly defined in practice.

Nonetheless, because the third method was by far the most prevalent, I have chosen to reconstruct in hypothetical fashion the diets that resulted from this feeding method, and then analyze them in order to address questions about the adequacy of slave nutrition. Table 1 depicts the two basic diets delivered to the slaves by this third method. For quantities of fish, beef, rice, and cornmeal, I am relying on the slave laws and the claims that the planters themselves made regarding the amounts of these foods made available to slaves (see the discussion in Chapter 4). Both the laws and the "claims" emerged during "amelioration," so we are obviously constructing an "ideal" diet for the slaves during "ideal" times. Consequently, if analysis reveals that even this regimen failed to deliver the chief nutrients to the slaves in sufficient quantities, then we may legitimately assume that most Caribbean slaves were seriously malnourished during the whole of Caribbean slavery.

The method behind the construction of Table 1 has been to assign to slaves an average of the amount of meat or fish and cereal that planters claimed they issued, or the law demanded that they issue and then "build up" the core allotment with those slave-grown supplements most universally available until an average caloric intake of about 3,000 daily is reached.

Many experts will quickly object that, ideal diet or not, a meat or fish ration of three pounds weekly is so excessive as to be ridiculous and this may well be the case. As mentioned previously, Richard Bean has calculated that Barbados at the end of the seventeenth century was importing a little under 100 pounds of fish annually per slave, which if evenly distributed throughout the slave population would have provided them with only a quarter of a pound daily. James Stephen found a similar discrepancy between planter claims and fish imports for Jamaica toward the end of the eighteenth century, while there are documents suggesting that during the middle of the nineteenth century, Cuba was importing some thirty-million pounds of jerked beef annually, which again, if evenly distributed over the slave population, would have provided about a quarter of a pound daily.[4]

On the other hand, Manuel Moreno Fraginals has stated rather emphatically that the "daily norm" for Cuban slaves was about 200 grams of jerked beef (one-half pound is equal to 227 grams), which would have meant a bit over three pounds weekly, and this is in line with planters' claims.[5] Thus I have chosen to reconcile the apparent discrepancy between planter claims and import data by assuming that planters were telling the truth as far as their slaves were concerned and that their slaves did receive around three pounds of meat or fish weekly, while other slaves who were expected to feed themselves (method 2) did not.

It may also be objected that the calorie intake is too low, which in fact it is for a young man laboring on a sugar plantation whose caloric

Table 1. *The "Apparent" Caribbean Slave Intake of the Chief Nutrients from*

Nutriments	Calories	Protein (g)	Fat (g)	Calcium (mg)	Phosphorus (mg)
Beef/Corn Core					
.42 lb. beef	387	65	12	38	791
1 pint cornmeal	884	22	8	42	544
Core and vegetable supplements (see below)	3,017	105.8	20	448	2,094
% RDA	—	192.3	—	56	262 }
% World standard	—	—	25	—	—
Fish/Rice Core					
.42 lb. fish	440	67	1	311	790
1 pint rice	1,416	26	2	94	366
Core and vegetable supplements (see below)	3,215	110	3	669	1,763
% RDA	—	200	—	87	200 }
% World standard	—	—	4	—	—
Vegetable Supplements					
½ lb. yams	197	4	—	39	135
½ lb. taro	236	3	—	187	218
1 lb. bananas	386	5	—	36	118
1 lb. plantains	540	5	—	32	136
¼ lb. cassava meal (beef/corn diet only)	387	1.8	—	74	152

Sources: Recommended Dietary Allowances 9th ed. (Washington, D.C., 1980); Catherine F. Adams, *Nutritive Value of Foods* (Washington, D.C., 1975); *Agriculture Handbook* (Washing-

needs would range between 3,200 and 4,000 daily. However, depending on the island, usually fewer than half of the slaves were engaged in sugar cultivation, their labor was at its most intense only seasonally during crop time, and of course the requirements of females are less than those of a male. Studies on the caloric intake of Africans in Africa have revealed that intake to average between 2,500 and 2,900 calories per day. Therefore an average of 3,000 calories for all adult slaves in the Caribbean would probably have been sufficient to supply their energy needs throughout most of the year.[6]

Thus, ideally, a slave was issued a bit less than a half pound of animal protein daily in the form of pickled or salt fish (common to the English Islands) or jerked beef (common to Cuba), as well as a pint of cereal in the form usually of cornmeal or rice.[7] The protein contained in the core diet would appear to have easily met today's recommended daily allowance (RDA) for this nutrient, but it would only have provided about a third of the slaves' daily caloric needs were he on a

Two Basic Diets for Slaves Aged Twenty-three to Fifty

	Iron (mg)	Vitamin A (IU)	Thiamine (mg)	Riboflavin (mg)	Niacin (mg)	Vitamin C (mg)
	9.7	—	0.13	0.60	7.2	—
	4.4	1180	0.74	0.20	4.6	—
	30.6	4,540	1.85	1.42	21.5	146.5
Male	306 ⎫					
Female	170 ⎭ 91	132	89	119	244
	—	—	—	—	—	—
	2.5	—	0.15	0.80	5.2	—
	3.2	—	0.28	0.12	6.2	—
	17.7	3,360	1.35	1.49	20.1	142
Male	177 ⎫					
Female	98 ⎭ 67	96	93	112	237
	—	—	—	—	—	—
	1.1	—	0.20	0.08	1.0	17
	4.5	—	0.22	0.04	1.8	16
	3.2	860	0.23	0.27	3.2	45
	3.2	2,500	0.27	0.18	2.7	64
	4.5	—	0.06	0.05	1.0	4.5

ton, D.C., 1950); and "Food Composition Tables of the Important Foodplants Used in West Africa," in *Protein Calorie Malnutrition*, ed. A. von Muralt (Heidelberg, 1969).

beef-corn core and about half of his caloric needs were he on a fish-rice core diet.

The remainder of the calories would have come from supplements to the core such as taro (eddo, dasheen), plantains (plátanos), yams (ñames), and bananas, to name the most important. Assuming then that a slave also consumed a half pound of yams daily along with a half pound of taro and a couple of pounds of plantains or bananas and that slaves on a beef-corn diet also consumed a bit of cassava meal, these supplements and the core would combine to supply the requisite 3,000 calories.

They would also seem to combine (as Table 1 suggests) to deliver all of the chief nutrients in sufficient amounts to call into question allegations that Caribbean slaves were badly nourished. Yet Table 1 is deceptive, for it reflects nothing of the chemistry of the foods in question, especially the chemistry of their metabolism, and it is based on RDAs that consider neither the differing needs of people living in the tropics in general nor those of persons of West African origin in particular.

Protein

Both the dried beef and fish would seem to be protein packed. Dried beef, for example, yields about half the fat and twice the protein of a similar portion of fresh beef, while of course most fish are famous for their low fat–high protein yield.[8]

A major difficulty with the fish, however, was that they were normally rancid when they reached slave cooking pots.[9] In the disgusted words of one observer, ". . . the herrings, in the state in which they are very commonly imported, and still more when progressively served out, often many months after their arrival, are little better than a mass of foetid matter, containing as little nutrition as the brine in which they lie."[10]

Modern experts on fish preservation confirm that the method of barrel curing commonly employed to preserve herring would have meant a product commonly rancid and bad smelling, although not necessarily "inedible."[11] Yet they also acknowledge that fish protein is "extremely unstable" and it seems highly possible that rancidity along with months of tropical heat while in storage exercised a deleterious effect on one or more of the amino acids in fish protein.[12] To some extent the curing process, coupled with prolonged storage, probably damaged the beef protein as well, which would have been unfortunate, for the remainder of the diet was not likely to make up much loss of complete protein. As we know, vegetable protein is incomplete and the supplements such as yams, taro, and plantains rank among the poorest of protein-yielding foods.[13]

As for the cereals, while corn is in a much better category, it is nonetheless deficient in two essential amino acids, tryptophan and lysine, while rice, like all cereals, is also deficient in lysine.[14] For all these reasons then, the slaves' protein intake was not so generous as Table 1 would make it appear. Moreover, the slaves doubtless would have had requirements much higher than the 55 grams, which constitutes today's RDA for peoples of the developed nations because of a sedentary lifestyle.[15] Yet it is also suggested that those engaged in any physical activity that causes perspiration, or those under stress should consume at least 100 to 125 grams of protein daily to maintain nitrogen balance.[16]

Were we to accept the figure of 125 protein grams as an appropriate RDA for the slaves, whose lifestyle was hardly sedentary, then those on a beef-cornmeal core diet would have received only 83 percent of their protein requirements, while those on a fish-rice core would have received 88 percent. Moreover this assumes that rancidity, curing, and prolonged storage in heat did not damage the animal protein, which it probably did. Finally we should also note that almost 40 percent of the protein in question is of the incomplete variety.

The point of this mathematical legerdemain is not to establish that slaves received only 83 or 88 percent of their protein needs, but rather to point out that even the ideal slave diet in the West Indies delivered barely enough protein to maintain good health, which suggests that some significant percentage of slaves probably suffered from inadequate protein intake. Moreover even those with adequate intake may have had difficulty in maintaining nitrogen balance for other reasons. The high salt content of dried fish or meat, we have speculated, must have created a hypertensive condition in many of those of West African origin whose bodies had developed the ability to retain sodium. This in turn would have depleted their potassium levels and potassium plays a catalytic role in protein metabolism. Finally both the dried meat and salted fish would have been extremely low in fats, which spare protein to perform its many functions, for fat is concentrated energy. The body's first need is for energy and, if necessary in order to obtain it, the body will degrade amino acids, thus sacrificing their most important function of making proteins.

In conclusion, I would also stress that, as in West Africa, there is testimony from the West Indies to suggest that protein rations to slave families were mostly consumed by the males, just as it apparently has been the custom for males to consume the bulk of the animal protein available in the Islands since the days of slavery. Yet the protein requirements for the young and for pregnant and lactating women are higher than those of adult males. Thus these are the individuals most likely to have been seriously protein deficient on the plantations of the West Indies.[17]

Fat

Having touched briefly on the low fat content of the slaves' diet, it seems appropriate to pursue the subject more vigorously, for without question the most crucial complicating factor in that diet was its extraordinarily low fat content. Today, with much of the Western world overfed nutritionally, we tend to take a dim view of dietary fats and either forget or ignore their many essential uses, among them, that of carriers for the fat-soluble vitamins A, D, E, and K.[18] Yet for most of the world's peoples a lack of sufficient dietary fats is a major nutritional problem and certainly this was true for those Caribbean slaves whose masters did not supply them with lard, or who did not regularly consume coconuts, avocados, or other fruits with a high fat content. In this case the core of the diet would have supplied almost all of the fats and as Table 1 shows, the lack of fat in the core meant at most only twenty grams daily for those consuming beef and corn and an impossibly meager three grams for those eating fish and rice. By contrast, the world standard established for fat intake indicates that from eighty to one hundred twenty-five grams constitutes a safe minimum.[19]

Vitamin A

The amount of vitamin A that slaves received, as indicated by Table 1, assumes (probably erroneously in many cases) that the corn in question is of the yellow rather than the white variety, which contains none of the vitamin. Nonetheless, although the amount is far from generous, even this is considerably overstated. As just noted, fats act as carriers for fat-soluble vitamin A and in fact are important for the conversion of carotene to vitamin A. Moreover rancidity has a devastating impact on the fat-soluble vitamins and those slaves consuming rancid fish would have almost automatically become vitamin A deficient.[20] Thus instead of being only mildly vitamin A deficient, as Table 1 suggests, many Caribbean slaves must have been severely deficient.[21]

Vitamin B₁

Thiamine levels can also be related to fat intake albeit in a lesser known and more complex kind of relationship. Thiamine is water soluble so fat has little to do with its absorption. But in the case of chronically low fat diets such as those of many Caribbean slaves, carbohydrates replace fats as the major energy source, and carbohydrates require thiamine for metabolization.[22]

Put another way, a low-fat, high-carbohydrate diet greatly accelerates the body's thiamine requirements. To employ a modern example, nutritionists in Puerto Rico recently discovered that although the nutriments consumed by their subjects contained an abundance of thiamine, the subjects themselves were deficient in the vitamin. Their report also stresses that the subjects were on a low-fat diet.[23]

Yet while a low fat intake boosted slave thiamine requirements far beyond the RDA of 1.2 milligrams upon which the calculations in Table 1 are based, other factors were at work to ensure that slaves did not actually receive the thiamine that Table 1 indicates. Thiamine is the least stable of the B vitamins and, as a consequence, is vulnerable to the meat and fish preservation processes of pickling, salting, and drying. Indeed both prolonged dehydration and alkaline solutions exert a destructive effect on thiamine.

Moreover the vitamin's lack of stability also means that, depending on the nutriment and the cooking process, much of it can be lost to heat, which is why the thiamine content of foods is almost always calculated before cooking. Thus Table 1 reflects the thiamine content of foods before cooking losses, which can run as high as 85 percent in meat to between 15 and 25 percent for cornmeal.[24]

Heat, however, was not the only agent destructive to thiamine in the cooking process as far as slaves were concerned, for their normal method of cooking was to boil and thiamine is highly water soluble. The fish or beef ration was generally placed in the family or communal pot where it simmered all day along with the yams, plantains, taro, and the cereal ration.[25] In the process considerable thiamine would have been leached out of the meat, grain, and vegetables.

Additionally those slaves whose normal cereal was rice would have been especially susceptible to thiamine deficiency for their rice was generally "polished" to prevent spoilage by stripping away the outer husk, which contains most of the thiamine in the grain.[26]

Finally, as if these factors singularly and in combination were not enough to occasion widespread thiamine deficiency among the slaves, there were still others to militate against a proper thiamine intake. Leaving fats aside, a diet heavy in carbohydrates accelerates thiamine requirements. So too does residence in hot or tropical regions, and thiamine is the most poorly stored of all vitamins, which means that occasional therapeutic injections such as might have been derived from roasted meats during holidays would quickly have been exhausted.[27]

To summarize then, thiamine deficiency to some degree must have plagued most Caribbean slaves, with many, especially those consuming rice, severely deficient in the vitamin. The problem, however, would not have been confined just to rice consumers largely because the low-fat diet would have sharply elevated thiamine requirements, as would the heavy carbohydrate content of that diet, along with tropical residence. Yet, while requirements for the vitamin were forced sharply upward, the dried and pickled nature of the animal protein coupled with cooking methods to reduce considerably the amount of thiamine delivered to the slaves.

Vitamins B_2 and B_3

Riboflavin and niacin intakes would have been improperly utilized by all those who were thiamine deficient because of the rule that the B vitamins are so interrelated that a deficiency of one reduces the efficiency of all and may even produce other B vitamin deficiencies.

In addition, there are numerous other reasons why slaves would have tended to be deficient in B_2 and B_3. As is the case with thiamine, both are vulnerable to cooking losses, although not to the same extent, while the drying of meats destroys riboflavin by exposing it to sunlight.[28] These losses alone would have sliced deeply into the already meager supply of riboflavin that Table 1 shows slaves as receiving, leaving them, as many of their present-day descendants, seriously deficient in the vitamin.[29]

Just as polished rice has become notorious for creating thiamine deficiency, so corn is firmly linked with niacin (and riboflavin) deficiency and therefore Table 1, which credits corn for about a quarter of the slaves' niacin intake, is particularly misleading. The niacin is contained in the corn all right, but unfortunately too well, in a chemically bound form that in the absence of special treatment (such as with lime water, traditionally used by Mexican and Central American Indians) denies the vitamin to the consumer.[30]

Yet it requires more than an inadequate intake of niacin to produce niacin deficiency in the human body, which can usually remedy the deficiency by converting tryptophan (an amino acid and niacin's precursor) to niacin. But once again the chemistry of corn manages to frustrate the body, this time because it contains an excess of leucine (another amino acid), which inhibits this process. The sum of these chemical relationships constitutes the reason why most peoples whose diets have centered too closely on corn have historically proved susceptible to niacin deficiency.[31]

In the case of the slaves, a dietary lack of riboflavin would have been another complicating factor, for riboflavin is also crucial to the process of converting tryptophan to niacin. [32] This means that slaves for whom corn was their principal cereal would probably have been marginally deficient in niacin, with their meat ration standing more or less alone in guarding against a severe deficiency. Were this ration cut substantially or withdrawn for any length of time, unmistakable signs of deficiency disease would have erupted.

Most slaves then would have been troubled with thiamine and riboflavin deficiency while some would have been susceptible to niacin deficiency. All of these cause specific illnesses, which will be sought among the slaves in Chapter 6. Meanwhile we should keep in mind that a general B-vitamin deficiency must have been widespread among the slaves and its effect would have been to impair the body's ability to utilize properly all of the carbohydrates, fats, and proteins that were consumed.[33]

Vitamin C

Given the popular view of the Caribbean Islands as fairly bristling with vitamin-C-packed fruits, it may seem downright foolhardy to argue that some slaves suffered a deficit of this vitamin. Moreover Table 1 depicts slaves receiving over three times their RDA. But, as with thiamine, the units of vitamin C shown in the fruit and vegetable supplements are only valid prior to cooking, for heat destroys vitamin C with losses of 60 percent or more in the normal process and upwards of 100 percent with prolonged cooking.[34]

Oxidation also destroys vitamin C and the iron cooking pots of the slaves would have destroyed vitamin C by oxidizing it.[35] Thus with the core diet providing no vitamin C and the supplements usually boiled for long periods of time in iron pots, slaves would probably have been vitamin C deficient had they not consumed uncooked fruits or vegetables as well.

Iron

Although the iron cooking pots used by slaves would have been harmful to vitamin C, their redeeming feature is that they would have injected iron into the foods cooked in them, thereby supplementing the already apparently substantial amount of iron shown in the diets in Table 1, particularly the diet containing the iron-rich dried beef. Yet once again the reality of the chemistry of the slave diet seems to have been at considerable variance with the illusion of sufficiency.

Individuals residing in the tropics are normally iron deficient, not necessarily because it is not forthcoming in their foods, but rather, it is suspected because tropical diets are normally quite high in phosphorus. Excess phosphorus can seriously hinder the body's ability to absorb iron by competing with iron for metal-binding sites in the intestinal mucosa and, as a glance at Table 1 will reveal, the slave diet was indeed high in phosphorus. In addition, tropical residents tend to lose a significant amount of iron through sweat and feces, which in turn raises their requirements.[36]

Then there were other chemical relationships to militate against iron absorption by the slaves. For example, the amino acids lysine and tryptophan promote iron absorption while calcium, if present in sufficient amounts, will actually combine with phosphorus to free iron for absorption. Yet, as we have already noted, both amino acids in question were undersupplied to the slaves while calcium, as we will see shortly, was also less than abundant in slave comestibles. Moreover iron from rice is poorly absorbed and iron from corn very poorly absorbed, while low vitamin C intakes can also contribute to an iron-deficient condition for one of the assignments of vitamin C is to keep iron in an absorbable state.[37]

Finally, as noted previously, modern nutritional surveys have revealed blacks at all ages – and in all income groups – to be consistently more iron deficient than whites in both warm and temperate climates, suggesting that genetics may also play an important role in their ability to absorb and utilize iron.[38]

Calcium and Phosphorus

These two elements are treated together because they must be in relative balance to function properly in the body. As Table 1 indicates, however, they were clearly out of balance in slave diets, which delivered an abundance of phosphorus and very little calcium. This imbalance would have worked against the absorption of the little calcium the diet did yield, thus further impoverishing the slaves' calcium supply and raising their requirements for the mineral.[39]

Had lactose been present in the slaves' diet, it could have assisted in the absorption of calcium, while the milk containing the lactose would have meant a substantial improvement in a calcium-poor diet. However, as discussed earlier, most slaves would have had difficulty in using milk, as do their modern-day descendants,[40] because of lactose intolerance even had it been available to them. Thus save for slave infants who were sometimes introduced early to animal milk to free their mothers for the fields, along with some fortunate slave youngsters whose diet included milk after weaning, the goat and bovine milk of the West Indies was consumed by the whites. Indeed, in discussing the "fluid part of the Negro diet," a contemporary physician stated flatly that it consisted almost "exclusively" of water with maybe a little rum added to the water on occasion.[41]

That the slave diet did not supply much calcium is not surprising, for as a rule tropical foods are low in the mineral. Moreover tropical residence tends to increase calcium requirements, for calcium like iron is lost at a higher rate in warm climates through perspiration and excretion. For Europeans this lack of dietary calcium over time, coupled with a high intake of phosphorus, would have been literally crippling, with porous and brittle bones the outcome. But as noted in Chapter 3, West Africans seem to have developed an ability to survive on a very low intake of calcium.[42] How well they survived the low calcium–high phosphorus regimen in the West Indies will be considered in the next chapter.

Mitigating Nutriments

Slaves had access to foods that are not reflected in Table 1, but that doubtless helped to mitigate to a greater or lesser extent many of the nutritional deficiencies described. In the Spanish Islands at least, many used onions in their dishes, which could have added somewhat to slave calcium intakes, although most of the onions' fairly substantial vitamin C content would have been lost in cooking. Red peppers were also in widespread use throughout the region and these, along with okra (which also delivers calcium), would have made a substantial contribution to the slaves' vitamin A intake, and while once again most of the vitamin C in these vegetables would have been lost, the vitamin C residuals in the cooking pots from peppers, onions, okra, and other vegetable supplements would have begun to add up.[43]

Slaves who lived in coffee-producing islands and drank a few cups every day probably were able to avoid niacin deficiency even if their diet did center closely on corn, while the molasses, often issued in sugar-producing regions, was brimming with calcium and, depending on its type, possibly with iron as well.[44]

The fava or horsebeans, kidney beans (*habichuelas coloradas*), pigeon peas (*gandules*), and black beans (*frijoles negros*) issued to many slaves on occasion would have contributed to their iron intake, but more important, they would have balanced the incomplete protein in rice or corn with their lysine contribution to the essential amino acids.[45]

Sorghum (guinea corn) was grown on many plantations for slave consumption[46] and had this replaced corn or rice as the slaves' principal cereal it would have delivered about a third more iron, although it would also have robbed the slaves of about one third of the calories provided by rice or corn.[47]

Cassava (*yucca, manioc*) was also grown for slave pots, particularly in the Spanish Islands. Its nutritional properties, however, especially its extremely low protein content, means that those slaves who were forced to depend on cassava for much of their nutrition would have taken in barely enough nutrients to sustain life.[48]

Malanga and *yautia* were other starchy roots grown in Cuba and Puerto Rico, respectively, and yielded about the same amount of B vitamins as taro, but much less calcium,[49] while cocos (*Colocasia antiquorum*) and other roots with similar nutritional yields were grown here and there in the British West Indies.[50] Sweet potatoes, which, depending on the variety, could have been an excellent source of vitamin A were "overshadowed" by other root crops in eighteenth-century Jamaica, while in Puerto Rico they have never been popular, not even in this century despite campaigns to introduce them into the island's diet.[51]

Coconuts where available could have helped considerably with the slaves' intake of fat, as would the avocado, while the papaya (pawpaw), avocado, and guava are rich in vitamins A and C.[52] The akee and mango arrived in the British West Indies during the late eighteenth century as part of a campaign to add new foods to the Islands and thereby lessen the possibility of slave famine in the future. The akee, of course, joined fish and rice to make a famous combination in Jamaica while the mango spread across the Caribbean, reaching Cuba by 1790.[53]

Breadfruit entered the Caribbean as a result of the same campaign and the grim determination of Captain William Bligh. Yet Bligh's efforts did not "bear fruit," at least not in the short run, since the breadfruit was "highly unappreciated" by the slaves.[54] It should be noted in passing, however, that the slaves' rejection of breadfruit was hardly a nutritional disaster for it is notoriously low in almost all nutrients.

Catalue (a kind of spinach), "dasheen," lemons, oranges, and grapefruit were also available to some slaves in some places some of the time

Table 2. *An Estimate of the Nutritional Status of Caribbean Slaves Following Analysis of Two "Ideal" Slave Diets*

Nutrient	Beef/Corn Core	Fish/Rice Core
Protein	Barely adequate	Barely adequate
Fat	Very low	Dangerously low
Calcium	Low	Low
Phosphorus	High	High
Iron		
Males	Adequate	Adequate
Females	Low to adequate	Low to adequate
Vitamin A	Very low	Dangerously low
Thiamine	Low	Dangerously low
Riboflavin	Very low	Very low
Niacin	Dangerously low	Low
Vitamin C	Barely adequate	Barely adequate

and their consumers certainly would have avoided vitamin C deficiency. However, as noted earlier in the chapter, Caribbean residence does not automatically mean voracious fruit consumption. Indeed, the consensus of nutritionists in this century is that Caribbean diets are more or less deficient in vitamin C, as well as vitamin A, niacin, thiamine, riboflavin, calcium, iron, and fats.[55] If, as John Parry has observed, the food habits of Caribbean blacks were "generally fixed" by the time of emancipation, then we may assume that the slave diet was similarly deficient in these nutrients except more so.[56]

This assumption in turn dovetails with our own analysis, as depicted in Table 2. Yet assumptions and even nutritional analyses are not substitutes for evidence, and it is evidence of malnutrition that will be the focus for much of the remainder of Part II as an attempt is made to achieve "matches" between the deficiencies that analysis has revealed and the diseases caused by those deficiencies.

CHAPTER 6

MALNUTRITION: MORBIDITY AND MORTALITY

It is evident that the Negro system is materially different from ours. It could not have escaped observation how diseases differ in their respective colours of white and black.

John Williamson (1817)[1]

Plantation-America offers a magnificent laboratory for the comparative approach.

Charles Wagley (1960)[2]

As the preceding chapter indicated, if Caribbean slaves had not consumed a fairly wide variety of supplemental foodstuffs, their basic diets (despite their ideal nature in terms of planter claims) would have provoked serious nutritional deficiencies. Moreover, the nutritional "analysis," which pointed up the slaves' inability to derive (and metabolize) adequate amounts of most of the chief nutrients was performed on an "ideal" diet during "ideal" times. Wars, economic circumstances, hurricanes, droughts, and outright famine increased the likelihood that the diet would frequently lack important components.[3]

The result should have been widespread diseases of nutritional nature. But deficiencies pointed up by theoretical nutritional analysis require confirmation in the form of actual nutritional ailments. This chapter represents an effort to search out those ailments and match suspected deficiencies with the diseases they create.

Vitamin A Deficiency and Night Blindness

Table 2 pronounced Caribbean slaves generally vitamin A deficient because of a low yield from their basic foodstuffs. Those consuming rancid fish should have been dangerously low in vitamin A because of the destructive effect of rancidity on the fat-soluble vitamins.

Vitamin A deficiency can produce a variety of symptoms such as rough skin, skin blemishes, and even a loss of a sense of smell, but by far the easiest symptom to discern in the medical literature on Caribbean slaves is eye problems.[4] "Sore eyes" for example were reported among the slaves throughout the history of Caribbean slavery and some physicians found the problem serious enough that they devoted many pages of their books on slave medicine to the subject.[5] Vitamin A deficiency causes the eye to become sore because it promotes a dryness that leads to cracking followed frequently by an invasion of dust or dirt and then infection. However, "sore eyes" alone among the slaves is not positive confirmation of vitamin A deficiency because a lack of other nutrients, especially riboflavin, can also produce a similar soreness.

We can be sure, however, that vitamin A deficiency played a prominent role in eye soreness when we discover that nyctalopia or night blindness was, in the words of a contemporary physician, "so frequently seen among the negroes."[6] Night blindness is a classic symptom of vitamin A deficiency for the eyes must have an adequate supply of vitamin A in the blood in order to regenerate "visual purple" (rhodopsin) after it is bleached by light. When vitamin A is undersupplied there is a significant "lag" in this process with the result night blindness. Given the vitamin-A-deficient nature of the food aboard slave ships, we have little reason to doubt statements that slaves often arrived from Africa with the disease, while observations that eye complaints, including night blindness, often reached epidemic proportions on plantations seems positive confirmation of the findings of our analysis of the slave diet, which indicated a serious vitamin A deficiency for many slaves.[7]

Vitamin C and Some Scurvy

Because of the relationship between vitamins A and C, a deficiency of the former should have resulted in a rapid loss of the latter, further exacerbating the "barely adequate" vitamin C intake for those slaves who ate few uncooked fruits or vegetables.[8] Yet vitamin C deficiency symptoms (caused by the breakdown of collagen) such as a tendency to bruise, wounds that were slow to heal, and loss of appetite are either difficult to spy in the medical literature of Caribbean slavery or they are firmly intertwined with other deficiency ailments. The bleeding gums of scurvy, however, are not difficult to spy and there is little question that the disease troubled some slaves.[9] Unfortunately scurvy was not adequately understood by most physicians of the era and consequently seldom diagnosed as a disease sui generis, which in turn may account for a lack of sufficient evidence to characterize the disease as widespread.[10] On the other hand, given the fact that well into this century Caribbean peoples (despite the fruits and vegetables available to them) have proved to be vitamin C deficient, it is certainly not unreasonable to assume that a majority of the slave population also failed to take in enough of the vitamin to promote good health and that a significant portion exhibited some deficiency symptoms.[11]

Calcium and Iron: Myriad Complaints

Vitamins A and C are both essential to calcium's absorption, while C is important in the breakdown of iron so that the body can use it. Thus deficiencies of A and C would have complicated even further the slaves' poor calcium intake, while a high phosphorus intake relative to calcium along with a diet low in vitamin C would have reduced considerably the slaves' ability to absorb iron.

This means that many slaves, especially females (with higher requirements) were probably iron deficient and consequently anemic. During the mid-twentieth century, iron deficiency (and anemia) was found to be common among the people of Barbados, whereas iron intake for Puerto Ricans was fair to adequate.[12] The difference is probably explicable in terms of diet, with the Puerto Ricans consuming more iron-rich foods such as beans, plantains, and meat, while the Barbados diet was lower in iron-rich foods because of a need to import most foodstuffs.[13] One suspects that similar patterns across the Caribbean during slavery may have produced "pockets" of iron-deficient slaves, and this in turn may have led to a characteristic craving for nonfoods discussed later in this chapter.

Modern Caribbean diets are also similar to those of the slaves in that they are characterized by a low consumption of fresh vegetables and dairy products.[14] The consequences (even if blacks have successfully adjusted to low calcium intakes) are widespread dental caries, peridontal disease, rheumatism, and surprisingly some full-blown cases of rickets, all of which testify that the calcium intake is too low or out of balance with magnesium, which, when lacking, also shares responsibility for many of these complaints.[15] Similarly during slavery physicians wrote that blacks were "peculiarly subject" to disorders of the bones, especially "bone ache" and that they had uniformly bad teeth.[16]

Vitamin B Deficiencies and Slave "Mood Swings"

Table 2 of the preceding chapter indicates that most slaves were more or less deficient in all of the B vitamins. Evidence of this general B vitamin deficiency (along with iron) is reflected in the peculiar phenomenon of apparently improved slave health during "crop time," when presumably the reverse should have held true, for slaves during the sugar harvest were called upon to perform extraordinarily hard labor for prolonged periods of time.

Nonetheless, it was firmly believed that a newly imported slave had a much better chance of survival if brought to the plantation during this period, while planters and physicians alike commented on the marks of vastly improved slave health including that "peculiar glossiness of the skin [which] is never seen to the same extent in any other season." They guessed that the reason for the apparent paradox was because of "the free and unrestrained use which they [the slaves] are allowed to make of the ripe canes, the cane liquor and the syrup" feeling that this acted as a "tonic" to "restore health and vigor to debilitated negroes."[17]

As Robert Dirks has pointed out, harvest time was also the time when many fruits and vegetables became available to the slaves; moreover, during this period planters tended to increase slave rations and thus slaves generally enjoyed their best nutritional intake of the year. But it may also be that the planters were correct in judging the efficacy of the tonic. For as contemporaries explained it, custom permitted slaves to drink as much as they wanted of the "hot liquor" from the "last copper" boiling kettle in the train and it was this kettle that contained a mixture of brown sugar and molasses rich in both the B vitamins and in iron.[18]

The phenomenon of slave good health and high spirits during crop time has not gone unnoticed by other students of slavery, who have pointed out that crop time was a time of excitement for the slaves. They have also voiced the suspicion that perhaps the availability of rum had something to do with the general cheerfulness, if not the improved health of the slaves. To this one might also add the possibility of a sugar "high" such as that sometimes exhibited by children after gorging themselves on candy. But we should not lose sight of the fact that the appearance of suddenly improved health, coupled with a greatly enhanced feeling of well-being, is a not unusual result of a sudden intake of vitamins by individuals chronically deficient in those vitamins. This is especially true of the B vitamins, which are active in providing the body with energy by converting carbohydrates into glucose and when in short supply tend to induce irritability, depression, even suicidal tendencies.[19]

No one doubts that such behavior, characteristic of depression, occurred frequently enough to belie the stereotypical image of the inevitably cheerful slave, for it was this behavior that often foreshadowed suicide, and the suicide rate is generally conceded to have been very high among the slaves, especially new arrivals who believed that they could accomplish a return to their homeland by dying.[20] Yet high suicide rates were not confined to the new arrivals nor even to slaves for that matter. Nineteenth-century Chinese contract laborers and free blacks also killed themselves at a sufficiently high rate to elicit comment, and of course high suicide rates continued to be a problem in the Caribbean even after slavery was abolished.[21]

This is not to say that despair did not affect the Chinese, who were too often treated as slaves, nor that free blacks during and after slavery had no reason to contemplate suicide. It is, however, to suggest that no study to our knowledge has been done on a history of suicide in the Caribbean and that when such a study does appear it may well turn out that a chronic shortage of the B vitamins (which doubtless was as characteristic of the diets of many Chinese and free blacks as it was of the slave diet) played a considerable role in a fair portion of those suicides.

Riboflavin and an Unclear Clinical Picture

Moving from the evidence and possible implications of general B vitamin deficiency to specific B vitamin shortages, we might first consider riboflavin, which has been the most widespread of the B vitamin deficiencies throughout the twentieth-century Caribbean.[22] It was doubtless also widespread during the days of slavery, particularly among those slaves whose source of animal protein was dried beef, for as we pointed out in the previous chapter, the drying process would have destroyed the beef's riboflavin content by exposing it to sunlight.[23]

There is, however, a real problem with identifying riboflavin deficiency symptoms among the slaves because for some reason, unlike deficiencies of niacin and thiamine, riboflavin shortages do not progress to the point of serious illness. The mild symptoms elicited such as visual fatigue and lesions of the lips and sores in the corners of the mouth were certainly not the sorts of things that would have bestirred the clinical curiosity of slave physicians whose attention was mainly focused on lesions of leprosy and yaws.[24]

On the other hand, it is important to remind ourselves that the slaves must have been riboflavin deficient and this deficiency in turn would have aggravated other B vitamin deficiencies, which do develop into life-threatening illnesses, because of the interrelated nature of the B vitamins.[25]

Niacin and Pellagra

In the case of niacin deficiency, riboflavin can and does play a role because it is needed for the bodily process of converting tryptophan to niacin.[26] Thus slaves whose intake of niacin was low (as would have been the case for those issued cornmeal) and who were also riboflavin deficient would have been hard pressed to make up this deficit by the conversion of tryptophan.[27] Still another impediment to this conversion process was inherent in corn because of its high leucine content since leucine inhibits the body's ability to produce niacin.[28]

Thus there is good reason to believe that slaves whose diet centered on corn would have been niacin deficient, even with their ration of animal protein. Without it, or when that ration was undersupplied, some significant number must have been severely niacin deficient and, consequently, pellagra prone.

Pellagra (from the Italian *pelle* [skin] *agra* [rough] is the classic disease that blossoms under these conditions and, as the name suggests, one of its classic symptoms is dermatitis while others are diarrhea, dementia, and death. These so called four D's of pellagra are also accompanied by myriad other symptoms ranging from mild lassitude and digestive disturbances, to more alarming indications such as a sore mouth, neck pains, a thickly coated tongue, and rough, scaly, hypersensitive skin to life-threatening signals such as severe cerebrospinal disturbances, delirium, hallucination, and a wasting stage, which generally results in death.[29]

Indeed it is this wide range of protean symptoms that prevented earlier physicians from recognizing pellagra as a disease in its own right, with the result that they tended to focus on the major symptom confronting them. Thus pellagra became a bowel complaint or a skin affliction or mental illness and so forth. Another characteristic of pellagra that forestalled early identification is its tendency to ebb and flow with the seasons. For example in the southern United States, pellagra tended to appear in the winter months when there were few supplements to the slaves' diet and then disappear with the late spring and early summer. In the West Indies, by contrast, the disease appeared in the spring, continued through the summer, and then disappeared when the winter brought a greater variety of food.[30]

Thus, in the words of the famous pellagrologist Joseph Goldberger, although fully developed cases of pellagra form "a picture which, when once seen, can hardly ever fail to be recognized even by one who is not a physician, the diagnosis of the disease is by no means always easy, because the fully developed cases form only a small proportion of the total."[31]

After pellagra was discovered to be a disease sui generis, it was immediately recognized among the poor on Barbados and Jamaica where the diets centered heavily on corn,[32] and then discovered on Trinidad, Tobago, St. Kitts, Nevis, St. Lucia, Antigua, and Puerto Rico.[33] This suggests that it must have been an even more severe problem among slaves whose diet was far more limited, but a problem masquerading as another illness, having one of pellagra's D's as a prominent symptom. Under the rubric of dermatitis, the disease "erysipelas" (also called St. Anthony's fire) becomes a possibility. The disease (an acute inflammatory affliction of the skin caused by various strains of streptococcus) produces dermatological symptoms easily confused with those of pellagra.

Thus a physician visiting Barbados shortly after slavery was abolished who reported that erysipelas was often epidemic there, along with diarrhea and dysentary, may in fact have been reporting pellagra.[34] If so, another visiting physician about two decades later, who commented on widespread "mania," may have described one of the effects of pellagra epidemics, for it has been asserted that between 4 and 10 percent of pellagra victims in the United States became permanently insane.[35]

An "erysipelas" epidemic that swept some Jamaican plantations in 1823, causing the skin to become darker and to hurt badly when touched and precipitating death and some insanity, seems very likely to have been pellagra and indeed resembles "Scott's palsy" described a century or so later among Jamaican plantation workers, which the noted authority on tropical medicine felt was a pellagra-related disease.[36]

According to a West Indian physician with a penchant for the pun, "the seat of the greatest part of Negro disorders . . . is in their bowels," while a modern authority states that the diarrhea and dysentery suffered by the slaves was often of a peculiar nature not suffered by whites.[37] Unquestionably diarrhea and dysentery were rife on West Indian plantations, and some was doubtless the result of pellagra (particularly in the case of those suffering from the diarrhea of a "peculiar nature not suffered by whites"), while some was also the result of conditions that produce pellagra. Indeed malnutrition alone causes diarrhea, while persons on a vegetable diet and especially one that centers on corn generally have the problem.[38] They are also susceptible to amebic dysentery, which must have been a serious problem of health on islands like Barbados where slaves drew their water from contaminated ponds, as the cisterns were mostly reserved for white use only.[39] The dysentery, in turn, would have precipitated further loss of the B vitamins, including niacin.

Similarly many of the dermatological symptoms displayed by slaves may have been caused by pellagra, yet have been called yaws or leprosy, or even "scabies" (the real disease is caused by mites), while in the Spanish Islands "bubas" was a term that indicated cutaneous difficulties (often yaws), but that also "covered a whole complex of illnesses."[40]

In this connection Robert Dirks, who has pursued pellagra in the British Islands, presents evidence that many cases called leprosy, yaws, and even "Barbados Leg" may in fact have been pellagra cases.[41] Clearly the problem with identifying pellagra in the West Indies is not a dearth of symptoms, but an abundance of symptoms indicative of all sorts of ailments, including infectious diseases and other nutritional ailments.

For example diarrhea can also be symptomatic of vitamin A deficiency, which we have already confirmed as an important deficiency of the slaves. Moreover vitamin A deficiency is associated with ergotism caused by a fungus in rye, which could easily have been present in the rye flour sometimes issued to slaves.[42] Thus diarrhea and cutaneous disorders suggestive of pellagra could have been produced by vitamin A deficiency, while tropical sprue (with pellagralike symptoms) and ulcers of all sorts suggest myriad nutritional deficiencies in many cases probably combining with, as well as concealing, pellagra.[43]

Thiamine and Beriberi; Mineral Deficiencies and Pica

Diarrhea can also be a prominent symptom of beriberi, which is caused by thiamine (vitamin B_1) deficiency. As we have already seen, the extremely low-fat diet of the slaves would have predisposed them to thiamine deficiency while increased requirements arising from tropical residence, cooking losses, and an imbalance in the slave's vitamin B intake must have doomed many to a deficiency serious enough to have precipitated beriberilike symptoms.

Like pellagra, beriberi, too, managed to escape identification as a disease for the longest while because of protean symptoms that misled physicians into believing that beriberi was actually a number of diseases. On the other hand, the etiology of beriberi was recognized earlier than that of pellagra and perhaps because recognition of its cause in 1885 came in the Far East, there is a tendency to think of beriberi as a disease exclusive to the rice-eating cultures of that area of the world.

Yet beriberi is no stranger to the Caribbean and in fact the first extensive report on the illness came in 1865 from the pen of Dr. Juan Hava, who reported beriberi raging on Cuban plantations. The symptoms he described – edema, loss of appetite, disturbed nerve functions, near paralysis, rapid heart beat, and labored respiration – left little doubt that the disease in question was beriberi, while significantly all the victims were blacks consuming a typical plantation diet.[44]

Six years later in 1870 a French physician had the opportunity to observe and try to treat the same disease, again on Cuban plantations.[45] In 1873 August Hirsch states that beriberi was still a problem in Cuba, raging "with great virulence" on two plantations near Palmyra where it was killing 60 to 75 percent of those attacked.[46]

Unquestionably then the thiamine intake of Cuban blacks was far from adequate and, for every case of blatant beriberi, there are usually hundreds or even thousands of less pronounced or subclinical cases.[47] Nor was the disease confined in the Caribbean to Cuba. It was also "recognized" in Puerto Rico in the 1920s, and with recognition came reports of numerous cases.[48] Certainly the disease frequented the French Islands. Indeed it is thought that beriberi was the *coupe de barre* that plagued Guadeloupe and St. Kitts during the years 1635 to 1640, while over 200 years later (1859) beriberi was still troubling Guadeloupe according to medical historians, who believe that a particularly serious epidemic swept the island in that year. And although beriberi was not "officially" reported until 1906, that report observed that the illness was "endemic" there and doubtless had been for some time. Similarly for the British West Indies, Robert Dirks has discovered beriberi to have been a periodic problem as well, perhaps extending as far back as the seventeenth century, although the first "official" diagnosis occurred in British Guiana in 1899. A decade and a half later, beriberi was reported as extensive in Jamaica where it was called "neuritis."[49]

One reason for a lack of continuity in beriberi reports has to do with the nature of the disease, which usually remains subclinical in a thiamine-deficient population, but erupts from time to time to rage in epidemic form. This eruption can be caused directly by a further decrease in intake of already undersupplied thiamine, or indirectly by, say, an outbreak of diarrhea or dysentery, which raises a people's thiamine requirements while diminishing their ability to utilize what they do take in.[50]

As it develops beriberi generally takes either a wet or a dry form. However, early signals that are common to both include an appetite loss, a vaguely defined malaise felt as a heaviness in the legs, and perhaps some difficulty in walking. The face and legs might swell a bit and the victims may experience palpitations of the heart. With some, a "pins and needles" sensation develops in the legs, while others complain of numbness.[51]

Frequently the disease progresses no further than this and the individual, although mildly incapacitated, continues to function more or less normally until or unless some intercurrent illness or complication such as diarrhea brings enough additional stress to trigger clinical wet or dry symptoms of beriberi.

In paraplegic or dry beriberi, weakness of the lower limbs increases and muscular coordination deteriorates so that the gait becomes exaggerated and "high stepping," although in extreme form muscular deterioration and weakness rob victims of their ability to walk entirely. In this state they are extremely susceptible to infection and tuberculosis or bacillary dysentery frequently descend to bring on death.[52]

By contrast, with wet beriberi there is little evidence of nervous system involvement. The onset is generally both swift and acute, with its major characteristic edema – a swelling of the legs and possibly the arms, hands, trunk, and face as well. Breathlessness and heart palpitations are marked as is the distention of the neck veins, which show visible pulsations. Indeed wet beriberi is also called cardiac beriberi for in this form sudden cardiac failure is not unusual.[53]

Because of some of these pronounced symptoms, beriberi is not as difficult to spy on West Indian plantations as pellagra. In fact one physician of the period writing of "dropsy" (an important if vaguely defined cause of slave mortality) helpfully used the term "beriberi" in describing an edema that "invades the system with serious effusion. . . . It bears a striking analogy to beriberi in some instances, and where the bloated appearance supervenes in certain cachetic cases the disease seems to me to be the same."[54]

Most observers, however, are not so helpful but write only of the various "dropsies" the slaves "sometimes. . .fall into. . .which generally prove mortal."[55] At the turn of the eighteenth century Hans Sloane wrote of a disease called the "dry dropsie," which he claimed was serious among the slaves of Barbados and Jamaica.[56] Apparently Sloane, by using the dry designation, was attempting to distinguish between swellings that subsequently burst open and those that do not, in which case his "dry dropsie" could easily have been wet beriberi.

Even more intriguing is the Abbé Raynal's description of a disease he observed among West Indian slaves toward the end of the eighteenth century. "They grow faint," he wrote, "and incapable of the least exercise. It is a languor and general relaxation of the whole machine. In this situation they are in such a state of despondence, that they suffer themselves to be knocked down, rather than walk." In addition Raynal commented on "the loathing which they have of mild and wholesome food," and reported that "their legs swell, their breath is obstructed and few of them survive this disorder."[57]

It seems probable that Raynal was describing beriberi of both the dry and the wet variety. A Jamaican physician writing a few years later seems also to have been describing wet beriberi when he wrote of a "dropsy" among slaves, which began at the ankles and then moved up the body to become a "universal swelling of the whole body."[58] Significantly one of his contemporaries wrote that rice "lately. . . has fallen into disuse . . .because it seems to cause bowel disorders and dropsical swellings" among the slaves.[59] This apparent relationship between thiamine-deficient rice and the "dropsical swellings" is compelling evidence that beriberi was an important cause of morbidity among the slaves.[60] But since beriberi does more than simply make people sick, it is worth noting "dropsy's" ability as a killer.

In Jamaica, mortality data for Worthy Park plantation indicate that between 1811 and 1824 "dropsy" was responsible for 10 percent of the slave deaths.[61] Barry Higman's sample of Jamaican slave mortality showed that "dropsy" along with "swellings" accounted for 13 percent of the deaths in St. James parish for the years 1817 to 1820, while "dropsy" and "bloated" were given as the cause of death for 14 percent of those who died on the Old Montpelier, New Montpelier, and Shettlewood estates between 1817 and 1829.[62]

In Barbados dropsy deaths constituted 8.2 percent of the slave deaths on the Newton plantation for which there were records during the years 1796 to 1825, while it accounted for 10 percent of those who died on the Codrington plantation.[63] In British Guiana, dropsy was credited with 9 percent of the slave deaths recorded for the years 1829 to 1832, while in the Havana diocese of Cuba a combination of *anasarca* (general dropsy) and *hidropesía* (dropsy) was credited for 6 percent of the blacks who were buried during the year 1843.[64]

Edema of course is symptomatic of numerous disorders besides wet beriberi and we certainly do not contend that all of the deaths subsumed under the cause "dropsy" were beriberi cases. Indeed some were probably hypertension cases of which fluid retention can be symptomatic, and as we saw, some slaves would doubtless have suffered from the disorder. Yet evidence that much of the "dropsy" was precipitated by poor nutrition exists in the prescription of planters and physicians alike for the "dropsie," which was quite simply "a very nutritious diet." Basic to the diet they claimed cured the "dropsies" was fresh meat, which contains thiamine and thiamine certainly would have cured dropsy whenever dropsy meant wet beriberi.[65]

Interestingly, physicians and planters also discovered that improved nutrition would cure what they believed to be the worst of all illnesses to afflict slaves, the *mal d' estomach*.[66] Known also as the *mal de estómago*, *hatiweri*, and *cachexia africana* across the Caribbean basin, no slave illness so intrigued and bewildered physicians, and one doctor even claimed in frustration that the man who discovered its cause "would deserve a statue."[67]

The most common explanation viewed the disease as caused by pica usage or "dirt eating." It was claimed that it could erupt on a plantation in epidemic form, sweeping away many slaves as the mania for consuming earth consumed them. Yet few actually witnessed slaves engaged in this "horribly disgusting" practice because "they always do it secretly and clandestinely" and "they will never acknowledge it."[68] Some contemporaries, moreover, doubted that dirt eating was an important factor in the etiology of the *mal d' estomach*. In the words of one, "it is generally imagined that these symptoms are occasioned by dirt eating . . . [yet] we have seen every symptom of the *mal de estomac* in Negroes, without being able to discover that they were also dirt eaters."[69]

This is not to say that slaves did not eat dirt or clay. On the contrary, some developed such a craving, for reasons to be discussed shortly, while others used pica because of custom – a custom the slaves had brought with them from Africa.[70] It is to say, however, that it is doubtful that dirt eating swept plantations killing slaves for the very good reason that the use of pica rarely kills anyone.[71]

However, beriberi (which, not incidentally, was known as the *mal d' estomach* in Ceylon) does kill, it appears in epidemic form, and a close look at the symptoms of the *mal d' estomach* seems to reveal beriberi of both the wet and dry variety. The illness began with a "great deal of torpor," a tiredness and inability to work, accompanied by a "loss of appetite." Next came "breathlessness on the least motion, attended with *visible pulsations of the carotids or arteries of the neck*" [italics mine], in which case the victim became "bloated." Alternatively the victim was likely to develop a certain "giddiness" or "vertigo" along with a "peculiar gait" and an "inability to go uphill."[72] These are not symptoms of pica usage, but they are classic symptoms of wet and dry beriberi, with the pulsation of the neck arteries and edema marking the former and the "peculiar gait" characteristic of the latter.[73]

The type that seems to have been most prevalent was wet (or cardiac) beriberi, described by physicians as an illness that "terminates in a dropsy," as first the legs became "swollen" and then often the face and arms too became "bloated." The disease was also characterized by "palpitations of the heart" and proved fatal in most of the pronounced cases, often by "suffocation," which suggests the edema of the lungs so common to beriberi.[74]

Historically, pregnant and lactating women (along with laboring men) have proved especially susceptible to the disease because of accelerated requirements for most nutrients including thiamine (30 to 50 percent more).[75] The *mal d' estomach* also revealed an affinity for pregnant women as well as "young girls. . .at a certain time in their lives, before their periodical evacuations appear."[76] Females on the verge of puberty would also be experiencing higher than normal nutritional requirements. "Deprived" children as well as slaves "past their prime" are also mentioned as susceptible to the *mal d' estomach* – those most likely to be last in line at the cooking pot and consequently less likely to come away with animal protein in their bowls.[77] Yet, as with "dropsy," the "match" achieved between distinctive symptoms of beriberi and those found in the descriptions of the *mal d' estomach* does not mean that all *mal d' estomach* cases were beriberi, and it remains to examine the other illnesses that could have been subsumed under the *mal d' estomach* category.

One West Indian physician reported that even a simple pain in the stomach could signify the *mal d' estomach* and such a pain is not a characteristic symptom of beriberi.[78] It is true that much slave "stomach pain" resulted from semantical confusion, for slaves tended to use "stomach pain" as a generic term to mean any pain in, or ailment of, the body. In Santo Domingo they even called yaws the *mal del estómago*.[79] But there were numerous ways in which the slaves could acquire a very legitimate stomach pain. One was by drinking "new" rum, while another was by the consumption of rum from stills that contained lead pipes and fastenings. The resulting sickness was frequently called the "dry belly ache" and in the latter case was often lead poisoning.[80] Other poisons could also have produced the "dry belly ache" such as the ackee fruit, which can be poisonous if not ripe. The poison in turn is soluble in cooking water and accentuated by alcohol, which may help to explain the apparent connection between the dry belly ache and alcohol consumption as far as some of the slaves were concerned. Poisonous ackee killed many in Jamaica until 1886 when the unripe fruit was discovered to be the source of the difficulty.[81] Other probable sources of the dry belly ache include nuts from the coral plant, which are poisonous, as is wild cassava (known as the belly-ache bush), while even cultivated cassava contains arsenic that must be removed before consumption. Finally, adulterated Jamaican ginger could easily have produced dry belly-ache symptoms.[82]

On the other hand some of the dry belly aches and *mal d' estomach* cases may have originated from pica usage. Blacks in Guiana reportedly ate *caovac*, a kind of yellow dirt, with no ill effects. But when they ate the *caovac* of the Islands it supposedly made them sick – so sick that planters forbade its consumption.[83] Elsewhere slaves preferred a "reddish clay" thought by one physician to contain "carbonate of lime" (and "carbonate of iron"), which he believed slaves ate to correct mineral deficiencies.[84]

He may well have been correct, for research on pica usage in Africa has revealed that some groups do eat soils containing minerals in which their normal diet is low such as calcium, iron, and potassium. Moreover, they also rely on soil consumption to control diarrhea.[85] Thus one student of geophagy in Africa has stated that "it seems clear that calcium from geophagy. . .plays a high-order incremental role that is nutritionally important in pregnancy. Furthermore, among the non-milking lactose intolerant and usually calcium deficient societies . . . of Africa, the marginal utility of mineral supplementation through clay eating assumes even greater significance."[86]

Since Caribbean slaves seem to have been similarly calcium deficient and because the "carbonate of lime" in "reddish clay" is a calcium-laden substance, it seems plausible that slaves in the Caribbean as modern-day Africans were responding to a bodily craving for a mineral they were seriously deficient in. The use of pica seems particularly important nutritionally for pregnant females and it was reported that among slave physicians "the strong propensity which pregnant females have to take alkaline [high in calcium] earths is generally known."[87]

That the slaves may have used pica to treat mineral deficiencies seems likely, especially when the earths consumed contained those minerals in which the slaves seem to have been the most deficient. But there is another hypothesis to deal with that remains firmly embedded in the literature, and this is that hookworm disease caused the dirt eating and the *mal d' estomach*. There are good reasons for the persistence. First of all the hookworm, *Necator americanus*, which has been widespread in the United States and the West Indies, is closely associated with the black who brought the parasite with him from Africa.[88] But more important, hookworm disease can produce "individuals exhibiting and persistently gratifying an unnatural craving for such things as earth, mud or lime. . . ," as well as iron deficiency anemia with symptoms including a "puffy face," "swollen feet and ankles," along with breathlessness, vertigo, apathy, and heart palpitations, not to mention heart failure.[89]

These, of course, are those same symptoms that suggested beriberi to us, even though textbooks on tropical medicine can still be found that link hookworm and dirt eating, while students of black history continue to assure us that hookworm "reduced thousands of Negroes to sick caricatures of their former selves."[90]

I do not deny that hookworm infection was probably widespread among the slaves and that hookworm disease troubled some. But as I stressed in Chapter 4, widespread hookworm disease, meaning a heavy load of worms causing severe iron deficiency anemia of the kind to elicit symptoms of appetite perversions, puffiness, vertigo, and all the rest, simply was not found among blacks by Rockefeller-funded investigators either in the United States or the West Indies, and the medical judgement today is that most people of West African origin have a tolerance for hookworm infection that whites do not possess.[91]

In this connection it is worth noting that hookworm disease was fairly common among British troops in the West Indies who did develop "perverted appetites," so physicians were accustomed to the phenomenon. Nonetheless they continued to insist that the *mal d' estomach* was peculiar to blacks.[92] Interestingly white troops serving the British crown in the West Indies in 1811 suffered a death rate of thirty per thousand from "cachetic" causes, much of which was probably hookworm disease; by contrast black troops died at the rate of only four per thousand from the same cause or causes, which may be taken as somewhat illustrative of their relative immunity to the illness.[93]

Moreover it should be kept in mind that most Caribbean blacks would have had their innate resistance buttressed with nutritional help in the form of an apparently adequate iron intake, thanks in no small part to their iron cooking utensils. In fact it is thought that a major reason for the freedom from hookworm anemia of the black populations of South and Central Africa has to do with the iron pots they use for cooking that supplement their iron intake. By contrast, in East Africa where iron pots are not used, there is "a considerable amount of hookworm anemia."[94]

Thus while there is every reason to believe that most slaves had a more or less adequate iron intake and therefore suffered little from hookworm disease, there is also a great deal of evidence that most slaves were thiamine deficient and suffered much from beriberi. Except for pica which seems to point to hookworm disease, the symptoms of the *mal d' estomach*, as noted, could mean either disease. Yet I also observed that physicians rarely saw individuals consuming pica; rather, they saw the symptoms of the *mal d' estomach* and assumed that the symptoms were precipitated by pica use.

The conclusions I have reached, then, are that slave pica usage did not occur with the frequency that slave physicians believed it did; that when it did occur it was a response to local mineral or vitamin deficiencies, rather than to uniformly widespread hookworm disease, against which slaves possessed both innate and nutritional resistance; that pica usage had little to do with the *mal d' estomach*[95] and that a substantial portion of the *mal d' estomach* cases were in fact wet or dry beriberi cases, probably often mingled with other deficiency diseases.

Summary

In summary, most of the vitamin and mineral deficiencies that an analysis of slave foodstuffs and the nutritional chemistry of their utilization pointed up have been verified by the presence of nutritional diseases among the slaves. Vitamin A deficiency was confirmed by the prevalence of night blindness and other symptoms; vitamin C deficiency seems not to have been uncommon because of the fairly regular references to scurvy, while calcium deficiency appears to have been the most important reason for widespread bone, and especially dental, complaints among the slaves. In this connection as well is the possibility that pica consumption was quite often linked to calcium deficiency. In addition, a general B vitamin deficiency seems to have been at the root of many of the slaves' mood "swings," while among the B vitamins, niacin deficiency seems confirmed by what appears to have been a fairly regular appearance of pellagra among slaves in areas where corn was consumed.

Of major interest among the B vitamin deficiency diseases, however, is beriberi, which nutritional analysis in Chapter 5 indicated had to be widespread among the slaves because of extensive thiamine deficiency. Yet, because beriberi was not known by West Indian physicians to be a disease sui generis, it would have "passed" as other diseases and I contend that, in view of their distinctive symptoms, "dropsy" and the mysterious *mal d' estomach* were very often beriberi in disguise. In making this assertion I have also argued, and attempted to demonstrate, that dirt eating was not part of the etiology of the *mal d' estomach*, nor was it a function of hookworm disease, but instead was a response to specific mineral deficiencies, especially calcium.

In the process of advancing these arguments, I have given beriberi a disproportionate share of attention, but not more than it deserves. For of all the major nutritional diseases save for PEM, beriberi is the only one that is capable of killing vast numbers of the very young. Following a look at slave demography in Chapter 7, Chapter 8 will again take up the question of illnesses among the slave young, whom malnutrition tormented twice, working much of its debilitating and often deadly effects through poor maternal nutrition before even touching the child via his own nutritional intake.

CHAPTER 7

SLAVE DEMOGRAPHY

Infant mortality [in the Leeward Islands] was in 1788 reckoned at about one-half the number of children born to slave women.

Elsa V. Goveia (1965)[1]

[It is an] astounding fact that while the slaves in the United States have increased tenfold, those of the. . .West Indies generally decreased in the proportion of five to two.

Josiah Clark Nott and George R. Gliddon (1857)[2]

As more specialized knowledge, especially that of a demographic nature, has been brought to bear on the study of slavery, the question of why most slave populations of the hemisphere failed to reproduce their numbers, while that of the United States grew at a brisk rate has become a central problem for those seeking a deeper understanding of New World slavery.

The problem of slave demography was also central for contemporary observers. Baron von Humboldt, for example, reported that, in early nineteenth-century Cuba, "I have heard discussed with the greatest coolness, the question of whether it was better for the proprietor not to overwork his slaves, and consequently have to replace them with less frequency, or whether he should get all he could out of them in a few years and thus have to purchase newly imported Africans more frequently."[3] Spanish authorities in Cuba believed that much of the failure of that island's slave population to grow stemmed from a tendency of planters to overwork slaves. For high slave mortality in turn created a continuing demand for fresh African cargoes, always weighted heavily in favor of males, and here they felt was the heart of the difficulty. The resulting imbalance of the sexes cut sharply into the potential for high slave fertility.[4]

Yet the problem was more subtle than this macro-overview would have it. Physicians in the British islands at a microlevel found that for some reason, "Black women are not so prolific as the white inhabitants and. . .their children. . .more frequently perish."[5] Reasons offered for both of these phenomena ranged from the assertion that black women were "less chaste and more liable to incurable obstructions of the monthly discharge," to a propensity of black women to abort or their infants to die soon after birth.[6]

Strangely, the contrast between this dismal portrait of slave demography in the Caribbean and the phenomenon of a rapidly reproducing slave population in the United States went largely ignored by slavery students until Philip Curtin recently focused some new quantitative light on the matter. Curtin pointed out that, although the Caribbean Islands absorbed over 40 percent of the slave imports to the hemisphere, as of the mid-20th century they contained only 20 percent of the hemisphere's Afro-American population. By contrast the United States, which had received less than 5 percent of the New World's African immigrants, counted among its citizens at mid-century about one third of the hemisphere's black population.[7]

This revelation had, among other things, the effect of redirecting scholarly attention from the comparative institutional and economic advantages and disadvantages of a particular slave system for the slave toward confronting directly fundamental questions of life, death, and physical well-being.[8] In particular it has challenged scholars to explain why the demographic experience of slaves in the United States was unique, and thus by implication challenged them to compile a truly holistic comparative study of hemispheric slavery.

Certainly when such a study appears many of the most compelling differences between Caribbean and U.S. slavery will cluster around a slave trade variable. For the Islands, the slave trade seems to have been absolutely essential for population growth throughout their years of commerical prosperity, beginning with Barbados in the middle seventeenth century and ending with Cuba some six decades into the nineteenth century. Conversely, during their years (1800–1860) of greatest prosperity, planters in the southern United States imported no slaves at all, yet saw their slave assets double their numbers, then double again, reaching a four million plus figure by the time of the Civil War.[9]

Most have blamed the slave trade twice for the inability of Caribbean slaves to reproduce: first, because as Humboldt indicated, many planters found it economical to be careless of slave lives and simply import new workers as their predecessors died; and second, as the Cuban government officials noted, the slave trade created a distinct imbalance in the sexes inimical to high fertility.[10]

Some might be inclined to tack onto the slave trade variable a disease environment variable as well, to account for the vast demographic differences between slave populations in the Islands and that of the southern United States. Yet not all West Indian slave populations failed to reproduce themselves. As Michael Craton has demonstrated, slaves on the Rolle plantation of Great Exuma Island in the Bahamas (and by implication most Bahamian slaves) enjoyed high levels of fertility and low levels of mortality; by contrast counterparts on Worthy Park plantation in Jamaica had the opposite demographic experience.[11] The latter were sugar slaves, the former were not and the stark contrast between the two seems to bear out the adage that sugar slavery was wasteful of human life both by shortening it considerably and by not encouraging births.[12]

Certainly this appears to have held true for Barbados, which was perhaps more totally given over to sugar monoculture than any other West Indian island. Between 1626 and 1807 Barbados imported some 387,000 slaves, yet in 1834 there were only 82,000 on the island to receive liberation.[13] The reason for this has not seemed elusive. Richard Sheridan has calculated that between the years 1676 and 1700 the Barbados slave population suffered a net natural decrease (an excess of deaths over births) of fully 4 percent annually, with the figure rising to 5 percent for the period 1701 to 1725.[14] These were flush times for Barbadian planters, who could afford to replace slaves as fast as they died. Later in the eighteenth century, however, times were not so flush. The island was beset by competition on all sides – especially from Jamaica within the Empire and St. Domingue without – wars were disrupting commerce including the slave trade, and as a consequence slave life became more highly prized and a policy of "amelioration" was adopted.

By the beginning of the nineteenth century, if not before, Barbadian slaves were achieving a natural increase, which might logically lead to the conclusion that planters' wishes had everything to do with slaves' reproduction. When Barbadian planters found it cheaper to import than to raise slaves they discouraged reproduction; when on the other hand circumstances increased the "value" of slaves on the island, planters encouraged reproduction and were duly rewarded with a natural growth of the slave population. The Jamaican example, however, raises a flag of caution. Barry Higman has calculated that during the eighteenth century Jamaican slaves suffered a net natural decrease of between 3 and 3.5 percent annually, suggesting that, relatively speaking, conditions during Jamaica's boom years were not as bad for slaves as they had been for Barbadian counterparts during that island's period of prosperity. Nonetheless, although Jamaican planters also appear to have embarked on the path of amelioration, they met with less success. Indeed, according to Higman's calculations, Jamaican blacks did not achieve a natural increase until sometime in the 1840s.[15]

Clearly then the suspicion seems justified that there were other factors influencing slave fertility besides planter wishes in the matter. Philip Curtin has made the interesting observation that natural growth seems to have been a function of the percentage of Creole or Island-born slaves in the population. In Curtin's words, "as a general tendency, the higher the proportion of African born in any slave population, the lower its rate of natural increase – or, as was more often the case, the higher its rate of natural decrease."[16] Unquestionably Curtin's observation seems to dovetail with the demographic experience of the slave populations under consideration. In Barbados of 1817, which was witnessing the natural growth of the slave population, only 7 percent of the slaves were African born.[17] By contrast, in 1770 Jamaica just prior to amelioration, fully 70 percent of the slaves were African born, while in the naturally growing slave population of United States of 1770, the percentage of African-born slaves had already fallen to 30 percent.[18]

Of course the percentage of Creole-born slaves in a population may only have been significant for slave fertility in that a high percentage, at least for West Indian sugar islands, indicated a cessation of the slave trade and a concomitant period of economic decline for the planters. This would tend to square with the argument of those who have pointed out that slave treatment (and by implication fertility) seems to have varied inversely with a slave society's stage of economic development.[19] The more intensive the system, the worse slaves were treated, and the less they reproduced, resulting in a greater need for "imports."[20]

Cuba, however, may have been something of an exception to the rule. Manuel Moreno Fraginals has reported recently that early in the nineteenth century, as Cuba became increasingly devoted to sugar production, the sex ratio on plantations sampled averaged 832 males for every 100 females – a ratio hardly conducive to a high rate of slave reproduction. However, by the mid 1820s, despite the increasing tempo of Cuban slavery, the planters had initiated a "good treatment" policy, a greater effort was made to ensure a balance of the sexes by importing more women, and the result was a sharp increase in slave fertility.[21]

If Moreno Fraginals is correct, then Cuba unlike Barbados managed the increased fertility with African-born women. Yet Jack Eblen's quantitative study of Cuba's black population suggests declining fertility for the period Moreno Fraginals would have it increasing, while my own work on Cuba census materials did not discover any significant change in slave fertility for the period in question.[22]

Thus, until Moreno Fraginals publishes the results of his investigations in Cuban archives, we are without a concrete example of African-born slave women achieving high rates of fertility on West Indian sugar plantations. On the other hand, we do have examples of African-born women doing no worse in this regard than Creole women. Richard Dunn, who examined the records of Mesopotamia Plantation in Jamaica, discovered no "pronounced" differences in fertility between African-born and Creole-born women, while Barry Higman found only slight differences reflected in the records of Jamaican plantations which he examined.[23] However, both studies seemed to confirm the low fertility of Jamaican slave women generally – so low that even in the early nineteenth century, Jamaican plantations had to be continually "restocked" with slaves.[24]

These differences in fertility between African-born and Creole-born women may serve to confirm our hypothesis that an inability to bear a child could have been a criterion for selection for the slave trade in West Africa. However the presence or absence of African-born women in a population does not seem by itself to suffice as a satisfactory explanation of low West Indian slave fertility, which makes the high rates achieved by slave women in the United States even more intriguing by comparison.

To date no explanation has been forthcoming. Rather most students of Caribbean slavery seem satisfied, for the moment at least, with the general notion that slavery became harsher as the man–land ratio increased in the Islands and as the plantation became more centralized. This harshness in turn somehow forestalled the natural growth of slave populations, which was no problem for the planters so long as there was a slave trade to provide an "unnatural" growth. The contrasting anomaly of the natural increase of the U.S. slave population also seems to defy explanation, although it tends to buttress considerably Eugene Genovese's broad contention that U.S. slavery was in itself something of an anomaly because of its peculiarly paternalistic nature.[25]

In a recent study David Littlefield has explained that paternalistic planters were not necessarily "uneconomic" in their tendency to conserve slave life and encourage its reproduction; rather, they viewed slaves as both labor and capital and were willing to "defer immediate, temporary earnings [from the labor component] for measured, long term gains" (the increase of capital) with one of the results high slave fertility.[26]

To be sure we have numerous examples of West Indian planters unwilling to settle for measured, long-term gains, such as the Nevis slaveholder who complained that low slave fertility, high infant mortality, the loss of a mother's labor, and the cost of raising slave young all militated against encouraging slave reproduction. However, against this we have the testimony of other West Indian planters who did wish slaves to reproduce, yet in the words of one, despite all encouragement "the children do not come."[27]

All of this, of course, brings us back again to the question of the extent to which planter attitudes could by themselves affect slave fertility in the first place, with historians now beginning to realize that any explanations of fertility based solely on planter attitudes are bound to fail because planters simply did not have that much control over the private lives of their slaves. Moreover, it has been argued that this lack of control was particularly pronounced for "nonpaternal-istic" planters of the West Indies who had "a comparative lack of concern about the private affairs of the bondsman, his household [and] social structure . . . "[28] When planters did intrude in slave af-fairs it seems to have been a positive type of interference to stimulate fertility by encouraging slave marriages.[29] Testimony that this sort of intrusion did increase fertility comes from Puerto Rico, where it was reported that these unions had effected a substantial natural growth of the slave population by the middle 1830s.[30] Yet would opposite attitudes have held true? Would planter discouragement of permanent slave unions at an earlier date have significantly discouraged slave fertility?

Baffled by these contradictions, investigators have concluded that "no simple economic explanation . . . can explain the secular trends of fertility in either the United States or the West Indies," and conse-quently have begun to investigate biosocial factors in a search for sup-plementary answers.[31]

One of the most intriguing explorations of this new terrain has been made by Herbert Klein and Stanley Engerman, who have suggested that lactation practices may well help to explain slave fertility differ-entials.[32] In West Africa the custom was to breast-feed infants for up to three years and lactation, they argue, would have provided some pro-tection against pregnancy for a good portion of the time the infant remained on the breast. Moreover many West African peoples held taboos against sexual intercourse while a female was lactating.

These West African cultural practices of course were carried to all those parts of the New World where slaves were employed. Yet Klein and Engerman argue that a continuing slave trade reinforced them in the Caribbean region, while the lack of a slave trade to the United States caused them to wither. Thus West African lactation practices in the West Indies, they suggest, may have resulted in a longer period between pregnancies for slave women and hence lower fertility than among slave women in the United States who only breast-fed for a year or so.

Another window in slave fertility has been opened by investigators who have devised a means of calculating the age of menarche (pu-berty) for slave females.[33] Thus far this has only been done for U.S. slaves, but presumably calculations will soon be available for West Indian slaves as well.[34] And it is strongly suspected by researchers that the age will in fact be higher for Caribbean slave women. Clearly the comparative focus is narrowing on differential fertility to account for the growth of the U.S. slave population on the one hand and the lack of a natural increase in the West Indies on the other. Indeed the hy-pothesis advanced recently by two investigators of the problem is that the "largest part of the explanation" for natural growth or its absence among slave populations "was the difference in fertility, not mortality."[35]

To test this hypothesis, researchers will doubtless be forced to turn to matters of nutrition, with some already voicing the suspicion that malnutrition lurks behind any accounting of West Indian slave fertility.[36] Certainly the suspicion seems, at least superficially, justified when factors such as the generally malnourished state of West Africans, their lower heights when compared with Creole-born counterparts, their high percentage of representation within West Indian slave populations, and the simple fact that West Indian slave populations failed to reproduce their numbers are all added together.

There is no doubt that malnutrition can depress fertility in a number of ways. Those calculating the age of menarche for example understand that malnutrition can retard physical development, which in turn delays the adolescent growth spurt and hence the age of menarche. Malnutrition can also disrupt the regular menstrual function and considerably delay postpartum recovery, which in turn impedes the ability to become impregnated again. Finally malnourishment can hasten the age of menopause.[37]

That malnutrition produced all of these impediments to pregnancy among West Indian slave women – particularly the African born – there is little doubt. Physicians and planters alike frequently complained that "obstructions of the menstrua" and "sterility" were common among slave females.[38] And when to the problems created by malnutrition, the impact of prolonged lactation on Caribbean slave fertility is added, a strong case has been made for low fertility that must be treated seriously.

Yet prolonged lactation seems to be the weaker half of the case. It is true that contemporary observers have verified that West Indian slave mothers did indeed nurse their young from two to even three years.[39] One physician commented dryly that "if permitted they will extend it . . . until, in their phraseology, the child can bring its mother a calabash full of water."[40]

The custom of prolonged lactation, however, was not confined to the African born but seems to have been practiced by Creole women as well, thus eliminating it as a factor to account for perceived differences in fertility between the two. In Barbados of 1824 when 5 percent or less of the slaves were African born and the slave trade had ceased for almost a generation, it was nonetheless reported that children were not weaned for an extended period, while there is much evidence that prolonged lactation among Caribbean peoples persisted until well into the twentieth century.[41]

Moreover, just as prolonged lactation does not seem a significant factor in differential fertility levels among West Indian slaves, it is doubtful that it can do much to explain the perceived differential between U.S. and West Indian slaves. The reason here is that studies on the contraceptive benefit of lactation have determined that generally this lasts no longer than a year.[42] Since North American slave mothers nursed for about a year, lactation by itself would seem to be fairly unimportant to comparative questions of slave fertility.[43]

More formidable however is the suggestion that African taboos against intercourse with a lactating woman would have cut into West Indian fertility.[44] Indeed it is precisely these taboos that modern-day demographers suggest may account for "pockets" of reduced fertility in West Africa.[45] The word "pocket," however, is stressed, for the presence of pockets indicates that the postnatal taboo is (and was) hardly uniformly practiced.[46]

It is important to note as well that the practice itself took root in a society that also practiced widespread polygamy, presumably at least in part a response to the considerably lower than normal West African sex ratio at birth and the heavier male than female mortality rate throughout infancy and childhood, all of which created a society with a surplus of females.[47] Obviously the slave trade, which sent far more men than women to the Americas, must have further exacerbated the imbalance of the sexes and consequently further reinforced the practice of polygamy in Africa – a situation that in turn made it easier for a male to sexually avoid a spouse during the period in which she was breast-feeding.[48]

But of course the slave trade, which helped to create a shortage of males in West Africa, created a surplus in the West Indies – such a surplus in fact that one suspects taboos calling for long periods of sexual abstinence for women were discarded fairly early in the history of New World slavery.[49] Another reason for this suspicion is the fact that mating between various African ethnic groups took place very early in the Caribbean.[50] Presumably this cultural homogenization saw much sifting out of cultural traits no longer useful in a new environment.

Yet these minor speculative carpings are not going to shed much light on the question of West Indian slave fertility nor for that matter on the larger question of why Caribbean slaves failed to reproduce their numbers. So instead of continuing in this vein, it appears advisable to turn elsewhere for enlightenment and the logical place to turn seems to be to a model – in this case a West African demographic model – where it is hoped that today's data may provide instruction on what took place in the Caribbean yesterday.

Unfortunately the comparison is quite legitimate. As we have seen, widespread malnutrition remains the chief problem facing modern West Africa and malnutrition was also an impediment to the health of many Caribbean slaves. Polygamy, prolonged lactation, and sexual taboos are all still very much a part of West African life and many of the major diseases suffered by the population are, as we have already noted, the same illnesses that dealt most harshly with Caribbean slaves.

Historically, as well as today, demographers have viewed West Africa as probably the most unhealthy place on the globe. Prior to this century "death rates were almost certainly the world's highest. . . and population numbers were sustained only by equally high birth rates, achieved by placing great cultural and social status on high fertility values."[51]

No one would argue that mortality rates have not fallen in West Africa during this century. Nonetheless those rates are still among the world's highest, largely because of infant and child mortality, and a very high rate of fertility is still absolutely crucial for population growth.[52] For purposes of this study it should be stressed that West African fertility is very high *despite* long periods of breast-feeding, social restrictions on intercourse during breast-feeding, much fetal mortality, and early sterility of women.[53]

The crude birth rate for the region today has been estimated at about fifty per thousand, a rate that includes those pockets of relatively low fertility previously noted.[54] The crude birth rate for U.S. slaves has been estimated to have been as high as fifty to fifty-five per thousand for the nineteenth century – rates that approximate those of modern West Africa.[55] By contrast, the birth rate for Creole born slaves in Jamaica has been estimated at only twenty-five to twenty-seven per thousand.[56] For all Jamaican slaves, African-born and Creole combined, the crude birth rate for the period 1817 to 1832 has been estimated at an average of about twenty-three per thousand.[57]

If the data from Jamaica can be taken as somewhat representative of Caribbean slave demography as a whole, then superficially it would seem that low slave fertility was indeed the key variable in the problem of little or no population growth in the region. Yet Barry Higman, who made the estimates, cautions that the rates are bound to be low for they are based on registered births only and "there was a good deal of underregistration among children less than two months old."[58] They are also bound to be low because of a notoriously high (if as yet unmeasured) rate of infant mortality – infants whose fleeting passage through this world went unacknowledged in both the birth and death registrations.[59]

To know, however, that because of underregistration and infant mortality the Jamaican rates are low is not the same thing as knowing what they actually were or should have been, so again a look at West Africa, or rather a state within West Africa, may provide some enlightenment. The 1957–58 census for Mopti within Mali revealed a crude birth rate of fifty-one per thousand, while it also disclosed an infant death rate of 354 per thousand live births.[60] Both rates are probably low, as are most West African demographic rates because of underreporting of both births and deaths. Nonetheless, assuming both to be accurate, then for the year 1957–58, Mopti, with a population of about 200,000, saw 10,200 births, of which 3,611 died as infants.[61]

Now let us assume for the moment that Mopti was a nineteenth century West Indian slave society that only registered the birth of every infant who did not die. In this case Mopti would have registered 6,589 births instead of 10,200 and the lower figure would have yielded a deceptively low crude birth rate of only thirty-three per thousand instead of fifty-one per thousand. It will of course be immediately noticed that a birth rate of thirty-three per thousand is not very far above the rate of twenty-five to twenty-seven calculated for Creole-born Jamaican slaves.

Nor is Mopti an extreme example of high infant mortality in West Africa.[62] In Nigeria it is estimated that between 40 and 50 percent of all infants born die shortly after birth, while the crude birth rate of Nigeria is around fifty per thousand population depending on the region.[63] However, were Nigeria's surviving infants aged one and under in the census taken as an indication of Nigerian fertility, the resulting calculation would assign a crude birth rate to Nigeria of between twenty-five and thirty instead of fifty per thousand.

Moving back to the plantations of the West Indies, some researchers have suggested that as many as one half of the slave infants born did not live out their first year of life.[64] Were this the case a crude birth rate of, say, twenty-six per thousand unadjusted for infant mortality would after adjustment yield an actual rate of slightly over fifty births per thousand population – a rate, not incidentally, similar to the adjusted estimate for U.S. slaves of between fifty and fifty-five per thousand.

Thus recourse to a West African model suggests that high infant mortality rather than low fertility may have been the real problem with slave populations unable to increase their numbers by natural means. Apparent impediments to high fertility such as prolonged lactation and sexual taboos as well as nutritionally related disorders such as delayed menarche and an early menopause all of which investigators suspect may have cut sharply into the fertility potential of West Indian slaves clearly have not resulted in low West African fertility, either historically or today.[65] However despite high fertility terribly high infant mortality rates in some parts of West Africa means deaths in some areas may actually be exceeding births, precisely as they did on most Caribbean slave plantations.[66]

Yet, West Africa's problem with high mortality rates runs far deeper than simply infant mortality, and once again the West African example can prove instructive for the Caribbean. As we saw previously, a peculiarity of the mortality profile of West Africa is that the rate of deaths among the young does not fall off rapidly after the initial incidence of infant mortality, but rather remains high and rises to peak again as the children fall victim to PEM or intercurrent diseases. Consequently demographers tell us that one of the "most striking features of African mortality is a heavy incidence of death in the second and third years of life."[67]

The mortality pattern of slave young in the Caribbean bears a striking resemblance to that of West Africa. As two investigators of slave mortality in Jamaica have pointed out, "it is evident that the majority of fatalities among slave children born at Worthy Park occurred not at birth, but in the children's early years."[68] Orlando Patterson also found Jamaican slave mortality in the under four-year-old age group to be excessive, as opposed simply to infant mortality,[69] while Barry Higman has puzzled over the fact that his mortality data on Jamaican slave children reveal that those deaths "peak at about 12 months" instead of much earlier.[70]

On the Codrington Plantation in Barbados, *at least* one of every two youngsters died before the age of five ("at least" is emphasized because presumably many infants who died during their first few days of life were not entered in the plantation records). Of these half or more died as children rather than infants.[71] Similarly the parish of St. Thomas saw 168 slave children aged ten and under buried during the years 1816 to 1834. Of these only thirty-six were less than one year of age, while in St. Philip's parish during the same years, of one hundred and six child burials only thirty-three were infants.[72] Finally, some contemporary physicians observed that slave child mortality was as heavy as infant mortality.[73]

Whether this is true, or whether the physicians simply saw more child mortality (since they were rarely called upon to deliver or treat infants), it was certainly the case that heavy child mortality was also a crucial factor militating against the growth of Caribbean slave populations. Let us present just one example drawn from the historical and archaeological records of the Newton Plantation of Barbados.[74] According to Jerome Handler and Robert Corruccini, who have examined the former and quite literally unearthed the latter, historical data indicate that about 50 percent of the infants born on the plantation survived to reach early childhood. However, early childhood was scarcely less dangerous according to the historical data, and these data are upheld by evidence gleaned from teeth excavated from a slave cemetery on the plantation that reveal growth arrest lines indicating a real battle for survival for youngsters shortly after weaning.

That many lost this battle the study leaves no doubt while implying that at least another 50 percent may well have become casualties at this point due in large part to weaning trauma. If true, then only about *a quarter* of the slaves born on the Newton Plantation survived the perils of infancy and early childhood.

Thus the demographic experience of slave youngsters does seem to parallel the West African pattern of both high infant and high child mortality suggesting that West Indian slave mortality, particularly that of the young, was the primary reason for the inability of West Indian slave populations to grow by natural means and that slave fertility was actually high.

Indeed it may have been very high, for as yet we have not considered stillbirths. Generally, stillbirths are not brought into measurements of fertility where the object is to gauge performance. Our interest, however, has focused in part on the extent to which prolonged lactation, sexual taboos, and the like may have affected performance, and thus a consideration of stillbirths, which indicate fecundity, seems germane at this point. We have already seen that in West Africa where a high frequency of prematurity is symptomatic of maternal malnutrition, the stillbirth rate is also high. In addition, we have suspected that slave women in the West Indies would have experienced a high rate of the toxemia of pregnancy, as do their descendants, and the toxemia of pregnancy is an important cause of stillbirths. Thus, from these two factors alone we might infer that slave mothers in the Caribbean experienced a soaring rate of stillbirths. But we also have data from the West Indian island of Antigua where compulsory birth, stillbirth, and death registration requirements were introduced in 1856 and a decennial census has been taken since 1857.[75] K.H. Uttley, the authority on the medical history of the island, reports that even on such a tiny island, some of the infants probably escaped registration and enumeration, and that stillbirths in particular were most likely underreported. Nonetheless, he judges the data for the decade 1867 to 1876 to be reasonably accurate, and those data include the recording of stillbirths with the number representing a whopping 12.5 percent of all births during the decade.

The West African model, in tandem with this high frequency of stillbirths in Antigua, suggests by inference that Caribbean fertility was indeed much higher than has generally been believed. But the problem is one of how much higher. Only for the islands of Cuba and Puerto Rico of the mid-nineteenth century do we have official censuses taken during slavery that give any real clue as to the number of slave young being born, and in the case of Puerto Rico, the size of the free colored population had, by this time, swollen to the point where the data on slaves alone is terribly skewed.[76]

In 1861 the Cuban census revealed that there were twenty-eight slave infants aged one year or less on the island for every 1,000 slaves. The Puerto Rican census data were similar in that they showed thirty slave and free colored infants aged one year or less for every thousand blacks on the Island. We know that both censuses are undercounts because of incomplete registration and baptismal data, and may safely assume that the infants would be the most likely to be undercounted.

Concentrating only on Cuba's census, which gives us better slave data, we also know that the twenty-eight slave infants per thousand slave population represent only the survivors of a group that had been thinned out considerably by mortality, with the bulk of that mortality occurring in the first few weeks of life. The question, of course, is how big was that group to begin with? Jack Eblen's demographic study of Cuba's nineteenth-century black population estimates the birth rate for the first six decades at between forty-five and fifty per thousand.[77] If we rather arbitrarily select fifty per thousand as the birth rate, and assume as well that the census did not count 20 percent of the infants, and that the forty per thousand who were counted suffered a loss rate of 30 percent, then we very neatly wind up with the twenty-eight infants per thousand slaves reported in the census. Certainly a 30 percent rate of infant loss can be justified on the basis of the West African model, the West Indian examples already examined, or the experience of Antigua after slavery, which during the decade 1867 to 1876 saw 30 percent of its births result in either stillbirth or death before the age of one year.[78] On the other hand, the assumption of a 20 percent undercount, which made the calculation come out so neatly, was nothing more than a wild guess.

But guess or not, the rate of loss and the guess as to the magnitude of the undercount do fit with Eblen's estimate, and if that estimate is reasonably accurate then, most assuredly, Cuban slave fertility was not low. Rather, it would have been on a level comparable to that of the slaves in the American South during the same time period, and this despite the Cuban slave population being top-heavy with males. For while the sex ratio for slaves in the United States stood at just over 100 males for every 100 females in 1860, during 1861 in Cuba, 144 slave males were counted for every 100 slave females, while the sex ratio for the black population as a whole stood at 122.[79]

There is a final way of glimpsing something of the probable fertility of Cuba's nineteenth-century slave population – that of measuring the number of infants per thousand females in the population of childbearing age – which, in view of the preponderance of males in the population, is a much better gauge of fertility. Thus, in Cuba during 1861 there were eighty-eight slave infants aged one year or less for every thousand slave females aged sixteen to fifty. By contrast, in the United States of the previous year 122 infants aged one and under had been counted for every thousand slave females in the fifteen- to forty-nine-year age group, or roughly 25 percent more slave infants per thousand women of childbearing age than in Cuba.

Superficially, it would seem that slave females in the United States were indeed more fertile than their Cuban sisters. But, as we continue to stress, this ignores the infant mortality variable. No one familiar with West Indian slavery would seriously argue that slaves in Cuba, and in sugar colonies generally, did not experience at least 25 percent more infant mortality than slaves in the United States, and when this is taken into account it would once again appear that Cuban slave fertility was on a level comparable to that of slaves in the American South.

This bit of numerical shuffling, of course, is hardly convincing by itself. Nor is mid-nineteenth-century Cuba intended to be representative of mid-seventeenth-century Barbados or mid-eighteenth-century Jamaica. Indeed, no single glimpse of the demographic experience of West Africans in their homeland or in the Caribbean is sufficiently reliable to resolve the problem of why West Indian slave populations failed to grow by natural means. However, after a few of such glimpses a picture begins to emerge that, if still somewhat blurred, nonetheless seems unmistakably to highlight the mortality rather than the fertility side of the demographic coin and in particular the infant portion of the mortality side.

Those who have viewed low fertility as the key have pointed to possible West African cultural causes such as prolonged lactation and sexual taboos during lactation along with nutritionally related impediments such as delayed menarche and early menopause. Nonetheless a look at West Africa, where these cultural practices persist and malnutrition is the region's greatest problem, indicates that the result is not low fertility among its peoples, but rather some of the highest fertility rates in the world. Unfortunately, however, West African peoples also sustain some of the world's highest infant and child mortality rates so that even in this modern age there are populations in the region that may be experiencing a natural decrease rather than an increase of their numbers. We have examined evidence suggesting that some West Indian slave populations suffered a similar fate. Contemporary accounts and modern studies alike all fairly bristle with references to extraordinarily high slave infant mortality, others have explained that "extraordinarily high" meant infant mortality in the 50 percentile range, and it would seem that child mortality on some plantations may have once again halved the survivors.[80]

At first this may seem an impossibly high percentage of dead infants, let alone young children, yet on Antigua, *after slavery*, 30 percent of all births resulted either in stillbirth or an infant mortality statistic within one year. Surely in this light a rate of 40 percent or higher for slave infants whose mothers were caught up in the rigors of sugar slavery does not seem unrealistic. And if Cuban or Jamaican or Puerto Rican data on birth rates are adjusted for infant mortality of this magnitude, then the data suggest that Caribbean slaves maintained a level of fertility at least equal to or even exceeding that of North American slaves.[81]

If true then the North American slave population grew at what seems to have been an astounding rate, not because of higher fertility than Caribbean counterparts, but because of much lower (although certainly not low) infant and child mortality. The final obvious question is why the differential and it is here that nutritional factors of both a general and a specific nature come into play. In general terms it is axiomatic that severe maternal malnutrition is the leading cause of stillbirths, prematurity, and low birthweight infants whose chances of survival are considerably less than those of heavier counterparts, and that malnutrition is today, and always has been, the leading cause of infant and child mortality. In specific terms, thiamine deficiency, which as we saw seems to have been widespread among the slaves, could easily have produced astronomically high infant and child mortality rates alone, although it would appear that other deficiencies, such as that of calcium, were also severe enough to have played a deadly role.

Thus the major difference between North American slave populations that grew by natural means and the West Indian slave populations that did not grow by natural means may well have been rooted in what the slaves consumed, with the most important difference one of protein consumption. Fat pork, which was the mainstay of slaves in the American South,[82] while hardly the best protein source one can think of, nevertheless was partly fat and it was this fat that made it possible for them to make use of many nutrients much more fully than their Caribbean counterparts whose diets were practically devoid of fats. Among these nutrients would have been thiamine.

In closing this chapter, it might be observed that if Caribbean slaves did manage the level of fertility that it appears they did, then planter attitudes toward slave reproduction probably had little impact on fertility. But planter attitudes had a great deal to do with infant and child mortality, for infant and child mortality was related to nutrition that was under planter control.

Thus, for example, in late eighteenth-century Jamaica, planters began a policy of "amelioration" with the hope of increasing their labor force through reproduction. This represented a change of planter attitude, yet as we have noted fertility did not increase. The reason, we would argue, is that it could not because it was already high. The problem with amelioration in Jamaica was that it came about as planters found themselves in increasingly dismal financial straits, and thus we might speculate that although some effort was made to improve the diet of the slaves, it was too little to correct many of the gross deficiencies of maternal nutrition. Hence high infant mortality would have continued to characterize Jamaican slave demography until emancipation when, as free men, Jamaican blacks could do something about improving their diet, and at this point the black population began to grow.[83] It grew because of reduced infant mortality due to better nutrition.

In Barbados, by contrast, amelioration was begun earlier with greater quantities of food and better quality a major part of the "amelioration" program. There planters were rewarded with a naturally growing slave population, again not because of increased fertility, but because of a significant reduction in infant and child mortality. For, as long as a master had control over a slave's life, he controlled to a large extent what he consumed. Thus with a diet in many ways a duplicate of the West African diet, and the disease environment also closely resembling that of West Africa, very little had changed for the slaves biologically except that they labored longer and harder, and consequently needed more calories for survival. And since little had changed, the terribly high infant and child mortality rates that had characterized the birth process on the West African side of the South Atlantic continued on the West Indian side.

CHAPTER 8

SLAVE INFANT AND CHILD
MORTALITY

While the infant mortality in a poor community may be 10 times
higher than in a prosperous one, the mortality in the 1 to 4 year age
group may be 50 times higher.

Sir Stanley Davidson et al (1975)[1]

The instances of [Jamaican slave mothers] who have had four, five,
six children, without succeeding in bringing up one, in spite of the
utmost attention and indulgence are very numerous.

M.G. Lewis (1816)[2]

As I have already suggested, the failure of the slave populations of the
West Indies to increase by natural means was not the result of low
fertility, but rather the consequence of a blending of genetic, cultural,
immunological, and especially nutritional factors, which quickly con-
verted so many birth statistics into death statistics that natural population growth was impossible. By examining the major causes of infant
and child mortality it is possible to glean some idea of the magnitude of
their destructiveness and also in some cases to see them begin to fade
as nutritional circumstances gradually improved for Caribbean blacks,
first as slaves and then as freemen. For convenience, as well as coher-
ence, the diseases to be examined are presented in the chronological
order that West Indian slave infants and children would have most
likely encountered them as they struggled for life during their first,
most hazardous, years.

Tetanus/Tetany

According to West Indian physicians and planters alike, the most important cause of infant death during the first week or two of life was
the illness called "jawfall," "trismus," or "locked jaw" in the British
Islands, *mocezuelo* in Puerto Rico, and *tetanos neonatorum* in Cuba. It
was also referred to colloquially as the "nine-day fits," for generally it
claimed the infant within the first nine days of life.[3]

Some of the terms, especially "jawfall" and "locked jaw," seemed contradictory, yet a Jamaican physician assured readers that the two were the "same complaint . . . a fixed spasm of the muscles of the jaw as in tetanus."[4] Explanations for its cause ranged from the belief that infants became too cold, to the conviction that smoky huts were to blame. Yet most physicians by the end of the eighteenth century had reached the conclusion that much of the difficulty revolved somehow around the "improper treatment of the navel string."[5]

In those many cases where the illness was in fact neonatal tetanus, the physicians were correct. Unfortunately, 200 years later the disease, although a needless cause of death, persists in much of the under-developed world. Investigators in Haiti, for example, reported as late as 1958 that cutting the umbilical cord of the newborn with such tools as an "unsterile machete, knife, scissors or broken piece of glass," then tying it with an "unsterile piece of string or wire," applying charcoal mixed with dirt to the cut stump, and then wrapping it with "leaves or any old piece of cloth" was responsible for neonatal tetanus claiming between 5 and 10 percent of the newborn in much of the country.[6]

Thus in Haiti, at least, little seems to have changed in the procedure for treating the umbilical stump from the days of slavery when the umbilical cord was cut with anything handy and then ashes or mud were placed on the stump, which was subsequently bound up with a "burnt rag."[7]

In the treatment of the umbilicus of the newborn, West Africans in the West Indies were victims of the culture of their homeland where neonatal tetanus was either rare or nonexistent. A physician in West Africa at the turn of the nineteenth century, for example, wondered why in the West Indies "negro children are very liable to locked jaw soon after birth [while] not a single instance of trismus in infants. . . occurred to my notice in Africa."[8]

But there were few large domesticated animals in most of West Africa, while in the West Indies there were numerous horses and oxen to drop tetanus spores in their manure.[9] The "jawfall" was credited with killing between one quarter and one half of the slave newborn,[10] while by contrast, physicians reported that the trismus "seldom or never visits a white child."[11] That neonatal tetanus was indeed "very bad" among black infants and claimed an astronomical number of them in the greater Antilles and Barbados was later confirmed by August Hirsch, who also reported that it was "not so common" in Trinidad and "rare" in St. Lucia.[12]

Yet Hirsch and the assertions of slave physicians notwithstanding, statistical data from around the Caribbean make it seem doubtful that neonatal tetanus alone snuffed out as many young lives as they believed it did. Antigua, for example, during the years 1877 to 1906 registered 3,734 births and neonatal tetanus attacked less than 9 percent of the newborn, killing only 324 infants.[13] In Cuba during the years 1900 to 1904, of 249,807 births only 6,487, or less than 3 percent, died from neonatal tetanus (although in rural regions the rate climbed to as high as 5 percent).[14]

In both Antigua and Cuba the data are reflective of the time before knowledge of the disease was widespread and before antiseptic procedures had been introduced. And although sanitary conditions must have been worse on plantations a century before, it seems doubtful that they were so much worse as to have produced 10 to 15 times more infant mortality than that suffered in turn-of-the-century Antigua or Cuba.[15]

Indeed, moving back into the days of Cuban slavery, we find that during the year 1843 the archdiocese of Havana counted 746 black infants who had died of "tetanos de los recién nacidos" (tetanus of the newborn), which when divided by 10,704 baptisms yields a rate of 7 percent, twice that of Cuba's rate some half a century later, but hardly anything approaching the death of a quarter to a half of all children born that some slave physicians blamed on the "jawfall."[16]

Similarly in Jamaica, for part of the parish of Clarendon during the year 1818, of 162 slave births, eight were listed as having "died within the month." There were also four deaths from lockjaw, although whether these were adult cases or infants is not clear.[17] But assuming that those who "died within the month" and the "lockjaw" deaths all represented neonatal tetanus statistics, the death rate was still only 7.4 percent.

Barry Higman also provides cause-of-death data for Jamaican plantations that fail to reveal neonatal tetanus as a major cause of death. However, he explains that probably a great many infant deaths went unrecorded when they occurred within the first few days of life and thus most of the unrecorded deaths would have been neonatal tetanus cases.[18]

A contemporary observer confirms that it was common practice to omit from the official statistics "any notice of such as die within the ninth day,"[19] while a midwife on a Jamaican plantation told her new master that "till nine days over we *no hope* of them" because of the "locked jaw" (italics his).[20] In addition, physicians on the spot reported that frequently trismus was used as a "catchall" cause of death category for all infants who died soon after birth.[21] Thus, in view of this, in view of the massive under-reporting of infant deaths, and in view of the reputation of trismus as a killer it is easy enough to believe that as many as a quarter of all infants born died of something called trismus during their first week or two of life. That many of these deaths were not actually neonatal tetanus is also easy to believe, given the fairly uniform death rate from this cause of between 5 and 10 percent throughout the nineteenth-century Caribbean.

Another reason for believing that the trismus category included many nonneonatal tetanus deaths has to do with the abrupt decline of the malady. An individual writing about Jamaican slavery just prior to abolition observed that as early as "about twenty years ago, a very great number of infants were lost by locked jaw" but that now "deaths from this cause have become rare."[22] He credited the improvement to the practice of bathing the infants more frequently, which physicians had earlier recommended.[23] Yet it is doubtful that bathing infants was very effective against neonatal tetanus since the water used by slaves was usually foul and the causative agent of tetanus is also found in water. Rather, one suspects that the decline was not in the incidence of neonatal tetanus, but instead that other diseases previously lumped into the trismus category had declined in importance.

This being the case there may be some significance in the time when the disease reportedly declined – the last decades of slavery, when amelioration was progressing and presumably, nutrition improving. There is a nutritional disease of infants that has often been confused with neonatal tetanus and this is the long misunderstood disease called tetany in which deficiencies of calcium, magnesium, and vitamin D have all been implicated, and whose symptoms are trismuslike convulsions, spasms of the voluntary muscles, and sometimes even rigidity.

The onset of neonatal tetany takes place between the third and the fourteenth days of life, which would have facilitated its confusion with the "nine day fits" as would the twitches and convulsions caused by a lack of calcium and/or magnesium, which have important assignments in muscular contraction and relaxation. Finally the very high mortality rate of 30 percent or more characteristic of neonatal tetany would also have doubtless assured its confusion with neonatal tetanus.[24]

As I have discussed earlier, the slave diet in the West Indies was very low in calcium while high in phosphorus relative to calcium, which would have considerably reduced the slaves' ability to absorb such calcium as was forthcoming from their diet. Moreover, as we saw, the West African diet was characterized by calcium deficiency. Thus Caribbean slave mothers, whether African or Creole born, were most likely calcium deficient even as they entered their first pregnancy. After multiple pregnancies, with calcium levels falling each time, many slave women must have become candidates for maternal tetany or at the very least begun to display those characteristic cravings of the calcium deficient that I explored in the discussion of the slave consumption of nonfoods containing calcium.[25]

As a general rule hypocalcemic tetany is not associated with breast-fed babies because the level of calcium in mother's milk seems "quite strictly maintained" regardless of maternal calcium status.[26] However, it has also been fairly well established that maternal serum calcium does fall with each succeeding pregnancy and mothers with a low calcium intake may well be rendered unable to deliver sufficient calcium to their infants.[27] True, calcium is "stored up by the fetus in the bones during the last three months of intrauterine life," but the amount stored can vary considerably depending on the calcium nutrition of the mother. If that amount is low, then the infant is in trouble, for the amount of calcium in breast milk is not enough to maintain skeletal growth "at the standard of calcification found at birth" without the contribution of the infant's stores.[28]

But – and here would have been the real difficulty given the probability of a high rate of prematurity among the slaves – if the infant is prematurely born then it has not had the time to build adequate calcium stores. Thus a slave infant born eight to ten weeks before term would have stored only about 30 percent of the calcium that a full-term infant stores. Neonatal tetany strikes hardest and most frequently at the prematurely born, and it has been estimated that somewhere between a quarter and a half of all preterm infants are hypocalcemic.[29]

Early neonatal tetany, which occurs during the first seventy-two hours of life, comes about when a mother cannot satisfy the premature infant's very high calcium demands,[30] and the "injudicious custom" of the slaves of putting the newborn on the breast of a woman who already was nursing her own child would have produced precisely this effect.[31] For the milk of a slave woman already nursing an infant, who we are told was "often a year old or perhaps older" would have probably declined both in quality and in calcium content, but in any event, it would have declined sufficiently in volume practically to guarantee neonatal tetany in the premature infant.[32]

It is possible that slave infants were also at risk of a later onset of neonatal tetany that can be triggered by magnesium deficiency, for it seems to be the case that the hypocalcemic infant fails to respond to a calcium intake if his body is deprived of sufficient magnesium.[33]

In Chapter 5 we made no effort to measure the magnesium intake of slaves, for the mineral is fairly widely distributed in foods, and the slaves' intake was probably adequate even though most of their foods – milled grains, root vegetables, and fruit – are poor sources. Nonetheless some slave infants must have been deprived of sufficient magnesium while in the womb and then later by a low content of their mother's milk because of the widespread diarrhea and dysenteries that tormented the slaves. For diarrhea causes severe malabsorption problems with magnesium and, to complicate matters, the premature infant is born with poor magnesium reserves and high magnesium requirements.[34]

Thus in light of slave difficulties with both calcium and magnesium it is probable that some significant percentage of the "neonatal tetanus" cases of slave infants were actually cases of neonatal tetany. Even today physicians confronted with an infant displaying symptoms of convulsions, stiffness in and spasms of the muscles, carp mouth (with the corners turned down) and rigid body, find it necessary to test with calcium injections to discover whether they are dealing with tetanus or tetany.[35] The chances are good that it will be diagnosed as the latter, for studies of neonatal convulsions have pinpointed tetany due to hypocalcemia as the culprit in between 20 and 55 percent of the cases, while as mentioned previously, tetany strikes between 26 and 50 percent of all premature infants.[36]

Given the foregoing, it seems significant to note that "convulsions" were also an important cause of death category for slave infants.[37] Finally, it is worth noting that some physicians were convinced that the "jawfall" stemmed from a variety of causes, while a few were already beginning to distinguish between "tetanic spasms" and tetanus.[38]

This is not, however, to imply that neonatal tetanus was not an important killer of Caribbean slave infants. It is only to suggest, given the nature of slave nutrition and especially the poor state of maternal nutrition, that tetany was doubtless responsible for many of the deaths that were registered as "jawfall" in the West Indies, just as we have argued elsewhere that tetany claimed many slave infants in the United States as well.[39] The fact that as slave nutrition improved during amelioration, deaths from "neonatal tetanus" began to fall does nothing to weaken our hypothesis since improved nutrition in the form of a greater variety of foods available should have resulted in both an increased slave calcium intake, and a lower incidence of prematurity.

Infantile Beriberi

This disease alone may have been crucial in the failure of the Caribbean slave population to grow by natural means.[40] Adult beriberi by itself would not have had that much of a demographic impact, just as pellagra, which seems to have been fairly widespread among slaves in the United States, had no significant impact.[41] But pellagra is seldom if ever transmitted to the young, for even if mothers are niacin deficient, human milk contains sufficient tryptophan (niacin's precursor) so that the infant can manufacture its own niacin. Yet a mother deficient in thiamine will not only give birth to a child with reduced bodily stores of the vitamin, but she also will be unable to correct that deficiency with her milk, which will also be thiamine deficient. Thus because thiamine deficiency seems to have been a severe problem of health for many slaves, their infants must have died in large numbers and this would definitely have had an important impact on Caribbean slave demography.

The question is how important. Slave physicians, of course, knew nothing of infantile beriberi as a separate disease entity, and in fact it remained hidden from medicine long after the adult variety had been recognized. One reason for this is that a woman does not have to display blatant beriberi symptoms for her infant to suffer from the disease, and in fact, in many cases she will reveal only a few, or even no outward signs of thiamine deficiency, which has caused beriberi researchers untold difficulties in linking infantile and adult beriberi.[42] Another difficulty with establishing the link is that beriberi symptoms in infants are generally very different from those manifested by adults and they vary depending on the time of the onset of the disease. Despite these difficulties, however, we know that because of widespread thiamine deficiency among their parents, slave infants who had successfully dodged tetanus or tetany must have been at risk from beriberi during three different stages of the first year of their young lives beginning at about one month of age.

The first or acute cardiac form of infantile beriberi normally mounts its attack from the end of the first through the fourth month of life. Its onset "is characteristically explosive, often in plump and well-nourished looking babies" beginning with restlessness and attacks of screaming, followed by vomiting, breathlessness, loss of appetite, and then convulsions and/or cardiac failure preceding death.[43] The next form, called "aphonic," is normally seen between the fifth and the seventh month of life. It customarily begins with fever, coughing, and perhaps choking – symptoms that plantation physicians would probably have associated with upper respiratory tract infection or bronchitis. A major symptom, however, is aphonia, where the baby seems to be crying but because of laryngeal complications utters no sound. The third "pseudomeningeal" form usually occurs in infants from eight to ten months of age, and is often characterized by a puffiness, although the "main emphasis" is on the central nervous system and "the clinical picture resembles tuberculous meningitis or an encephalitis."[44] Thus infantile beriberi presents a variety of symptoms, and to slave physicians it would have suggested a number of diseases depending on its form and the extent to which the victim was thiamine deprived.

Today beriberi researchers look for infant victims under cause-of-death rubrics such as "convulsions," congenital disability, acute bronchitis, acute meningitis, and enteritis.[45] Moreover, they are aided in pinpointing areas likely to have an abnormally large number of deaths in these categories by certain unusual patterns of infant mortality. For one thing the frequency of infant mortality is very high. At the turn of this century in the Philippines, for example, where the disease was (and still is) a chronic problem, about half of all infants born did not live out the first year of life, infantile beriberi being the major reason. Even in the late 1950s some 25,000 beriberi deaths were being reported annually, with infants comprising three quarters of the victims. Perhaps the most distinctive characteristic, however, is that a population with widespread beriberi will tend to include an abnormally high number of mothers who, because of chronic thiamine deficiency, have a history of losing one child after another within the first year of life.[46]

The Caribbean plantation world qualifies as an area of potential infantile beriberi on both counts. We have thus far examined infant deaths in the first week or two of life and discovered that tetanus/tetany killed perhaps as many as a quarter of the newborn. But as investigators of Worthy Park in Jamaica have observed, the majority of deaths of the slave young that took place on this plantation did not occur at birth or shortly thereafter and if, as we contend, infantile beriberi was a major killer in the region, then a continuing high level of infant mortality after the first month of life should have been the case on numerous plantations.[47]

Certainly the Jamaican estates of Matthew Lewis provide a striking example of high infant mortality at all stages throughout the first year, despite the fact that Lewis regarded himself, and seems to have been regarded by others, as a humane and quite progressive planter where matters of slave well-being were concerned.[48] Nonetheless, his journal is peppered with entries suggesting much infant and child mortality, and, more significantly for our purposes, those entries reveal multiple deaths of infants born of the same women, which conforms with a maternal history of thiamine-deficient milk killing one infant after another.

Examples include one woman who had given birth to fifteen children, yet saw only two survive, a woman who had "borne ten children yet has now but one alive" and still another who "has borne seven and but one has lived to puberty." In addition, Lewis lamented the "instances of those who have had four, five, six children without succeeding in bringing up one."[49]

Among these "instances" was the case of a "most affectionate woman" who had "borne four children" only to lose them all. She almost lost her fifth baby as well because its "manner of breathing" was peculiar. The baby survived because it was taken away from the mother (whom Lewis suspected of dropping it) and given to the plantation doctor for a "proper mode of treatment."[50]

Peculiar breathing of course can be symptomatic of many ailments. But when the symptom is displayed in a baby whose mother has already lost four previous infants, it takes on a special significance for it is one of the major signals of infantile beriberi. Perhaps equally significant is the fact that, deprived of its mother (and her milk), the infant survived. We cannot know what the "proper mode of treatment" consisted of, but can suspect that in the hands of a physician other foods besides mother's milk (and perhaps another woman's milk) became part of the infant's diet and delivered enough thiamine to avert death.

Many other plantations across the Caribbean witnessed the same phenomenon of high infant mortality and individual mothers losing numerous infants. On Worthy Park, records revealed that "only 19 of the 89 women had managed to keep alive all of the children born to them." Fully "70 women had lost various numbers of children. Of the exceptional nineteen women whose children had all survived, fifteen had in fact been delivered of only a single child."[51] On the Poey Plantation in Cuba it was calculated that only one third of the pregnant women brought "offspring to maturity," while visitors to the island frequently commented on slave women who had lost numerous infants.[52]

Because the Caribbean slave population does seem to be characterized by the peculiar infant mortality patterns suggesting infantile beriberi, we might, at this point, follow the routine of modern-day investigators and look into the various causes of infant death categories. The category "convulsions" and/or "fits" is particularly interesting for it suggests some of the most prominent symptoms that beriberi investigators look for. Both convulsions and fits were important killers of slave infants and earlier we observed that many cases occurring during the first days of life may well have been tetany. However, convulsions and fits also occurred late in babyhood and in this case are frequently mentioned in connection with "teething."[53] In the words of a Jamaican physician, the cutting of teeth was "not unaccompanied with danger, as it causes numerous complaints, the most common of which are purgings, fevers and convulsions." He adds that convulsions are the "most dangerous of the complaints of infants."[54]

Yet teething was not the cause of convulsions. Today medical authorities state emphatically that despite "old wives' tales, sometimes still propagated by the medical profession, teething is not the cause of diarrhea, fever, or convulsions; rather the phenomenon is too often conveniently blamed for something much more serious."[55]

Generally infants' teeth begin to make their appearance at about the time that the risk of beriberi declines, for with teeth comes less dependence on the breast and the introduction of other foods into the baby's regimen, which increases its chances of an adequate thiamine intake. However, as we have already discussed in terms of slave fertility, as well as West African infant feeding practices, the custom of prolonged lactation was well entrenched among slave women. Thus, in many cases, slave babies were probably not introduced to new foods at this point and consequently, given widespread thiamine deficiency among the slaves, the convulsions could easily have marked the onset of beriberi.[56]

We mentioned earlier in this discussion that the "pseudomeningeal" form of beriberi, which usually attacks infants between eight and ten months of age, presents a clinical picture very much like that of tuberculous meningitis. Thus, had there been beriberi researchers looking at

Cuba's mortality statistics of the 1840s, they would have cast skeptical eyes on those who branded "tisis" or tuberculosis as a major killer of the black young on the island.[57] On the one hand, it is doubtful that physicians a century and a half ago could have recognized tuberculosis in youngsters, for modern medicine asserts that "the differences between the pathological and clinical manifestations [of tuberculosis] in children and adults are so pronounced as to suggest two entirely different disease processes." On the other hand, about the only symptom that physicians could have spied that would have suggested tuberculosis to them would have been meningitis.[58] Thus there exists the possibility that many of Cuba's "tisis" deaths among the very young were, in fact, beriberi – a possibility enhanced considerably when it is recalled that it was in Cuba a couple of decades later that the first "official" beriberi epidemics in the Caribbean were observed.

If many of these tuberculosis deaths in children were actually beriberi deaths, then much of the fault would have rested with prolonged lactation, which would have prevented even youngsters one year of age and older from consuming enough other foodstuffs to avoid the thiamine deficiency created by their mother's milk. Certainly this practice did not escape the suspicious eyes of physicians and planters, who worried that the "milk becomes unfit" after prolonged lactation and credited the practice with many infant ailments.[59] As we have seen, the milk must have caused much more morbidity and mortality than even they suspected.

Weaning and Protein Energy Malnutrition (PEM)

If the slave infant successfully avoided tetanus, tetany, and infantile beriberi, he entered his second year of life having run a gauntlet in which we suspect that upward of half of his age mates had already fallen. Yet with the approach of the time of weaning came still another serious nutritional threat to the child's life. Up to the time of weaning the baby may have accompanied his mother to the fields strapped to her back, or he may have been raised in a nursery. But either way, his mother was probably available for nourishment either on demand or at regular intervals.

But with weaning, the child entered the plantation's "weaning house" or "rearing hospital" (generally operated by elderly slave women) and had to adjust to a new regimen.[60] The food given to slave youngsters was quite similar to that given to West African youngsters today, and seems to have been fairly standard fare across the Caribbean, consisting of a gruel ("atole" in Cuba) made of corn meal or flour, soups, and perhaps milk.[61] The food was prepared and simmered in large pots – "pot feeding" they called it – exactly like that of adult slaves, with the important exception that the youngsters' pots contained little or no meat; indeed physicians warned against serving meat to the young.[62]

Thus the slave children were weaned to a high-carbohydrate–low-protein diet, much as West African children are today. And the consequence of this practice in West Africa is widespread protein energy malnutrition (PEM). Milk, when it was available, would have provided enough protein for slave children to avoid the illness, but at this point in some cases falling lactase levels would have prevented the use of that milk. Studies of different African peoples have revealed a high correlation between groups characterized by low lactase levels and severe infant and child malnutrition, suggesting that lactose intolerance, which some youngsters develop even in the first year of life, can be a predisposing factor to PEM.[63]

Another such factor is "weanling diarrhea," which occurs in children who receive little or no protein in their new diet, but instead "are fed with derivations of cereals or other vegetable products." In this case the diarrhea would have prevented even those slave children whose lactase levels were still high from digesting lactose, while the diarrhea would have robbed their bodies of many of the nutrients they were taking in.[64]

Pathogens would also have precipitated PEM in slave children. Epidemic diseases such as whooping cough or measles are frequently responsible for placing enough additional stress on malnourished bodies to trigger the disease as do malaria parasites or a heavy load of worms, which many slave children would have been acquiring at about this time. Moreover the low intake of vitamin A and the dietary absence of fats necessary for vitamin A utilization would have encouraged worm proliferation in slave children, for parasites multiply much faster in vitamin-A-deficient individuals, and the levels of serum A in youngsters suffering from PEM has been discovered to be significantly lower than levels in normal children.[65]

Earlier, when looking at West Africa, we discussed PEM and its symptomatic poles, marasmus and kwashiorkor. Because marasmus signifies outright starvation, it is doubtful that many cases of this type were seen on the plantations of the Caribbean. Yet it is probable that many developed symptoms of kwashiorkor, just as do many of their modern-day counterparts. For example, in Jamaica it has been estimated that between 35,000 and 50,000 youngsters are suffering from PEM (mostly kwashiorkor) and that between 50 and 85 percent of all children's deaths on the island are related to the disease. In Haiti, depending on the classification employed, it appears that most youngsters endure PEM in some form, exactly as they do in West Africa.[66]

Thus when West Indian physicians wrote of symptoms in slave children such as an "inordinate swelled belly, the legs and arms reduced in size and muscle," or the "swelling of youngsters' stomachs to a prenatural size. . . known under the vulgar name of pot belly," we may safely assume that they were describing kwashiorkor.[67] That physicians implied the condition was common among the slave young suggests how widespread kwashiorkor actually was on the plantations. It is estimated that for every classic case, such as those just described, there are ninety-nine subclinical cases with less pronounced symptoms that can burst forth at any time when stimulated by a dietary change for the worse or by intercurrent disease that raises nutritional requirements.[68]

In regions where kwashiorkor is prevalent, deaths are frequently attributed to diarrhea or worms and these two causes of death seem to have accounted for the bulk of the deaths of the slave young who had not perished as infants.[69] Bronchopneumonia is also a frequent outcome of kwashiorkor, while of course any youngster suffering from a prekwashiorkor condition, not to mention kwashiorkor, would have been much more likely to contract and much less able to resist any infectious diseases that came his way, which is probably one important reason why African children typically seem to suffer from these diseases at an earlier age than their European counterparts.[70]

Infectious Diseases

Certainly there were some infectious diseases that seemed to punish slave children with unusual severity, and certainly too, slave children would have been vulnerable at an early age. Despite prolonged lactation the mother's antibodies would have begun ceasing to shield the child after about six months. Moreover lactating ability begins to decline at this point and the protein in the mother's milk no longer meets all of the infant's needs. Thus without a rich source of supplementary nourishment the slave young would have suddenly become vulnerable to infectious disease and this vulnerability as we just saw, was likely to continue through weaning into early childhood.[71]

Whooping cough was one illness that, according to physicians, struck much harder at slave children than at white youngsters, which is to be expected, for "an undernourished child contracting whooping cough is certainly more likely to die of this disease than a healthy child similarly infected."[72]

This may be a reason why blacks have historically proved more susceptible to the disease than whites, and even though whooping cough is not known for frequenting the world's tropical regions, it has unerringly sought out black youngsters in the West Indies. Thus for the years 1857 through 1956 the disease was a regular visitor to Antigua and claims responsibility for 1 percent of all the island's deaths during this period, which means a considerably higher percentage of the deaths of those aged nine and under.[73]

For the years of slavery Hirsch gathered reports of the disease, show-ing it to have been epidemic in Barbados in 1753, Grenada in 1798, St. Bartholomew in 1804, 1809, and 1812, and suggesting that Guadeloupe was an endemic focus.[74] The published reports gathered by Hirsch, however, represent only a few of many epidemics that must have swept the Islands, adding to the misery of slave children as well as to the death tolls.

Another ailment that is not particularly common in the tropics but nonetheless sought out slave youngsters was the "putrid sore throat" or diphtheria. "Women and children get it most" reported a physician, and "indeed they are almost its only victims; for although men do not entirely escape, they are much less apt to perish under this disorder."[75] The description conforms to diphtheria's decided preference for fe-males and the young, so we may be reasonably certain that it does not represent a misdiagnosis of tonsillitis, nondiphtheritic croup, or some other illness with which diphtheria has often been confused.[76] Yet we have no way of measuring the impact of the illness upon the slaves. For even as the description was being penned, the disease was already in decline and, save for an 1856 pandemic, would pass into extinction as far as the West Indies, at least, were concerned.[77]

There were, of course, other illnesses such as malaria, measles, and mumps, but these tormented white youngsters as well as black chil-dren and thus are not mentioned by West Indian physicians as almost exclusively the property of the blacks, while yaws, which was very much a disease of black children as well as adults, will be taken up in the next chapter.

Low Birthweight

Before moving along to adult diseases, however, we should take note briefly of a final condition that would have predisposed many slave infants to illnesses of both a nutritional and infectious nature. The condition is the susceptibility discussed previously of black infants to a low birthweight (LBW), which impairs their chances of survival. We noted that West Indian black infants today are born with weights sig-nificantly lower than those of white infants, or even of black counter-parts living in the United States. Much of the reason for this has to do with prematurity, for if the birthweights of only full-term infants are averaged, as for example those of Jamaica, we find them substantially above the 2,500-gram definition of a LBW baby.[78]

Because premature LBW babies are frequently the product of a mal-nourished mother, we can safely assume that many slave infants were indeed LBW babies.[79] We have seen that the West Indian slaves were vitamin A deficient and vitamin A shortages can have "dire effects on pregnancy." Riboflavin and consequently all the B vitamin requirements increase during pregnancy, yet the entire B complex was also undersupplied to the slaves, and poor maternal nutrition of this nature sharply increases the chances of having a premature baby.[80] It also increases the chances of a stillbirth, for when malnourished mothers go into labor, the process can easily be prolonged by as much as five hours with all the attendant hazards for both mother and infant of prolonged labor.[81]

Finally, problems of prolonged labor and prematurity would not cease with a successful birth. Infants whose heritage of malnutrition put them at risk of these phenomena would also have been extremely susceptible not only to the diseases we have discussed but to mental retardation as well.[82]

Amelioration and Disease Incidence

By now there should be little doubt that maternal and infant malnutrition combined in many places to destroy slave infants at a rate sufficiently high to significantly retard population growth among Caribbean slave populations. Indeed the crucial role nutrition played in the demography of Caribbean slavery is suggested by an exception to the usual reports of ill-fed slaves.

In this case a visitor to Antigua just prior to the American revolution wrote in her journal that her host was a planter who "has not bought . . . a slave for upwards of twenty years [because of] a daily increase of riches by the slaves born to him on his own plantation." The reason for these "riches" seems fairly evident. His slaves were "well-fed" if for no other reason than that he was a rarity among planters, one who raised cattle so his slaves could have "fresh meat."[83] Thus his slaves, unlike many in the Caribbean, would have taken in enough fats and vitamin B to avoid those diseases that militated so strongly against the survival of slave infants.

By contrast, let us again consider the Lewis plantations in Jamaica where slaves were "expected to feed themselves," except for allowances of salt fish.[84] One of Lewis's major complaints was that although he owned "upwards of 330 negroes. . . not more than 12 or 13 children have been added annually to the lists of births."[85] Interestingly thirteen children annually would have given his slaves a misleadingly low crude birth rate of thirty-nine per thousand, for Lewis acknowledged that "I have lost several infants" who were not even counted as births.[86]

Unfortunately we cannot discover how many these "several" amounted to. During January of 1816 alone he recorded the loss of three infants and then seems to have lost interest in keeping track.[87] Assuming, however, that no more perished in that year his slaves would still have managed a rate of reproduction activity that translates into a crude birth rate of forty-eight per thousand and in addition Lewis does mention slave miscarriages and stillbirths, which means still more "almost realized" natality.[88]

Indeed what we may well be seeing on the Lewis Plantation is Caribbean slave fertility in microcosm – fertility that the previous chapter hypothesized was very high. But we are also witnessing the very high infant mortality that we have presented evidence to suggest was actually so high as to forestall natural population growth, and it will be recalled that it was the Lewis plantation which contained a number of slave mothers whose history of losing one child after another was suggestive of infantile beriberi. Clearly Lewis's problem was not low fertility, but rather extremely high infant mortality. That diet was an important factor in this mortality seems probable in that the salt fish and slave-grown vegetables would have constituted one of the basic slave diets that we analyzed and found wanting. That slave mothers were suffering from severe nutritional disorders seems confirmed by the high frequency of miscarriages and stillbirths Lewis laments, not to mention the mothers who witnessed the multiple deaths of their infants.

In conclusion, the evidence although sketchy and too often impressionistic when marshalled for the whole of the Caribbean does become sufficiently robust to permit a telling indictment of malnutrition as not only a significant problem of slave health, but also as a central factor in the slaves' inability to reproduce their numbers. If some of the "matches" between nutritional deficiency and disease are less than perfect, they nonetheless match well enough to become important pieces in filling in the heretofore complex puzzle of why Caribbean slave populations, unlike that of the United States, failed to grow by natural means. The answer seems to be that around half of all slaves born in the West Indies did not survive infancy, while many more perished in early childhood, with tetany, infantile beriberi, and PEM foremost among their major killers.[89] It remains to consider still more hazards to the health of those who managed to survive this weeding-out process in the West Indies so reminiscent of that of West Africa.

CHAPTER 9

BLACK DISEASES AND WHITE MEDICINE

The Negro can never feel the hardships of want. . . . In sickness he is provided with medical attention, and every attention and care is bestowed upon him which his situation requires.

Committee of the Legislature of Dominica (1823)[1]

Sorry am I that the subject requires me to say, that no part of Negro management has been more neglected, or erroneously performed than that which regards the treatment of the sick.

Dr. Robert Collins (1811)[2]

An interesting article, "Some Disease Patterns in West Indian Immigrants," was published in 1962 by a London physician. His purpose in writing was to warn colleagues that in treating these newcomers they were likely to "encounter some rather unusual disease patterns."[3] Among the "new" illnesses general practitioners were told to be on the lookout for were "old" curses that had tormented the prospective patients' ancestors for centuries. Prominent among them were dysenteries, particularly amebic dysentery, and while schistosomiasis, filariasis, and other worm infections are also treated, the most remarkable aspect of the essay is that it can find so few "unusual disease patterns" to discuss.[4] In fact, none of the illnesses that we saw decimating the slave young are mentioned, nor are leprosy, yaws, and other "exotic" ailments that tormented the slaves. It is not that these diseases have become extinct, and cannot be found in the Caribbean today. But most have become rare in the region, for infectious diseases as well as those of a frankly nutritional origin fade in the face of better nutrition.[5]

The following pages focus on some of the most important of these infectious diseases that were prevalent during slavery. Some such as cholera were killers; others such as yaws generally were not. But almost all were sufficiently black related to indicate a much different biological experience for blacks as opposed to whites in the West Indies.

Leprosy, Yaws, and Their Mimics

Called alternately "kocubea," "coco-bay," "cocabay," "lazarino," "lepra," the "joint evil," and the "king's evil," leprosy was known to slave physicians and planters as "one of the most horrible of Negro diseases."[6] They believed that the disease had been brought to the Americas from Africa and it would seem that this judgment was correct.[7] Moreover, Africa was also the home of other illnesses that were called leprosy in the West Indies, for leprosy quickly became a generic term connoting all sorts of illnesses including those created by New World parasites and nutritional circumstances.

When a West Indian physician wrote of a disease that began among the slaves with white spots near the ends of the extremities – spots that in turn became ulcerous, began to swell, with a finger or toe or foot then dropping off until "in the end it reduces the miserable sufferer to a mere trunk,"[8] he was probably describing leprosy. But when another described *cocabay* as a condition in which "different parts of the [patient's] body swell, he is covered with a leprous scurf, his spirits sink into deep dejection, he loaths his food, and yet his miserable existence is prolonged for years,"[9] he could easily have been viewing wet beriberi or elephantiasis.

Indeed physicians pondered the extent to which elephantiasis, leprosy, and *cocabay* were different, with the latter often used synonymously for the "joint evil," which more often than not meant a condition in which the victim's toes dropped off, "almost without pain and always without fever."[10]

There were in fact several afflictions that mimicked leprosy. One was ainhum, an affliction peculiar to blacks caused by a linear constriction of a toe (especially the little toe), with the constriction eventually amputating the toe.[11] A contemporary observer explained that the loss of the toe (or toes) happened gradually and "with no pain." The toe swelled, and after a few years either became gangrenous or just dropped off.[12]

Still another threat to the toes of the slaves came from the chigoe flea (*Pulex penetrans*), jigger, sand flea, etc., the female of which burrows into the skin of the feet, and if not removed causes ulceration that can lead to spontaneous amputation of digits. A physician of the period described the process succinctly enough when he stated that "the Negroes often let them [chigoes] collect and remain in their feet until their toes rot off."[13]

Interestingly, Oviedo in the sixteenth century wrote of blacks losing their toes and even feet because of the "niguas" (chigoes), which he described as "very tiny, much smaller than the smallest flea."[14] Doubtless only blacks suffered much from foot infection because only blacks went barefoot.[15] The chigoe was branded the cause of much slave lameness, as well as the "most general of Negro infirmities," by Matthew Lewis. But as a "pathfinder for tetanus" the parasite was responsible for much mortality as well as lameness.[16] One Caribbean physician made the connection by speculating that blacks were somehow "more subject" to tetanus because of bare feet although another felt chigoes did little harm because of the black's method for removing them with a knife, performing the "operation with greater dexterity than it could have been done [by] the most skillful surgeon of Europe."[17] One suspects, however, that despite the surgical skill, in an age before antiseptic procedures the "operation" frequently rendered the patient even more liable to tetanus.

Another parasite that caused slaves considerable discomfort was "scabies." Here the lesions developed between the fingernail and the hands and, particularly if they ulcerated, were doubtless also confused on occasion with leprosy. Moreover, some kinds of scabies infections are frequently encountered in leprosy patients.[18] In Africa scabies was known as "craw-craw," and newly captured slaves were reported to be infested with the mites. Naturally the mites made the middle passage with their hosts, becoming very prevalent on slave ships and often endemic among West Indian blacks.[19]

All of these infections could easily have become ulcerated or gangrenous and passed as leprosy, as could tropical ulcer, leishmaniasis, amebic and mycotic infections, beriberi, pellagra, and yaws. But the point is simply that it is extremely doubtful that leprosy was as widespread among the slaves as physicians believed it to be. Of 357 slave deaths in St. James Parish, Jamaica, during the years 1817 to 1820, 10 were attributed to "coco-bay" or 1 of every 36 deaths. On the Newton Plantation of 169 deaths, leprosy was blamed for 11 and the "joint evil" for 1 more, making the score 1 of every 14 deaths, while in British Guiana during the years 1829 to 1832, leprosy was blamed for 270 out of 6,154 slave deaths or 1 out of every 23.[20]

In other records however, leprosy and "cocabay" are absent as causes of death.[21] On the one hand, this conforms to leprosy's tendency to appear in pockets rather than to be uniformly spread throughout a population. But on the other, it may mean that some planters and physicians were accustomed to blaming leprosy for deaths while others were not. In point of fact, however, leprosy is seldom the cause of death and later in the nineteenth century, as diagnosis in the Caribbean presumably became more precise, other diseases passing as leprosy began to disappear and the leprosy "death rate" dropped remarkably.

In Antigua, for example, leprosy was given as the cause of death for only 1 out of every 200 deaths for the years 1857 through 1926, while in Cuba records from the archdiocese of Havana in 1843 list only 23 deaths from "elefanciasis" (the original name for leprosy) out of 13,462 deceased, or only 1 out of almost every 600 deaths.[22] Indeed, between 1800 and 1899 only 1,393 patients were treated at the Leper (San Lázaro) Hospital in Havana, and while this hospital was not the only place of treatment for the disease in Cuba, the relatively few cases tend to reenforce the suspicion that real leprosy was neither as widespread nor as serious a problem of black health as physicians believed it to be.[23]

The extent to which yaws was called leprosy and vice versa is difficult to ascertain. Physicians who wrote descriptions of the illness emphasizing that there would be one "pustule" larger than the rest that they called "the *master*" or "*mamma* yaw" and that yaws was a disease one could only host once clearly knew yaws when they confronted it.[24]

Yet their emphasis on the nonrecurrence of yaws in an individual may have caused them to be deceived by the different stages of the disease. Following infection there is an incubation period of from two to eight weeks before the initial lesion or the mother yaw makes an appearance. A few weeks (up to about four months) later, secondary lesions begin to blossom and a kind of yellowish crust develops on the lesions. Successive lesions may endure for as long as two or three years, while those on the lips and soles of the feet might continue even longer. But, generally after a few months the secondary lesions heal and the individual's bout with yaws is over.

For some, however, a tertiary stage awaits – but one that normally reveals itself only after a more or less symptom-free interval of several years. In this stage destructive bone lesions are frequent, joint lesions not uncommon, and nodules as well as ulcers erupt on the body.[25] Obviously this third stage of yaws could be and doubtless was often confused with leprosy both because of its superficial resemblance and because many physicians would have discounted a yaws diagnosis on the basis that the patient could not suffer from it twice.

Just as with leprosy, yaws is not normally a fatal disease, yet a number of slave deaths were allegedly caused by yaws. In part of Clarendon, Jamaica, during the year 1818, 6 deaths out of 141 were attributed to yaws, or 1 of every 23 deaths. Between the years 1817 and 1829 yaws was credited with killing 9 of the 288 deceased of another group of Jamaican plantations (1 of every 32 deaths) and, in still another group yaws was blamed for 1 of every 45 deaths. In British Guiana a sample of slave mortality revealed yaws as responsible for 1 of every 34 deaths.[26]

In some places the incidence of and mortality from yaws appears tied to the slave trade, implying that the disease was kept alive by a West African reservoir. Edward Long, for example, asserted that yaws alone was responsible for about a third of the mortality sustained by newly imported slaves. This seems a substantial exaggeration, yet it may mean that some slaves were imported from regions that did not include yaws in their disease environments and consequently were encountering the illness for the first time.[27] The new imports would have been mostly young adults and yaws, like many diseases that are normally diseases of childhood, deals much more severely with adults. This, coupled with the shock of the middle passage, nutritional debilitation, and a change of diet may have weakened many to the point where yaws either became exceptionally lethal or combined with some other disease, with a resulting harvest of many more victims than normal.

Yet we cannot be certain that Long was actually referring to the disease yaws, for in the British Caribbean physicians seem to have used "yaws" as a generic term to include all "scrofulous" complaints, while counterparts elsewhere used the term "leprosy" in the same fashion.[28] Nor were the physicians in the Spanish Islands any more precise, for there the terms "bubas" and "bobos" meant "a whole complex of illnesses. . . the symptoms of which were sore spots and swollen glands."[29] Thus, given the absence of diagnostic precision, it has been asserted that even elephantiasis was called leprosy.[30] But elephantiasis, we have observed, was in some cases actually wet beriberi, and because both leprosy and yaws are not nearly so fatal as plantation death records would have them, the suspicion is sharpened that perhaps a sizable proportion of the so-called leprosy deaths were beriberi, just as numerous cases diagnosed as yaws may actually have represented the skin lesions of pellagra. Moreover, infectious and nutritional disease may also have intertwined. For example, neuritic leprosy and beriberi frequently occur together, and one is easily confused with the other. Similarly acute pellagra cases in which "the skin lesions may progress to vesticulation, cracking, exudation and crusting with ulceration and sometimes secondary infection" could easily have been confused with or occurred simultaneously with yaws.[31]

The fact that both "leprosy" and "yaws" were regarded by physicians as strictly black-related diseases suggests that to some extent both were in fact misdiagnosed nutritional ailments, for it was the slaves, as opposed to the whites, who consumed a diet that would have predisposed them to beriberi or pellagra. On the other hand, the slaves also seem to have been innately susceptible to both yaws and leprosy – a phenomenon not lost on slave physicians, who commented that whites were not subject to these illnesses "even though black women suckle white children." Moreover, even when whites in the Islands did on occasion contract the yaws they "have generally a much milder disease," while in Africa it has been alleged that Africans suffered much more that whites from leprosy.[32]

In like fashion, the apparently abrupt decline of "yaws" and "leprosy" following the end of the slave trade[33] could be linked to epidemiological factors – the capping of the West African reservoir of the illnesses – or it could be related to improving nutrition during amelioration and the period following the end of slavery. One suspects, however, that both epidemiological and nutritional factors are inextricably linked in the etiologies of both the infectious diseases and their nutritional mimics. In Haiti, for example, where nutritional circumstances have improved very little since slavery, leprosy continues to be a problem and yaws has been estimated to assault about half of the population.[34]

Lung Ailments

This coalition of nutritional, immunological, epidemiological, and genetic factors that seems to have been present in the etiologies of slave skin lesions also prevailed in the susceptibility of slaves to lung ailments. For example, in the matter of cold intolerance that may have been a predisposing factor, it seems that despite their tropical location West Indian blacks were frequently troubled by cold and suffered from it much more than whites.[35] According to one planter "when the sun is not above the horizon the Negro always feels very chilly" and consequently slaves slept with "plenty of bed clothes," while maintaining fires burning in their huts all night "without which," in the words of another observer "a Negro cannot sleep with comfort."[36]

It is true that planters and physicians used the slaves' relative intolerance for cold as a convenient rationale to explain away much slave mortality,[37] and yet in this case expediency and truth may have accidentally coincided. From a nutritional standpoint, I noted previously that the slave fat intake was extraordinarily low. We should also note that from fats come the body lipids and fatty acids that keep the body temperature up, and consequently individuals on a low-fat diet, are ill-prepared to deal with cold.[38] In addition, dietary fats provide the essential materials for the absorption of the fat-soluble vitamins and act as carriers of the vitamins as well.[39] Given the fat-soluble vitamin A deficiency among the slaves, it seems significant that vitamin A deficiency has been pinpointed as an important factor in lung disease susceptibility and that administration of the vitamin has proved effective in treatment.[40]

From a possible genetic standpoint we have already noted that blacks seem innately less able to tolerate cold, and therefore this combination of nutritional and genetic factors is probably partly to blame for the blacks' very high incidence of lung ailments historically. But leaving genetics and nutrition aside for the moment, there are sound immunological reasons why Caribbean slaves should have proved susceptible to lung ailments such as tuberculosis. For one thing, it was a European disease, which West Africans had escaped entirely until relatively recently since it is essentially a disease of urban people.[41] Thus, even after it was imported to a mostly rural West Africa, it would have spread so slowly that probably most slaves reaching the West Indies had had no previous contact with it.

Tuberculosis runs a much different course, and therefore is more difficult to identify in the historical record in inexperienced peoples, than in those whose ancestors have "lived" with the illness. The problem then becomes one of recognizing the disease in the Caribbean.

This task is made easier because of the experience of blacks in the United States with tuberculosis. In the antebellum South, physicians believed the disease to be rare among the slaves.[42] By contrast, their postbellum successors expressed alarm that tuberculosis was so rife among blacks that it might eradicate the entire population. The juxtaposition of these views gives the impression of a sudden epidemic among American blacks. Yet, as it turns out, tuberculosis was actually not rare among the slaves but rather was simply unrecognizable to the physicians who treated them.

It was useful in understanding the phenomenon to look at the early twentieth-century experience with tuberculosis of a remote Indian tribe in western Canada. Following their late exposure to the disease, the first and second generations to suffer from it manifested few pulmonary symptoms (which physicians were trained to recognize), but rather revealed an extensive glandular involvement. It was only with the third generation that the disease began to settle into the lungs and with the fourth generation symptoms of glandular involvement had fallen to less than 1 percent of the cases.[43]

What had happened was this. In the inexperienced first and second generations of Canadian Indians, the bacilli of tuberculosis met with resistance so sluggish and ineffective that they were able to race pell-mell through lymph channels and spread to numerous organs. However, the bodies of the third and fourth generations had gained the ability to combat the disease, which is done most effectively by localizing it in the lungs. It was this latter form of the disease with which physicians were familiar. The symptoms presented by the first and second generations, by contrast, were foreign to them and were only diagnosed as tuberculosis by microscopic analysis.

Antebellum slave physicians of course had no such techniques and consequently, when confronted with an illness among the slaves revealing extensive glandular involvement, they thought it to be a peculiarly Negro disease and called it "struma Africana," "cachexia Africana," or "scrofula."[44] But by the time their postbellum successors grappled with the disease, it had settled into the lungs, was easily identifiable as tuberculosis or "consumption," as many called it, and thus it seemed as if the disease had appeared out of nowhere to assault Afro-Americans.

Although data are much more sketchy for the Caribbean than for the

American South it would seem that tuberculosis ran a similar course through blacks in that region as well. It is not, for example, very discernible early in the blacks' career in the West Indies. Richard Dunn explains that tuberculosis was less "rampant in the Indies during the seventeenth century than at home [England]," while Pitman does not mention the illness as an important cause of death during the first decades of the eighteenth century in the British West Indies.[45]

During this time the disease would have manifested itself in deceptive ways from a physician's standpoint. Quite conceivably it made frequent appearances as tuberculosis of the urinary tract that doctors would most likely have called gonorrhea, or abdominal swellings, which they may have called dirt eating, or tuberculosis of the joints (joint evil), or even leprosy, for leprosy, while seldom fatal, frequently leads to tuberculosis, which is.[46] Thus tuberculosis, too, was undoubtedly misdiagnosed as leprosy, venereal disease, and dirt eating.

However, at about the turn of the nineteenth century, tuberculosis began to become more recognizable. During approximately two decades bridging the turn of the century the Newton Plantation in Barbados recorded 169 slave deaths, of which 14 were caused by "consumption" and another 8 by "scrofula."[47] Clearly tuberculosis (consumption) was no longer a stranger to Barbadian plantations and, on the Newton Estate at least, was responsible for 1 of every 12 recorded deaths. When "scrofula" is added, the rate becomes 1 of every 8 deaths, which is significant in light of the population mix of Creole and African born. Barbados was the oldest sugar island in the Caribbean and therefore had a long established Creole-born population that would have had the opportunity to gain experience with tuberculosis. But it also still had a sizable African-born population that, with little experience, would have manifested symptoms of "extensive glandular involvement" or "scrofula."

In Jamaica, by contrast, which was a much newer sugar island, it was the opinion of observers that there was very little consumption among the slaves. Yet the data do not bear this out. "Consumption" was blamed for 44 of the 786 slave deaths listed by Higman for the period 1817 to 1820 or 1 out of every 18. On Worthy Park, the disease was responsible for 1 of every 15 deaths while in British Guiana a mixture of asthma, catarrh, consumption and pleurisy was responsible for 1 of every 11 slave deaths.[48]

Scrofula, however, is not given as a cause of death in the Jamaican data nor in records from British Guiana. Presumably unrecognized tuberculosis deaths in these "newer" sugar regions were subsumed under "cachexies" and "swellings." Yet had "scrofula" been diagnosed, scrofula and consumption deaths together would probably have approached the rate of Barbados, because it was at precisely this time that "recognizable" tuberculosis seems to have been spreading under the very noses of physicians and would soon explode in Caribbean blacks just as it exploded in blacks in the postbellum American South.

Thus by 1843 in Cuba *tisis* (tuberculosis) had assumed responsibility for 1 of every 7 deaths (1,037 of 7,272 deaths) of blacks in the Havana diocese to become overwhelmingly the single biggest killer of Africans in Cuba.[49] Two decades later it was reported from Barbados that the disease was "common," while shortly afterwards Hirsch informs us that tuberculosis among adults and scrofula among children were claiming huge numbers of Caribbean blacks and were on the increase.[50]

By the turn of the twentieth century, the Puerto Rican death rate from tuberculosis was 160 per 100,000 live population, and by the middle 1930s it had climbed to 258 per 100,000 (compared to a rate of 47 per 100,000 for the United States), with the blacks of Puerto Rico proving much more susceptible to the disease than the whites. In crowded Havana the death rate from tuberculosis became astronomical, with an average of 800 per 100,000 population dying annually, during the years 1872 to 1890, with the rate still at 312 per 100,000 in 1914.[51]

As explained, much of the black susceptibility was the result of inexperience. Much, too, had to do with culture. A Rockefeller-funded physician who surveyed the Caribbean in 1917 explained that black tuberculosis susceptibility stemmed from their "universal custom" of sealing all windows "at night for superstitious reasons, with the result that once a disease such as tuberculosis infected a member of the family, they all became infected."[52]

Yet surely poor nutrition was another major factor. It has been observed that the relationship between nutrition and infection is best documented in tuberculosis and evidence exists that, with a high-protein diet, even relatively inexperienced peoples are able virtually to shrug it off. For example, a comparison was made between two East African tribes, one of which ate meat while the diet of the other tribe was almost exclusively vegetable in nature. The tribe that ate meat had a tuberculosis incidence of 1 percent, while the one that ate little animal protein had an incidence of 6 percent.[53]

Related evidence comes from studies demonstrating that the major reason for the decline of tuberculosis mortality in eighteenth- and nineteenth-century England was a rising standard of living and hence better nutrition,[54] while a powerful correlation has been drawn in parts of Argentina between a high incidence of tuberculosis and a poor diet.[55]

In the case of bacterial pneumonia, we have already noted its historical attraction to black victims since its introduction to Africa. But because there are many kinds of pneumonia and many causative agents, it is a hopeless task to discover precisely what was behind the various pneumonialike illnesses that plagued West Indian slaves. "Epidemic catarrh" reputedly killed slaves on a fairly regular basis right after the

New Year began; yet, while some physicians intended "catarrh" to mean an illness with lung symptoms, others used the term to mean influenza, which was also occasionally epidemic and harvested many lives.[56] More certain is the term "pleurisy," which was the cause of one out of every thirty slave deaths given by Higman for Jamaica, while pneumonia and pleurisy together killed one of every nineteen blacks who died in the Havana diocese during 1843.[57] The latter rate is more representative of the blacks' susceptibility to a disease that today kills more of them in West Africa than any other illness.[58] All of this suggests that susceptibility, coupled with malnutrition that predisposes to respiratory difficulties, should have provided a similarly high rate of pneumonia deaths throughout much of the slavery period.[59]

Certainly rates were high in the late nineteenth- and twentieth-century West Indies. Hirsch, in surveying susceptibility to pneumonia, found blacks very liable to the disease, as compared with whites, and "most subject" to it in Cuba, Santo Domingo, St. Thomas, and Trinidad. Johnson maintains pneumonia was a chief cause of death among Caribbean blacks at the beginning of this century, while Lowenthal presents data for mid-century Barbados showing respiratory illnesses to be a chief cause of death on that island.[60]

During slavery, however, causes of death such as "fever," "catarrh," "lung abscess," "debility," and "cold" do as much to conceal pneumonia as they do to reveal it and we can only assume, for the reasons already outlined, that it was a much more important cause of slave death than the data indicate.

Other Slave Killers

While tuberculosis and perhaps pneumonia were increasing in virulence, smallpox, which had previously been a terrible killer in the Islands, was on the wane, largely because of massive efforts at vaccination.[61] In Jamaica by the last quarter of the eighteenth century, the technique for inoculation had been perfected by a local physician named Quier and by the first decades of the nineteenth century blacks and whites alike were being vaccinated by Jenner's vaccine in wholesale lots.[62]

Prior to this prophylactic activity it was reported that smallpox tended to fall with greater weight on blacks than whites.[63] However, this may well have been more a matter of a black numerical majority on the one hand, and greater exposure, on the other, than of heightened susceptibility, for smallpox had by this time been present in Africa for centuries and, in fact, most of the smallpox reaching the West Indies was introduced from Africa via the slave trade.[64]

This is probably much of the reason why Cuba, whose slave trade endured for a good part of the nineteenth century, continued to be troubled with smallpox while other islands were spared. Yet it was clear from the manner in which the disease reportedly swept plantations that many Cuban planters did not vaccinate.[65] By contrast, on Worthy Park in Jamaica, of 222 slave deaths for the years 1811 to 1834 smallpox was blamed for only 4, while Antigua recorded its last epidemic in 1865.[66]

In the seventeenth century and much of the eighteenth, however, smallpox was truly formidable. An epidemic that struck Santo Domingo in 1666 was said to have "devastated" the slave population, while an epidemic of 1732 in Puerto Rico allegedly killed so many slaves that there were scarcely enough survivors to keep plantations operating. Epidemics of 1738, 1740, and 1741 also swept Santo Domingo winnowing the slaves on that island, while epidemics of 1732, 1747, 1776, 1792–93, 1801, and 1803–04 did the same in Puerto Rico. The smallpox also "raged with great violence" in Jamaica from time to time, with a notable outbreak in 1759 that created a decrease in the slave population despite massive immigration.[67]

However, the irregular epidemic appearances of smallpox almost certainly prevented it from attaining the status of a major killer. While it raged it took a terrible toll on an island. But its momentary ferocity could not match the mortality statistics produced by the quiet but infinitely more deadly endemic illnesses. Aside from the nutritional ailments already discussed, one such endemic disease must have been typhoid, called the "low nervous fever," which shared credit with pneumonia for most of the slave "fever" deaths. The problem is that typhoid was not distinguished from typhus until the middle of the nineteenth century and West Indian physicians, who saw much typhus among military personnel and presumably much typhoid among the slaves, made little effort to disentangle those fevers from the bundle of fevers tormenting the whole of the Caribbean basin.[68]

Yet we know that terribly fouled water was in many places the only water available to slaves and that, despite late nineteenth-century efforts to alleviate this situation, typhoid continued to be a major Caribbean health problem on some islands until well into this century. Thus, in Antigua for example, the typhoid death rate for the years 1897 through 1926 fluctuated between a mere 19 and 24 per 100,000 live population, while that of Havana climbed as high as 425 per 100,000 during epidemic years, such as that of 1898, and averaged 260 per 100,000 during bad years, such as those of 1856 to 1858. In turn-of-the-century Barbados and Jamaica, typhoid was reported as an important killer of the population. Indeed as late as 1930 the typhoid death rate in Kingston was estimated to be at least 111 per 100,000.[69] Moreover, there is some evidence to indicate that blacks may have been more susceptible to typhoid than whites, which if true may implicate thiamine, riboflavin, and vitamin A deficiencies, for their deficiency can predispose to the disease.[70] To further buttress a possible connection, the West Indian diet remains deficient in these nutrients in the few places where typhoid remains endemic to this day.[71]

In any event there can be no doubt that the West Indies, which were collectively a hotbed of typhoid even in this century, were similarly afflicted with the disease during the days of slavery and that a fair portion of slave "fevers," as well as some of their diarrheas and dysenteries, would today have been diagnosed as typhoid.

During three dreadful epidemics of the nineteenth century, however, most of these diarrheas and dysenteries were accurately diagnosed as cholera, whose major symptom is diarrhea precipitated by a toxin released by the *Vibrio cholerae* into the small intestine. The consequence in about half of the nineteenth-century cases was a terrible dehydration, which produced in progressive fashion, powerful muscular cramps and ruptured capillaries, lethargy, stupor, shock, and finally death.[72]

Cholera vibrios are transmitted via human feces that contaminate food and especially water. Thus the nineteenth-century Caribbean islands, where human excreta was disposed of in a casual manner if at all, would inevitably prove ripe for cholera's invasion. Gardens were fertilized with human waste, public water supplies were vulnerable to contamination, and many drank from ponds and stagnant pools.[73]

The world's second, and the western hemisphere's first pandemic of Asiatic cholera reached Cuba in February of 1833. It arrived in the bowels of the crew of a ship that had just left the cholera-ravaged United States and lingered in Cuba until 1836. During a savage first year of residence in and around Havana it killed at least 19,000 blacks and some 4,000 whites. The remainder of its visit was spent in outlying parts of the island where fewer records were kept on the mortality that it inflicted. Nonetheless, there seems little doubt that, before subsiding, the disease had killed at least 22,000 of the island's slaves, or about 8 percent of the slave population.[74]

Cuba was the only Caribbean island to feel cholera's sting in the 1830s. In the 1850s it was only the first of many. Between 1850 and 1854 Cuba may have lost as many as 34,000 slaves, while relatively few whites perished from the disease.[75] From Cuba and from the United States the disease spread throughout the Caribbean, killing between 40,000 and 50,000 in Jamaica, between 20,000 and 25,000 in Barbados, and at least 26,000 in Puerto Rico, to provide only some of the more dramatic mortality statistics.[76] And finally, the disease appeared one last time in Cuba alone of the Caribbean islands in 1867 to claim a few thousand more lives before leaving the region forever.[77]

It also left something of a mystery, for in every one of its many appearances it killed far more blacks than whites – so many more that it too came to be thought of as a black man's disease. Of course on islands such as Jamaica or Barbados that were overwhelmingly black anyway it was more difficult to spy cholera's discriminatory course. But in Cuba it was more apparent, while in Puerto Rico's statistics the pattern was starkly revealed: during the years 1855 to 1856 cholera had killed only 2.4 percent of the whites, but 8.3 percent of the free coloreds and fully 9.2 percent of the slaves.[78]

The question, of course, is what rendered a black in Puerto Rico or Cuba some four or five times more likely to become a cholera fatality than a white. The answer once again seems to include a number of factors. Up to a point, cholera's discriminatory behavior can be explained in terms of environment. First, it was a disease that thrived in crowded and dirty surroundings – the surroundings of the poor, who suffered most from the disease in Europe, and certainly the surroundings of most blacks in the nineteenth-century Caribbean, whether they were in the cities or on the plantations.[79] Second, cholera's normal method of establishing a beachhead on a West Indian island was to infect the region around a major port, and blacks inevitably predominated near the wharves and docks of a city. Third, blacks, whether slaves or freedmen, were most likely to have those occupations which would expose them to the disease, from stevedores on the waterfronts, to food handlers at all stages of that food's progression from gardens and groves, sea and farms, to the table.

Thus, as a general rule, blacks constituted a demographic majority in the face of the disease and this doubtless goes far toward explaining the blacks' increased susceptibility to the disease. There exist, however, other data that reveal another kind of susceptibility. Once cholera was acquired, blacks were much more likely to die from the disease than whites. For example, in Puerto Rico during the 1855 epidemic, cholera swept a racially mixed military unit. Within 24 hours 12.5 percent of the whites had died, but during this same period fully 46 percent of the blacks had perished.[80] We do not know the outcome of those who survived these first 24 hours, but perhaps can make a guess based on the records of a hospital in the Bahamas that during the same epidemic saw 60 percent of its almost all black patients die of cholera, while by contrast, in a Cuban military hospital where the cholera patients were almost all whites, 60 percent recovered.[81]

Indifferent medical care for blacks certainly cannot explain the differential, for the treatment for cholera by purging, which was standard procedure then, put the physicians in league with the disease in dispatching the cholera victim.[82] But quite possibly malnutrition can help with the explanation. For it has just been recently discovered that individuals with normal gastric acidity are usually able to avoid cholera because their gastric acid destroys cholera vibrios before they can reach the small intestine and begin their destructive work. Yet malnutrition would have made Caribbean blacks prone to a gastric hypoacidic (low

gastric acid) condition, and consequently would not only have enhanced their chances of contracting cholera, but also would have considerably increased the likelihood of their dying from it.[83]

Jewish physicians who made numerous observations on starving patients in the Warsaw ghetto noticed among other things that these
patients had an almost total lack of stomach acid, and these observations were subsequently confirmed by studies done on volunteers at
the University of Minnesota. Thus the undernourished and the malnourished are frequently bereft of the body's "first line of defense"
against cholera, and certainly Caribbean blacks were much more likely
than whites to fall into the undernourished as well as the malnourished category.[84]

Genetic Illnesses and Demographic Implications

Sickle trait, as we have noted, protected its possessor against falciparum malaria. There is an unfortunate price for this protection that is
extracted when two recipients of sickle trait mate, for the odds are that
one of every four of their offspring will be a victim of sickle cell anemia. During slavery this disease would have killed approximately 25
percent of its victims before the age of two, and about half before they
reached the age of five.[85]

As I pointed out in Chapter 1, perhaps a quarter of all blacks reaching the Caribbean would have carried sickle trait, which would mean
that between 1 and 2 percent of all slave infants would have been born
with sickle cell anemia. Slave physicians had no notion of the genetic
disease and thus, despite its fairly distinctive symptoms, it went unnoticed in the awful caldron of slave infant and child mortality. Because of the tremendous susceptibility of sickle cell anemia victims to
pneumonia and meningitis, these diseases probably received credit for
many of the deaths actually caused by sickle cell anemia.[86]

Credit also would have gone to "convulsions" and even "tetanus"
because of the symptoms produced by painful hemolytic crises. Yet
even sickle trait (as opposed to anemia) may have precipitated mortality among the slaves in the form of deaths from pneumonia, fever, and
diarrhea, for it has been discovered that possession of the trait can
predispose the individual to respiratory complaints and salmonella infection (including typhoid), which in turn may help to explain the
higher incidence of these illnesses among Caribbean slaves.[87]

I also stated in Chapter 1 that upwards of a quarter of the slaves
would have carried the G6PD deficiency trait, which, although
thought to be normally benign, can heighten hemolytic susceptibility
during intercurrent infectious illness. Thus G6PD deficiency probably
bears some significant amount of responsibility for the slaves' allegedly greater susceptibility to infectious disease. It is possible, as

well, that the possessors of some variants of G6PD deficiency would have suffered the gravest clinical manifestation of the anomaly, hemolysis precipitated by consuming the fava or "horsebeans," which appeared occasionally in the slaves's diet, although as stated previously most of the G6PD deficiency variants in blacks do not predispose them to "favism."[88]

It is important to note in closing my remarks on these blood anomalies, that even in their benign form they would also have had an impact on infant mortality. Mothers with these traits tend to have lower birthweight babies than the norm, perhaps because of a lack of oxygenation for the fetus or because of maternal anemia.[89] Low birthweight babies and particularly prematurely born infants in turn are normally iron deficient and, as mother's milk contains little iron, the premature slave infant would have been inexorably doomed to iron deficiency anemia, with a reduced ability to fight off infection.[90] Thus genetic anomalies would have combined with nutritional deprivation and infectious disease quite literally to make life impossible for some of the slave young.

There is a final consequence of the tremendous nutritional stress on the slave population to be considered at this point, and that has to do with the superior ability of females to survive such stress. We saw earlier in West Africa, for example, that despite the male's chances of being better fed than the females, he nonetheless perished at a faster rate than the female. And we glimpsed the phenomenon once again during the middle passage, which the female was more likely to survive than the male. In the Caribbean the situation was the same, and students of slavery in the region have commented on the ability of female slaves to outlive males by a considerable margin.[91]

Sex ratios for the Islands make the point dramatically. Despite having been the terminus of a slave trade that had supplied many more males than females, Barbados in 1817, now stripped of its slave trade, contained only 86 black males for every 100 females.[92] True, some slaves had been sold off the island, but the decrease in the percentage of males in the population from a sizable majority to a minority in a relatively few years is very suggestive of the black female's superior ability to survive. Perhaps even more startling was the demographic experience in Jamaica, which had made much more use of the slave trade in the years immediately prior to its abolition than had Barbados, yet in 1817, despite the importation of cargoes weighted much more heavily with males, had a slave sex ratio of only 100.[93]

We have also observed that a much higher female survival rate has continued to characterize the Caribbean islands. Thus, while acknowledging that the data are skewed by immigration (Trinidad, for example, which offers employment to many Caribbean males has a sex ratio of 104), it may be instructive to look at recent sex ratios throughout the Islands. That of Barbados is 90; for the Bahamas it is 98; for Haiti,

94; Jamaica, 96; and St. Lucia and Antigua both contain 89 males for every 100 females. That the situation has remained fairly constant can be seen in earlier sex ratios: In 1931 the sex ratio in the Bahamas was 87; in Barbados, 67; in Jamaica of 1921 the sex ratio was 88 (in 1943 it was 94); in St. Lucia and Antigua during the same year it was 90 and 71 respectively.[94]

Clearly the fluctuations reflect male migration patterns, but the important point is that all sex ratios are significantly below 100, and in part this is due to the male's impaired ability to survive relative to the female. The example of Antigua may help to shed some light on the question. Between 1857 and 1956 the island witnessed 62,175 male and 60,139 female live births, for a sex ratio of 103.[95] This is in conformity with the observation of demographers that for reasons still to be explained the black sex ratio at birth is normally 103 while that of whites is 106.[96] For Antigua, at least, much of the reason can be credited to a high rate of male as opposed to female fetal mortality. The sex ratio for the stillborn (10,838 stillbirths during the period) was 118 stillborn males for every 100 females.

However, the Antigua male's disadvantage in terms of survival did not end with his predominance in the stillbirth category. The ratio of infants who died prior to age one was 111 males for every 100 females, while 103 males for every 100 females died between ages one and four, and the trend continued throughout a lifetime with "the male mortality at all ages, and with few exceptions. . .greater than females"; the result has been that almost all-black Antigua has always had, since the days of slavery, "a larger number of females in the population, especially in adult life."[97]

A final example of the black male disadvantage in terms of survival can be seen in the Black Caribs of Honduras. This group, which has retained the African genotype by virtue of little intermarriage with either whites or Indians today has only 83 males per hundred females in the age cohort 0–4, and this low ratio falls to only seventy-six males per hundred females for those entering their third decade of life.[98]

Having seen the phenomenon of the male disadvantage first in West Africa, and now in the West Indies, we can fairly conclude that it was this phenomenon that was largely responsible for bringing down black sex ratios so abruptly following the end of the slave trade. In Cuba, for example, the combined sex ratio for slaves and free coloreds was 123 in 1861; by 1899 the sex ratio for blacks had fallen to 94.[99]

We might also reasonably conclude that the slave male's inability to survive as well as the female was in part responsible for a continued demand for slaves from Africa. But this demand was met with more and more cargoes of mostly males, who would also perish more quickly than females, and this continued shipment of perishable males combined with the extraordinarily high infant and child mortality to ensure that there would be no slave population growth in the Islands, and consequently that the Islands would have to rely continually on Africa for labor.

That black Caribbean populations were able to grow by natural means was dramatically demonstrated following the end of slavery. But what had changed? Modern medicine was still decades away from making headway against any of the diseases of the region. Hard plantation labor was still being performed by blacks on many islands such as Barbados, yet the free blacks of Barbados steadily increased their numbers.[100] The only thing that had changed materially was the ability of Caribbean blacks to choose their own diet as freedmen. And with that ability came enough in the way of extra nutrients to cut considerably into the heavy infant and child mortality rates, by reducing the incidence of maternal malnutrition.

This does not mean, however, that the problem of nutritional stress was ended. For although nutrition improved as individuals had greater dietary choices following slavery, it was still poor, largely because nutritional choices, although enhanced, were nonetheless limited by poverty. Thus because nutritional stress continued, the male disadvantage also continued.

Medical Care

Certainly improved medical care was not the reason for an improved demographic picture for blacks in the immediate post emancipation period; in fact it was not until this century that medicine was actually able to begin to cope with Caribbean health problems, and public health procedures were implemented to lower the incidence of those problems.[101]

During slavery we receive contrasting views of general slave health. On the one hand there was "the opinion of . . . the planters that the robust bodies of the negroes . . . were constantly ready for the necessary work of the fields," while on the other we discover planters complaining that their hospitals were always full.[102]

It seems that most plantations on all islands did have a hospital, "sickhouse," or "hothouse" under the daily or at least weekly supervision of a doctor.[103] The doctor generally was contracted for on an annual basis, which seems to have averaged from $400 to $800 yearly per plantation. Others were paid on a per-slave basis, which netted the physician about $2.00 per slave annually.[104] Thus physicians who had a large practice (and many did judging from complaints that some physicians took responsibility for more than 4,000 slaves per year) could quickly become wealthy, which apparently many did, at least in the British islands.[105]

The situation was apparently not so lucrative in the Spanish islands where medicine was not, at that time, thought to be a proper career for a gentleman, let alone slave medicine. Thus in Santo Domingo a royal decree of 1797 authorized mulattos to practice medicine because of a shortage of white physicians, while in Cuba it was observed that medicine was a field open even to blacks.[106]

This is not to say, however, that blacks did not play an important role in their own medical care throughout the Caribbean. Almost invariably each plantation had one or more slave "doctors" or "doctor women," as well as a group of midwives, all generally elderly. The slave "doctor" or "doctoress" would normally treat minor wounds and fevers, and together with midwives deliver the infants and provide postnatal care for both mother and child.[107] That this black staff was deemed crucial can be seen in the words of one physician, who stated that "an intelligent healthy Negro man and woman are . . . considered necessary to dispense medicines, dressings, etc. in the hospital and they form very important acquisitions to every estate, under the direction of a practitioner."[108]

The extent to which white physicians and black staff actually aided the sick and abetted the birth process is another matter. We have already taken note of the fearful infant mortality caused in part by the unhygienic practices of medical attendants. In Puerto Rico an observer went so far as to state that white physicians actually added to the death toll with their incompetence. By contrast, in Jamaica a white physician charged black staff with the same incompetence claiming that the "hothouse" doctors and "doctoresses" collectively constituted "a most fearful fraternity," which among other things should never have "charge of the bulk of what medicines may be on the estate."[109] He added that not only were they "egregiously ignorant [but] most obstinately addicted to their own way; but still if they find damage fast approaching most probably brought on by their own tampering they will cunningly run to the overseer, tell him of the dangerous case, and that he should send for the doctor; and when he arrives, when sinking nature is nearly lost . . . or [if the patient] expires shortly after his arrival, they dexterously assert that if he had followed their advice all would have been well."[110]

Clearly there was a bit of professional rivalry among plantation healers, and one suspects that physicians too blamed black assistants for their failures. Yet the system was also to blame, for physicians were under pressure from overseers to keep labor laboring and thus, if after an examination "the pulse neither indicates a fever, nor the frequency of the stools a flux, he [the physician] concludes that there is no disorder, and the Negro is dismissed to the fields."[111]

Slave hospitals likewise left much to be desired. Illustrative is the claim of Dr. Collins that "in the sickhouses [the slaves] are indulged with all the facilities in the world to die."[112] Yet apparently not all slaves agreed that hospital facilities were that bad since many feigned sickness to gain admittance, the classic example occurring on Lewis's Plantation in Jamaica whose hospital was jammed after the slaves discovered him to be a bit too indulgent. Lewis, however, was also shrewd and discovered that he had only to throw a party for the slaves to empty the hospital.[113]

Malingering, unfortunately, did not always have such a happy outcome. Dr. R.R. Madden reported that "the Negroes are prone to shamming when they want to escape from labor, but the result of that propensity is that every sick Negro is suspected of being a shammer."[114] Nonetheless, it seems that even without the "shammers" slave hospitals never lacked patients, for rates of morbidity were very high especially during the grueling work of "croptime." Moreno Fraginals states, for example, that in Cuba it was "normal" for 15 to 20 percent of a gang to be in the hospital during normal times, with that percentage rising to 40 percent by the end of the sugar harvest.[115] In Jamaica, according to Patterson, there was a "large number of invalid slaves to be found on almost every estate," while in Barbados it was estimated at the turn of the nineteenth century that slaves averaged at least nineteen sick days per year.[116]

There were various notions of what made slaves ill besides disease. A Frenchman visiting Puerto Rico incredibly blamed much slave sickness on a "lack of exercise" and then contradictorily (and a bit enviously perhaps) on "the passions of lovemaking carried to the ultimate extreme."[117] In addition he mentioned the "immoderate use of liquor" and drunkenness among the slaves, and here he may have been closer to the mark even if his portrayal of the slave as a leisurely individual with time on his hands to pursue women and drink is definitely at odds with the standard picture of plantation slavery. Slave drunkenness, however, is mentioned frequently, with one observer going so far as to claim that alcohol was one of the causes of the natural decrease of the slave population. He lamented, however, that "their universal passion for rum" could not be thwarted because it was so "plentiful and easily obtained."[118] In view of these comments there seems little reason to doubt that "hangovers" sent more than a few agonized slaves in search of a hospital bed for a few hours away from the broiling sun, while excessive alcohol consumption over time may have damaged black livers and pancreata, just as it did the organs of island whites.

But lovemaking and drunkenness aside, physicians often had difficulty in diagnosing slave sickness because of the tendency of the latter to be "fatalistic" and uncooperative when ill, even going so far as to conceal one illness by naming another. In part the latter was, according to one historian, the result of a language barrier between whites and blacks concerning various parts of the body. But much of the fatalism was a function of a religious belief in a world of conflicting spirits and forces over which the individual had little personal control.[119]

This in turn furnished another reason for deceiving physicians, because slaves had their own medicine quite apart from and doubtless in many cases more effective than white medicine – more effective because its practitioners were deemed to have some control over spirits and forces.[120] In addition, black preventive medicine was in many ways more advanced than the white variety. Blacks from the Gold Coast, for example, had brought with them the technique of innoculating for yaws ("borrowing the yaws"), while smallpox inoculation was practiced among some groups in Africa long before it was discovered by Europeans.[121] For curative purposes Edward Long reported that slaves used "lime juice, cardamons, the roots, branches, leaves, bark, and gums of trees and about thirty different herbs," and while Long was less than impressed with the *materia medica* of the slaves, we have subsequently discovered how much we can learn from yesterday's "natural medicine."[122]

In truth the slaves would probably have been better off with their own practitioners, for white medicine in the West Indies was, to put it charitably, of low quality. Part of the difficulty was that prior to the nineteenth century there was no education or "proof of qualifications" required to practice medicine, few older colleagues to teach young practitioners something of anatomy and tropical medicine, and no local medical journals as vehicles for sharing knowledge.[123] Part of the difficulty, too, was the low state of the medical arts in general, which, until something was known of germ theory, was speculative, intuitive, and when aggressive methods such as purging and phlebotomy were employed often more effective in killing the patient than in curing him.

In surgery the physicians were also less than successful, as evidenced by statements to the effect that when a slave had his hand mangled in a machine, or a limb that required amputation he was written off in advance by everyone, including the physician who performed the surgery.[124] In the face of leprosy, yaws, and their mimics, physicians were equally helpless except to recommend quarantine procedures, which in effect meant the banishment of a victim to a "yaws house" or "leprosy hut" where, especially with leprosy, he became a lonely outcast.[125]

There was, however, at least one flash of brilliance in the physicians' observations and this was their recognition that many diseases of the slaves could be cured by a better diet. Unfortunately their recommendations for a better and more varied slave diet usually went unheeded until epidemic disease appeared, whereupon the slaves' diet was often hurriedly improved, if only for the duration of the epidemic.[126]

In fact this exception to slave feeding practices during epidemics serves to emphasize the rule that generally slaves were badly nourished. Perhaps this was the reason why a poor man like Tomás Terry in Cuba could build a fortune by buying "sick Negroes for a song, nurse them back to health and sell them at prices ranging from eight hundred to a thousand dollars a head."[127] The "nursing" consisted mostly of merely feeding them well.

PART III

PATHOGENS AND POLITICS

INTRODUCTION

In some countries foreigners and natives are as differently affected by certain contagious disorders as if they had been different animals. . .

Charles Darwin (1836)[1]

We need to remind ourselves – those of us in the Western world at
least – that to live long enough to be haunted by the specter of cancer
or heart disease is a very rare and very recent privilege. We no longer
need concern ourselves with epidemic disasters that could easily spoil
that privilege by carrying away 10, 20, even 40 percent of the members
of a community, nor must we live in fear of lingering, hideously disfig-
uring diseases, which would condemn us to a living death whose
termination by cancer or heart failure would be seen as a blessing.

This study has treated a different time when such illnesses were an
omnipresent fact of life in a region then regarded more as a disease-
ridden hell than an earthly paradise. We have seen why this was the
case for blacks. Chapter 10 shows why it was also the case for whites
by examining their relationship with yellow fever and malaria in the
area. In so doing, it picks up the threads of the treatment begun in
Chapter 1 that demonstrated the role that yellow fever and malaria
resistance played in the enslavement of the black. One concern of
Chapter 10 is to reveal as fully as possible the extent to which blacks
did indeed seem resistant to these diseases relative to whites. Another
concern is to show in the process how this pair of tropical killers
victimized blacks despite this resistance, or perhaps better because of
it, while they also influenced the geopolitical and demographic history
of the West Indies in ways not yet fully appreciated.

The final chapter of the book explores the questions of how a mark-
edly different black and white disease experience in the West Indies
may have shaped slave societies and fostered racism, before taking up
what is perhaps the most saliently tragic aspect to the biological history
of the West African in the West Indies.

That history began with a diaspora because blacks were needed to
colonize a region in which, after pathogenic poisoning, the Indians
could not survive and the Europeans could not thrive demographically.

159

The West Africans did both. They survived the biologically devastating circumstances of slavery, as perhaps no other people could, and after slavery, began to thrive demographically despite poverty and racial oppression.

Yet the cleansing of the West Indies, in this century, of diseases that killed whites, opened the region to massive white exploitation of a kind never before possible. The ironic result has been that the black, whose hardiness was crucial to the colonization of the region in the first place, was suddenly no longer crucial, and in fact, despite his demographic preponderance in the West Indies, not even very important. Yet at the same time those qualities that contributed so heavily to his ability to survive hardship have now, with improved nutrition and modern medicine, contributed to a swelling population.

To relieve pressure on the Islands, many have voluntarily engaged in another black diaspora to the homelands of people who for so long exploited the Caribbean. But those who so desperately needed the black yesterday are turning him away today. With no modern diaspora to correct the consequences of the original black diaspora, the black West Indian's respite from a centuries-old cycle of poor nutrition, poor health, and abysmally high infant and child mortality rates may be very brief indeed.

CHAPTER 10

FEVERS AND RACE

To those who are impelled by necessity, or induced by interest, to visit the torrid zone, and relinquish the blessings which flow from exercise in the delightful climates of the earth, in temperate regions; to those who exchange their native countries, which yield the free and unbounded enjoyments of spontaneous health, for such as no care, nor art, can ever make agreeable; – some cautions may be necessary – some precedents useful.

Benjamin Moseley (1789)[1]

The problem of whether there exists any disposition or immunity, in a particular race or population can only be solved when two or more races, or population groups, live side by side in contact with each other and under as similar circumstances as possible without any mixing of blood.

Folke Henschen (1966)[2]

Black-related diseases have occupied most of our attention to this point. We have seen Caribbean blacks dying of myriad ailments that ranged from epidemic cholera to endemic nutritional ailments to the chronic illnesses that accompanied them from Africa. Whites, by contrast, were troubled little by most of these diseases. Yet their demographic performance in the West Indies was even more dismal than that of their servants. In the words of Philip Curtin, "We know in a vague way that, in the Caribbean, the net natural decrease for Europeans was higher than it was for Africans, but not by how much or how long this situation persisted."[3]

This "situation" was not, as we know from Chapter 1, created by indigenous diseases; nor was it the creation of numerous illnesses of varied etiologies, such as those that plagued the slaves. Rather, major responsibility is borne by only two illnesses, both of them of African origin and both far more deadly to whites than to blacks. Yet although the diseases in question – falciparum malaria and yellow fever – were essentially "white related," they nonetheless shaped black history in

161

Table 3. *Deaths in Havana, 1646–1650*

Year	Deaths	Death Rate (per 1,000)
1646	87	19
1647	106	23
1648	134	29
1649	562	122
1650	148	32

Table 3-A. *Havana Deaths by Month and Race, 1649*

Month	Whites	Blacks
January	7	1
February	10	—
March	3	—
April	3	—
May	4	—
June	2	2
July	7	5
August	208	4
September	235	8
October	24	3
November	20	—
December	13	3
Totals	536	26

Source: Jorge Eduardo Leroy y Cassa, *La primera epidemia de fiebre amarilla en la Habana, en 1649* (Habana, 1930), 39–40.

the Caribbean in many – sometimes blatant, sometimes subtle, but as yet, mostly unappreciated – ways.

A quick glance at Table 3 will reveal how the relative salubrity of early Havana was suddenly shattered by that city's first yellow fever epidemic. To be sure, an annual death rate of twenty to thirty per thousand could not be considered good by today's standards. But Havana then, as a frontier community, was enjoying a remarkably low death rate, or at least it was until 1649 when mortality suddenly skyrocketed. Yet as will be seen in Table 3-A, that mortality skyrocketed only for whites. The city's blacks were affected much less by yellow fever, although they were certainly not untouched.[4] On the other hand, a significant percentage of those affected were probably not actually black, but rather the mulatto products of miscegenation in a society heavily weighted with Spanish males.

At the other end of yellow fever's career in the West Indies, K.H.

Uttley has presented data on yellow fever mortality for Antigua during the years 1857 to 1895. These data reveal that 84 percent of the yellow fever deaths on the island during the years in question were white deaths, even though 96 percent of the population was black.[5] Again, although blacks did not escape the disease entirely (and again one suspects that many of those who did not were "colored" as opposed to black), as a group they displayed a relative immunity to the disease that whites did not enjoy.

I have presented data bracketing yellow fever's West Indian life span to make the same point briefly that I have made in some detail in other publications, as well as in Chapter 1, and which is that blacks possessed an innate yellow fever immunity that whites did not have. Clearly neither whites nor blacks in Havana of 1649 had had the opportunity to acquire immunity to a disease that was making its West Indian debut – at least they had no such opportunity in the West Indies, and most blacks in Havana at that time were doubtless Creole born. Similarly both blacks and whites in nineteenth-century Antigua would have had equal opportunity to acquire immunity, and consequently should have died at equal rates from the disease. But because whites monopolized the death rolls, despite this equal opportunity for acquired immunity, there is little doubt that the blacks' most important line of defense against yellow fever was innate rather than acquired.

During the two-and-a-half centuries between Cuba's early experience with the disease and its last few decades in Antigua, black yellow fever resistance in the Caribbean seems even more pronounced. But this was mostly an illusion, created not so much by an even more steadfast black resistance to the disease, but rather by a dramatic white susceptibility as the region filled with transient Europeans who died in droves from the illness.

Creole-born whites, however, as a rule did not die, for they, to use their term, had become "acclimated." They attained this state of grace by hosting the disease and surviving it, for yellow fever, like many illnesses, is permitted only one assault on the individual. Moreover, as with many illnesses, yellow fever, while a vigorous slayer of adults, tends to treat the young quite gently. Thus, for most Creoles, "acclimation" was a matter of entertaining yellow fever as a child and in the process earning a lifetime of immunity to it.

Blacks could and did "acquire" immunity in like fashion, for their innate resistance did not keep them from taking yellow fever. But it did keep them from dying of it by generally blessing them with a mild, almost symptom free case of the disease much like the experience of white children. Thus they too earned an immunity more or less painlessly.

However for yellow fever's chief victims – the newly arrived Europeans – the process was anything but painless. They were the ones to display yellow fever's classic symptoms which signalled death for so many. The symptoms appeared suddenly, often with no warning. They began with severe pains in the head, back and limbs, progressed to extreme prostration and jaundice (hence the appellation yellow fever) and then to internal hemorrhage, with the victim vomiting blood (hence the Spanish *vomito negro*) and finally to coma and death.[6]

Conveniently for yellow fever, which is generally an urban disease when it troubles man, most of the "unacclimated" reaching the West Indies, whether immigrant, businessman, soldier, or sailor, took up urban residence, and in places like Havana, where enough of these individuals arrived with regularity, the disease would ultimately become sufficiently omnipresent to be called endemic.

Conversely, it was the absence of large urban populations capable of hosting the disease on a sustained basis that helps to account for yellow fever's relatively tardiness in taking up Caribbean residence. Yet long before its advent, dwellers in rural and urban areas alike were already suffering from a far more ubiquitous illness, falciparum malaria, which produced the "bilious remittent malarial fevers" so often confused with yellow fever, particularly when the victims hemorrhaged internally.[7]

Thus, after yellow fever's arrival, these tropical killers were not always distinguished, with yellow fever sometimes receiving undue credit for rural outbreaks and malaria unjustly blamed for sweeping a seacoast town.[8] The confusion among physicians can be seen in their assertion that "Creoles and Negroes are not subject to . . . [yellow fever] in its most malignant form; when it invades them it appears under a remittent or intermittent type."[9]

In some cases individuals making this distinction may have been witnessing the mild yellow fever of the blacks or white Creole youngsters. But mostly, one suspects, they are describing malaria, which the Creoles suffered much from and the blacks far less because of their genetic protection. We know that blacks would have been almost totally immune to vivax malaria and relatively immune to *Plasmodium falciparum* because of both innate and acquired immunity. Thus an observer pondering the matter of black malarial protection was close to the mark when he concluded that "there is unquestionably in his constitution or organic frame a something, we know not what, an influence or power of resistance which makes him proof against malaria, and the destructive fevers resulting from what we call malaria when acting on white men."[10]

Not all Caribbean Islands were equally plagued with malaria. Hirsch identified Cuba, Jamaica, and Santo Domingo as well as Guadeloupe, Dominica, Martinique, St. Lucia, Grenada, Trinidad, and Tobago as those "chiefly affected," whereas he termed the disease "rare" in the Bahamas, Antigua, St. Vincent, and Barbados.[11] Actually the disease may well have been more than just rare in Barbados; it may have been nonexistent, as it apparently also was on St. Kitts and Anguilla. For in Barbados visitors enthusiastically commented on the "freedom from insect life" and it seems that the island was indeed free of mosquitoes capable of bearing malaria, with much of the credit due to a tiny fish that inhabited its ponds and streams and fed on mosquito larvae.[12] Physicians, however, gave credit to the "clearing" of the island's timber and its intensive cultivation, claiming that prior to this effort the island was troubled with "intermittent fevers."[13]

Unfortunately, the *Aëdes aegypti* population was aided by this clearing process and little troubled by the fish since it breeds in mud puddles, open containers of water, or any stagnant body of water. Thus the *Aëdes* was well settled into Barbados when yellow fever began arriving in the blood of infected individuals and it was deadly effective in spreading the virus among the island's crowded populace. The result was that the first epidemic of 1647–49 may have killed as many as 6,000, and by the dawn of the eighteenth century, thousands more had died.[14] Indeed, for a time the disease proved so destructive to the islanders that it became known as the "Barbados Distemper." This nickname quickly faded, however, after the intensifying slave trade of the late seventeenth and early eighteenth centuries began delivering the illness to almost every corner of the Caribbean, whereupon many began to call it simply the "white man's death."[15]

As we discussed in Chapter 1, black fever resistance served as an important reason as well as rationale for slavery, and West Indian planters, physicians, and visitors alike never ceased to marvel at the black's ability to withstand yellow fever and malaria. Moreover they never ceased to remind governments at home that because of this ability blacks were absolutely essential for hard work in hot climates.[16]

Ironically the blacks' fever resistance also led to their employment in defending the very islands upon which they had been enslaved. For in truth, because of European susceptibility, yellow fever and malaria had more to say about the outcome of West Indian military engagements than all of the admirals and generals on the spot or territory-hungry governments at home. In the process these diseases also inflicted considerably more mortality on armies and navies than armies and navies did on one another.

Cuba's first yellow fever epidemic, for example, not only killed civilians – it also wiped out a third of the garrison at Havana and pruned somewhat the crew of the fleet then in port,[17] and this may not have been yellow fever's first harvest of military personnel in the West Indies. A prominent historian of the Caribbean, who feels yellow fever was already present in the region prior to 1647, argues that it was this disease that drove the English away from San Juan, Puerto Rico, after their capture of that city in 1598.[18] In addition he asserts that yellow fever continued to hound the English by killing thousands of them

after their 1655 capture of Jamaica and that the disease was responsible
for the renewing of entire seventeenth-century British garrisons in the
West Indies every two years.[19]

French forces received their first real baptism under yellow fever's
fire in 1655 as 1,500 men were landed to occupy St. Lucia. According to
Francisco Guerra, a few months later only 89 remained alive. Yellow
fever had not been the only illness to wreak this havoc, but it had been
the major one,[20] and following 1655, war between England and France
and Spain became a four-sided affair with yellow fever at war with the
other three sides. An English fleet of eleven ships was sent to Barbados
during the 1690–1691 period only to be driven away by yellow fever
before it had the opportunity to meet the French.[21] In 1695 the English
tried their luck again, this time in an effort to capture Cap-François in
St. Domingue; they succeeded but did not enjoy the spoils for yellow
fever drove them off. The disease also triumphed over a stubborn
British blockade of Porto Bello by killing three rear admirals, ten ships'
captains, fifty lieutenants, and around 4,000 men.[22]

North Americans who accompanied Admiral Vernon in his 1741 expedition against Cartegena during the War of Jenkin's Ear had their first
real encounter with yellow fever as they witnessed a 12,000-man army
suddenly reduced by 8,500 men, with yellow fever leading the diseases
that did the damage.[23] Ironically the survivors of this campaign soon
discovered that lightning could indeed strike them twice as they were
incorporated into a face-saving effort to take Santiago, Cuba. Yellow
fever halved the English forces before the attack was called off.[24]

Back in Cuban waters in 1762, the British once again encountered
yellow fever as they laid siege to Havana. That siege was almost
broken by the disease that invalided well over half of the 15,000-man
force while a subsequent attack launched from Jamaica against Spaniards in Nicaragua resulted in fewer than 600 men out of seventeen
battalions "fit for duty," although this time apparently malaria led the
counterattack.[25]

Obviously great plans of state for the Caribbean region more often
than not foundered in a sea of pathogens. Those plans of course were
dictated by the mercantilistic *Weltanschauung* of the age, which pre-
scribed grabbing all one could from the other fellow while holding on
tightly to what one already had. Yet not only were England's offensive
operations regularly throttled by fevers, but those same fevers were
also insidiously chipping away at an ability to defend her West Indian
possessions. Thus, in the spring of 1782, with Jamaica anticipating a
French attack, an army physician worried that although some 7,000
men had been sent to the island in the three preceding years, there
were now no more than 2,000 able to man Jamaica's defenses. He
asserted that the average troop mortality rate was about 25 percent,
"none at enemy's hands," and concluded that all the dying the troops

were doing was extremely dangerous for the island.[26] In this same vein a colleague complained about the "dreadful mortality of British troops ever since Great Britain has been in possession of West India colonies" and went so far as to wonder if they were actually worth the price.[27]

Yet that price would shortly be reduced, thanks to experiments already set in motion. One such experiment involved North Americans. After the British capture of Savannah, Georgia in 1779, white loyalists and black slaves in the area had been welded together into "the South Carolina" regiment and following the war the regiment was relocated in Jamaica. The whites abandoned the unit to join the planter class, while the blacks, who chose to remain as soldiers, were shipped off to the Windward and Leeward Islands.[28] Blacks then had become a legitimate part of the English military.

Meanwhile, other blacks or rather individuals with an "admixture of Negro blood" were among the mostly white Jamaican volunteers who accompanied the all-white regular army in a secret expedition against Nicaragua launched in 1780. Disease quite literally destroyed the effort. However, it did not escape notice that the mulattoes had fared better with disease than anyone else.[29] Finally, Barbados, which had long used free blacks in its militia, took an important step in 1782 by raising an all-black unit – the Prince of Wales Corps of free mulattoes – to buttress the island's defenses.[30]

The experiments proved successful from the standpoint of the whites in that armed blacks and mulattoes did not turn those arms against them and army physicians, long aware of the black's ability to resist the fevers that slew European troops so vigorously, began a campaign to make the use of black troops in the Islands a matter of policy – a policy that would help to ease the "terrible mortality of white troops."[31]

The campaign proved successful when London, faced with a need for troops in Europe, and heavy mortality among those in the West Indies, issued a request in 1795 that colonial legislatures form black regiments. The request could not have arrived at a worse time. London might have been worried about the course the French Revolution was taking on the Continent, but West Indian planters were absolutely terrified by its local manifestation in the form of the St. Domingue slave revolt. To arm large numbers of their own blacks at that particular moment seemed nothing short of madness.[32]

However, despite their fears, West Indian planters could not avoid gloating that the revolution was destroying their most formidable competitor, which prior to the slave revolt had been exporting almost as much sugar as all of the British Islands combined.[33] Thus, with the prospect of real prosperity ahead, the planter class came to feel that their islands were worth protecting at almost any price. Moreover, a recent yellow fever epidemic had once more raised serious questions about the ability of British troops to pay that price. The epidemic, which had reached Grenada from an island off the African Coast, had subsequently swept British garrisons across the West Indies and in its aftermath came grave doubts that the survivors were sufficiently numerous to defend the Islands, let alone mount an offensive operation, which, in the words of a naval physician, was "considered as little better than a forlorn hope."[34]

The much debated outcome was the birth of twelve West Indian regiments of black troops, with the first formed in 1795 and composed in part of the survivors of the old South Carolina regiment.[35] The other units were to be formed as need became apparent and there was no lack of apparent need, for the next decade saw yellow fever raging across the Caribbean like a biblical plague.

During the years 1793 to 1796 alone, the British army in the West Indies lost some 80,000 men, with over half of them victims of yellow fever. Much of this mortality had resulted from the British invasion of St. Domingue. For a brief period they met with success. Then they met with yellow fever.[36] Initial losses were between 10,000 and 12,500 and by the time the expeditionary forces were withdrawn, some 45,000 to 50,000 soldiers and sailors had perished.[37]

Britian's attempt to claim the former French colony was succeeded by Napoleon's attempt to reclaim it. French forces, led by Napoleon's brother-in-law, invaded in 1802. Whether by accident or design, they seemed ignorant of the disastrous outcome of the previous English effort. Francisco Guerra describes the mood of the French as that of a holiday outing with the promise of promotions adding an exciting spice. The mood changed abruptly as yellow fever once more counterattacked and ground up an army. Within ten months after landing on St. Domingue, the French had lost about 40,000 men, including 1,500 officers and Napoleon's brother-in-law.[38] Whether it is true, as one historian has asserted, that "without yellow fever Haiti would still be French" we can never know.[39] But it does seem that this particular French army at this particular time, when yellow fever was so virulent, "would have been . . . defeated . . . had never a shot been fired by either side."[40]

Unfortunately for the French, yellow fever was not content with the damage it inflicted on them at St. Domingue, but pursued their withdrawing forces to Martinique and Guadeloupe, where it destroyed all thoughts of another campaign by raging among them for the next three years. During these same years the disease also impartially decimated British garrisons where, depending on location in the Caribbean, between 15 and 70 percent of the troops were lost. Noncombatants also felt yellow fever's fury, as American seamen were almost routinely dying in the port of Havana.[41]

With the memory of the now obviously successful St. Domingue slave revolt fresh in mind, island whites continued to fret about the black troops that they felt had been forced upon them. They did grudgingly concede the crucial role of the "Blackshot" Regiment in ending the "Maroon War" in Jamaica, and openly acknowledged that for some reason white soldiers, particularly those fresh from Europe, quickly "sickened and died" while the black troops did not.[42] However, it was not until almost four decades of the nineteenth century had elapsed that these general impressions were confirmed by statistical evidence and the fullness of the wisdom of employing black troops became apparent. For in 1835 Major Alexander Tulloch was ordered to begin a series of statistical studies on morbidity and mortality in the British army – studies that today, in the words of Philip Curtin, provide "by far the best data we now have or are likely to discover."[43]

The report, published in 1838, starkly revealed an extraordinary difference in the experience of blacks and whites with the diseases of the Caribbean.[44] White troops, for example, in the Jamaican command had suffered an average annual death rate during the years 1817 to 1836 of 121 per thousand mean strength; moreover, according to Tulloch, "when we come to include certain omissions the ratio is as high as 143."[45] For black troops, by contrast, the death rate was only 30 per thousand mean strength per annum, with the reason for the striking difference in mortality largely the work of "fevers." Indeed "fevers," which had killed whites at the rate of 102 per thousand, had only killed blacks at the rate of 8 per thousand. By region the impact of "fevers," particularly yellow fever, was even more striking. In the Bahamas, which had seen much yellow fever, the white death rate was 200 per thousand, the blacks only 41, and "fever" was the cause of 80 percent of the white deaths. In the Windward and Leeward command, which had seen substantially less yellow fever during these years, the white annual mortality rate was 93.5 per thousand, while again the black rate was 40, indicating how little the presence or absence of yellow fever affected black mortality.

In Table 4 death rates are presented by race for both the Jamaican and the Windward and Leeward commands. They illustrate vividly black resistance and white susceptibility to yellow fever, particularly during severe epidemics such as that which occurred in Jamaica during the years 1831 to 1832. Conversely, the data for the Windward and Leeward command after 1822, along with data in Table 5 on the Eastern Caribbean, show mortality mostly without yellow fever's contribution, thus highlighting black immunities to the less dramatic but equally deadly tropical killer, falciparum malaria. Also highlighting white susceptibility is the absence of malaria in Barbados, St. Vincent, and Antigua, and the consequent relatively low white death rates, as opposed to the mortality generated among the white troops on Dominica, St. Lucia, Grenada, Tobago, and Trinidad mentioned by Hirsch as among the islands "chiefly affected" by the disease.[46] Black resistance

Table 4. *Deaths per Thousand Mean Strength per Annum by Race for Troops Serving the British Crown in the Jamaican and Windward and Leeward Commands, 1817–1836*

Year	Jamaican Command		Windward and Leeward Command	
	White	Black	White	Black
1817	88	45	162	46
1818	89	36	126	37
1819	294	34	83	63
1820	153	46	105	38
1821	116	42	109	40
1822	171	25	77	43
1823	65	37	49	37
1824	84	39	70	29
1825	307	18	76	35
1826	80	47	68	43
1827	224	44	85	26
1828	74	16	81	36
1829	62	28	58	46
1830	97	14	65	40
1831	133	45	69	36
1832	111	8	64	36
1833	86	15	50	37
1834	93	8	43	33
1835	75	13	57	37
1836	61	26	77	35
Death rate	121.3	30	78.5	40

Source: Alexander M. Tulloch, "Statistical Report on the Sickness, Mortality, and Invaliding Among the Troops in the West Indies," in Great Britain, *Parliamentary Papers*, XL, 1837–1838 (*Accounts and Papers*), V (London, 1838).

to malaria can also be clearly seen in that the death rate of black troops on malaria-free Barbados was actually higher than it was on malaria-ridden St. Lucia and Dominica. The rates, however, also confirm our earlier observation regarding black susceptibility to enteric illnesses and once more emphasize the lethal quality of water on Barbados.

Tulloch's study served also to dramatize the insalubrious nature of the West Indies by contrasting death rates of soldiers stationed there with that of those serving in the British Isles, which stood at a mere fifteen per thousand. Moreover, it must be remembered that the years 1817 to 1836, which were the years that Tulloch's study for the most part focussed on, were years of peace in the Caribbean. The report pointed out that during the wartime period of 1796 to 1807 white troops had died at a rate of 244 per thousand per annum, while the black rate was 59. The St. Domingue debacle lay at the root of much of

Table 5. *Death Rates per Thousand Mean Strength
per Annum by Race for Troops Serving the British Crown in
the Eastern Caribbean, 1817–1836*

Island	White	Black
Trinidad	106	40
Tobago	153	34
Grenada	62	28
St. Vincent	55	36
Barbados	58	46
St. Lucia	122	42
Dominica	137	40
Antigua	41	29

Source: Alexander M. Tulloch, "Statistical Report on the Sickness, Mortality, and Invaliding Among the Troops in the West Indies," in Great Britain, *Parliamentary Papers*, XL, 1837–1838 (*Accounts and Papers*), V (London, 1838).

Table 6. *Mortality Rates for French Troops at Martinique and Guadeloupe per Thousand Mean Strength per Annum, 1802–1807*

Year	Martinique	Guadeloupe
1802	570	600
1803	440	460
1804	300	290
1805	400	490
1806	83	100
1807	103	150

Source: Alexandre Moreau de Jonnes, "Observations pour servir a l'histoire de la fièvre jaune des Antilles suivies de tables de la mortalité des troupes Europeènes dans les Indes-Occidentales," *Bulletin de la Société Medicale d' Emulation* 6 (1817), 237–47.

the increased mortality over the peacetime rates. Much too, however, was the consequence of troop movements from one place to another where still more troops were congregating, all of which greatly increased the chances of yellow fever infection.

Yet dreadful as the experience of the English troops seems to have been, it was overshadowed by that of their French counterparts, whose death rates, as reported in Table 6 grimly reflect the magnitude of the cost of their abortive attempt to invade St. Domingue in 1802 and 1803, as well as the effects of yellow fever's pursuit back to the French garrisons.

Of course none of these troop mortality rates reflect normal Caribbean mortality levels. They are offered only to indicate the magnitude of the blacks' ability to survive yellow fever and malaria when serving side by side with whites who possessed no such ability. With no previous opportunity to acquire immunities prior to their arrival in the West Indies, the assignment of whites to the region was tantamount to a death sentence, which surely the home governments must have understood, at least by the early years of the nineteenth century. Ragatz, for example, has observed that of the 19,676 troops sent to the British West Indies in 1796, fully 17,173 were dead within five years.[47]

Roberts has stated that "the troops sent to the West Indies were among the worst available," which probably means, among other things, that they were in poor physical health to begin with, and this poor health coupled with the absolute "genius" of their commanders for locating garrisons "on waste land near marshes" was bound to have produced a high rate of mortality.[48]

On the other hand, the health of black troops in the Caribbean was also precarious. For like the white troops, they too were migrants of sorts moving into disease environments with which they were often unfamiliar. Thus their death rates, although low relative to whites, were nonetheless high relative to the rates of plantation slaves, which, at least for the British Islands, ranged between twenty-five and thirty-three per thousand for those aged three years and older during the early nineteenth century.[49]

It is true that the original black companies (formed in 1795 and shortly thereafter) were "recruited through purchase from some of the best conditioned slaves on the islands." But later regiments were composed mostly of contraband slaves captured by the British navy before they reached the West Indies as a part of England's campaign against the slave trade.[50] Like the slaves, they proved susceptible to "dropsy," diseases of the lungs, and bowel complaints, which together accounted for most black troop mortality. And, also like the slaves, they were resistant to fevers.[51]

Thus one's chances of a full lifetime were considerably greater in the pre-twentieth-century Caribbean if one's skin were black than if one were a white with no yellow fever and malaria protection. Physicians from the middle of the eighteenth century on, warned that "strangers" reaching the West Indies could expect to be assaulted by fevers, yet the strangers continued to pour into those islands that were sugar rich, many willingly to seek their fortunes, many more unwillingly to defend those fortunes.[52] However, as an island faltered in the race for riches, and its soils became impoverished, and its planter class inert, the warnings ceased as there were no longer any strangers to be forewarned.

Thus one could, without any knowledge of politics and economics, unerringly select the most prosperous Caribbean island on the basis of the frequency of its yellow fever epidemics, and for the nineteenth century the yellow fever capital of the Caribbean was Cuba. Fresh blood was constantly infused into the island in the form of Asian

Table 7. *Yellow Fever Deaths in Havana, 1876–1900*

Year	Deaths	Year	Deaths
1876	1,619	1889	303
1877	1,374	1890	308
1878	1,559	1891	356
1879	1,444	1892	357
1880	645	1893	496
1881	485	1894	382
1882	729	1895	553
1883	849	1896	1,282
1884	511	1897	858
1885	165	1898	136
1886	167	1899	103
1887	532	1900	310
1888	468		
Total			15,991

Source: Jorge E. Leroy y Cassá, *Estadística de veinticinco años de fiebre amarilla* (Havana, 1904), 25.

contract laborers, white laborers from Catholic Europe, and the Canary Islands, and refugees from revolution-torn Latin America.[53] The result was that Cuba's 311,051 whites counted in the census of 1827 swelled to well over a million by 1887,[54] despite the fact that yellow fever was invariably on hand to perform initiation rites. Indeed people expected to get the disease – it was called the "fever of acclimation" – and with incredible optimism they also expected to survive it.[55]

Many thousands did not. During 1843, 466 yellow fever deaths, all whites, occurred in the diocese of Havana alone and this was a healthy year. Between 1855 and 1859, 9,341 yellow fever deaths took place in the island's civilian hospitals, while another 5,127 perished in military hospitals.[56] In fact, during the 1850s, it was estimated that at least a quarter of all soldiers sent from Spain died sooner or later from the yellow plague, which represented quite an effort on the part of the disease since the soldiers were also perishing in large numbers from cholera, smallpox, typhoid, and malaria.[57]

However, after the 1850s, deaths from yellow fever began to decline across the Caribbean. It has been speculated that much of the reason had to do with the improvement in a town's water supply, eliminating the need for storage vats that provided ideal mosquito breeding grounds.[58] But one suspects that the most important factor was a simple lack of susceptible individuals, since by this time the region had, save for Cuba, become a stagnant backwater of Empire that attracted few newcomers.

Indeed, as Table 7 illustrates, it was the newcomers that kept the disease alive in Cuba, particularly the Spanish soldiers who poured into the island during the years 1876 to 1878 to end the Ten Years' War (1868–1878) and returned in 1896 to oppose Cuba's renewed struggle for independence. In fact, almost half of Havana's yellow fever deaths during the entire quarter century occurred during only five years of military activity.

Yet despite yellow fever's continued presence in Cuba, the mortality levels it precipitated even among the soldiers were in no way as horrendous as those of most eighteenth-century Caribbean epidemics, which may suggest that milder strains of the illness were more common during these years.[59] In any event, yellow fever, even in Cuba, was definitely on the wane when Reed and his colleagues drew together the work of an Englishman, Ross, an American, Carter, and a Cuban, Finlay, and with something known of its etiology and much about its epidemiology the career of yellow fever was brought to a close for most of the Caribbean.[60]

Knowledge of the disease, however, did not yield the reason for the blacks' ability to resist it so spectacularly as, for example, they had done in Havana during the years 1899 to 1901 when Havana buried 451 white yellow-fever victims and only one black. Medical speculation of the day ranged from the hypothesis that the blacks' use of oil on their bodies kept the mosquitoes at bay to the notion that offensive body odors had the same effect. Other variations had the black skin too thick for the mosquitoes to penetrate, and in addition to these wrongheaded (and racist) speculations there were also some badly reasoned arguments that credited acquired immunity.[61]

Against the acquired immunity arguments, however, stood examples such as that of isolated Bermuda, which saw much black resistance to the illness that had struck there in the early 1850s, or the example of inland Memphis, Tennessee, whose blacks proved relatively resistant to the epidemic that swept the city in 1878.[62] In both cases, blacks had not had the opportunity to acquire immunity in wholesale fashion.

Thus governments as well as businesses in the nineteenth and twentieth centuries continued to avail themselves of the services of blacks for immunological reasons. In the early 1860s, for example, white French troops were again dying of yellow fever in the Caribbean basin, this time on the coast of Mexico. Hence, a black batallion was hurriedly sent to join them – a battalion that displayed "almost complete immunity" to the illnesses that were killing whites.[63]

In that same decade Jamaican laborers began their first of many journeys to Panama where yellow fever had killed some 9,000 workers, claiming, it was alleged, "a life for every railroad tie." In the 1880s more Jamaican workers arrived, this time to work on the French canal, for the French laborers at the time were suffering an "official" death toll of sixty-three per thousand and an actual death toll substantially higher. The blacks as usual proved resistant to the fevers that killed as many as 20,000 individuals before the French finally gave up.[64]

Shortly after the Americans began construction of their canal, William Gorgas arrived, fresh from a successful mosquito eradication program to stop yellow fever in Havana, with orders to make the canal zone yellow fever free as well. He succeeded in 1905 and thus eliminated one enemy that had defeated the French attempt. Nonetheless, the following year 800 of every 1,000 workers on the canal were sick and death rates were reaching forty per thousand because malaria, the other great tropical killer, remained stubbornly entrenched. Thus once more the call went out from Panama for black laborers and the West Indian islands responded by sending workers from Jamaica, Barbados, St. Lucia, Antigua, Martinique, Guadeloupe, some 44,000 in all, and this was just the first wave.[65]

The exact number of black immigrants to Panama will probably never be known. We do, however, know something of their genetic makeup and consequently know that black malarial resistance played a crucial role in the construction of a canal normally credited exclusively to North American ingenuity.[66]

There are other ironies, small and large, connected with disease and race in the Caribbean. William Gorgas told the Cornell class of 1907 that it would not be long before "life in the tropics for the Anglo-Saxon will be more healthful than in the Temperate Zones."[67] He was correct, for the eradication of mosquitoes also eradicated yellow fever and malaria, the two most formidable disease barriers to *Anglo-Saxon* life in the tropics. The emphasis on the term Anglo-Saxon, however, raises serious questions about the motives behind America's so-called humanitarian campaign to bring health to the tropics.[68]

Cuba and Panama, for example, were quickly cleared of diseases that killed whites, while little was done about diseases that killed the bulk of the Cubans or Panamanians. Puerto Rico, on the other hand, although American territory, was largely ignored (save for the important exception of the Rockefeller International Health Board campaign to eradicate hookworm, yaws, and other Caribbean illnesses) and malaria remained the island's biggest killer well into this century, while Haiti is fever ridden yet today.

With the cleansing of Cuba, American capital rushed into the island's sugar industry and between the years 1912 and 1924 some quarter of a million Jamaicans and Haitians were imported to do the work.[69] The old rationale, however, that black disease resistance made their presence crucial was gone. Blacks had proved whites correct in their judgment of their ability to survive in the tropics by doing precisely that, and after the yoke of slavery had been lifted, by increasing their numbers at such a rate that migration out of islands such as Barbados had become an absolute economic necessity.[70]

But this demographic triumph was the only victory the blacks enjoyed. For although their ability to labor and survive in the West Indies had made the colonization of the Islands possible in the first place, they had remained politically powerless and economically destitute. As a numerous, needy but powerless people, there was little choice but to continue doing the white man's work.

CHAPTER 11

EPILOGUE: DIET, DISEASE, AND DISPLACEMENT

Reproaching the victim for the consequences of his victimization antedated slavery and has outlived it.

Sidney W. Mintz (1974)[1]

Demographic predominance is no panacea; problems of colour continue to affect West Indian society, culture and personality.

David Lowenthal (1972)[2]

At their most virulent, diseases such as yellow fever and malaria were killers of hundreds of thousands of Europeans in the West Indies. In this century the diseases have receded, due to preventive and therapeutic medicine, and memories have dimmed of the terror they wrought. However, the current low state of these diseases is not assured for the future. Yellow fever remains very much alive in the treetops of nearby South America and there is still no specific treatment for the disease; malaria is on the offensive throughout the world and mosquito vectors for both yellow fever and malaria are plentiful throughout the Caribbean.[3]

Were both diseases once again to assume hurricane intensity and sweep the Islands, they would surely overwhelm modern medicine, at least temporarily. Were it yellow fever, hospitals could overflow and only a small percentage of the victims might ever reach exhausted physicians and nurses. The imagination can conjure up scenes of airports and docks jammed with persons attempting to flee and riots when no planes or boats appeared because the island was quarantined. The cities would fall quiet as individuals huddled fearfully indoors – a quiet broken only by the sound of trucks, pressed into service for transporting the dead.

Fanciful or not the scenario may help those of us in this century to comprehend the terror of a yellow fever epidemic in centuries past. Moreover, the terror now, as then, would be largely the property of whites, for there is no reason to believe that blacks have lost their capacity for resisting the disease in a few short decades. Thus the cities

177

would not fall completely quiet, for blacks would rediscover this gift and their presence in the streets might well stir resentments in whites, even fear in those islands where whites form a small minority.

Suppose further that the blacks took some real satisfaction in the "white man's death." They did yesterday, claiming that whites were seized with terror every time they fell victim to fever and that they were much more likely to die of the former than the latter. "Fear kills Bawkra," said the slaves and certainly the literature of the period reveals a constant white preoccupation with fevers and death.[4]

Yet the slaves could hardly be blamed, for whites also took racial satisfaction in the "shocking disorders" of yaws or leprosy, which were monopolized by blacks. It was these "loathsome and disgusting" diseases, which, along with dirt eating, also "horribly disgusting," were taken by whites as prima facie evidence of black subhumanity. In fact, even black fever resistance was seen in this light. After all, none of the "lower animals" seemed to suffer from yellow fever or malaria.[5]

Indeed for medicine the "lower animal" explanation was an easy explanation for an otherwise difficult paradox, created by the fact that differential reactions to fevers did not "square" with medical theory of the time. It had earlier fit neatly enough with "humoral" theory, which viewed illness as the result of bodily fluids out of balance. Any minor internal crisis such as teething or menstruation could precipitate a destruction of "humoral" equilibrium, to say nothing of a major external crisis such as change of climate. Thus whites, accustomed to the temperate zones, could expect serious "humoral" disruptions in the tropics, whereas the "humors" of blacks long accustomed to the tropics would remain placidly in balance.

However, as tropical medicine became more empirically oriented, it was noticed that whites were far more likely to contract fevers close to swamps or low-lying marshy areas where "a moist foggy atmosphere" was "exhaled," or around waterfronts where the air was laden with unpleasantness.[6] Humoral theory contained no really satisfactory explanation for this and physicians gradually began to hold that fevers were triggered by "poisonous effluvium" oozing from damp places and laden with "morbific and peccant matter."[7]

On the other hand, while this "miasmatic theory" was clearly more appropriate to the circumstances surrounding the onset of fevers in the Caribbean, it was no help in explaining why blacks so successfully escaped the "poisonous effluvium," since presumably it was color blind and poisonous to everyone human, black and white – unless of course the black was a lower grade of human, or even subhuman. This, then, was the direction in which the speculations of physicians and laymen alike began to drift, with blacks emerging from these speculations as brutish, animal-like, insensitive to pain, and certainly biologically different from whites.[8]

We have seen the important role fever resistance played in the blacks' enslavement; surely it played a significant role in racism as well. For whites, particularly by the time of the age of the Enlightenment, were forced to convince themselves that blacks were a lower species of man in order to rationalize their enslavement. Fever resistance provided a nucleus of such rationalization and black disease susceptibilities were grouped around this nucleus to form its substance. In addition to this dawning "scientific racism," however, there also arose the popular notion that blacks were a dirty, disease-ridden people who spread illnesses as well as suffered from them. On Hispaniola and Martinique quarantine measures were early adopted to keep out the diseases carried by slaves. The South Sea Company received considerable criticism from whites in Jamaica because it "us'd [sic] to land all their Negroes brought in here for refreshment, which infected the inhabitants with all their malignant fevers, smallpox and other dangerous distempers." In St. Domingue slave ships were restricted to an out-of-the way port after 1776, while Puerto Rico continually imposed the tightest possible restrictions on all vessels.[9]

The extent to which these popular, as well as "scientific" views of black disease susceptibilities and immunities shaped whites' view of blacks must remain a matter of speculation, just as the extent to which black-related diseases brought on by poor nutrition, poverty, and genetic heritage have continued to shape this view must remain in the speculative realm. One suspects, however, that they may have played much more of a role in white racism than has been imagined and quite possibly they still play more of a role than many whites in the Islands realize or care to acknowledge. On the other hand, the literature of the Caribbean does not reveal anything approaching the virulent scientific racism that was constructed by physicians in the Antebellum South and that has continued to tarnish North American race relations, not to mention black health care, throughout this century.[10]

We are on more solid ground when we begin to consider the ways in which fevers and black fever resistance shaped the demographic history of the West Indies. I pointed out in the first chapter of this study that yellow fever and malaria in tandem did much to assure an overwhelmingly black predominance in the region. This was not, however, solely the result of the massive importation of fever-resistant Africans. For in addition the fevers contributed to something of a white exodus from the Islands.

Illustrative is the example of Barbados, which in 1643 contained 37,000 whites, in 1655, 23,000 whites and 20,000 blacks, and in 1712 counted only 12,500 whites along with 42,000 blacks.[11] The usual explanation for the rapid decline in the number of island whites revolves around the onset of the sugar revolution, the growth of large plantations at the expense of small landholders, and concomitant dimming economic opportunity for most whites. That explanation ignores, however, the abrupt appearance on the island of yellow fever in 1647, which contributed significantly to the decline of the whites by killing upwards of 6,000 of them by 1655 and driving many more away. Needless to say, its periodic reappearance following these initial outbreaks did much to discourage white settlement on the island.[12]

This pattern of white population peaking and declining was followed in the Leewards and in Jamaica about three decades later.[13] It was as if some critical mass of whites was necessary to support yellow fever and malaria, and after the "mass" was achieved those illnesses began actively to reduce the population. Thus Pitman, looking at the British West Indies and the Danish Virgin Islands of the eighteenth century, concluded that the "white race" was suffering a net natural decrease; Abenon's examination of Guadeloupe revealed the same for that population, while Handler's study of Barbados in the early nineteenth century indicated that only the slaves were increasing; whites by contrast were decreasing.[14]

In fact, this pattern seems to have been the same everywhere in the Caribbean, save in the Spanish Antilles, where the white population grew from about 12,000 in 1510 to some 200,000 by the end of the eighteenth century.[15] In the nineteenth century, of course, massive white immigration from Catholic Europe, revolution-torn Haiti, and Latin America began to occur, and it was this migration that helped to ensure the survival of the European phenotype in the majority of the inhabitants in Puerto Rico, Cuba, and even the Dominican Republic.

But it is the growth of the white population prior to this nineteenth-century influx that is of special interest, for it bespeaks a significantly different demographic experience for the Iberians, which may indicate, as we suggested in Chapter 1, that the Iberians were more able to tolerate the West Indian fevers or that the Spaniards' willingness to interbreed with the Africans may have gained the products of these unions some fever protection.

Consider again the words of Abbé Raynal, who wrote that "of ten men that go into the Islands, four English die; three French, three Dutch, three Danes, and one Spaniard."[16] Certainly popular wisdom, which condemned 30 to 40 percent of the northern Europeans who ventured into the Caribbean to a quick death, must have given pause to many a potential immigrant, not to mention seamen who needed only to read some of the material written on the risks they ran to take up farming or almost any other occupation.[17]

But in addition to forestalling immigration, West Indian fevers doubtless had much to do with creating absenteeism among West Indian planters and consequently much to do with shaping both slave societies and Island governments. Indeed the phenomenon of absentee proprietors on Jamaica has been viewed as at the root of much slave mistreatment, responsible for the "gross mismanagement of the economic affairs of the Island," a major reason for the problem of "the gross lack of proper education in the Island," and to blame for the failure of the island to retain its "best people," who might have prevented economic stagnation.[18]

In the view of some, Jamaica was sorely in need of "best people." Many of its planters were "semiliterate," descendants of former indentured servants, the troops reaching the island have been described as "the very scum of the Earth," and "most of them fit only. . .to fill a pit with," while the lower-class whites were, according to Long at any rate, "the very dregs of the three Kingdoms."[19] The "best people," however, were those planters who, having made their fortune, left for England so as to live to enjoy it and let attorneys and overseers run the risk of a fever death while they ran the plantations. Yet this managerial group, which normally took a percentage of the profits, was more interested in a quick return from immediate output than it was in long-run growth. The basic formula for achieving a quick return was to minimize costs and maximize the application of labor, which meant underfed and overworked slaves.[20]

On the other hand, because of the disease environment, even planters who remained to manage their estates had a sense of immediacy about their role. From their early days on Barbados, to the end of slavery in Jamaica, Island whites have been portrayed as a hard-living, heavy-drinking lot, who "lived fast, spent recklessly, played desperately and died young," and in the words of Richard Dunn, "everyone seemed caught up in a race between quick wealth and a quick death."[21] Planters caught up in such a race, with dissipation a refuge from the reality of their actuarily precarious position, were not likely to be overly concerned with the lives of their slaves, or with the quality of those lives.

In fact, the island's disease environment must have helped to foster a planter callousness toward, or at the very least an indifference to, the welfare of their bondsmen – an attitude very much the antithesis of the paternalistic attitude that characterized so many planters in the southern states of North America. But there yellow fever and malaria were not so life threatening. True yellow fever made regular appearances at coastal cities such as New Orleans, Charleston, and Savannah, but during slavery, it seldom reached inland to destroy rural residents whereas it would sweep small islands such as Barbados, killing planters and urban dwellers alike. Moreover falciparum malaria was confined principally to coastal areas or swampy inland areas in the American South and the predominant malaria type in North America was the much less lethal vivax malaria.[22]

Thus, although yellow fever and malaria certainly militated against any reputation the South might have developed for salubrity, the area was infinitely less fever ridden than the islands of the West Indies. As a result North American planters could and did take a long-range view of their own future in both personal and economic terms, which meant relatively good treatment for their slaves.[23] By contrast, West Indian planters and their representatives, because of heavy white mortality in the Islands, too often acted in economic terms as if there were no tomorrow. The consequences for slaves were overwork, poor nutrition, and all too frequently, for the young in particular, no tomorrow.

Further influencing this shortsighted outlook of West Indian planters, as opposed to the more "mature" outlook of North American planters, may have been the fact that the latter were indeed more mature in terms of age. For in the Islands yellow fever and malaria, by virtue of their implacable attacks on white adults, created a very youthful population.[24]

Somewhat equidistant between United States planters who, for the most part, lived on their estates and Jamaican planters, who more often lived abroad, were the planters in Cuba, who evinced no desire to return to the mother country but did manifest the Latin love of city life. Thus Cuban planters were absentee in the sense that they resided in Havana, or Matanzas, entrusting the day-to-day management of the estate to others (often family members) and visiting their properties infrequently.[25] Observers split on their judgment of this system, with one claiming that the Cuban planter "may be considered quite as much an absentee as the Jamaica planter. . . ," while another thought this method, which removed the planter from his estate by just a few miles instead of thousands, quite effective in avoiding "the ruinous practice of absenteeism which prepared for the British West Indies that sudden ruin. . ."[26]

In truth, however, Cuban planters, absentee or not, also appear to have "unpaternalistically" opted for short-run profits with considerable slave wear and tear the result. Much of the reason seems to have stemmed from political and economic uncertainty created by the island's contraband slave trade.[27] But whatever the reason, absenteeism, by removing the planter from daily personal contact with his slaves, must also have removed him from maintaining that sense of personal responsibility for slave welfare that proved so effective in mitigating slavery in the United States and thus put Cuban slavery much closer to the Jamaican variety.

Interestingly, however, as with Jamaica, epidemiological factors may also have played a considerable part in Cuban absenteeism, even though at first blush it would appear that planters, by electing to reside in a yellow fever capital such as nineteenth-century Havana, had to be totally oblivious to matters of personal health. But by this time the "bundle" of fevers, which had terrorized whites, had been unraveled to reveal only two – yellow fever and malaria.[28] Cuban planters, who were overwhelmingly Creole born (or West Indian born in the case of those who had relocated after the revolution in St. Domingue), knew themselves to be immune to the former, knew also that their children should acquire their own immunity as early as possible, and consequently felt safe in Havana. Conversely they felt considerably less safe on their estates because of malaria, for as I pointed out earlier, Cuba was among those Caribbean Islands most plagued by falciparum malaria, a disease to which the planters were definitely not immune.

Perhaps because Cuba's "best people" took refuge in the cities of Cuba, absenteeism of the Cuban variety did not engender the attitude that the island was not a fit place to live. By contrast, Douglas Hall has argued convincingly that absenteeism in the British West Indies created precisely this notion – a notion that has continued to permeate the Islands and has, as a consequence, resulted in the loss of important human and physical resources.[29]

Thus the Caribbean disease environment not only shaped the institution of slavery in significant ways, but it also shaped perceptions of the Islands in ways that have continued to have an adverse impact upon them. We have seen as well how the differential experience with disease by race may have influenced racial perceptions, particularly the white's view of the black, spawning a legacy of white racism while poor black health has continued throughout this century to interact synergistically in perpetuating both.

Poverty and ignorance are also important ingredients in the unhappy mixture. A lack of education and consequently a lack of knowledge about nutrition, illness, and the body have kept old destructive customs regarding childbirth alive and maintained notions of disease inflicted by black magic or even by foods with "strong" or "weak" or "hot" or "cold" qualities. Consequently, a sick man who believes himself to be cursed can see no reason for consulting a medical doctor; Haitian babies, children, and teenagers are deprived of or deprive themselves of important nutriments in an effort to avoid all sorts of ailments ranging from teething to acne, while an alarming number of Jamaican mothers and "nanas" believe that food has nothing to do with the marasmus of children.[30]

Anyone who has spent time on the streets of Port-au-Prince or Kingston or even Bridgetown has seen more frank cases of protein energy malnutrition than he or she cares to recall; doubtless that individual is also familiar with the exasperation of whites pressed to explain those cases – an exasperation that is often rooted in racism. Indeed it is this exasperation on the part of whites and coloreds alike regarding black customs and beliefs that bears part of the responsibility for the "brain drain" of physicians that has taken place in the Caribbean (as it has in much of the Third World) and has resulted in more Haitian physicians, for example, practicing in Montreal than in all of Haiti or more Surinamer doctors in the Netherlands than in Surinam.[31]

Table 8. *Selected Demographic and Nutritional Data from the 1960s and*

Country	Population	Sex Ratio	"Mixed" or African in Origin (%)	Crude Birth Rate	Crude Death Rate	Infant Mortality Rate	Still Birth Rate (per 100,000 live births)
Barbados	265,200	90	95	25.2	8.2	39.4	14.4
Cuba	9,404,899	96	26	27.7	6.5	28.9	11.3
Dominican Republic	4,006,405	100	85	32.6	6.5	81.3	17.4
Haiti	4,918,695	94	99	45–50	20–25	—	—
Jamaica	1,813,594	96	95	28.9	6.0	36.7	11.1
Puerto Rico	1,329,949	96	20	28.3	5.9	42.0	13.4
United States	203,235,298	95	10	26.6	5.4	16.1	11.5

	Calcium (% RDA) (milligrams)		Iron (% RDA) (milligrams)		Vitamin B$_1$(% RDA) (milligrams)	
Barbados	654	(82)	15.4	(85.5)	1.24	(113.0)
Cuba	640	(80)	12.5	(69.4)	1.11	(101.0)
Dominican Republic	409	(51)	12.0	(67)	0.96	(87.2)
Haiti	347	(43)	19.6	(109)	1.49	(135.45)
Jamaica	568	(71)	14.0	(78)	1.09	(99.0)
Puerto Rico	—	—	—	—	—	—
United States	949	(120)	19.5	(108)	1.79	(163.0)

Sources: Claudio Veliz (ed.), *Latin America and the Caribbean: A Handbook* (New York, 1968); *The Caribbean Yearbook* (Toronto, 1978); *FAO Production Yearbook:* Vol. 33, 1979 (Rome, 1980); *Demographic Yearbook* (New York, 1980).

Yet the so-called medical brain drain has not been so damaging to the masses as one might expect.[32] For physicians trained in what is variously called Western or clinical or capitalist medicine are by inclination and training oriented toward the few who can afford them rather than the many who cannot, and toward the lavish application of technology to treat what might be termed "diseases of the well-to-do" who live long enough to acquire them (such as cancer or cardiovascular ailments), as opposed to preventive medicine, which, by focusing on nutrition and enteric diseases, can preserve so many lives of the very young.

Thus the classic example of a medical "brain drain" occurred in post-revolutionary Cuba, which witnessed the exodus of somewhere around half of the island's physicians. Yet paradoxically Cuba's health delivery system improved and stands today as the best in the region.[33] The major changes wrought by the Castro government were in the emphasis placed on preventive medicine, which made impressive gains in protecting the island's children from infectious and parasitic illnesses; on better nutrition for all segments of society, which has been

1970s for Six Caribbean Countries and for the United States

Number of Persons per Physician	Number of Persons per Hospital Bed	Calories	Fat (grams)	Protein (grams)	Protein (% of RDA)	Vegetable Protein (grams)	Animal Protein (grams)
				Nutritional Intake Daily			
2,600	170	3,172	91.7	82.7	(118.1)	36.2	46.5
1,200	170	2,636	54.2	68.7	(98.0)	35.1	33.6
1,600	440	2,107	49.5	42.9	(61.1)	28.2	14.7
10,600	1,800	2,040	29.5	49.1	(70.1)	42.0	7.1
2,000	235	2,663	64.0	70.5	(101.0)	38.0	32.5
1,300	200	—	—	—	—	—	—
500	62	3,537	163.8	106.2	(152.0)	33.5	72.7

Vitamin B_2 (% RDA) (milligrams)		Vitamin B_3 (% RDA) (milligrams)		Vitamin C (% RDA) (milligrams)		Vitamin A (% RDA) (Intern. units)	
1.31	(101.0)	17.7	(118)	62	(103.3)	1,840	(37.0)
1.30	(100.0)	14.2	(95)	87	(145.0)	1,914	(38.3)
0.89	(68.46)	11.5	(77)	109	(182.0)	2,649	(53.0)
0.85	(65.4)	12.7	(85)	116	(193.3)	4,231	(85.0)
1.07	(82.3)	15.0	(100)	104	(173.3)	2,383	(48.0)
—	—	—	—	—	—	—	—
2.11	(162.3)	23.7	(158)	145	(242.0)	3,136	(63.0)

less successful but at least seems to have eliminated most nutritional ailments of the young; and on a much more uniform distribution of a health delivery system that previously was concentrated largely in Havana.[34]

Ironically the Castro government has also helped to improve the health of West Indians throughout the Caribbean, for in its determination to avoid another Castro the United States has poured much money into Caribbean health and nutrition programs. This injection of funds has served to accelerate an ongoing trend of improving Caribbean health, which has continued throughout the century. Infant mortality rates, which averaged 303 per thousand live births in Barbados of 1919, and 162 in Puerto Rico of 1920–1921, and between 121 and 87 in Jamaica of 1939 to 1948, had plummeted to levels well below 50 per thousand by the late 1960s or early 1970s (see Table 8) and in the Caribbean today are (save for Hispaniola) for the most part below 20 per thousand live births.[35]

Yet one of the most tragic ironies in the tragically ironic story of the black diaspora to the Caribbean is that the region quite literally cannot afford this good health. For now that the age-old problem of high levels of black infant and child mortality is being resolved, the black population, which has grown steadily since slavery, is mushrooming and in turn accelerating another diaspora.[36]

This Caribbean diaspora has resulted in there being more Cubans in Miami than in Cuba's second city, Santiago de Cuba, while New York has become the "second city" for Jamaica, the Dominican Republic, Puerto Rico, Haiti, and Barbados. In addition London has taken in multitudes of West Indians since 1948, and many have also reached France and the Netherlands.[37] Unfortunately this emigration has reinforced the feeling that the Islands are not a good place to live and that the only way to get ahead is to get out.[38] Moreover it has increased the black's poor image of himself, at times reinforced "delusions of whiteness" among the expatriates, and thus proved destructive of both racial and national identity.[39]

Despite emigration, however, the Island populations are still swelling and with sharply reduced infant mortality will continue to swell; this, coupled with the continued preemption of land for sugar at the expense of food crops, will place impossible pressure on local resources and dictate the need for more and more imported food that the common people simply cannot afford. Put plainly, the black West Indians' vastly improved health has brought them face to face with the classic Malthusian dilemma and, unless the demographic picture changes radically and very soon, there is no good reason to believe that their health will not once more abruptly deteriorate.

In fact, because of pressure on the food supply, it must deteriorate for it seems certain that most of the improvement in Caribbean health has come about because of improved nutrition. To be sure the medical system has also played an important role. However that system in most islands, as was the case in pre-Castro Cuba, does not reach out much farther than the major cities, and consequently the physician and hospital-bed ratios shown in Table 8 are deceptive since both physicians and hospitals are chiefly urban phenomena.

Yet even though Caribbean nutrition is much improved, it remains a relative improvement only, while for a few countries such as Haiti, the improvement is mostly illusory. Haiti's per capita income for example is $260.00 annually. However, 80 percent of the population earns less than $30.00 annually.[40] Consequently the per capita intake of nutrients for Haiti shown in Table 8 must be similarly skewed, with most of the population in serious nutritional trouble.

Although not of the magnitude of the Haitian data, similar distortions apply to per capita nutritional data for other islands and the nutritional picture that Table 8 reveals is marginal even in these "best of times" for Caribbean blacks. Much nutritional intake is of a seasonal nature, as for example when vitamin C and A yielding fruits and vegetables are available. Thus vitamin C and A intakes in particular are considerably lower on a year-round basis. Calcium intakes are low and iron is undersupplied; indeed, with iron cooking untensils falling into disuse, modern blacks are, on the average, taking in significantly less iron than their slave ancestors. Fat intakes, although higher than during slavery, are still low enough to create absorption difficulties with the fat-soluble vitamins while B vitamin intake ranges from quite good to dangerously low, depending on the island.

Moreover, intakes of the B vitamin are largely due to the consumption of imported animal protein just as in the days of slavery, and one fears that as populations increase, this protein source will become even more unavailable to all but the middle- and upper-income groups able to afford the inevitably higher prices.

In 1950 enormous concern was expressed for "the problem of over population in the Caribbean [which] is a very serious one," and a deteriorating standard of living was envisoned unless measures were taken to reduce fertility on one hand and resettle "surplus" populations on the other.[41] A quarter of a century later birth rates remained "characteristic of pre-industrial societies" although migration had relieved enough of the pressure so that the Islands with tourist dollars at least were able actually to see a considerable increase in their standard of living.[42]

Today, however, migration itself is threatened. The recent Nationality Bill in England has made it clear that "black colonial subjects . . . are not wanted in the Mother Country," while the United States, in view of a world wide recession and massive cutbacks in social programs for its own citizens, "is again considering a very restrictive policy reminiscent of the 1920s."[43]

Should the migration safety valve be blocked, the catastrophic results would be sharply increased population pressure and sharply decreased economic means as remittances from the emigrants would dry up. One has no difficulty in envisioning the political and social consequences of this shattering of rising expectations.

The consequences in black health would be equally disastrous, as black West Indians after a brief respite would be once more reunited with their heritage of malnutrition. Infant mortality rates would again soar, birth weights would fall even lower, PEM would be rampant, with high child mortality the immediate consequence and intellectual decrement the long-term result. And once again Caribbean blacks would no doubt be blamed for their own misfortune.

NOTES

Abbreviations for Archival Sources

AHN   Archivo Historico Nacional (Madrid, Spain)
AGPR   Archivo General de Puerto Rico (San Juan, Puerto Rico)
IHB   International Health Board (North Tarrytown, New York)
RAC   Rockefeller Archive Center (North Tarrytown, New York)
RSC   Rockefeller Sanitary Commission (North Tarrytown, New York)
RSGPR   Records of the Spanish Governors of Puerto Rico

Journal Abbreviations

AA   *American Anthropologist*
ADC   *Archives of the Diseases of Childhood*
AfA   *African Affairs*
AHB   *Annals of Human Biology*
AHR   *American Historical Review*
AIHMT   *Anais do Instituto de Higiene e Medicina Tropical*
AIM   *Annals of Internal Medicine*
AIMT   *Anais do Instituto de Medicina Tropical*
AJA   *American Journal of Anthropology*
AJCN   *American Journal of Clinical Nutrition*
AJE   *American Journal of Epidemiology*
AJHG   *American Journal of Human Genetics*
AJM   *American Journal of Medicine*
AJPA   *American Journal of Physical Anthropology*
AJPH   *American Journal of Public Health*
BAJMPS   *British American Journal of Medical and Physical Science*
BCGP   *Boletim Cultural da Guiné Portuguesa*
BHM   *Bulletin of the History of Medicine*
BHPR   *Boletin Historico de Puerto Rico*
BJPSM   *British Journal of Preventive and Social Medicine*
BMJ   *British Medical Journal*
BWHO   *Bulletin of the World Health Organization*
CMJ   *Caribbean Medical Journal*
EHR   *Economic History Review*
HAHR   *Hispanic American Historical Review*
HB   *Human Biology*

JADA	*Journal of the American Dietetic Association*
JAfH	*Journal of African History*
JAMA	*Journal of the American Medical Association*
JCH	*Journal of Caribbean History*
JHM	*Journal of the History of Medicine and Allied Sciences*
JHMJ	*Johns Hopkins Medical Journal*
JHR	*Journal of Human Relations*
JIH	*Journal of Interdisciplinary History*
JN	*Journal of Nutrition*
JNH	*Journal of Negro History*
JNMA	*Journal of the National Medical Association*
JP	*Journal of Pediatrics*
JPA	*Journal of Physical Anthropology*
JTMH	*Journal of Tropical Medicine and Hygiene*
JTP	*Journal of Tropical Pediatrics*
NEJM	*New England Journal of Medicine*
NOMSJ	*New Orleans Medical and Surgical Journal*
PED	*Pediatrics*
PHR	*Public Health Reports*
PMJ	*Postgraduate Medical Journal*
PR	*Pediatric Research*
PSQ	*Political Science Quarterly*
RHA	*Revista de Historia de America*
SES	*Social and Economic Studies*
SSM	*Social Science and Medicine*
SSR	*Sociology and Social Research*
TRSTMH	*Transactions of the Royal Society of Tropical Medicine and Hygiene*
WAMJ	*West African Medical Journal*
WIJTMH	*West Indian Journal of Tropical Medicine and Hygiene*
WIMJ	*West Indian Medical Journal*
WMQ	*William and Mary Quarterly*

Part I. Introduction

1   Charles Robert Darwin, *The Origin of Species by Means of Natural Selection; or the Preservation of Favoured Races in the Struggle for Life* (London, 1859).

2   William H. McNeill, *Plagues and Peoples* (Garden City, N.Y., 1976).

3   Philip D. Curtin, *The Atlantic Slave Trade: A Census* (Madison, Wis., 1969), 25, 71, 84.

4   Dennis G. Carlson, "African Fever, Prophylactic Quinine, and Statistical Analysis: Factors in the European Penetration of a Hostile West African Environment," *BHM* 51 (1977), 386–96.

5   This scenario was first sketched for us by David Brion Davis and discussed in Kenneth F. Kiple and Virginia H. King, *Another Dimension to the Black Diaspora: Diet, Disease, and Racism* (New York, 1981), 67.

Chapter 1. The Peoples and Their Pathogens

1   G. Pouchet, *The Plurality of the Human Race*, 2d ed., tr. and ed. H. J. Beavau (London, 1864), 92.

2   Charles Darwin, *The Voyages of the Beagle* (New York, 1909), 459.

3   For the English migrants see, for example, Kenneth A. Lockridge, "The Population

of Dedham, Massachusetts, 1636–1736," *EHR* 9 (1966), 318–44 and "A New England Town: The First Hundred Years" (New York, 1970). See also John Demus, *A Little Commonwealth: Family Life in Plymouth Colony* (New York, 1970).

4   Alfred W. Crosby, "Ecological Imperialism: The Overseas Migration of Western Europeans as a Biological Phenomenon," *Texas Quarterly* 21 (1978), 11 and passim.

5   In the Dominican Republic, for example, the 1950 census classified 28.1 percent of the population as white, 11.5 percent as "Negro," and 60.4 percent as "colored." Cuba in 1943 classified 74 percent of its population as white. By contrast, the 1946 census of Barbados called 77 percent of its population black, 18 percent colored, and 5 percent white, percentages quite similar to those of Jamaica. See Dir. General de Estadística, *Censo nacional de población, 1960* (Dominican Republic, 1961), part 1; *Censo de 1943* (Havana, 1945), 746; David Lowenthal, "The Population of Barbados," *SES* 6 (1957), 467; George W. Roberts, *The Population of Jamaica* (Cambridge, Eng., 1957).

6   Good general histories of the peninsula can be found in Jaime Vicens Vives et al., *Historia social y economica de España y America*, 4 vols. (Barcelona, 1957–58) and A.H. de Oliveira Marques, *História de Portugal*, 3 vols. (Lisbon, 1972–73).

7   Philip D. Curtin, *The Atlantic Slave Trade: A Census* (Madison, Wis., 1969), 20; see also Herbert Klein (*The Middle Passage* [Princeton, 1978], 5–6 and n. 4), who cites estimates of as many as 140,000 slaves imported by the Portuguese to Europe between 1450 and 1505. For blacks in Iberia, see José António Saco, *Historia de la esclavitud de la raza africana en el nuevo mundo y en especial en los paises americo-hispanos*, 4 vols. (Madrid, 1974) 1:164; Victor Alba, *The Latin Americans* (New York, 1969), 24; and Ruth Pike, "Sevillan Society in the Sixteenth Century: Slaves and Freedmen," *HAHR* 47 (1967), 344–59.

8   The major work at present and the source of many of our speculations is that by Joaquín Villalba, *Epidemiologia española* . . . (Madrid, 1802). See also J.A.F. Ozanam, *Histoire médicale générale* . . . , 2d ed., 4 vols. (Paris, 1835).

9   Arno G. Motulsky and Jean M. Campbell-Kraut, "Population Genetics of Glucose-6-Phosphate Dehydrogenase Deficiency of the Red Cell," in *Proceedings of the Conference on Genetic Polymorphisms and Geographic Variations in Disease*, ed. Baruch S. Blumberg (New York, 1961), 175; Jacques M. May, "The Ecology of Malaria," in *Studies in Disease Ecology*, ed. Jacques M. May (New York, 1961), 198–9; Frank B. Livingstone, *Abnormal Hemoglobins in Human Populations* (Chicago, 1967), 306; E.H. Hudson, "Treponematosis and African Slavery," *British Journal of Venereal Disease* 40 (1964), 44.

10   Abbé Guillaume Raynal, *A Philosophical and Political History of the Settlements and Trade of the Europeans in the East and West Indies*, 8 vols., tr. J.O. Justamond (London, 1788) 5: 350–3.

11   Linda Newson, *Aboriginal and Spanish Colonial Trinidad*, (London, 1976), 120–3; John H. Parry (*The Spanish Seaborne Empire* [New York, 1966], 235) points out that although there was a steady increase of "the white or reportedly white population of the Indies," it is difficult to ascertain how much of this was due to migration and how much to a natural increase. Finally, in the words of Julian Bishko ("The Iberian Background of Latin American History: Recent Progress and Continuing Problems," *HAHR* 36 [1956], 64–65), "as far as the history of the Iberian population in relation to overseas colonization is concerned, almost everything remains to be done."

12   Save perhaps for syphilis. The debate over the origin of syphilis is hoary with age. Indeed it seems as if the Europeans arrived in the New World one day and began arguing about how, when, and where they had contracted it the next. At first the facts appeared to credit the American Indians for cursing Europeans, and then the world, with at least one major-league pathogen, for the illness supposedly made its initial widespread European appearance in 1493–94 during those "Italian wars" that pitted the Spanish against the French. Outraged at becoming infected, everyone initially blamed the Italians, who were closest, by calling it "the disease of Naples."

However, the outbreak was so virulent among the French army, which included German, Swiss, Hungarian, Polish, and English contingents, that they were forced to abandon the military campaign. The demobilized troops soon spread the disease all over Europe, whereupon it became known as the "French disease." Yet there were some who noted the coincidence of the outbreak of epidemic syphilis with the return of Columbus and his men from their first New World voyage, giving birth to the Columbian theory of the origin of syphilis. It reigned for centuries with little opposition for a very good reason. Syphilis acted like a new disease in Europe by following the classic course of a new disease among inexperienced peoples. It raged among Europeans for a time with extraordinary virulence and then gradually became milder in subsequent generations, so that by the eighteenth century it had settled down to become more or less the disease we know today.

The antithesis of the Columbian theory is that the disease did exist in Europe prior to 1492 but in a less virulent state. Yet largely because most European physicians felt that they were dealing with a new disease, this notion made little headway. At least it made no headway until this century when a new theory was advanced to cast the entire question into confusion by lending support to a European, or perhaps better, a non-American origin of the disease. As a result, we now have a third position on the origin of syphilis somewhat intermediate between the older opposing views.

This so-called Unitarian position derived from the discovery that the spirochetes causing syphilis and yaws are indistinguishable under a microscope and cannot be differentiated in a laboratory. One conclusion flowing from this discovery is that these pathogens are very closely related. Another conclusion – that of the "Unitarians" – is that they are the same pathogen, with yaws and syphilis being different manifestations of the same disease, which they call treponematosis. According to this theory, venereal syphilis evolved out of endemic syphilis, which in turn evolved out of the original manifestation of the disease – yaws. Venereal syphilis was just making its first European appearance when Columbus returned from the New World and consequently he and his men received the blame for importing it.

Against this argument, however, are bone lesions, very probably the work of syphilis, which have been found in pre-Columbian Indian remains. Moreover the Spaniards, who quizzed the Indians about their history with the disease, wrote that they swore to have suffered from syphilis since time immemorial. Finally the Spaniards claimed that the Indians seemed to suffer much less from the illness than they did and tolerance for a pathogen normally suggests a long acquaintance with it. Therefore America's claim to being the homeland of the disease remains a strong one. Yet the arguments of the "Unitarians" are also very convincing. It may be that Columbus joined together two worlds, both of which included syphilis in their disease environments, but that the infection was quite new in the Old World, and quite old in the New. Our summary is based largely on "The Early History of Syphilis: A Reappraisal" by Alfred W. Crosby, Jr., in his study of *The Columbian Exchange: Biological and Cultural Consequences of 1492* (Westport, Conn., 1972), 122–64. For a summation of the case for an Old World origin of syphilis, see Charles Clayton Dennie, *The Gift of Columbus* (Kansas City, Mo., 1936), 13–35 and passim. For a brief but cogent statement of the claims for a New World origin, consult Saul Jarcho, "Some Observations on Disease in Prehistoric North America," *BHM* 38 (1964), 11–15. And for the Unitarian argument, see E.H. Hudson, "Treponematosis," in chap. 27C in *Oxford Medicine* (London, 1946); "Treponematosis and Man's Social Evolution," *AA* 67 (1965), 885–901; "Treponematosis in Perspective," *BWHO* 32 (1965), 735–48; Thomas A. Cockburn, "The Origin of the Treponematoses," *BWHO* 24 (1961), 221–8. Finally, see Francisco Guerra, "Medicina colonial en Hispanoamerica," in *Historia universal de la medicina*, 7 vols., eds. Pedro Lain Entralgo et al. (Barcelona, 1971–75) 4: 346.

13   Henry F. Dobyns, "Estimating Aboriginal American Populations: An Appraisal of

Techniques with a New Hemispheric Estimate," *Current Anthropology* 7 (1966), 415; Francisco López de Gómara, *Historia general de las Indias* (Madrid, 1941), fol. xxvi, verso xxvii, recto xvi.

14 Crosby, *Columbian Exchange*, 39; C.W. Dixon, *Smallpox* (London, 1962), 192; P.M. Ashburn, *The Ranks of Death: A Medical History of the Conquest of America* (New York, 1947). For a quick appreciation of the Indian holocaust wrought by European disease, see also Woodrow Borah and Sherburne F. Cook, *The Aboriginal Population of Central Mexico on the Eve of the Spanish Conquest* (Berkeley, 1963); Sherburne Cook and Woodrow Borah, *Essays in Population History: Mexico and the Caribbean* (Berkeley, Calif., 1971); Henry F. Dobyns, "An Outline of Andean Epidemic History to 1720," *BHM* 37 (1963), 493–515; and José G. Rigau-Perez, "Smallpox Epidemics in Puerto Rico during the Prevaccine Era (1518–1803)," *JHM* 37 (1982), 424–7. We have no precise data to document the destructiveness of the hurricane of diseases that swept the original West Indians. But we can make educated guesses as to the extent of the catastrophe based on the experience of other peoples for whom we do have records. Smallpox, for example, when introduced to Iceland in 1707 killed 18,000 out of a total population of 50,000. If the New World's first "official" smallpox epidemic – that of 1518 – made a similar levy on the already disappearing Indians, then the terrible depopulation reported by early chroniclers such as Oviedo, Las Casas, and Herrera for Hispaniola and Cuba do not seem all that exaggerated. Moreover measles, when first introduced to the Fiji Islands in 1875, killed 40,000 of a population of 150,000. Because of this obvious virulence among a virgin people, the disease probably passed in the Americas as smallpox, as well as joining forces with it to deplete further the aboriginal populations of the Caribbean.

Finally these diseases had to be introduced and reintroduced from without, whereas vivax malaria, when it arrived as it probably did with the first Europeans, came to stay. Thus malaria may have been a factor in the declining Indian population when smallpox and measles first reached the Americas. An example of the impact of malaria alone on an indigenous population with no resistance is offered by the island of Mauritius where, during the years 1867–68 in Port Louis alone, over 22,000 of a population of 80,000 died within a thirteen-month period after malaria was introduced. See Gonzalo Fernández de Oviedo, *Historia general y natural de las Indias, islas y tierra firme del mar oceano* . . . , 4 vols. (Madrid, 1851–55), 1:103; Bartolomé de las Casas, *Historia de las Indias*, 3 vols. (Mexico, 1951), 3:270, 558; Antonio de Herrera y Tordesillas, *Historia general de los hechos de los Castellanos en las islas y tierra firme en el mar oceano*, 17 vols. (Buenos Aires, 1945), 3:374–6. For Cuba's 1529 epidemic, see Ramiro Guerra y Sanchez et al. (*Historia de la nacion Cubana*, 10 vols. [Havana, 1952], 1:229–30), who provides a mortality ratio of one Indian out of three. However, see also Henry F. Dobyns ("An Outline of Andean Epidemic History," *BHM* 37 [1963], 498), who suggests that it was measles not smallpox that was epidemic in Cuba in 1529. For Santo Domingo on Hispaniola, Las Casas (*Historia* 3:558) reported a decline of the Indian population from 60,000 in 1508 to between 13,000 and 14,000 by 1514. For smallpox in Puerto Rico, see "Los primeros casos de viruelas en la isla," *BHPR* 9 (1922), 147. For smallpox in Iceland and other examples of its staggering impact on virgin peoples, see E. Wagner Stearn and Allen E. Stearn, *The Effect of Smallpox on the Destiny of the Amerindian* (Boston, 1945), 14 and passim.

15 William H. McNeill (*Plagues and Peoples* [Garden City, N.Y., 1976], 51), for example points out that humans share about thirty-five diseases with horses, forty-two with pigs, forty-six with sheep and goats, fifty with cattle, and sixty-five with dogs. Among these are influenza (shared with hogs), smallpox (related to cowpox), and measles (probably related to rinderpest and/or canine distemper).

16 McNeill, ibid., gives a cogent and well-reasoned description of this process.

17 Sherburne F. Cook, "The Incidence and Significance of Disease among the Aztecs

and Related Tribes," *HAHR* 36 (1946), 220–35. See Thomas A. Cockburn ("The Evolution of Infectious Disease," *International Record of Medicine* 172 [1959], 493–508) for theories on the development of disease resistance. But see also Thomas D. Dublin and Baruch S. Blumberg, "An Epidemiologic Approach to Inherited Disease Susceptibility," *PHR* 74 (1961), 499–503.

18 Macfarlane Burnet and David O. White, *Natural History of Infectious Disease* (Cambridge, Eng., 1972), 83; Alfred W. Crosby, "Virgin Soil Epidemics as a Factor in the Aboriginal Depopulation in America," *WMQ* 33 (1976), 294.

19 Crosby, ibid., 295 and passim.

20 Crosby, "Ecological Imperialism," 21.

21 For good introductions to man's diseases and the means by which peoples have developed immunities to them, see Burnet and White, *History of Infectious Disease,* 78, 83, and passim; Francis L. Black, "Infectious Diseases in Primitive Societies," *Science* 187 (1975), 515–18; Cockburn, "Evolution of Infectious Disease," 493–508; and Abraham M. Lillienfeld, *Foundations of Epidemiology* (New York, 1976).

22 Judith Friedlander, "Malaria and Demography in the Lowlands of Mexico: An Ethnohistorical Approach," in *Culture, Disease, and Healing,* ed. David Landy (New York, 1977), 113–19; Woodrow Borah and Sherburne F. Cook, *The Aboriginal Population of Central Mexico on the Eve of the Spanish Conquest* (Berkeley, Calif., 1963), 89 and passim; Cook, "Incidence and Significance of Disease," 233; J.H. Parry and P.M. Sherlock, *A Short History of the West Indies,* 3d ed. (London, 1971), vi–vii; McNeill, *Plagues and Peoples,* 213–14. It should be noted here for the sake of accuracy that in Puerto Rico and a few of the Eastern Caribbean islands some Arawaks and Caribs managed to survive until the nineteenth century.

23 Sir Philip Sherlock, "The West Indian Experience," in *Eighteenth-Century Florida and the Caribbean,* ed. Samuel Proctor (Gainesville, Fla., 1976), 44–5; Eugenio Fernández Méndez, "Las Encomiendas y esclavitud de los indios de Puerto Rico, 1508–1550," *Anuario de estudios Americanos* 23 (1966), 377–443; Edwin A. Levine, "The Seed of Slavery in the New World: An Examination of the Factors Leading to the Impressment of Indian Labor in Hispaniola," *RHA* 69 (1965), 1–68.

24 Kenneth F. Kiple, "The Negro in Spanish America," in *Encyclopedia of Latin America,* ed. Helen Delpar (New York, 1974), 409–13.

25 Leslie B. Rout, Jr., *The African Experience in Spanish America* (Cambridge, Eng., 1976), 23; Saco, *Historia de la esclavitud* 1:169; Las Casas, *Historia* 3:275–6.

26 Magnus Mörner, *Race Mixture in the History of Latin America* (Boston, 1967), 19; Manuel Moreno Fraginals, "Africa in Cuba: A Quantitative Analysis of the African Population in the Island of Cuba," in *Comparative Perspectives on Slavery in New World Plantation Societies,* eds. Vera Rubin and Arthur Tuden (New York, 1977), 198; Friedlander, "Malaria and Demography," 118.

27 Great Britain Naval Intelligence Division, *French West Africa,* vol. 1: *The Federation* (Oxford, 1943), 158; William Malcolm Hailey, *An African Survey* (London, 1957), 1122; George H.T. Kimble, *Tropical Africa,* 2 vols. (New York, 1960), 2: 47; Stevenson Lyle Cummins, *Primitive Tuberculosis* (London, 1939), 14–22; John Charles Caldwell (ed.), *Population Growth and Socio-Economic Change in West Africa* (New York, 1975), 4; K. David Patterson and Gerald W. Hartwig, "The Disease Factor: An Introductory Overview," in *Disease in African History,* eds. Gerald W. Hartwig and K. David Patterson (Durham, N.C., 1978). 3–21; and Kenneth F. Kiple and Virginia H. King, *Another Dimension to the Black Diaspora: Diet, Disease, and Racism* (New York, 1981), chap. 1. For a look at West Africa through eighteenth- and nineteenth-century eyes, see John Atkins, *The Navy Surgeon . . .* (London, 1758) and William Freeman Daniell, *Sketches of the Medical Topography and Native Diseases of the Gulf of Guinea, Western Africa* (London, 1849). Indispensable to a consideration of West African disease are August Hirsch, *Handbook of Geographical and Historical Pathology,* 3 vols. (London,

1883–86) and R. Hoeppli, *Parasitic Disease in Africa and the Western Hemisphere: Early Documentation and Transmission by the Slave Trade* (Basel, 1969).

28 The term "white man's grave" was first used by F. Harrison Rankin in his book *The White Man's Grave: A Visit to Sierra Leone, in 1834* (London, 1836).

29 Kenneth G. Davies, "The Living and The Dead: White Mortality in West Africa 1684–1732," in *Race and Slavery in the Western Hemisphere: Quantitative Studies*, eds. Stanley L. Engerman and Eugene D. Genovese (Princeton, N.J., 1975), 97; H.M. Feinberg, "New Data on European Mortality in West Africa: The Dutch on the Gold Coast, 1719–1760," *JAfH* 15 (1974), 362–67; Philip D. Curtin, "Epidemiology and the Slave Trade," *PSQ* 83 (1968), 202–3; Daniell, *Sketches*, 11–12, 60, 72; William Pym, *Observations upon . . . Yellow Fever* (London, 1848), 270 and passim.

30 Curtin, "Epidemiology," 203–4.

31 Michael Gelfand, "Rivers of Death in Africa," *Central African Journal* (supplement), 11 (1965), 24–25.

32 Unless otherwise specified, the following discussion is based on Kiple and King, *Another Dimension*, chap. 1, to which the reader is referred for a more detailed discussion of black resistance to malaria. For more specialized studies on various aspects of the problem, consult Louis H. Miller and Richard Carter, "A Review: Innate Resistance in Malaria," *Experimental Parasitology* 40 (1965), 132–46; Graham R. Serjeant, *The Clinical Features of Sickle Cell Disease* (Amsterdam, 1974); Frank B. Livingstone, "Malaria and Human Polymorphisms," *Annual Review of Genetics* 5 (1971), 33–64; P.C.C. Garnham, *Malaria Parasites and Other Haemosporidia* (Oxford, 1966); Bracha Ramot et al. eds., *Genetic Polymorphisms and Diseases in Man* (New York, 1974); William H. Bullock and Pongrac N. Jilly, "Hematology," in *Textbook of Black Related Diseases*, ed. Richard A. Williams (New York, 1975), 199–316; and B. Ringelhann et al., "A New Look at the Protection of Hemoglobin AS and AC Against *Plasmodium Falciparum* Infection: A Census Tract Approach," *AJHG* 28 (1976), 270–9.

33 Louis H. Miller, "Malaria," in *Infectious Disease*, ed. Paul D. Hoeprich (Hagerstown, Md., 1972), 1120. To a large extent longevity is determined by the environment of the victim of sickle cell anemia because of a heightened susceptibility to intercurrent diseases. Thus, in underdeveloped regions of Africa, most die in early infancy. In the United States and the West Indies, on the other hand, only about half of the victims die before age twenty, although most of the rest are dead by ages forty to forty-five. Robert B. Scott, "Health Care Priority and Sickle Cell Anemia," *JAMA* 214 (1970), 731–4; Arno G. Motulsky, "Frequency of Sickling Disorders in U.S. Blacks," *NEJM* 288 (1973), 31–3; Serjeant, *Sickle Cell*, 58.

34 However, studies conducted on American blacks in Vietnam finally established conclusively that G6PD deficiency did confer protection against falciparum malaria. See, for example, Thomas Butler, "G6PD Deficiency and Malaria in Black Americans in Vietnam," *Military Medicine* 138 (1973), 153–5.

35 Bullock and Jilly, "Hematology," 283–4; N. Nagaratnam, Chitra S. Subawickrama, and Therese Kariyawasam, "Viral Infections in G6PD Deficiency," *Tropical and Geographical Medicine* 22 (1970), 179–82; Ernest Beutler, "Glucose-6-Phosphate Dehydrogenase Deficiency," in *Hematology*, 2d ed., eds., William J. Williams et al. (New York, 1977), 466–79; Arno G. Motulsky, "Theoretical and Clinical Problems of Glucose-6-Phosphate Dehydrogenase Deficiency: Its Occurrence in Africans and its Combination with Hemoglobinopathy," in *Abnormal Haemoglobins in Africa*, ed. J.H.P. Jonxis (Philadelphia, 1965), 146, 157.

36 Serjeant, *Sickle Cell*, 28, 34–43; Roger A. Lewis, *Sickle States: Clinical Features in West Africans* (Accra, Ghana, 1970), 39–40.

37 For abnormal hemoglobins in the Caribbean, see the appropriate tables in Livingstone, *Abnormal Hemoglobins*; see also L.N. Went et al., "The Incidence of Abnor-

mal Haemoglobins in Jamaica," *Nature* 180 (1957), 1131–2; Serjeant, *Sickle Cell*, 36–7, tables; L.N. Went and J.E. MacIver, "Investigations of Abnormal Haemoglobins in West Jamaica" *WIMJ* 5 (1956), 247–55; D.W. Rogers et al., "Early Deaths in Jamaican Children with Sickle Cell Disease," *BMJ* 1 (1978), 1515–16; R.M. Suarez et al., "Distribution of Abnormal Hemoglobins in Puerto Rico and Survival Studies of Red Blood Cells Using Cr^{51}," *Blood* 14 (1959), 255–61; Hortensia Molino Franchossi y Edmundo Lopez Hidalgo, "Incidencia de anemia por sickle-cell durante los dos ultimos años en el hospital de Pinar del Rio," *Revista Cubana de Pediatria* 37 (1965), 477–8; L. Eredero et al, "Development of a Method of Screening for Hemoglobins for the Purpose of Genetic Consultation in Cuba–Results of an Analysis of 24,000 Blood Samples," *Genetika* 14 (1978), 1079–84; H. Fabritius, J. Milan, and Y. Le Corroller, "Depistage systematique des hemoglobinopathies chez les donneurs de sang de la Guadeloupe (Antilles Françaises)," *Revue Française de Transfusion et d'Immuno-hematologie* 21 (1978), 937–50; and M.U. Henry, "The Hemoglobinopathies in Trinidad," *CMJ* 25 (1963), 26–40.

38   Hirsch, *Handbook* 1:230.

39   I.L. Firschein, "Population Dynamics of the Sickle Cell Trait in the Black Caribs of British Honduras, Central America," *AJHG* 13 (1961), 233–54. Examples of how racial mixing does reduce the frequency of sickle trait can be found throughout the Caribbean. In a group of Afro-Caucasian schoolchildren in Jamaica, for example, the trait was found in only 5.6 percent of those tested (as opposed to a black Jamaican frequency of at least 11 percent). In Puerto Rico where the population is more "brown" than black or white, studies have uncovered a range of frequencies between 2.3 and 5.5 percent, while among the "colored" population of Havana the rate was 5.6 percent. See James V. Neel, "Inferences Concerning Evolutionary Forces from Genetic Data," in *Genetic Polymorphisms*, eds. Ramot et al., 403; see also T. Edward Reed, "Caucasian Genes in American Negroes," *Science* 165 (1969), 762–8; and Serjeant, *Sickle Cell*, 36–7, tables.

40   L.N. Went and J.E. MacIver, "Thalassemia in the West Indies," *Blood* 17 (1961), 166–79; Motulsky and Campbell-Kraut, "Population Genetics," 169.

41   However, G6PD deficiency occurring among West Africans seems to be produced by a gene that maintains a higher enzyme level than is maintained in Caucasians with G6PD deficiency, and consequently the condition is not as dangerous to blacks. For the "Negro type" of G6PD deficiency, see Motulsky, "Theoretical and Clinical Problems," 144.

42   Louis H. Miller et al., "The Resistance Factor to *Plasmodium Vivax* in Blacks; The Duffy-Blood-Group Genotype, $F_y^a\ F_y^b$," *NEJM* 295 (1976), 302–4.

43   Ibid; S.G. Welch, I.A. McGregor and K. Williams, "The Duffy Blood Group and Malaria Prevalence in Gambian West Africas," *TRSTMH* 71 (1977), 295–6.

44   And they were probably even better prepared than we know at present. Lucio Luzzatto ("Studies of Polymorphic Traits for the Characterization of Populations: African Populations South of the Sahara," in *Genetic Polymorphisms*, eds., Ramot et al., 65) points out that at least seven genes at present have been identified as "uniquely" African. Some are explicable now in terms of malaria protection. Others probably will be in the future. For an example of efforts in this direction, see S.K. Martin et al., "Low Erythrocyte Pyridoxal-Kinase Activity in Blacks: Its Possible Relation to *Falciparum Malaria*," *Lancet* 1:8062 (1978), 466–8.

45   For malaria in Europe see Arturo Castiglioni, *Storia della Medicina* (Milano, 1927), 566 and passim.

46   For varying views on the question of malaria's arrival in the New World, see Frederick L. Dunn, "On the Antiquity of Malaria in the Western Hemisphere," *HB* 37 (1965), 385–93; Jarcho, "Observations on Disease," 1–18 and L.J. Bruce-Chwatt, "Paleogenesis and Paleo-epidemiology of Primate Malaria," *BWHO* 32 (1965), 363–87.

47 W.H.R. Lumsden, "Probable Insect Vectors of Yellow Fever Virus, from Monkey to Man, in Bwamba County, Uganda," *Bulletin of Entomological Research* 42 (1951), 317 and passim; James W. Mosley, "Yellow Fever," in *Infectious Disease*, ed. Hoeprich, 655; Telford H. Work, "Virus Diseases in the Tropics," in *Manual of Tropical Medicine*, eds. George W. Hunter, Wiliam W. Frye, and J. Clyde Swartzwelder (Philadelphia, 1956), 31; Richard M. Taylor, "Epidemiology," in *Yellow Fever*, ed. George Strode (New York, 1951), 451 and passim; Hailey, *African Survey*, 1131.

48 William P. MacArthur, "Historical Notes on Some Epidemic Diseases Associated with Jaundice," *British Medical Bulletin* 13 (1957), 146–9.

49 Kenneth F. Kiple and Virginia H. Kiple, "Black Yellow Fever Immunities, Innate and Acquired as Revealed in the American South," *Social Science History* 1 (1977), 419–36, and Kiple and King, *Another Dimension*, chap. 2.

50 Kiple and King, *Another Dimension*, chap. 2.

51 Taylor, "Epidemiology," 592–3; McNeill, *Plagues and Peoples*, 213; Scott, "Influence of the Slave Trade," 178.

52 Work, "Virus Diseases," 31; A.W. Brown, "Yellow Fever, Dengue and Dengue Haemorrhagic Fever," in *A World Geography of Human Diseases*, ed. G. Melvyn Howe (London, 1977), 298–9.

53 Kiple and Kiple, "Yellow Fever Immunities," 426.

54 Among these conditions may have been the presence of sugar cane cultivation. See this interesting argument by James D. Goodyear, "The Sugar Connection: A New Perspective on the History of Yellow Fever," *BHM* 52 (1978), 5–21. But early authorities such as Ozanam (*Histoire médicale* 1:227) and even Carlos Juan Finlay (*Obras completas*, 4 vols. [Havana, 1964], 2:111–18) held yellow fever responsible for many white deaths during Spain's first years on Hispaniola. Later authorities, however, have discredited this view. See especially Carter, *Yellow Fever*, passim and Ashburn, *Ranks of Death*, 129–40. Nonetheless there seems to be a consensus of sorts that yellow fever's "unofficial" Caribbean debut occurred in Puerto Rico at the end of the sixteenth century (Sir Harry Johnson, *The Negro in the New World* [New York, 1919], 211–12, note). For this and other possible early New World yellow fever epidemics, see Francisco Guerra, "The Influence of Disease on Race, Logistics and Colonization in the Antilles," *JTMH* 69 (1966), 31 and M. Foster Farley, *An Account of History of Strangers' Fever in Charleston 1699–1876* (Washington, D.C., 1978), 13. For a listing of the "official" epidemics, see Hirsch, *Handbook* 1:318–31.

55 Most writers have the disease making its New World debut in the Yucatan in 1648. Yet when Richard Ligon (*A True and Exact History of the Island of Barbados* [London, 1657]) arrived in Barbados in 1647 he found the disease raging there. From Barbados it spread to St. Kitts and Guadeloupe (Alan Burns, *History of the British West Indies* [London, 1954], 32), and then to the Yucatan (Diego Lopez de Cogolludo, *Historia de Yucatan*, 2 vols. [Mexico, 1867] 2:561–2). It reached Cuba the following year (Jorge Leroy y Cassa, *La primera epidemia de fiebre amarilla en la Habana, en 1649* [Habana, 1930] and Jacobo de la Pezuela y Lobo, *Historia de la isla de Cuba*, 4 vols. [Madrid, 1868] 2:106–9).

56 John Poyer, *The History of Barbados* (London, 1808), 155; "Antiguedad del vomito negro en la isla de Cuba (estracto de una memoria escrita en Cuba en 1703)," *Repertorio médico-habanero y boletín científico* 2 (1842), 30; Jorge Leroy y Cassa, *La mortandad en la Habana durante el siglo XVII* (Habana, 1930).

57 Gary Puckrein, "Climate, Health and Black Labor in the English Americas," *American Studies* 13 (1979), 189–90; Ashburn, *Ranks of Death*, 40. This is not to say that whites could not and did not acquire immunities to both malaria and yellow fever. See Chapter 10.

58 Scott, "Influence of the Slave Trade," 183–4.

59 Cockburn, "Origin of Treponematoses," 225.

60   George L. Lythcott, Calvin Sinnette, and Donald R. Hopkins, "Pediatrics," in *Textbook of Black Related Diseases*, ed. Williams, 159; Julian Herman Lewis, *The Biology of the Negro* (Chicago, 1942), 255–7; George P. Paul, *Report on Ankylostomiasis Infection Survey of Barbados* (New York, 1917), 49.

61   R.R. Willcox, "Venereal Diseases," in *Geography of Human Diseases*, ed. Howe, 208.

62   Matthew Gregory Lewis, *Journal of a West Indian Proprietor, 1815–1817* (London, 1929), 144.

63   Michael Gelfand, *The Sick African*, 3d ed. (Capetown, 1957), 137–54; Thomas Dancer, *The Medical Assistant or Jamaica Practice of Physic . . .* (Kingstown, Jamaica, 1809), 239.

64   R. Storrs, "The White Man's Grave in the Eighteenth Century," *Journal of the Royal Army Medical Corps* 53 (1927), 227; Hirsch, *Handbook* 3:614–16.

65   Lythcott, Sinnette, and Hopkins, "Pediatrics," in *Textbook of Black-Related Diseases*, ed. Williams, 163.

66   Todd L. Savitt, *Medicine and Slavery: the Health Care of Blacks in Ante-Bellum Virginia* (Urbana, Ill,. 1978), 75.

67   Edward E. Mays, "Pulmonary Diseases," in *Textbook of Black Related Diseases*, ed. Williams, 416.

68   Thomas Adams and Benjamin G. Covino, "Racial Variations to a Standardized Cold Stress," *Journal of Applied Physiology* 12 (1958), 9–12; Paul T. Baker, "American Negro-White Differences in the Thermal Insulative Aspects of Body Fat," *HB* 31 (1959), 316–24 and "Racial Differences in Heat Tolerance," *AJPA* 16 (1958), 287–305; John H. Phillips and George E. Burch, "A Review of Cardiovascular Diseases in the White and Negro Races," *Medicine* 39 (1960), 245–6.

Chapter 2. West African Diet and Disease

1   S.M. Garn, "Culture and the Direction of Human Evolution," *HB* 35 (1963), 235.

2   R.G. Hendrickse, "Some Observations on the Social Background to Malnutrition in Tropical Africa," *AFA* 65 (1966), 342.

3   For the growth "lag" in children, see John Spurgeon, E. Matilde Meredith, and Howard V. Meredith, "Body Size and Form of Children of Predominantly Black Ancestry Living in West and Central Africa, North and South America, and The West Indies," *AHB* 5 (1978), 234. For adults, see P.B. Eveleth and J.M. Tanner, *Worldwide Variations in Human Growth* (Cambridge, Eng., 1976), chap. 4. Malnutrition as West Africa's most pressing problem has been a constant theme over the last four decades or so. See, for example, C.K. Meek, W.M. Macmillan, and E.R.J. Hussey, *Europe and West Africa: Some Problems and Adjustments* (London, 1940), 32–3; George H.T. Kimble, *Tropical Africa*, 2 vols. (New York, 1960), 2:41; and Bo Valquist, "Nutrition as a Priority in African Development," *AJCN* 25 (1972), 345–7.

4   Phyllis Eveleth and J.M. Tanner, *Worldwide Variations in Human Growth* (Oxford, 1976), 274; Albert Damon, "Secular Trend in Height and Weight within Old American Families at Harvard, 1870–1965. 1. Within Twelve Four-Generation Families," *AJPA* 29 (1968), 45–50; J.M. Tanner, "Early Maturation in Man," *Scientific American* 218 (1968), 26–7.

5   Robert W. Fogel, Stanley L. Engerman, and James Trussell, "Exploring the Uses of Data on Height," *Social Science History* 6 (1982), 416; Robert W. Fogel and Stanley L. Engerman, "Recent Findings in the Study of Slave Demography and Family Structure," *SSR* 63 (1979), 566–89; Barry Higman, "Growth in Afro-Caribbean Slave Populations," *AJPA* 50 (1979), 373–85; Manuel Moreno Fraginals, "Africa in Cuba: A Quantitative Analysis of the African Population in the Island of Cuba," in *Comparative Perspectives on Slavery in New World Plantation Societies*, eds. Vera Rubin and Arthur Tuden (New York, 1977), 187–204; David Eltis, "Nutritional Trends in Africa and the Americas: Heights of Africans, 1819–1839," *JIH* 12 (1982), 453–75; Gerald

Friedman, "The Heights of Slaves in Trinidad," *Social Science History*, 6 (1982), 482–515.

6 William Greulich, "Growth of Children of the Same Race Under Different Environmental Conditions," *Science* 127 (1958), 515–16; J.M. Tanner, "Growing Up," *Scientific American* 229 (1973), 35–43.

7 This is not to exclude other nutritional deficiencies such as provitamin A, iodine, or calcium/phosphorus, which have been implicated in retarding physical growth. It is only to single out what seems clearly to be the most widespread and pervasive factor.

8 A good and readable introduction to proteins is Aaron M. Altschul, *Proteins, Their Chemistry and Politics* (New York, 1965). For a more complex examination, see Anthony A. Albanese, *Protein and Amino Acid Nutrition* (New York, 1959).

9 Altschul, *Proteins*, 118; A.E. Harper, "Basic Concepts," in *Improvements of Protein Nutrition*, ed. Committee on Amino Acids, Food and Nutrition Board, National Research Council (Washington, D.C., 1974), 7, 12, 15.

10 Great Britain, Economic Advisory Council, Committee on Nutrition in the Colonial Empire, *Nutrition in the Colonial Empire*, 2 parts (London, 1939) 1:13, 29 and 2:33ff; Tadeuz Lewicki, *West African Food in the Middle Ages: According to Arabic Sources* (London, 1974), 79; Elizabeth Isichei, *A History of the Igbo People* (New York, 1976), 224; Juan Papadakis, *Crop Ecological Survey in West Africa* (*Liberia, Ivory Coast, Ghana, Togo, Dahomey, Nigeria*), 2 vols. (Rome, 1966) 1:72; James L. Newman, "Dietary and Nutritional Conditions," in *Contemporary Africa: Geography and Change*, eds. C. Gregory Knight and James L. Newman (Englewood Cliffs, N.J., 1976), 71–80; Pierre Cantrelle, "Mortality," in *Population Growth and Socio-Economic Change in West Africa*, ed. John C. Caldwell (New York, 1975), 99.

11 Papadakis, *Survey in West Africa* 1:72; Isichei, *Igbo People*, 224.

12 Kimble, *Tropical Africa* 2:44; Michael Latham, *Human Nutrition in Tropical Africa* (Rome, 1965), 191; Isichei, *Igbo People*, 224; Lewicki, *West African Food in the Middle Ages*, 127; Cantrelle, "Mortality," 99.

13 H.F. Welbourne, *Nutrition in Tropical Countries* (London, 1963), 39; W.B. Morgan and J.C. Pugh, *West Africa* (London, 1969), 136; T.R. Batten, *Problems of African Development* (London, 1960), 122.

14 Firman E. Bear, "Soil and Man," in *Hunger and Food*, ed. Josué de Castro (London, 1958), 40–50; H.L. Richardson, "The Use of Fertilizers," in *The Soil Resources of Tropical Africa*, ed. R.P. Moss (London, 1968), 138; R.J. Harrison Church, *West Africa: A Study of the Environment and of Man's Use of It* (London, 1963), 87; Great Britain Naval Intelligence Division, *French West Africa*, Vol. 1, *The Federation* (London, 1943), 80; Bruce F. Johnston, *The Staple Food Economies of Western Tropical Africa* (Stanford, Calif., 1958), 161–3; J. Dresch, "Questions Ouest-Africaines," *BCGP* 5 (1950), 1–2.

15 Oliver Davies, *West Africa before the Europeans: Archaeology and Prehistory* (London, 1967), 149; William Malcolm Hailey, *An African Survey* (London, 1957), 822; Basil Davidson, *The African Genius: An Introduction to African Cultural and Social History* (Boston, 1969), 33; Paul Lovejoy, "Indigenous African Slavery," *Historical Reflections/ Reflexions Historiques* 6 (1979), 20–61; Alfred W. Crosby, *The Columbian Exchange: Biological and Cultural Consequences of 1492* (Westport, Conn., 1972), 186–8.

16 Meek, Macmillan, and Hussey, *Europe and West Africa*, 17; Hailey, *African Survey*, 822; Jill R. Dias, "Famine and Disease in the History of Angola, 1830–1930," *JAfH* 21 (1981), 349–78; Joseph Miller, "Disease and Famine in the Agriculturally Marginal Zones of West-Central Africa," *JAfH* 23 (1982), 17–61.

17 World Health Organization, "Africa's Health," *JHR* 8 (1960), 437–42; J.C. Carothers, "The African Mind in Health and Disease," *JHR* 8 (1960), 443–54; Jacques M. May and Donna L. McLellan, *The Ecology of Malnutrition in the French Speaking Countries of West Africa and Madagascar* (New York, 1968), 10–11; Valquist, "Nutrition as a Prior-

ity in African Development," 345–7; Newman, "Dietary and Nutritional Conditions," 71–80.

18 See Chapter 6 for a more complete discussion of pellagra, beriberi, and nutritional chemistry.

19 Michael Gelfand, *The Sick African* (Capetown, 1957), 359; see also his *Diet and Tradition in an African Culture* (Edinburgh, 1971), 207; Kimble, *Tropical Africa* 2:42; Isichei, *Igbo People*, 197–8; Meek, Macmillan, and Hussey, *Europe and West Africa*, 32–3; K.V. Bailey, "Malnutrition in the African Region," *WHO Chronicle* 29 (1975), 354–64; J.C. Carothers, "The African Mind in Health and Disease," *JHR* 8 (1960), 445; Great Britain, *Nutrition in the Colonial Empire* 2:40; Davidson Nicol, "A Pilot Nutrition Survey in Nigeria," *WAMJ* 2 (1953), I25; B.M. Nicol, "Maintenance and Improvement of the Diets of the Nigerian Population," *III Conferência Interafricana de Nutrição (Luanda)* (Angola and Portugal, 1956), 2:239–43; Olumbe Bassir, "Nutrition in Nigeria," *WAMJ* 2 (1953), 31.

20 Nicol, "Pilot Nutrition Survey in Nigeria," 125.

21 Rui Álvaro Vieira, "Pesquisa de Vitamina C na Urina dos Indígenas Bijagós da Guiné Portuguesa," *BCGP* 12 (1957), 552–3.

22 D.B. Jelliffe, "Infant Feeding among the Yoruba of Ibadan," *WAMJ* 2 (1953), 119; B. Nicol, "Maintenance and Improvement of the Diets," 239–43; Susan Ofor Atta, "Social and Cultural Factors Encountered in the Work on Nutrition in African Communities," *III Conferência Interafricana de Nutrição (Luanda)* 2:335–41; "Nutritional Policy for Nigeria," *WAMJ* 7 (1958), 48.

23 J.A. Close, "Quelques Résultats d'une enquête alimentaire au Ruanda-Urundi," and Fernando Tomás Gonçalves, "Nutrição e Condições de Higiene dos Aborígenes do Bilene," and José António Pereira Nunes, "Aspectos de uma Necessidade Alimentar Criada pelo 'Stress,' " and O.A. Roels, O. Debeir, and M. Trout, "Vitamin A Deficiency in the Region of Astrida," all in *III Conferência Interafricana de Nutrição (Luanda)* 1:466, 2:545–9, 2:709–40, 2:491–500; J.C. Endozien, "Biochemical Normals in Nigerians: Chemical Composition of the Blood of Adults," *WAMJ* 9 (1960), 204–7; Carlos Santos Reis, "Contribuição para o Estudo de Nutrição dos Povos da Guiné-Bissau; IV A Missão de Estudos Nutricionais de 1959/1960," *AIHMT* 5 (1977–78), 371–8; Bassir, "Nutrition in Nigeria," 40.

24 J.F. Brock and M. Autret, "Kwashiorkor in Africa," *Bulletin of the World Health Organization* 5 (1953), 33; Close, "Quelques Résultats," 545–9; Roels, Debeir, and Trout, "Vitamin A Deficiency," 491–500; Jelliffe, "Infant Feeding," 119; Tito Serra Simões, "O Problema da Alimentação dos Trabalhadores Negros," *AIMT I* (1943–4), 335.

25 Gonçalves, "Nutrição," 2:709–40; Fernando Coutinho Costa, "Contribuição para o Estudo do Regime Alimentar dos Bijagós," *III Conferência Interafricana de Nutrição (Luanda)*, 2:685–708; B. Nicol, "Maintenance and Improvement of the Diets," 239–43.

26 Carlos Trincão, L.T. de Almeida Franco, and Egídio Gouveia, "Anemias Gravídicas nas Indígenas da Guiné Portuguesa: Inquérito nas Tribos do Interior," *AIMT* 13 (1956), 101; D. Nicol, "Pilot Nutrition Survey in Nigeria," 123–8.

27 Cicely D. Williams, "Kwashiorkor," *JAMA* 153 (1953), 1280–5; Sohan L. Manocha, *Malnutrition and Retarded Human Development* (Springfield, Ill., 1972), 19, 23; Merrill S. Read, "Malnutrition, Hunger, and Behavior," *JADA* 63 (1973), 379–85; Remy Clairin, "The Assessment of Infant and Child Mortality from the Data Available in Africa," in *The Population of Tropical Africa*, eds. Caldwell and Okonjo, 200; Paul Gyorgy, "Biochemical Aspects of Human Milk," *AJCN* 24 (1971), 970–5; Leonardo J. Mata and Richard G. Wyatt, "The Uniqueness of Human Milk: Host Resistance to Infection," *AJCN* 24 (1971), 249–59.

28 James L. Newman, "Dietary Behavior and Protein-Energy-Malnutrition in Africa South of the Sahara: Some Themes for Medical Geography," in *Conceptual and Meth-*

odological Issues in Medical Geography, ed. Melinda S. Meade (Chapel Hill, N.C., 1980), 79.

29 Hubert Carey Trowell, *Non-Infective Disease in Africans* (London, 1960), 332; Newman, "Dietary Behavior and Protein-Energy-Malnutrition," 79.

30 Williams, "Kwashiorkor," 1284; Derrick B. Jelliffe, *Infant Nutrition in the Subtropics and Tropics,* 2d ed. (Geneva, 1968), 9, and "Infant Feeding," 120; J.F. Brock and M. Autret, "Kwashiorkor, in Africa," Part I, *WAMJ* 2 (1953), 151–63.

31 Ann McElroy and Patricia K. Townsend, *Medical Anthropology in Ecological Perspective* (North Scituate, Mass., 1979), 230; Kimble, *Tropical Africa* 2:42, 44; Newman, "Dietary and Nutritional Conditions," 77; Latham, *Nutrition in Tropical Africa,* 104–9; Great Britain, *Nutrition in the Colonial Empire* 2:36.

32 J.H. Walters and Dean A. Smith, "Oedematous Beri-Beri in Gambian Palm Wine Tappers," *WAMJ* 1 (1952), 21–8; Bernardo Bruto da Costa, "Casos de beri-beri em São Thomé," *Archivos de Hygiene e Pathologia Exóticas* 3 (1910–13), 79–87; Ayres Kopke, "Beri-beri em S. Thomé," *Archivos de Hygiene e Pathologia Exóticas,"* 1(1905–8), 92–9; Joaquim Xabregas and António de Sousa Santos, "O Problema Alimentar no Colonato do Vale do Loge," *III Conferência Interafricana de Nutrição* (*Luanda*) 2: 533–8.

33 Xabregas and Santos, "O Problema Alimentar," 533–8.

34 Kimble, *Tropical Africa* 2:42; Isichei, *Igbo People,* 197–8; Great Britain, *Nutrition in the Colonial Empire* 2:40; D. Nicol, "Pilot Nutrition Survey in Nigeria," 127; B. Nicol, "Maintenance and Improvement of the Diets," 239–43; Bassir, "Nutrition in Nigeria," 35,40.

35 Bailey, "Malnutrition," 354–64; Great Britain, *Nutrition in the Colonial Empire* 2:40; D. Nicol, "Pilot Nutrition Survey in Nigeria," 125; Hailey, *African Survey,* 1070; J.C. Chartres, "Onchocerciasis: Incubation Period, Clinical Course and Treatment at First Hand," *WAMJ* 4 (1955), 130–5; A.W. Woodruff, "Recent Advances in Tropical Medicine No. 2 – Loa Loa and Loiasis," *WAMJ* 1(1952), 45–55; "Nutritional Policy for Nigeria," 48.

36 D. Nicol, "Pilot Nutrition Survey for Nigeria," 125; Vieira, "Pesquisa de vitamina C," 552–3.

37 D. Nicol, "Pilot Nutrition Survey in Nigeria," 126; Carlos Trincão et al., "Anemias Gravídicas nas Indígenas da Guiné Portuguesa. Inquéritos nas Tribos do Litoral," *Clínica Contemporânea* 7 (1953), 101.

38 G.M. Edington, "Haemosiderosis and Anaemia in the Gold Coast African," *WAMJ* 3 (1954), 66–70.

39 Hailey, *African Survey,* 1119; Latham, *Human Nutrition in Africa,* 45–7; Nevin S. Scrimshaw, Carl E. Taylor, and John E. Gordon, *Interactions of Nutrition and Infection* (Geneva, 1968), 30, 32.

40 Okechukwu Ikejiani, "A Laboratory Epidemiological Study of Certain Infectious Diseases in Nigeria," *WAMJ* 8 (1959), 37–42.

41 R. Cook, "The General Nutritional Problems of Africa," *African Affairs* 65 (1966), 337–8; Bassir, "Nutrition in Nigeria," 39; D. B. Jelliffe, "Clinical Rickets in Ibadan, Nigeria," *TRSTMH* 45 (1951), 119–24.

42 Geoffrey Taylor, "Osteomalacia and Calcium Deficiency," *BMJ* 1 (1976), 960.

43 K. Holemans and A. Lambrechts, "Besoins énergétiques et plastiques ainsi que leur couverture chez le nourrisson du Kuango," *III Conferência Interafricana de Nutrição* (*Luanda*) 1:55–8; O. Bassir, "Nutritional Studies on Breast Milk of Nigerian Women," *WAMJ* 5 (1956), 88–96; Atta, "Social and Cultural Factors," 338; Cicely D. Williams, "Introductory Observations on Kwashiorkor," *WAMJ* 7 (1958), 6.

44 Edington, "Haemosiderosis and Anaemia," 67 table; Ikedinachuku Okpala, "The Incidence of Intestinal Parasites among School Children in Lagos, Nigeria," *WAMJ* 5 (1956), 169 table.

45 J. Fraga de Azevedo, "Soil-Transmitted Helminths in the Portuguese Republic (European and African Provinces)," *AIMT* 21 (1964), 273–312.

46 Ikejiani, "Laboratory Epidemiological Study," 337–42.

47 See, for example, G. Jorge Janz et al., "Estudos sobre a Influência do Parasitismo sobre o Estado de Nutrição," *III Conferência Interafricana de Nutrição (Luanda)* 1: 221–30.

48 Silva Telles, "The Prophylaxis of Paludism in the Portuguese Colonies," *Arquivos de Higiene e Patologia Exóticas* 7 (1925), 439–44; Ikejiani, "Laboratory Epidemiological Study," 38–9; Leonard J. Bruce-Chwatt, "Malaria in Nigeria (Part I)," *WAMJ* 1 (1952), 109.

49 M.J. Colbourne and F.N. Wright, "Malaria in the Gold Coast (Part I)," *WAMJ* 4 (1955), 3–17.

50 Ibid, 170–1; Bruce-Chwatt, "Malaria in Nigeria (Part I)," 109.

51 Edington, "Haemosiderosis and Anaemia," 67.

52 J. Fraga de Azevedo, "The Human Trypanosomiasis in Africa–The Contribution of Portugal for its Knowledge," in *Recent Works on Sleeping Sickness in Portuguese Overseas Territories* (Lisboa, 1974), 574; João Cardosa, Jr., *Subsídios para a Matéria Médica e Terapêutica das Possessões Ultramarinas*, 2 vols. (Lisboa, 1902), 1:117–18.

53 Atta, "Social and Cultural Factors," 335–6.

54 Henry Richards, "Child Loss in Tema, Gold Coast," *WAMJ* 4 (1955), 154–5; Costa, "Contribuição," 2:695.

55 Richards, "Child Loss," 154–5; Trincão et al., "Anemias gravídicas . . . Guiné . . . do Litoral," 101; Bruce M. Nicol, "Fertility and Food in Northern Nigeria," *WAMJ* 8 (1959), 18–27.

56 Carlos Santos Reis, "Contribuição para o estudo do estado de nutrição dos povos da Guiné Portuguesa," *AIMT* 19 (1962), 84.

57 M.A. Majekodunmi, "Effects of Malnutrition during Pregnancy and Lactation," *WAMJ* 7 (1958), 30–2; Jelliffe, "Infant Feeding," 116; Oscar Felsenfeld, *The Epidemiology of Tropical Diseases* (Springfield, Ill., 1966), 413; Joe D. Wray, "Maternal Nutrition, Breast-feeding and Infant Survival," in *Nutrition and Human Reproduction*, ed. Mosley, 203, 205, 206–9; Aaron Lechtig et al., "Effect of Maternal Nutrition on Infant Mortality," *Nutrition and Human Reproduction*, ed. Mosley, 161; Joseph C. Edozien, M.A. Rahimkhan, and Carol I. Waslien, "Human Protein Deficiency: Results of a Nigerian Village Study," *JN* 106 (1976), 319.

58 Williams, "Introductory Observations," 5–9; Atta, "Social and Cultural Factors," 338; Costa, "Contribuição," 694; Jelliffe, "Infant Feeding," 114–22; Carlos Santos Reis, "Contribuição para o Estudo do Estado de Nutrição dos Povos da Guiné Portuguesa 3. Inquérito Etnográfico à Alimentação Materno-Infantil," *AIMT* 21 (1964), 127.

59 Jelliffe, "Infant Feeding," 116; Reis, "Contribuição 3," 124–5; Costa "Contribuição," 694.

60 G. Jorge Janz and Gabriela L. Pinto, "A Composição do Leite num Grupo de Mães Africanas e a sua Relação com o Estado de Nutrição," *III Conferência Interafricana de Nutrição (Luanda)* 1: 127–35; Holemans and Lambrechts, "Besoins énergétiques," 1: 55–58; Bassir, "Nutritional Studies on Breast Milk," 88–96; D.B. Jelliffe, "Some Aspects of Tropical Paediatrics," *WAMJ* 2 (1953), 194–5; James L. Newman, "Dietary Behavior and Protein-Energy-Malnutrition in Africa South of the Sahara: Some Themes for Medical Geography," in *Conceptual and Methodological Issues in Medical Geography*, ed. Melinda S. Meade (Chapel Hill, N.C., 1980), 82–3; Cantrelle, "Mortality," 108; Wray, "Maternal Nutrition," 218; Solien de Gonzalez, "Lactation and Pregnancy," 873.

61 Charles C. Hughes and John M. Hunter, "Disease and 'Development' in Africa," *SSM* 3 (1970), 465; Cook, General Nutritional Problems of Africa," 335; Hendrickse,

"Observations on the Social Background to Malnutrition in Tropical Africa," 344; Jelliffe, "Infant Feeding," 119–20, Gonçalves, "Nutrição," 2:709–40 passim.

62 Hendrickse, "Observations on the Social Background to Malnutrition in Tropical Africa," 343–4; Atta, "Cultural and Social Factors," 235–6; B. Nicol, "Maintenance and Improvement of the Diets," 239–43; Beverly Winikoff, "Nutrition, Population, and Health: Some Implications for Policy," *Science* 200:4344 (1978), 896.

63 D.C. Morley, "Childhood Tuberculosis in a Rural Area of West Africa," *WAMJ* 8 (1959), 225–9.

64 W. Brass, "Introduction: Bio-Social Factors in African Demography," in *The Population Factor in African Studies*, eds. R.P. Moss and R.J.A.R. Rathbone (London, 1975), 92; Cantrelle, "Mortality," 107.

65 Richards, "Child Loss," 154–5; Costa, "Contribuição," 685–708; Bruce M. Nicol, "Fertility and Food in Northern Nigeria," *WAMJ* 8 (1959), 18–27.

66 Hughes and Hunter, "Disease and 'Development' in Africa," 448; Great Britain, *Nutrition in the Colonial Empire* 2:33 and passim.

67 Brock and Autret, "Kwashiorkor in Africa", 42–35; Bassir, "Nutrition in Nigeria," 40; Newman, "Dietary and Nutritional Conditions," 74; Lewicki, *West African Food in the Middle Ages*, 126–7.

68 Costa, "Contribuição," 685–708; B. Reiff, "Plasma and Urinary Vitamin C Levels in Adult Nigerians, with a Note on the Ascorbic Acid Content of some Nigerian Foodstuffs," *WAMJ* 8 (1959), 149–51.

69 Jelliffe, "Infant Feeding," 118.

70 R. Cook, "The General Nutritional Problems of Africa," *AFA* 65 (1966), 334; Hughes and Hunter, "Diseases and 'Development' in Africa," 448.

71 John C. Super, "Sources and Methods for the Study of Historical Nutrition in Latin America," *Historical Methods* 14 (1981), 27.

72 Hughes and Hunter, "Disease and 'Development' in Africa," 465–6; K. David Patterson and Gerald W. Hartwig, "The Disease Factor: An Introductory Overview," in *Disease in African History*, eds. Gerald W. Hartwig and K. David Patterson (Durham, N.C., 1978), 13–14.

73 Patterson and Hartwig, "Disease Factor," 11, 13–15.

74 See Chapter 7 for more on West African lactation practices.

75 For examples see William Freeman Daniell, *Sketches of the Medical Topography and Native Diseases of the Gulf of Guinea, Western Africa* (London, 1849), 48; Donald D. Wax, "A Philadelphia Surgeon on a Slaving Voyage to Africa," *Pennsylvania Magazine of History and Biology* 92 (1968), 465–93, passim; Philip D. Curtin, ed., *Africa Remembered: Narratives by West Africans from the Era of the Slave Trade* (Madison, Wis., 1967), 260; and P.M. Ashburn, *The Ranks of Death: A Medical History of the Conquest of America* (New York, 1947), 36–7.

Chapter 3. The Parameters of West African Survival

1 Norman Kretchmer, "The Geography and Biology of Lactose Digestion and Malabsorption," *PMJ* 53 (1977), 70.

2 Richard Allen Williams, "Black Related Diseases: An Overview," *Journal of Black Health Perspectives* 1 (1974), 39.

3 For a summary of these studies, see Robert M. Malina, "Biological Substrata," in *Comparative Studies of Blacks and Whites in the United States*, eds. Kent S. Miller and Ralph Mason Dreger (New York, 1973), 59–60.

4 Robert H. Hutcheson, "Iron Deficiency Anemia in Tennessee among Rural Poor Children," *PHR* 83 (1968), 939–43.

5 They feel, in other words, that this condition in blacks may result from a genetic

condition. See for example Peter Dallman, "New Approaches to Screening for Iron Deficiency," *JP* 90 (1977), 678–81; Stanley M. Garn and Dianne C. Clark, "Problems in the Nutritional Assessment of Black Individuals," *AJPH* 66 (1976), 262–7; Stanley M. Garn et al., "Apportioning Black-White Hemoglobin and Hematocrit Differences in Pregnancy" (letter to editor), *AJCN* 30 (1977), 461–2; Michael J. Kraemer et al., "Response to Letter ('The Magnitude and the Implications of Apparent Race Differences in Hemoglobin Values') by Dr. Garn and Co-workers," *AJCN* 28 (1975), 566; Michael J. Kraemer et al., "Race-related Differences in Peripheral Blood and in Bone Marrow Cell Populations of American Black and American White Infants," *JNMA* 69 (1977), 327–31.

6   Aaron E. Masawe, Josephia M. Muindi, and Godfrey B.R. Swai, "Infections in Iron Deficiency and other Types of Anemia in the Tropics," *Lancet* 2 (1974), 316.

7   Arno G. Motulsky, "Frequency of Sickling Disorders in U.S. Blacks," *NEJM* 288 (1973), 31–3.

8   Virgil F. Fairbanks, John L. Fahey, and Ernest Beutler, *Clinical Disorders of Iron Metabolism*, 2d ed. (New York, 1971), 238.

9   Margaret F. Gutelius, "The Problem of Iron Deficiency Anemia in Preschool Negro Children," *AJPH* 59 (1969), 290–5.

10 O. Ransome-Kuti, "Lactose Intolerance – A Review," *PMJ* 53 (1977), 73–87; T. Matsumura, T. Kuroume, and K. Amanda, "Close Relationship between Lactose Intolerance and Allergy to Milk Protein," *The Journal of Asthma Research* 9 (1971), 24.

11 For an excellent look at the geographic distribution of lactose intolerance, consult Frederick J. Simoons, "New Light on Ethnic Differences in Adult Lactose Intolerance," *Digestive Diseases* 18 (1973), 595–611.

12 David M. Paige and George G. Graham, "Nutritional Implications of Lactose Malabsorption," *PR* 6 (1972), 329.

13 For comparative purposes, in India 80 percent of the adults are lactose intolerant; in China the figure is 90 percent. See John M. Hunter, "Geography, Genetics, and Culture History: The Case of Lactose Intolerance," *Geographical Review* 61 (1971), 605–8.

14 Gebhard Flatz and Hanz Werner Rotthauwe, "Lactose Nutrition and Natural Selection," *Lancet* 2:7820 (1973), 76–7. Not necessarily incompatible with this hypothesis is the suggestion that those who do exhibit lactase activity as adults may "be inheritors of a dominant mutation of a regulatory gene controlling lactase synthesis, . . ." a process that began in the Near East and India some 10,000 years ago; Kretchmer, "Geography and Biology of Lactose Digestion and Malabsorption," 70.

15 J.J. Pieters and R. Van Rens, "Lactose Malabsorption and Milk Tolerance in Kenyan School-Age Children," *Tropical and Geographical Medicine* 25 (1973), 365–71.

16 Theodore M. Bayless and Norton S. Rosensweig, "Incidence and Implications of Lactase Deficiency and Milk Intolerance in White and Negro Populations," *JHMJ* 121 (1967), 54–64.

17 John D. Johnson, Norman Kretchmer, and Frederick J. Simoons, "Lactose Malabsorption: Its Biology and History," *Advanced Pediatrics* 21 (1974), 197–237.

18 Robert D. McCracken, "Lactase Deficiency: An Example of Dietary Evolution," *Current Anthropology* 12 (1971), 479–517; C.C. Desilva and N.Q. Baptist, *Tropical Nutritional Disorders of Infants and Children* (Springfield, Ill., 1969), 34–5; G.C. Cook, "Lactase Activity in Newborn and Infant Baganda," *BMJ* 1 (1967), 529.

19 A.E. Davis and T. Bolin, "Lactose Intolerance in Asians," *Nature*, 216 (1967), 1244–5; Paige and Graham, "Nutritional Implications," 329; Martin H. Floch, "Whither Bovine Milk?" *AJCN* 22 (1969), 214–17.

20 George Paul, *Report on Ankylostomiasis Infection Survey on Barbados* (New York, 1917), 26; H. Muench, "Final Report of the Hookworm Infection Survey of St. Christopher

(St. Kitts), British West Indies, 1925", RAC, IHB, 439, Series 21 Leeward Islands, Box 44, folder 271; Kal Wagenheim, *Puerto Rico: A Profile* (New York, 1970), 178; M.T. Ashcroft, I.C. Buchanan, and H.G. Lovell, "Heights and Weights of Primary School Children in St. Christopher-Nevis-Anguilla, West Indies," *WIJTMH* 68 (1965), 277.

21   U.S. Department of Health, Education, and Welfare, *Ten-state Nutrition Survey, 1968–1970*, 5 vols. DHEW Pub. No. (HSM) 72-8130-34 (Washington, D.C., 1972) 5: tables 241–6, hereinafter referred to as *TSNS*; Public Health Services, Health Resources Administration, *Preliminary Findings of the First Health and Nutrition Examination Survey, United States, 1971–1972. Dietary Intake and Biochemical Findings.* DHEW Pub. No. (HRA) 75-1219-1 (Washington, D.C., 1974), hereinafter referred to as *HANES*; Jacques M. May and Donna L. McLellan, *The Ecology of Malnutrition in the Caribbean* (New York, 1973), 122, 175, 220, 221, 331–2 and passim; Michael Latham et al., *Scope Manual on Nutrition* (Kalamazoo, Mich, 1972); Alexander R.P. Walker, "The Human Requirements of Calcium: Should Low Intakes be Supplemented?" *AJCN* 25 (1972), 518–30; Geoffrey Taylor, "Osteomalacia and Calcium Deficiency" (letter), *BMJ* 1:6015 (1976), 960.

22   M. Isabel Irwin and Eldon W. Kienholz, "A Conspectus of Research on Calcium Requirements of Man," *JN* 103 (1973), 1019–95; Marshall T. Newman, "Ecology and Nutritional Stress," in *Culture, Disease and Healing*, ed. David Landy (New York, 1977), 322.

23   Robert M. Neer, "The Evolutionary Significance of Vitamin D, Skin Pigment, and Ultraviolet Light," *AJPA* 43 (1975), 409–16; John H. Phillips and George E. Burch, "A Review of Cardiovascular Diseases in the White and Negro Races," *Medicine* 39 (1960), 245.

24   For a discussion, see Kenneth F. Kiple and Virginia H. King, *Another Dimension to the Black Diaspora: Diet, Disease and Racism* (New York, 1981), 104–6 and passim. Although not within the purview of this study, it is worth noting that pigment affecting the biosynthesis of vitamin D is a major reason for sometimes dangerously elevated lead levels in black children. See John M. Hunter, "The Summer Disease: Some Field Evidence on Seasonality in Childhood Lead Poisoning," *SSM* 12 (1978), 85–94 and "The Summer Disease: An Integrative Model of the Seasonality Aspects of Childhood Lead Poisoning," *SSM* 11 (1977), 691–703.

25   John D. Kirschmann, ed., *Nutrition Almanac* (New York, 1975), 160–1; Felix Bronner, "Vitamin D Deficiency and Rickets," *AJCN* 29 (1976), 1307–14; Irwin and Kienholz, "Conspectus of Research," 1021.

26   R. Cook, "The General Nutritional Problems of Africa," *African Affairs* 65 (1966), 337–8; Collin George Miller and Winston Chotkaw, "Vitamin D Deficiency Rickets in Jamaican Children," *ADC* 51 (1976), 217.

27   John G. Haddad and Theodore J. Hahn, "Natural and Synthetic Sources of Circulating 26-Hydroxyvitamin D in Man," *Nature* 244 (1973), 515–17; Oscar Felsenfeld, *The Epidemiology of Tropical Diseases* (Springfield, Ill., 1966); Reginald C. Tsang and William Oh, "Neonatal Hypocalcemia in Low Birth Weight Infants," *PED* 45 (1970), 773–81; Jennifer Jowsey, "Osteoporosis: Its Nature and the Role of Diet," *PMJ* 59 (1976), 75–9

28   Sir Stanley Davidson et al., *Human Nutrition and Dietetics*, 6th ed. (Edinburgh, 1975), 318.

29   L.W. Aurand and A.E. Woods, *Food Chemistry* (Westport, Conn. 1973), 253.

30   B.S. Platt, *Nutrition in the British West Indies* (London, 1946), 18.

31   Frances A. Johnston, Thelma J. McMillan, and Erica R. Evans, "Perspiration as a Factor Influencing the Requirement for Calcium and Iron," *JN* 42 (1950), 291; Irwin and Kienholz, "Conspectus of Research," 1031–2.

32 Phillips and Burch, "Review of Cardiovascular Diseases," 245. Blacks are, however, capable of higher rates of perspiration than whites because of a greater number of sweat glands, which serve to keep the body cooler in the tropics.

33 Jacques M. May and Donna L. McLellan, *The Ecology of Malnutrition in the French Speaking Countries of West Africa and Madagascar* (New York, 1968), 23, 67, 109, 149, 223–4 and passim; Hubert Carey Trowell, *Non-Infective Disease in Africa* (London, 1960), 371–4; Walker, "Human Requirements of Calcium," 520–3.

34 P.M. Morgan et al., "Dental Health of Louisiana Residents Based on the Ten-State Nutrition Survey," *PHR* 90 (1975), 173–8; Walker, "Human Requirements of Calcium," 523; Stanley J. Birge et al., "Osteoporosis, Intestinal Lactase Deficiency and Low Dietary Calcium Intake," *NEJM* 276 (1967), 445–8.

35 George M. Owen et al., "A Study of Nutritional Status of Preschool Children in the United States, 1968–1970," *PED* 53 (1974), 597–646.

36 G. Jorge Janz, "O Peso dos Recém-Nascidos Africanos em Relação com o estado da Carência das Maês," *III Conferência Interafricana de Nutrição (Luanda)* (Angola and Portugal, 1956), 365–73, and G. Jorge Janz et al., "O Peso do Recém-Nascido Africano da Guiné Portuguesa," *AIMT* 16 (1979), 73–80; Helen C. Chase and Mary E. Byrnes, "Trends in Prematurity, United States: 1950–67," DHEW Pub. No. (HSM) 72-1039 (Washington, D.C., 1972); Helen C. Chase "Infant Mortality and Weight at Birth: 1960 United States Birth Cohort," *AJPH* 59 (1969), 1618–28; Helen C. Chase, "Time Trends in Low Birth Weight in the United States, 1950–1974," in *Epidemiology of Prematurity*, eds. Dwayne M. Reed and Fiona L. Stanley (Baltimore, 1977), 17–37; Joseph Chinnici and Raymond C. Sansing, "Mortality Rates, Optimal and Discriminating Birth Weights between White and Non-White Single Births in Virginia (1955–1973)," *HB* 49 (1977), 335–48; George I. Lythcott, Calvin H. Sinnette, and Donald R. Hopkins, "Pediatrics," in *Textbook of Black-Related Diseases*, ed. Richard Allen Williams (New York, 1975), 135; Howard V. Meredith, "North American Negro Infants: Size at Birth and Growth During the First Postnatal Year," *HB* 24 (1972), 290–308; Gerald Wiener and Toby Milton, "Demographic Correlates of Low Birth Weight," *AJE* 91 (1970), 260–72.

37 Leroy R. Weekes, "Obstetrics and Gynecology," in *Textbook of Black-Related Diseases*, ed. Williams, 102.

38 Carl L. Erhardt and Helen C. Chase, "A Study of Risks, Medical Care and Infant Mortality. II. Ethnic Group, Education of Mother, and Birth Weight," *AJPH* 63 (1973), 26; Chase, "Time Trends in Low Birth Weight," 20–4, 28.

39 See Malina's bibliographic discussion of the question in "Biological Substrata," 67–8.

40 Carl L. Erhardt, "Influence of Weight and Gestation on Perinatal and Neonatal Mortality by Ethnic Group," *AJPH* 54 (1964), 1849.

41 Weiner and Milton, "Demographic Correlates of Low Birth Weight," 27; A. Frederick North and Hugh M. McDonald, "Why are Neonatal Mortality Rates Lower in Small Black Infants Than in White Infants in Similar Birth Weight?" *JP* 90 (1977), 809–10; Stanley M. Garn, Helen A. Shaw, and Kinne D. McCabe, "Effects of Socio-economic Status and Race on Weight-Defined and Gestational Prematurity in the United States," in *Epidemiology of Prematurity*, eds. Reed and Stanley, 136–7.

42 Jerry L. Weaver, "The Case of Black Infant Mortality," *Journal of Health Policy* 1 (1977), 439.

43 Sanford Brown et al., "Low Birth Weight in Babies Born to Mothers with Sickle Cell Trait," *JAMA* 221 (1972), 1404–5.

44 Lythcott, Sinnette, and Hopkins, "Pediatrics," 131–2; Frank Falkner, ed., *Key Issues in Infant Mortality* (Bethesda, Md., 1969), 18.

45 Nicholson J. Eastman, *Obstetrics* (New York, 1956), 187; A.V. Wells, "Study of Birth Weights of Babies Born in Barbados, West Indies," *WIMJ* 12 (1963), 194–9; P. Desai,

W.E. Miall, and K.L. Standard, "A Five Year Study of Infant Growth in Rural Jamaica," *WIMJ* 18 (1969), 210–21; Ashcroft, Buchanan, and Lovell, "Heights and Weights," 277–83; M.T. Ashcroft and H.C. Lovell, "Heights and Weights of Jamaican Primary School Children," *JTP* 12 (1966), 37–43; Stephen A. Richardson, "Physical Growth of Jamaican School Children Who Were Severely Malnourished Before 2 Years of Age," *Journal of Biosocial Science* 7 (1975), 445–62; Robert Cook, "Nutrition and Mortality Under Five Years in the Caribbean Area," *JTP* 15 (1969), 109–17; J.H. Spurgeon, et al., "Body size and Form of Children of Predominantly Black Ancestry Living in West and Central Africa, North and South America and the West Indies," *Annals of Human Biology* 5 (1978), 229–46.

46 Weaver, "Black Infant Mortality," 435; Lythcott, Sinnette and Hopkins, "Pediatrics," 131.

47 Richardson, "Physical Growth," 445.

48 Garn and Clark, "Nutritional Assessment of Black Individuals," 262; J.M. Tanner, *Foetus into Man: Physical Growth from Conception to Maturity* (London, 1978), 59–60.

49 Nancy Bayley, "Comparisons of Mental and Motor Test Scores for Ages 1–15 Months by Sex, Birth Order, Race, Geographical Location, and Education of Parents," *Child Development* 36 (1965), 379–411; Trowell, *Non-Infective Disease in Africa*, 322–4.

50 Stanley M. Garn and Diane C. Clark, "Nutrition, Growth, Development, and Maturation: Findings from the Ten-State Nutrition Survey of 1968–1970," PED 56 (1975), 314.

51 Ibid. See also Garn and Clark, "Nutritional Assessment of Black Individuals," 265; and S.M. Garn, et al., "Negro–Caucasoid Differences in Permanent Tooth Emergence at a Constant Income Level," *Archives of Oral Biology* 18 (1973), 609–15.

52 Garn and Clark, "Nutrition, Growth, Development, and Maturation," 314; Cicely D. Williams, "Varieties of Unbalanced Diet and Their Effect on Nutrition," in *Hunger and Food*, ed. Josué de Castro (London, 1958), 93.

53 Nancie L. Solien de Gonzalez, "Lactation and Pregnancy: A Hypothesis," *AA* 66 (1964), 873; R.G. Hendrickse, "Some Observations on the Social Background to Malnutrition in Tropical Africa," *AFA* 68 (1966), 342–4; William Freeman Daniell, *Sketches of the Medical Topography and Native Diseases of the Gulf of Guinea, West Africa* (London, 1849), 54–5.

54 S.H. Cohn, et al., "Comparative Skeletal Mass and Radial Bone Mineral Content in Black and White Women," *Metabolism* 26 (1977), 171–8; R.L. Allen and David L. Nickel, "The Negro and Learning to Swim; The Buoyancy Problem Related to Biological Differences," *Journal of Negro Education* 38 (1969), 404–11, esp. 406.

55 Mildred Trotter, George E. Broman, and Roy R. Peterson, "Densities of Bones of White and Negro Skeletons," *Journal of Bone and Joint Surgery* 42A (1960), 56; Davidson, et al., *Human Nutrition and Dietetics*, 116. The phenomenon of blacks on a low-calcium diet enjoying a low incidence of calcium deficiency disease has also been reported in South Africa according to the Scientific Council for Africa South of the Sahara, *Nutrition Research in Africa South of the Sahara* (London, 1956), 79.

56 O.O. Akinkugbe, *High Blood Pressure in the African* (London, 1972), 14–22; E. Boyce, Jr., "Biological Patterns by Race, Sex, Body Weight and Skin Color," *JAMA* 213 (1970), 1637–43; Richard Allen Williams, "Cardiology," in *Textbook of Black Related Diseases*, ed. Williams, 361; Phillips and Burch, "Review of Cardiovascular Diseases," 352; Jack Slater, "Hypertension: Bigger Killer of Blacks," *Ebony* 28 (1973), 76.

57 Earlier studies, such as that by G.M. Saunders and H. Bancroft ("Blood Pressure Studies on Negro and White Men and Women living in the Virgin Islands of the United States," *American Heart Journal* 23 [1942], 410–23), found the blood pressure of blacks much greater than that of whites on the Islands. It was also found that Virgin Island blacks had a greater incidence of hypertension than blacks in the

United States. B.H. Kean and J.F. Hammill ("Anthropathology of Arterial Tension," *AIM* 83 [1949], 355–62) and B.H. Kean ("Blood Pressure Studies on West Indians and Panamanians. . ." *AIM* 68 [1941], 466–75) also report higher rates among Panamanians with some black admixture and the highest rates of all among West Indian blacks. For a logical explanation of this phenomenon, I am relying, unless otherwise indicated, on the work of Thomas Wilson, a Ph.D. candidate at Bowling Green State University, whose dissertation deals with the question of "History and Hypertension: The Case of the Afro-Americans."

58 Davidson, et al., *Human Nutrition and Dietetics*, 663; Josué de Castro, *The Geography of Hunger* (Boston, 1952), 48; Todd L. Savitt, *Medicine and Slavery: The Diseases and Health Care of Blacks in Antebellum Virginia* (Urbana, Ill., 1978), 41; Gilbert B. Forbes, "Sodium," in *Mineral Metabolism*, eds. Cyril Lewis Comar and Felix Bronner, 4 vols. (New York, 1969), 2b:29.

59 Shaul G. Massry, Peter Weidmann, and Francisco Llach, "Blood Calcium Levels and Hypertension," *Contributions in Nephrology* 8 (1977), 117–25; E.E. Hellerstein, et al. "Studies on the Relationship between Dietary Magnesium, Quality and Quantity of Fat, Hypercholesterolemia and Lipidosis," *JN* 71 (1960), 339. See also P. Harris and L. Opie (eds.), *Calcium and the Heart* (London, 1971), passim; G.R. Kellman, *Applied Cardiovascular Physiology*, 2d ed. (London, 1977), 42–3; and Warren E.C. Wacker and Bert L. Vallee, "Magnesium," in *Mineral Metabolism*, eds. Comar and Bronner 1a:495–7.

60 Edward Long, *The History of Jamaica*, 2 vols. (London, 1774) 2:526; Bryan Edwards, *The History, Civil and Commercial, of the British Colonies in the West Indies*, 4th ed., 3 vols. (London, 1807) 2:158–9; Matthew Gregory Lewis, *Journal of a West India Proprietor* (London, 1834), 106.

61 *Miniconsultation on the Mental and Physical Health Problems of Black Women* (Washington, D.C., 1974), 2; Weekes, "Obstetrics and Gynecology," 104; Committee on Maternal Nutrition/Food and Nutrition Board, National Research Council, *Maternal Nutrition and the Course of Pregnancy* (Washington, D.C., 1970), 163–71.

62 Weekes, "Obstetrics and Gynecology," 104; *Health Problems of Black Women* 4; see also Frank A. Finnerty, Jr., "Editorial: Hypertension is Different in Blacks," *JAMA* 216 (1971), 1634–5 and "Toxemia of Pregnancy as Seen by an Internist: An Analysis of 1081 Patients," *AIM* 44 (1956), 358–75.

63 J.D. Fage, "Slavery and the Slave Trade in the Context of West African History," *JAfH* 10 (1969), 393–404; M.J. Herskovits, *The New World Negro* (Bloomington, Ind., 1966), 118; A.G. Hopkins, *An Economic History of West Africa* (London, 1973), 23–6.

64 T. Lynn Smith, *Fundamentals of Population Study* (Chicago, 1960), 196–7; L.W.G. Malcolm, "Sex Ratio in African Peoples," *AA* 26 (1924), 469; C. Tietze, "A Note on the Sex Ratios of Abortions," *HB* 20 (1946), 156–60.

65 Malcolm, "Sex Ratios," 455; Esmat I. Hammond, "Studies in Fetal Differentials in Mortality, II. Differentials in Mortality by Sex and Race," *AJPH* 55 (1965), 1152; Richard Naeye et al., "Neonatal Mortality, The Male Disadvantage," *PED* 48 (1971), 902–6.

66 Fage, "Slavery and the Slave Trade," 400; Simon and Phoebe Ottenberg, *Cultures and Societies of Africa* (New York, 1960), 30; Herbert S. Klein, *The Middle Passage: Comparative Studies in the Atlantic Slave Trade* (Princeton, N.J., 1978), 240; Frank Wesley Pitman, "Slavery on British West India Plantations in the Eighteenth Century," *JNH* 11 (1926), 637; Michael Craton and James Walvin, *A Jamaican Plantation: The History of Worthy Park, 1670–1970* (Toronto, 1970), 138.

67 Philip D. Curtin, *Economic Change in Pre-Colonial Africa: Senegambia in the Era of the Slave Trade*, 2 vols. (Madison, Wis., 1974) 1:175–6; Walter Rodney, "African Slavery and Other Forms of Social Oppression on the Upper Guinea Coast in the Context of the Atlantic Slave Trade," *JAfH* 7 (1966), 437; Klein, *Middle Passage*, 241.

68 Klein, *Middle Passage*, 240–2. For an earlier statement of the argument, see Frank Tannenbaum, *Slave and Citizen: The Negro in the Americas* (New York, 1946), 35–6. For confirmation from a slave trader that his African sources insisted he take three males for every female, see Captain William Snelgrave, *A New Account of Some Parts of Guinea and the Slave Trade* (London, 1734), 73.

69 Rodney, "African Slavery," 435.

70 Robert Collins, *Practical Rules for the Management and Medical Treatment of Negro Slaves, in the Sugar Colonies* (London, 1811), 133, 134, 325; James Grainger, *An Essay on the More Common West India Diseases* . . . (London, 1764), 7–8; Francisco Eujenio Moscoso Puello, *Apuntes para la historia de la medicina de la isla de Santo Domingo* (Santo Domingo, 1977), 41.

Part II. Introduction

1 U.N., "Women in Food Production, Food Handling and Nutrition (with Special Emphasis on Africa)," *Protein-Calorie Advisory Group Bulletin* 7 (1977), 40.

2 For the diets of whites, see Richard S. Dunn, *Sugar and Slaves: The Rise of the Planter Class in the English West Indies, 1634–1713* (Chapel Hill, N.C., 1972), 275–81; Michael Craton and James Walvin, *A Jamaica Plantation: The History of Worthy Park* (Toronto, 1970), 135; Lowell Joseph Ragatz, *The Fall of the Planter Class in the British Caribbean, 1763–1833* (New York, 1928), 7–8; Robert Renny, *A History of Jamaica* (London, 1807); and Frank Wesley Pitman, *The Development of the British West Indies, 1700–1763* (New Haven, Conn., 1917), 13, 386. For a first-hand description of meals and food items served, see *Journal of a Lady of Quality*, ed. Evangeline Walker Andrews (New Haven, Conn., 1927), 95–8 and passim. For "Food Imports into the British West Indies: 1680–1845," consult the study by Richard N. Bean in *Comparative Perspectives on Slavery in New World Plantation Societies*, eds. Vera Rubin and Arthur Tuden (New York, 1977), 581–90. Finally, for assurances that in the English Islands "the poorest white person seems to consider himself nearly on a level with the richest," and presumably ate on "nearly" such a level, see Bryan Edwards, *The History; Civil and Commercial of the British Colonies in the West Indies*, 3 vols. (New York, 1964) 1:7–8. By contrast, although some house slaves probably enjoyed a better diet than the average, status did not necessarily mean a better diet for blacks. For example, white troops serving the British Crown in the West Indies were issued a pound of fresh meat every two days in addition to salt meat rations. Yet black troops were specifically denied fresh meat and only received the salted rations. See, for example, *Correspondence Relating to the Issue of Fresh Meat Rations to the Troops in Jamaica . . . and Bermuda* (London, 1840), 68, 99.

For the Spanish Islands, almost any traveler's account describes foods available and there seems no question that the wealthy and middle classes ate well. However, in both Puerto Rico and Cuba there was not the sharp dichotomy between black and white that existed in the English Islands and the racially mixed lower classes, although free, seem frequently to have eaten little better than slaves. Doubtless this is a major reason why in Cuba, at any rate, the "Whites" seem to have suffered a higher rate of apparently nutritionally related illnesses, which, as will be seen, victimized blacks almost exclusively in the English Islands.

Chapter 4. The Middle Passage and Malnutrition

1 Wilberforce letter quoted in Thomas Fowell Buxton, *The African Slave Trade and its Remedy* (London, 1840), 122.

2 George Orwell, *The Road to Wigam Pier* (London, 1937), 91.

3 For a description of these "horse trading" methods as well as the "scramble", see Daniel P. Mannix, *Black Cargoes* (New York, 1962), 128–30.

4 Nathan Irvin Huggins, *Black Odyssey* (New York, 1977), 53–4; Frank Wesley Pitman, "Slavery on British West India Plantations in the Eighteenth Century," *JNH* 11 (1926), 632; Elizabeth Donnan, ed., *Documents Illustrative of the History of the Slave Trade to America* (Washington, D.C., 1930–5) 1:206–9.

5 Frank Wesley Pitman, *The Development of the British West Indies 1700–1763* (New Haven, 1917), 78; Orlando Patterson, *The Sociology of Slavery* (London, 1967), 137–8; Philip Curtin, *The Atlantic Slave Trade: A Census* (Madison, Wis., 1969), 161.

6 For slave height data we are relying on B.W. Higman ("Growth in Afro-Caribbean Slave Populations," *AJPA* 50 [1979], 373–86), who has been in the forefront in examining the heights of some 25,000 slaves born in Africa, Trinidad, and elsewhere in the Caribbean. For determining averages, the heights of only those aged twenty-five to forty years were included "in order to exclude late-developers and height-reduction in later life" (375). Throughout the study, Higman carefully considers and then eliminates from consideration a number of reasons why his data could be misleading or unrepresentative.

7 Pitman, *Development of the British West Indies*, 69; Alexander Falconbridge, *An Account of the Slave Trade on the Coast of Africa* (London, 1788), 21, 22, 29, 53, 54. This surgeon in the slave trade was remarkably alert to the importance of nutrition. At the time of his writing (1788) it seems that some corn was grown on the Windward Coast as well. He reported that both Windward and Gold Coast blacks were very "hardy" (as opposed to "Eboes" from Bonny) and that the former raised hogs and goats. Charles C. Hughes and John M. Hunter ("Disease and 'Development' in Africa," *SSM* 3 [1970], 474) discuss the low nutritional yield of cassava and corn. However, see also Richard Annaud and Philip L. Romero ("Protein in Foodstuffs: Historical Perspective and Modern Measurement," *American Laboratory* Oct. [1976], 44), who point out that even high-yielding cereals such as wheat, rice, and corn "leave sub-Saharan Africans seriously malnourished." Finally, see Pierre Cantrelle ("Mortality," in *Population Growth and Socio-Economic Change in West Africa*, ed., John C. Caldwell [New York], 99–100) for nutrition by region in modern West Africa, which seems quite similar to that of the slave days.

8 Higman, "Growth," 374, table; Falconbridge, *Account of the Slave Trade*, 53–4.

9 There are, of course, dangers in attempting to make correlations such as these, for the nutriments in some sectors of West Africa have changed over the past few centuries. See, for example, Jean Hiernaux, *La Diversité humaine en Afrique subSaharienne: recherches biologiques* (Bruxelles, 1968). Nor for that matter can we be certain of the actual origins of slaves arriving in the New World. For a discussion see Leslie B. Rout (*The African Experience in Spanish America: 1502 to the Present Day* [Cambridge, Eng., 1976], 27–32) for Spanish America. For the British West Indies see Patterson (*Sociology of Slavery*, 113–26), and for a general overview see Curtin, *Atlantic Slave Trade*, 156ff.

10 James Grainger, *An Essay on the Most Common West India Diseases* (London, 1764), 111–15; Robert Collins, *Practical Rules for the Management and Medical Treatment of Negro Slaves in the Sugar Colonies* (London, 1811), 236; Edward Long, *The History of Jamaica*, 3 vols. (London, 1774) 2:403.

11 Long, *History of Jamaica* 2:403; Sir Stanley Davidson, et al., *Human Nutrition and Dietetics* (Edinburgh, 1975), 285.

12 Calculated from data in Higman, "Growth," 374, table.

13 R. Hoeppli, *Parasitic Diseases in Africa and the Western Hemisphere; Early Documentation and Transmission by the Slave Trade* (Basel, 1969); Johannes Postma, "Mortality in the

Dutch Slave Trade, 1675–1795," in *The Uncommon Market: Essays in the Economic History of The Atlantic Slave Trade*, eds. Henry A. Gemery and Jan S. Hogendorn (New York, 1979), 242.

14 Curtin, *Atlantic Slave Trade*, 278; Herbert S. Klein, *The Middle Passage* (Princeton, N.J., 1978), 64–5, 160–3, 173–4 and passim. For in-transit mortality in *The French Slave Trade in The Eighteenth Century; An Old Regime Business* (Madison, Wis., 1979), see the study by Robert Louis Stein, who places it around 13 percent (99). For "Mortality in the Dutch Slave Trade, 1675–1795," see Johannes Postma (273), who places it at 17 percent. For some of the methodological problems in calculating mortality, see the splendid study by Joseph C. Miller, "Mortality in the Atlantic Slave Trade: Statistical Evidence on Causality," *JIH* 11 (1981), 385–423.

15 Dauril Alden and Joseph C. Miller, "Unwanted Cargoes: The Origins and Dissemination of Smallpox via the Slave Trade to Brazil," paper delivered at the American Historical Association annual meeting 1982, Washington D.C. Miller ("Mortality in the Atlantic Slave Trade," 407 and passim) suspects that nutritional deficiencies of a severe and life-threatening nature were frequently suffered by slaves prior to boarding slaving ships. Moreover, in his study of "Legal Portuguese Slaving From Angola, Some Preliminary Indications of Volume and Directions, 1760–1830," (*Revue Française d' histoire d' Outre-Mer* 52 [1975], 156 and passim), Miller has pointed out that harvest failures would have substantially reduced the nutritional status of slaves in certain years, which in turn would have influenced mortality rates aboard ship. Miller's observations are for Angola, but may be germane for some West African regions.

16 Klein (*Middle Passage*, 157, table) has calculated an average of sixty-one days' sailing time from Africa to Jamaica for the end of the eighteenth century. Stein (*French Slave Trade*, 107) suggests the elapsed time from Africa to the Caribbean for French Slavers was two to three months.

17 Klein (*Middle Passage*, 157, table) calculates an average stay on the Coast of 114 days; Stein (*French Slave Trade*, 86) indicates that the stay of French slavers was somewhat longer. Mannix [*Black Cargoes*, 107] reported an average stay of six months to a year on the Gold Coast. Postma ("Mortality in the Dutch Slave Trade," 244) has discovered an average on the coast of seven and a half months.

18 Colin Palmer, *Human Cargoes: The British Slave Trade to Spanish America, 1700–1739* (Urbana, Ill., 1981), 50; Miller, "Mortality in the Atlantic Slave Trade," 412; Postma, "Mortality in the Dutch Slave Trade," 252; Stein, *French Slave Trade*, 100–2; Mannix, *Black Cargoes*, 122; P.M. Ashburn, *The Ranks of Death* (New York, 1947), 65, 137.

19 Palmer, *Human Cargoes*, 50; Klein, *Middle Passage*, 229; Ashburn, *Ranks of Death*, 36–37; Pitman, *Development of the British West Indies*, 68; John Riland, *Memoirs of a West-India Planter* (London, 1827), 56; Falconbridge, *Account of the Slave Trade*, 21; Hugh Crow, *Memoirs of the Late Captain Hugh Crow . . .* (London, 1830); Robert Renny, *A History of Jamaica . . .* (London, 1807), 173–4.

20 Klein, *Middle Passage*, 153; Stein, *French Slave Trade*, 107; Ashburn, *Ranks of Death*, 36; Mannix, *Black Cargoes*, 128; Donnan, ed., *Documents* 1:206–9.

21 Herbert S. Klein and Stanley L. Engerman, "A Note on Mortality in the French Slave Trade in the Eighteenth Century," in *The Uncommon Market*, eds. Gemery and Hogendorn, 270.

22 Stein, *French Slave Trade*, 96.

23 Miller, "Mortality in the Atlantic Slave Trade," 398–401 and passim. The opposite relationship has seemed the more logical one to those unfamiliar with the circumstances of the slave trade and especially to those who have sought, for various reasons, to sensationalize the more lurid aspects of the middle passage. See also Curtin (*Atlantic Slave Trade*, 279), who refers to the generalization "that the loss at sea dropped with the passage of time."

24 Miller, "Mortality in the Atlantic Slave Trade," 412.

25 Klein, *Middle Passage*, 240–1 and passim; Stein, *French Slave Trade*, 100; Postma, "Mortality in the Dutch Slave Trade," 249–50.

26 For contemporary descriptions of West African waters, which were far from placid, see the correspondence of captains and excerpts from ship logs in *New England Merchants in Africa: A History Through Documents 1802–1865*, eds. Norman R. Bennett and George E. Brooks (Boston, 1965), 21, 27, 64–5, 80–1, 107, 109, and 131.

27 Charles Wilcocks and P.C.E. Manson-Bahr (*Manson's Tropical Diseases*, 17th ed. [Baltimore, 1974], 247) report an infection rate from *Ascaris* as high as 95 percent in some West African regions.

28 Josué de Castro, *The Geography of Hunger* (Boston, 1952), 46.

29 Bacillary dysentery has a short incubation period of seven days or less, whereas amebic dysentery has a longer (twenty- to ninety-day) period of incubation (Wilcocks and Manson-Bahr, *Manson's Tropical Diseases*, 162–73, 520–8). See also George W. Hunter, William W. Frye, and J. Clyde Swartzwelder, *A Manual of Tropical Medicine*, 4th ed. (1966), 294.

30 David Eltis ("Free and Coerced Transatlantic Migrations: Some Comparisons," *The American Historical Review* 88 [1983], 276) and Klein (*Middle Passage*, 202–3 and 234–5) both indicate that dysentery was the major cause of death aboard slave ships. See also Postma, "Mortality in the Dutch Slave Trade," 252; Ashburn, *Ranks of Death*, 34, 162–3; and Donald Wax ("A Philadelphia Surgeon on a Slavery Voyage to Africa," *Pennsylvania Magazine of History and Biography* 92 [1968], 465–93 and passim) whose narrative reveals both worms and dysentery to be major causes of death aboard ship. Finally see Donnan (*Documents* 1:206–209) for cramps and "dropsy" (as well as flux) among the slaves, which suggest the abdominal symptoms of worm infection.

31 Hoeppli, *Parasitic Diseases*, 64; Palmer, *Human Cargoes*, 52, 56; Friedrich Heinrich Alexander von Humboldt, *The Island of Cuba*, (trans.), J.S. Thrasher (New York, 1856), 229.

32 See Huggins (*Black Odyssey*, 50–1), Mannix (*Black Cargoes*, 120), and Falconbridge (*Account of the Slave Trade*, 31–2) for a discussion of "fixed melancholy." See Davidson et al. [*Human Nutrition and Dietetics*, 94–8] for the process of dehydration and its symptoms. Joseph Miller, who kindly read and criticized a draft of this chapter, is responsible for urging that the effects of dehydration on slaves be considered (personal correspondence).

33 See Davidson et al (*Human Nutrition and Dietetics*, 285–7) for the symptoms of personality derangement that accompany starvation; see also Myron Winick, ed., *Hunger Disease Studies by Jewish Physicians in the Warsaw Ghetto* (New York, 1979), 43 and passim. In addition see the lengthy letter of Captain General Leopoldo O'Donnell on the subject of suicides (in many cases by not eating) of newly arrived slaves in Cuba, "O'Donnel al secretario de estado y del despacho," 31 marzo de 1844 AHN Ultramar, leg. 4620, no. 31. Finally, see Gwendolyn Midlo Hall, *Social Control in Slave Plantation Societies: A Comparison of St. Domingue and Cuba* (Baltimore, 1971), 20–3, and Mannix, *Black Cargoes*, 120–2.

34 Patterson, *Sociology of Slavery*, 99.

35 J.M. Tanner, *Foetus into Man: Physical Growth from Conception to Maturity* (Cambridge, Mass, 1978), 48; Ancel Keys et al., *The Biology of Human Starvation*, 2 vols. (Minneapolis, 1950) 1:171–4.

36 Pitman, *Development of the British West Indies*, 69; Falconbridge, *Account of the Slave Trade*, 21, 22, 29.

37 Falconbridge, *Account of the Slave Trade*, 53, 54.

38 Humboldt, *Island of Cuba*, 195, 227–29.

39 Patterson, *Sociology of Slavery*, 98; see also Collins, *Practical Rules*, 44–5.

40 Miller, "Mortality in the Atlantic Slave Trade," 414.

41 Robert W. Fogel and Stanley L. Engerman, "Recent Findings in the Study of Slave Demography and Family Structure," *SSR* 63 (1979), 567; E. Phillip Leveen, "A Quantitative Analysis of the Impact of British Suppression Policies on the Volume of the Nineteenth Century Atlantic Slave Trade," in *Race and Slavery in the Western Hemisphere: Quantitative Studies*, eds. Stanley L. Engerman and Eugene D. Genovese (Princeton, 1975), 76n. It should be noted that 25 percent mortality was probably characteristic of the late eighteenth and nineteenth centuries. Earlier in the century estimates exist of seasoning mortality as high as 50 percent; Charles Leslie, *A New and Exact Account of Jamaica* . . . (Edinburgh, 1740), 312.

42 See note 29 above; see also Hoeppli, *Parasitic Diseases*, 64 for assurance that amebic dysentery was a major problem of health in West Africa and may in fact have been an African disease.

43 Michael Craton, "Jamaican Slave Mortality: Fresh Light from Worthy Park, Longville and the Tharp Estates," *JCH* 3 (1971), 20, 26.

44 Patterson, *Sociology of Slavery*, 99; Ashburn, *Ranks of Death*, 157–65.

45 Hunter, Frye, and Swartzwelder, *Manual of Tropical Medicine*, 302.

46 Grainger, *Essay . . . on West India Diseases*, 8.

47 Collins, *Practical Rules*, 51.

48 For Jamaica, see M.G. Lewis, *Journal of a West India Proprietor, 1815–1817* (London, 1929), 105; Pitman, "Slavery on the British West India Plantations," 608; Bryan Edwards, *The History, Civil and Commercial of the British Colonies in the West Indies*, 4th ed., 3 vols. (London, 1807) 2:159; John H. Parry, "Plantation and Provision Ground: An Historical Sketch of the Introduction of Food Crops into Jamaica," *Revista de historia de America*, 39 (1955), 1–20. For Puerto Rico, see Berta Cabanillas de Rodriguez, *El Puertorriqueño y su alimentación a través de su historia (siglos XVI al XIX)* (San Juan, 1973), 276; Luis M. Díaz Soler, *Historia de la esclavitud negra en Puerto Rico* (Madrid, 1953); and for Cuba see Manuel Moreno Fraginals, *El ingenio; el complejo económico social Cubano del azúcar 1760–1860* (La Habana, 1964); Demoticus Philalethes, *Yankee Travels through the Island of Cuba; or, The Men and Government, the Laws and Customs of Cuba, as Seen by American Eyes* (New York, 1856), 26–8; Maturin Murray Ballou, *Due South; or, Cuba Past and Present* (Boston and New York, 1855), 301.

49 Lewis, *Journal*, 99; Collins, *Practical Rules*, 54; Hans Sloane, *A Voyage to the Islands Madera, Barbados, Niéves, S. Christophers and Jamaica* . . . , 2 vols. (London, 1707) 1:47.

50 Patterson, *Sociology of Slavery*, 100; see also Robert Dirks, who links low blood sugar with cold susceptibility in chap. 3 of his forthcoming *Black Saturnalia*, an ethnohistory of the British West Indian slave culture.

51 Michael Craton and James Walvin, *A Jamaican Plantation: The History of Worthy Park, 1670–1970* (Toronto, 1970), 133.

52 Edwards, *History* 2: 161; Richard S. Dunn, *Sugar and Slaves: The Rise of the Planter Class in the English West Indies, 1624–1713* (Chapel Hill, N.C., 1972), 278.

53 Claude Levy, *Emancipation, Sugar, Federalism: Barbados and the West Indies, 1833–1876* (Gainesville, Fla., 1980), 9.

54 J. Harry Bennett, *Bondsmen and Bishops; Slavery and Apprenticeship on the Codrington Plantations of Barbados, 1710–1838* (Berkeley, Calif., 1958), 37; Richard Pares, *Yankees and Creoles: The Trade Between North America and the West Indies before the American Revolution* (Cambridge, Mass., 1956), 39.

55 Jerome S. Handler, "An Archaeological Investigation of the Domestic Life of Plantation Slaves," in *Journal of the Barbados Museum and Historical Society*. 34:4 (1974), 69; Claude Levy, "Slavery and The Emancipation Movement in Barbados, 1650–1833," *JNH* 55:1 (1970), 5; E.M. Shibstone, *Instructions for the Management of a Plantation in Barbados and for the Treatment of Negroes*, etc. (London, 1786).

56 Shibstone, (*Instructions*, 25) and Collins, (*Practical Rules*, 87ff) both exhorted overseers to make certain that slaves did in fact tend provision grounds.

57 Edwards, *History* 2:161–2.
58 Cabanillas, *El Puertorriqueño y su alimentación*, 276, 290 and passim; Collins, *Practical Rules*, 99.
59 Edwards, *History* 2:162.
60 Ibid., 2:160–1.
61 Michael Craton, "Jamaican Slavery," in *Race and Slavery in the Western Hemisphere*, eds. Engerman and Genovese, 254; Richard B. Sheridan, "The Crisis of Slave Subsistence in the British West Indies During and After the American Revolution," *WMQ* 33 (1976), 640.
62 Craton and Walvin, *Jamaican Plantation*, 135.
63 Sheridan, "Crisis of Slave Subsistence," 635; Pitman, "Slavery on British West India Plantations," 608.
64 Collins, *Practical Rules*, 76–80.
65 *A Report of a Committee of the Council of Barbados, Appointed to Inquire into the Actual Condition of the Slaves* (London, 1824), 106, 113.
66 Elsa Goveia, "The West Indian Slave Laws of the Eighteenth Century," *Revista de Ciencias Sociales*, 4 (1960), 75–106; "Documento para la historia de la esclavitud de los negros en Puerto Rico–reglamento del Gobernador Don Miguel de la Torre en 1826," *BHPR* 10 (1923), 265.
67 Jorge D. Flinter, *Examen del estado actual de los esclavos de la isla de Puerto Rico bajo el gobierno Español* (New York, 1832), 37.
68 David Turnbull, *Travels in the West: Cuba, with Notices of Puerto Rico and the Slave Trade* (London, 1840), 285.
69 Francisco Morales Padron, "La vida cotidiana en una hacienda de esclavos," *Revista del Instituto de Cultura Puertorriqueña* 4:10 (1961), 27; Manuel Moreno Fraginals, "Africa in Cuba: A Quantitative Analysis of the African Populations in the Island of Cuba," in *Comparative Perspectives on Slavery in New World Plantation Societies*, eds. Vera Rubin and Arthur Tuden (New York, 1977), 198; Ramiro Guerra y Sanchez, et al., *Historia de la Nación Cubana*, 10 vols. (La Habana, 1952) 3:305.
70 Moreno Fraginals, "Africa in Cuba," 198; Guerra y Sanchez et al., *Historia* 3:305; Flinter, *Estado . . . de los Esclavos*, 37; Morales Padron, *Vida cotidiana*, 27; James Stephen, *The Slavery of the British West India Colonies Delineated . . .* , 2 vols. (London, 1824–30) 2:281; Elsa V. Goveia, *Slave Society in the British Leeward Islands at the End of the 18th Century* (New Haven, Conn., 1965), 138–93; Collins, *Practical Rules*, 75; Bennett, *Bondsmen*, 37. There is testimony, however, that frequently plantains, not corn, were the principal foodstuff for slaves in Jamaica. See, for example, Renny, *History of Jamaica*, 177.
71 See H.F. Welbourne (*Nutrition in Tropical Countries* [London, 1963], 42) for the merits of and difficulties in raising these crops. Collins (*Practical Rules*, 95) reports that with care yams could be preserved from June until October. For the importance of these crops in the diets of slaves in the Spanish Islands, see Flinter, *Estado . . . de los esclavos*, 37, 244; Fray Iñigo Abbad y Lasierra, *Historia geográfica, civil y natural de la isla de San Juan Bautista de Puerto Rico* (San Juan, 1886), 183; and Samuel Hazard, *Cuba with Pen and Pencil* (Hartford, Conn., 1871), 95.
72 Sidney W. Mintz and Richard Price, *An Anthropological Approach to the Afro-American Past: A Caribbean Perspective* (Philadelphia, 1976), 38; Patterson, *Sociology of Slavery*, 216–23; William Beckford, *A Descriptive Account of . . . Jamaica*, 2 vols. (London, 1790) 2:153; William Sells, *Remarks on the Condition of the Slaves in the Island of Jamaica* (London, 1823), 12; John Steven Cabot Abbott, *South and North; or Impressions Received During a Trip to Cuba and the South* (New York, 1860), 40–1, 136; Maturin M. Ballou, *History of Cuba; or, Notes of a Traveller in the Tropics . . .* (Boston, 1854), 301; Levy, *Emancipation, Sugar and Federalism*, 5; Handler, "Domestic Life of Plantation Slaves," 69; Pitman, "Slavery on British West India Plantations," 608, 625.

73   Higman, "Growth in Afro-Caribbean Slave Populations," 383; Gerald C. Friedman, "The Heights of Slaves in Trinidad," *Social Science History* 6 (1982), 503 and passim.
74   Robert A. Margo and Richard H. Steckel, "The Height of American Slaves: New Evidence on Slave Nutrition and Health," *Social Science History* 6 (1982), 516–38; Robert W. Fogel, Stanley L. Engerman, and James Trussell, "Exploring the Uses of Data on Height: The Analysis of Long Term Trends in Nutrition, Labor Welfare and Labor Productivity," *Social Science History* 6 (1982), 416.
75   Kenneth F. Kiple and Virginia H. King, *Another Dimension to the Black Diaspora: Diet, Disease, and Racism* (New York, 1981), 81–3.
76   Richard N. Bean, "Food Imports into the British West Indies: 1680–1845," in *Comparative Perspectives on Slavery in New World Plantation Societies*, eds. Rubin and Tuden, 587; Jerome S. Handler and Frederick W. Lange, *Plantation Slavery in Barbados* (Cambridge, Eng., 1977), 87; Bennett, *Bondsmen*, 37. For Jamaica, see Stephen, *Slavery of the British West India Colonies* 2:286.
77   Higman, "Growth in Afro-Caribbean Slave Populations," 383. See also Michael Craton, "Hobbesian or Panglossian? The Two Extremes of Slave Conditions in the British Caribbean 1783 to 1834," *WMQ* 35 (1978), 324–56.
78   Higman, "Growth in Afro-Caribbean Slave Populations," 383.
79   See Chapter 5 for an analysis of the basic slave diets.
80   John W. Blassingame, ed., *Slave Testimony: Two Centuries of Letters, Speeches, Interviews, and Autobiographies* (Baton Rouge, La., 1977), 259–60; Abbad y Lasierra, *Historia*, 183; Francisco Eujenio Moscoso Puello, *Apuntes para la historia de la medicina de la isla de Santo Domingo* (Santo Domingo, 1977), 39; Jean Barthelemy Danzille, *Observations sur les maladies des nègres, leurs causes, leurs traitements, et les moyens de les prevenir* 2d ed., 2 vols., (Paris, 1892) 1:24.
81   Grainger, *Essay . . . on West India Diseases*, 71; Collins, *Practical Rules*, 100; Stephen, *Slavery of the British West India Colonies* 2:281; "Circular del gobierno superior civil de la isla de Cuba," 31 Mayo de 1844, AHN Ultramar, Leg. 17, No 17; Secretaria del gobierno superior civil de la isla de Cuba, "Espediente sobre las causas que influyen en el frecuente suicidio de los esclavos, 1846," AHN Ultramar Leg. 3550; "Reglamento de esclavos . . . en 1826," *BHPR* 10 (1923), 265; Humphrey E. Lamur, "Demography of Surinam Plantation Slaves in the Last Decade before Emancipation: The Case of Catharina Sophia," in *Comparative Perspectives on Slavery in New World Plantation Societies*, eds. Rubin and Tuden, 171.
82   Collins, *Practical Rules*, 74–81; Patterson, *Sociology of Slavery*, 217.
83   Dunn, *Sugar and Slaves*, 248; Craton, "Hobbesian or Panglossian?" 345; E. van den Boogaart and P.C. Emmer, "Plantation Slavery in Surinam in the Last Decade before Emancipation: The Case of Catharina Sophia," in *Comparative Perspectives on Slavery in New World Plantation Societies*, eds. Rubin and Tuden, 205–25.
84   John Brathwaite, "Odd Pages from Old Records," *Journal of the Barbados Museum and Historical Society* 18 (1950), 26; David Lowenthal, "The Population of Barbados," *SES* 6 (1957), 451–2; Sheridan, "Crisis of Slave Subsistence," 615–41; Bennett, *Bondsmen*, 37–8, 100–1; Richard Sheridan, *Sugar and Slavery: An Economic History of the British West Indies, 1623–1775* (Baltimore, 1974), 245; Patterson, *Sociology of Slavery*, 218.
85   Lowell Joseph Ragatz, *The Fall of the Planter Class in the British Caribbean 1763–1833* (New York, 1928), 190–1 and passim.
86   See Chapter 7.
87   Robert Dirks, "Resource Fluctuations and Competitive Transformations in West Indian Slave Societies," in *Extinction and Survival in Human Populations*, eds. Charles D. Laughlin, Jr. and Ivan A. Brady (New York, 1978), 141–2.
88   Stephen, *Slavery of the British West India Colonies* 1:95–6 and passim; Lewis, *Journal*, 173; Edwards, *History* 2:161–62; Collins, *Practical Rules*, 99.
89   Wilcocks and Manson-Bahr, *Manson's Tropical Diseases*, 256; Hoeppli, *Parasitic Dis-*

eases, 113–14. There are two types of hookworms that affect man. One, *Ancylostoma duodenale*, the Old World hookworm, is prevalent in southern Europe and northern Africa as well as much of the Far East and the Pacific. The other, *A. americanum or Necator americanus*, also occurs in Africa, Asia, and the South Pacific, and is the predominant human hookworm in the Americas.

90 The Rockefeller Archive Center in Pocantico Hills, North Tarrytown, New York contains a wealth of information on hookworm eradication in the American South, the Caribbean, and Brazil. The original survey in the American South was done "without racial distinction" because of the explosive racial situation in the South and because of a feeling in some quarters that "the Negro is the worst carrier of the infection" that could only add to the explosiveness if scientifically confirmed. See RAC, RSC, "Report of the Assistant Secretary for Eradication of Hookworm Disease," in *Quarterly Reports*, Vol. 1, June 1910, December 1914, p. 13, and "Wickliffe Rose to Wm. W. Dinsmore," June 17, 1912 RAC, RSC, Series 2, Box 2, Folder 52. Nonetheless, physicians quickly noticed a black resistance to hookworm disease. See, for example, the observations of R.H. Knowlton on "Hookworm," p. 11, or those by Charles A. Kofoid to a Dr. Meyer, January 6, 1919, both in RAC, IHB, Series 2, 200 U.S.A., Box 3, Folder 18. Later in the Caribbean and Brazil where surveys were carried out by race, black resistance to hookworm disease was confirmed countless times. For subsequent studies, which supported these earlier findings, see Geoffrey M. Jeffery et al., "Study of Intestinal Helminth Infections in a Coastal South Carolina Area," *PHR* 78 (1963), 49; A.E. Keller, W.S. Leathers, and H.C. Ricks, "An Investigation of the Incidence and Intensity of Infestation of Hookworm in Mississippi," *American Journal of Hygiene* 19 (1934), 629–56. See also the Rockefeller resurveys conducted in the 1920s, which were done by race and revealed a rate of white infection twice to three times that of blacks. They are summarized in W.P. Jacocks, "Hookworm Surveys and Resurveys, 1910–1915, 1920–1923" in RAC, Sanitary Commission, Series 200, Box 3, Folder 21. Finally, for black hookworm resistance see Julian Herman Lewis, *The Biology of the Negro* (Chicago, 1942), 255–7 and Gilbert F. Otto, "Hookworm," in *Maxcy-Rosenau-Preventive Medicine and Public Health*, 19th ed., ed. Philip E. Sartwell (New York, 1973), 221.

91 Michael Gelfand, *The Sick African* (Capetown, 1957), 125–36; Aaron E.J. Masawe and G. Swal, "Iron Deficiency and Infection," *Lancet* 1 (1975), 1241; Mary Ellison, *The Black Experience: American Blacks Since 1865* (New York, 1974), 56; David Lee Chandler, "Health and Slavery: A Study of Health Conditions Among Negro Slaves in the Viceroyalty of the New Granada and its Associated Slave Trade, 1600–1810," unpublished Ph.D. dissertation (Tulane University, La., 1972), 220.

92 Asa C. Chandler and Clark P. Read, *Introduction to Parasitology with Special Reference to the Parasites of Man*, 10th ed. (New York, 1961), 428. Elizabeth Barrett-Connor, "Anemia and Infection," *AJM* 52 (1972), 243.

93 George I. Lythcott, Calvin H. Sinnette, and Donald R. Hopkins, "Pediatrics," in *Textbook of Black-Related Diseases*, ed. Richard Allen Williams (New York, 1975), 178–9.

94 Greer Williams, *The Plague Killers* (New York, 1969), 9.

95 C.C. Bass, "The Symptoms and Diagnosis of Hookworm Disease," *NOMSJ* (1910), 252. See also John Ettling (*The Germ of Laziness* [Cambridge, Mass., 1981] 4, 172–6) for his comments on the phenomenon of black hookworm resistance in the South.

96 "Despatch from the Governor of Barbados with Enclosures by Dr. Hutson, Inspector of Health, with Regard to the Prevalence of Ankylostomiasis in Certain Districts," RAC, IHB, Series 2, 435 Barbados, Box 43, Folder 12; George P. Paul, *Report of Ankylostomiasis Infection Survey of Barbados* (New York, 1917), 45.

97 H. Muench, "Final Report on the Hookworm Infection Survey of St. Christopher (St. Kitts) British West Indies 1935," RAC, IHB, 439 Leeward Islands, Box 44, Folder

271; H. Muench, "Final Report on the Hookworm Infection Survey of Dominica, British West Indies, April–July 1924," RAC, IHB, Series 2, 455 Windward Islands, Box 45, Folder 281; "Report on Work for the Relief and Control of Uncinariasis in Trinidad from August 11, 1914 to March 31, 1915," RAC, IHB, Series 2, 451, Trinidad and Tobago, Box 45, Folder 274; M.E. Conner, "Report on Hookworm Infection Survey of Jamaica from June 14 to July 31, 1918," RAC, IHB, Series 2, 437 Jamaica, Box 43, Folder 262; Paul, *Report*, 49.

98 Robert W. Hegman, "Porto Rico as a Field for the Study and Investigation of Tropical Disease," unpublished paper, RAC, IHB, Series 2, 243, Puerto Rico, Box 39, Folder 130; M.T. Ashcroft, "A History and General Survey of the Helminth and Protozoal Infections of the West Indies," *Annals of Tropical Medicine and Parasitology* 59 (1965), 481; (n.a.) "Ankylostomiasis" (address delivered before Trinidad Estates in 1914), RAC, IHB, Series 2, 451 Trinidad and Tobago, Box 45, Folder 276.

99 Hunter, Frye, and Swartzwelder, *Manual of Tropical Medicine*, 441, 439.

100 Moscoso Puello, *Historia de la Medicina*, 39.

101 Lythcott, Sinnette, and Hopkins, "Pediatrics," 177; Todd L. Savitt, *Medicine and Slavery; the Diseases and Health Care of Blacks in Antebellum Virginia* (Urbana, Ill., 1978), 64–5; Robert P. Parsons, "History of Haitian Medicine," *Annals of Medical History* 1 (1929), 295. The Rockefeller Surveys for hookworm infection were often expanded to include *Ascaris* and *Trichuris* infection as well. See, for example, the survey of Grenada where of 31,706 examined for hookworm, 79 percent proved positive for *Ascaris* and 73 percent for *Trichuris*: H.S. Colwell, "Reports on Work for the Relief of Hookworm Disease in Grenada from December 1, 1914 to December 31, 1917," RAC, IHB Series 2, 455 Windward Islands, Box 46, Folder 283.

102 Wilcocks and Manson-Bahr, *Manson's Tropical Diseases*, 273.

103 Hunter, Frye, and Swartzwelder, *Manual of Tropical Medicine*, 435; Lythcott, Sinnette, and Hopkins, "Pediatrics," 177.

104 Henry L. Barnett, ed., *Pediatrics*, 15th ed. (New York, 1972), 801–2; Hunter, Frye, and Swartzwelder, *Manual of Tropical Medicine*, 430–3.

105 Grainger, *Essay . . . on West India Diseases*, 7; John Williamson, *Medical and Miscellaneous Observations Relative to the West India Islands*, 2 vols. (Edinburgh, 1817) 1:52; William Hillary, *Observations on the Changes of the Air and the Concomitant Epidemical Diseases in the Island of Barbados* (London, 1759), 318–22. See also the appropriate pages of Benjamin Moseley, *A Treatise on Tropical Diseases* (London, 1789) and James Thomson, *A Treatise on the Diseases of Negroes as they Occur in the Island of Jamaica; With Observations on the Country Remedies* (Jamaica, 1820). Some U.S. physicians also viewed worms as an important killer of slaves. See for example P. Tidyman, "A Sketch of the Most Remarkable Diseases of the Negroes of the Southern States, with an Account of the Method of Treating Them Accompanied by Physiological Observations," *Philadelphia Journal of the Medical and Physical Sciences*, 12 (1826), 331 and Daniel Drake, "Diseases of the Negro Population – in a letter to Rev. Mr. Pinney," *Southern Medical and Surgical Journal*, new series, vol. 1 (1845), 341.

106 William Malcolm Hailey, *An African Survey* (London, 1957), 1119; Hughes and Hunter, "Diseases and 'Development' in Africa," 448; J.P. Carter et al., "Nutrition and Parasitism Among Rural Pre-School Children in South Carolina," *JNMA* 62:3 (1970), 190; Leonard Greenbaum, "Bilharziasis/Schistosomiasis," *Phoenix* 1 (1961) 3; Nevin S. Scrimshaw, Carl E. Taylor, and John E. Gordon, *Interactions of Nutrition and Infection* (Geneva, 1968), 47, 102, 106; John R.K. Robson, *Malnutrition: Its Causation and Control*, 2 vols. (New York, 1972) 1:113; C.C. DeSilva and N.Q. Baptist, *Tropical Nutritional Disorders of Infants and Children* (Springfield, Ill., 1969), 23.

107 Sloane, *Voyage to the Islands* 1:115, 126; Hillary, *Diseases in the Island of Barbados*, 319; The method was still used in the Caribbean during this century although not

recommended by the medical profession, for if the worm is broken, serious infection can result. Thomas T. Mackie, George W. Hunter, and C. Brooke Worth, *A Manual of Tropical Medicine*, 2d ed. (Philadelphia, 1954), 454. Today, however, the guinea worm seems to have disappeared from the West Indies. Ashcroft, "Helminth and Protozoan Infections," 484.

108 Hoeppli, *Parasitic Diseases*, 121. For the disease among slaves in the Charleston region of the southern United States, see Todd L. Savitt, "Filariasis in the United States," *JHM* 32 (1977), 140–50.

109 Wilcocks and Manson-Bahr, *Manson's Tropical Diseases*, 194; Oscar Felsenfeld, *Synopsis of Clinical Tropical Medicine* (St. Louis, 1965), 243.

110 Wilcox and Manson-Bahr, *Manson's Tropical Diseases*, 198. On the other hand, Oscar Felsenfeld (*The Epidemiology of Tropical Diseases* [Springfield, Ill., 1966], 265) points out that males in the regions where the mosquito vectors are found are usually less heavily dressed than females.

111 Hillary, *Diseases in the Island of Barbados*, 304–17; John Stewart, *An Account of Jamaica* (London, 1808), 270.

112 J. Bovell, "Observations on the Climate of Barbados, and its Influence on Disease; Together with Remarks on Ankylostomiasis or Barbados Leg," *BAJMPS* 4 (1848), 170.

113 August Hirsch, *Handbook of Geographical and Historical Pathology*, 3 vols. (London, 1883) 3:725; E.R. Stitt, "Our Disease Inheritance from Slavery," *United States Medical Bulletin* 4 (1928), 811. Despite its nineteenth-century prevalence in Cuba, filariasis seems to have receded greatly with the end of the slave trade and is not much of a problem today. Nor is it a problem in Trinidad and in Jamaica where the filarial worm "has never been transmitted." Ashcroft ("Helminth and Protozoal Infections," 481–2) also reports that blacks seem to be racially susceptible to microfilaremia.

Chapter 5. Plantation Nutrition

1 H. Hoetink, *Caribbean Race Relations: A Study of Two Variants* (London, 1967), 2.

2 I.P. Pavlov, "Physiology of Digestion," in *Nobel Lectures – Physiology of Medicine, 1901–1921* (New York, 1967), 140–55.

3 B.W. Higman, "Growth in Afro-Caribbean Slave Populations," *AJPA* 50 (1979), 382.

4 R.N. Bean, "The Imports of Fish to Barbados in 1698," *Journal of the Barbados Museum and Historical Society* 35 (1975), 17–21; James Stephen, *The Slavery of the British West India Colonies Delineated*, 2 vols. (London, 1824), 2:286. The Cuban import figures, an average of the years 1848–50, have been taken from John S. Thrasher, "Cuba and Louisiana, Letter to Samuel J. Peters," published in *The New Orleans Picayune*, May 7, 1854. They in turn were divided by the slave population of the 1846 Census as found in Kenneth F. Kiple, *Blacks in Colonial Cuba 1774–1899* (Gainesville, Florida, 1976), appendix.

5 Manuel Moreno Fraginals, "Africa in Cuba: A Quantitative Analysis of the African Population in the Island of Cuba," in *Comparative Perspectives on Slavery in New World Plantation Societies*, eds. Vera Rubin and Arthur Tuden (New York, 1977), 198.

6 Food and Agriculture Organization of the United Nations, *Calorie Requirements* (Washington D.C., 1950), 23–4; J.A. Close, "Quelques Résultats d'une enquête alimentaire au Ruanda-Urundi," *III Conferência interafricana de nutrião (Luanda)* (Angola and Portugal, 1956) 2:545–59; B.M. Nicol, "Maintenance and Improvement of the Diets of the Nigerian Population," *III Conferência interafricana de nutrição* 2:239–43.

7 Puerto Rico does not seem to have imported large quantities of beef from Buenos Aires as Cuba did. Other grains issued from time to time in place of rice or corn include guinea corn, rye meal, wheat flour, and dried beans, with guinea corn the

most frequent. Its nutritional properties, however, approximate those of corn (maize) so closely that there was no need to construct a separate breakdown.

8   Melville Sahyum (ed.), *Proteins and Amino Acids in Nutrition* (New York, 1948), 474, table; Benjamin Stanley Platt, *Nutrition in the British West Indies* (London, 1946), 22.

9   Michael Craton and James Walvin, *A Jamaican Plantation: A History of Worthy Park, 1670–1970* (London, 1970), 135; Edward Long, *The History of Jamaica*, 2 vols. (London, 1774), 2:413.

10 Stephen, *Slavery of the British West India Colonies* 2:282.

11 G.H.O. Burgess, et al. (eds.), *Developments in Handling and Processing Fish* (London, 1965), 56.

12 Ibid., 60; Aaron Altschul, *Proteins, Their Chemistry and Politics* (New York, 1965), 152–61.

13 Sir Stanley Davidson et al., *Human Nutrition and Dietetics* (Edinburgh, 1975), 65. For the method of jerking beef, see Reay Tannahill, *Food in History* (New York, 1973), 275.

14 Ricardo Bressani, "The Importance of Corn for Human Nutrition in Latin America and Other Countries," *Conference on Nutritional Improvement of Corn, Proceedings* (Guatamala, 1972): Altschul, *Proteins*, 273–4.

15 Nevin S. Scrimshaw, "Shattuck Lecture – Strengths and Weaknesses of the Committee Approach: An Analysis of Past and Present Recommended Dietary Allowances for Protein in Health and Disease," *NEJM* 294 (1976), 201–3.

16 Scrimshaw (ibid.) adds that for this reason nitrogen losses are underestimated for individuals in the tropics. See also C. Frank Consolazio et al., "Protein Metabolism during Intensive Physical Training in the Young Adult," *AJCN* 28 (1975), 29–33, and Mark D. Altschule (ed.), *Nutritional Factors in General Medicine: Effects of Stress and Distorted Diets* (Springfield, Ill., 1978), 21.

17 Stephen, *Slavery of the British West India Colonies* 2:307; Carlos Larrazabal Blanco, *Los negros y la esclavitud en Santo Domingo* (Santo Domingo, 1975), 107; Altschul, *Proteins*, 198–202; Michael S. Laguerre, "Haitian Americans," in *Ethnicity and Medical Care*, ed. Alan Harwood (Cambridge, Mass., 1981), 178; Great Britain, Economic Advisory Council, Committee on Nutrition in the Colonial Empire, *Nutrition in the Colonial Empire*, 2 parts (London, 1939) 2:92.

18 Altschule, *Nutritional Factors*, 31.

19 League of Nations Technical Commission on Nutrition, *The Problems of Nutrition* (Geneva, 1936), 4.

20 Leonard W. Aurand and A.E. Woods, *Food Chemistry* (Westport, Conn., 1973), 122; Davidson et al., *Human Nutrition and Dietetics*, 144.

21 It is true that vitamin A can be stored by the body, and because sweet potatoes (many kinds of which are high in vitamin A) were sometimes consumed seasonally, doubtless some slaves had higher levels of vitamin A than the analysis suggests. On the other hand, when vitamin A is no longer ingested, it is rapidly eliminated from the liver and consequently even 'storage' of vitamin A only benefits the individual for two or three months (Henrik Dam and Ebbe Søndergaard, "Fat-Soluble Vitamins," in *Nutrition*, eds., George H. Beaton and Earle Willard McHenry, 3 vols. [New York, 1964] 2:9). Moreover it seems that blacks maintain a lower serum level of vitamin A (despite a normal level in the liver), which has led some researchers to believe that the blacks' ability to mobilize the vitamin may be somehow impaired or at least different from that of whites (P.J. Leonard and J.G. Banwell, "The Absorption of Vitamin A as an Index of Malabsorption in African Subjects," *East African Medical Journal* 41 [1964], 501–4). If so, the difference probably lies in the interplay of sunlight on black skin. See W.M. Politzer and E.H. Clover, "Serum Vitamin A Concentration in Healthy White and Bantu Adults Living Under Normal Conditions on the Witwatersrand," *South African Medical Journal* 41 (1967), 1012–15.

22 L.E. Lloyd, B.E. McDonald, and E.W. Crampton, *Fundamentals of Nutrition*, 2nd ed. (San Francisco, 1978), 166; Roger J. Williams et al., *The Biochemistry of B Vitamins* (New York, 1950), 276–82; Aurand and Woods, *Food Chemistry*, 210.

23 Nelson A. Fernandez, et al., "Nutrition Survey of Two Rural Puerto Rican Areas Before and After a Community Improvement Program," *AJCN* 22 (1969), 1639–51.

24 Aurand and Woods, *Food Chemistry*, 211; Lloyd, McDonald, and Crampton, *Fundamentals of Nutrition*, 163; Sylvia Cover and William H. Smith, "Retention of Thiamine and Pantothenic Acid in Pork after Stewing," *Food Research*, 17 (1952), 148–52; E.E. Rice, "The Nutritional Content and Value of Meat and Meat Products," in *The Science of Meat and Meat Products*, 2d ed., eds. J.F. Price and B.S. Schweigert (San Francisco, 1971).

25 A. Barclay, *A Practical View of the Present State of Slavery in the West Indies*, 2d ed. (London, 1827), 307; R.J. Levis, *Diary of a Spring Holiday in Cuba* (Philadelphia, 1872), 49; Francisco Morales Padron "La vida cotidiana en una hacienda de esclavos," *Revista del instituto de cultura puertoriqueña* 4 (1961), 27; William Beckford, *A Descriptive Account of . . . Jamaica*, 2 vols. (London, 1790) 2:148–9; [John Stewart] *An Account of Jamaica* (London, 1808), 231–2; Long, *History of Jamaica* 2:413 .

26 Diva Sanjur (*Puerto Rican Food Habits: A Socio-Cultural Approach* [Ithaca, 1971], 23) explains that it is only the recent technique of enriching rice by replacing the thiamine lost in the polishing process that stands between many in the Caribbean today and the thiamine deficiency that would result from their fish and rice diets.

27 Lloyd, McDonald, and Crampton, *Fundamentals of Nutrition*, 163; H.H. Mitchell and Marjorie Edman, *Nutrition and Climatic Stress* (Springfield, Ill., 1951), 92; Grace A. Goldsmith, "The B Vitamins: Thiamine, Riboflavin, Niacin," in *Nutrition: A Comprehensive Treatise*, eds. George H. Beaton and Earle Willard McHenry, 3 vols. (New York, 1964–66), 2:120.

28 Williams, *Biochemistry of the B Vitamins*, 33 and passim; John D. Kirschmann (ed.), *Nutrition Almanac*, rev. ed. (New York, 1979), 23.

29 Ivan D. Beghin, W. Fougere, and K.W. King, "L'Ariboflavinose en Haiti," *Archivos Latinoamericanos de nutrición* 17 (1967), 95–107.

30 That niacin in corn is bound was the discovery of E. Kodichek. See his "The Effect of Alkaline Hydrolysis of Maize on the Availability of its Nicotinic Acid to the Pig," *British Journal of Nutrition* 10 (1956), 51–67 and "Nicotinic Acid and the Pellagra Problem," *Bibliotheca et nutritio dieta* 4 (1962), 109–27. For a recent summary of the state of research on the disease see M.R. Barakat, "Pellagra," *WHO Monograph Series* 62 (1976), 126–35.

31 M.K. Horwitt, "Niacin-Tryptophan Requirements of Man," *JADA* 34 (1958), 914–19; Kamala Krishnaswamy and Coluther Gopalan, "Effect of Isoleucine on Skin and Electroencephalogram in Pellagra," *Lancet* 2 (1971), 1167–9; Constance Kies, and Hazel M. Fox, "Interrelationships of Leucine with Lysine, Tryptophan and Niacin as They Influence Protein Value of Cereal Grains for Humans," *Cereal Chemistry* 49 (1972), 223–31; C. Gopalan and K.S. Jaya Rao, "Pellagra and Amino Acid Imbalance," *Vitamins and Hormones* 33 (1975), 505–28.

32 Margaret S. Chaney and Margaret L. Ross, *Nutrition*, 8th ed. (Boston, 1971), 267; N.B.S. Raghuramulu, Narasinga Rao, and C. Gopalan, "Amino Acid Imbalance and Tryptophan-Niacin Metabolism. I. Effect of Excess Leucine on the Urinary Excretion of Tryptophan-Niacin Metabolites in Rats," *JN* 86 (1965), 100–6.

33 F.A. Robinson, *The Vitamin B Complex* (New York, 1951); Chaney and Ross, *Nutrition*, 278.

34 For the differences in vitamin C content between uncooked and cooked foods such as the sweet potato, which per pound raw contains 69 mg of vitamin C, but only 26 mg after being boiled in the skin, see Catherine F. Adams, *Nutritive Value of American Foods in Common Units*, USDA Agriculture Handbook N 456 (Washington, D.C., 1975), 257–8 and passim.

35 Eleanor Noss Whitney and Eva May Nunnelley Hamilton, *Understanding Nutrition* (St. Paul, Minn., 1977), 321. It is doubtful that any slaves had copper kettles, but copper utensils too destroy vitamin C. See Kirschmann (ed.), *Nutrition Almanac*, 44. For assurance that slaves were issued iron pots, see Frank Wesley Pitman, "Slavery on British West India Plantations in the Eighteenth Century," *JNH* 11 (1926), 595 and J. Harry Bennett, *Bondsmen and Bishops* (Berkeley, Calif., 1958), 33.

36 Bela Ringlehann, Felix Konety-Ahulu, and Silas R.A. Docu, "Studies on Iron Metabolism in Sickle Cell Anaemia, Sickle Cell Haemoglobin C Disease, and Haemoglobin C Disease Using a Large Volume Liquid Scintillation Counter," *Journal of Clinical Pathology* 23 (1970), 132; Marshall T. Newman, "Ecology and Nutritional Stress," in *Culture, Disease, and Healing: Studies in Medical Anthropology*, ed. David Landy (New York, 1977), 320; Miguel Lyrisse and Carlos Martinez-Torres, "Food Iron Absorption: Iron Supplementation of Food," in *Progress in Hematology*, eds. Elmer B. Brown and Carl V. Moore (New York, 1971), 140 and passim; Virgil F. Fairbanks, John L. Fahey, and Ernest Beutler, *Clinical Disorders of Iron Metabolism*, 2d rev. ed. (New York, 1971), 238.

37 Layrisse and Martinez-Torres, "Food Iron Absorption," 140; Kirschmann (ed.), *Nutrition Almanac*, 71; Whitney and Hamilton, *Understanding Nutrition*, 314; B. Brozovid, "Absorption of Iron," in *Intestinal Absorption in Man*, eds. Ian McColl and G.E. Sladen (New York, 1975), 279–80; James D. Cook, "Absorption of Food Iron," *Federation Proceedings* 36(7)(1977), 2028–32; Ann Ashworth et al., "Absorption of Iron from Maize (*Zea mays* L.) and Soya Beans (*Glycine hispada* Max.) in Jamaican Infants," *British Journal of Nutrition* 29 (1973), 269; Adam Turnbull, "Iron Absorption," in *Iron in Biochemistry and Medicine*, eds. A. Jacobs and M. Worwood (New York, 1974), 371–4.

38 See Chapter 3.

39 D.M. Hegsted, "Calcium, Phosphorus and Magnesium," in *Modern Nutrition in Health and Disease: Dietotherapy*, 4th ed., eds. Michael G. Wohl and Robert S. Goodhart (Philadelphia, 1971), 323–38.

40 See Frederick J. Simoons ("New Light on Ethnic Differences in Adult Lactose Intolerance," *Digestive Diseases* 18 [1973]) for lactose intolerance rates in the Caribbean.

41 Michael Craton, "Jamaican Slave Mortality," in *Race and Slavery in the Western Hemisphere: Quantitative Studies*, eds. Stanley L. Engerman and Eugene D. Genovese (Princeton, N.J., 1975), 254; Pitman, "Slavery on British West India Plantations," 625; M.G. Lewis, *Journal of a West India Proprietor, 1815–1817* (London, 1929) 166–7; Robert Collins, *Practical Rules for the Management and Medical Treatment of Negro Slaves, in the Sugar Colonies* (London, 1811), 101.

42 H. Cullumbine, et al., "Mineral Metabolism on Rice Diets," *British Journal of Nutrition* 4 (1950), 101–11; Firman E. Bear, "Soil and Man," in *Hunger and Food*, ed. Josué de Castro (London, 1958), 45; Mitchell and Edman, *Nutrition and Climatic Stress*, 94.

43 Berta Cabanillas de Rodriguez, *El Puertorriqueño y su alimentacion a través de su historia* (*siglos xvi al xix*) (San Juan, 1973), 339; "Food Composition Tables of the Important Foodplants used in West Africa," in *Protein-Calorie Malnutrition*, ed. A. von Muralt (Heidelberg, 1969), 158, 166.

44 Richard S. Dunn, *Sugar and Slaves; The Rise of the Planter Class in the English West Indies, 1624–1713* (Chapel Hill, N.C., 1972), 279; [E.M. Shibstone] *Instructions for the Management of a Plantation in Barbadoes and for the Treatment of Negroes, etc.* (London, 1786), 26; *Report of a Committee of the Council of Barbadoes, Appointed to Inquire into the Actual Condition of the Slaves* (London, 1824), 106, 113.

45 Slaves received dried peas or beans only if they were grown locally for there is little mention in the literature of imported legumes. See Sanjur, *Puerto Rican Food Habits*, 25, 26 for the fruitful marriage of beans and rice. Sidney W. Mintz (*Caribbean Transformations* [Chicago, 1974], 227), however, reports that the dish would have been a "luxury" during the slave days.

46 John Brathwaite, "Odd Pages from Old Records," *Journal of the Barbados Museum and Historical Society* 18 (1950), 26; John Williamson, *Medical and Miscellaneous Observations Relative to the West India Islands*, 2 vols. (Edinburgh, 1817), 1:137.

47 Computed from "Food Composition Tables of the Important Foodplants Used in West Africa," in *Protein-Calorie Malnutrition*, ed. von Muralt, 158.

48 Fray Iñigo Abbad y Lasierra, *Historia geográfica, civil y natural de la isla de San Juan Bautista de Puerto Rico* (San Juan, 1886), 183; Larrazabel Blanco, *La esclavitud en Santo Domingo*, 107; Davidson, *Human Nutrition and Dietetics*, 271; H.F. Welbourne, *Nutrition in Tropical Countries* (London, 1963), 43.

49 Government of Puerto Rico, Department of Education, *Tropical Foods* 3 (1925) 16; Sanjur, *Puerto Rican Food Habits* 23, table. Food values have been calculated for yautia. The assumption is that Cuba's malinga and Puerto Rico's yautia were the same plant, *Xanthosoma sagittae-folium*, of which there are both a white and yellow variety, with the yellow containing a fair amount of vitamin A. See Juan J. Angulo, Cesar Fuentes, and Margarita Johnson, "The Carotene Content of Cuban Foods," *JN* 31 (1946), 466.

50 John Parry, "Plantation and Provision Ground," *RHA* 39 (1955), 13.

51 Ibid., 12; Sanjur, *Puerto Rican Food Habits*, 21.

52 "Food Composition Tables of the Important Foodplants Used in West Africa," in *Protein-Calorie Malnutrition*, ed. von Muralt, 176.

53 Parry, "Plantation and Provision Ground," 16–17; Jose Antonio Saco, *Colección de papeles científicos, históricos, políticos y de otros ramos sobre la isla de Cuba . . .* , 3 vols. (Paris, 1858) 1:387–8; Angulo, Fuentes, and Johnson, "Carotene Content of Cuban Foods," 468 and table.

54 Collins, *Practical Rules*, 96–7; Parry, "Plantation and Provision Ground," 18–19.

55 Conrado Asenjo et al., "Ascorbic Acid and Dehydroascorbic Acid in Some Raw and Cooked Puerto Rican Starch Foods," *Food Research* 17 (1952), 132; Conrado F. Asenjo, "Niacin Content of Tropical Foods," *Journal of Food Science* 15 (1950), 465–70; Conrado F. Asenjo, "Thiamin Content of Tropical Foods," *Food Research* 13 (1948), 94–9; M.T. Ashcroft, I.C. Buchanan, and H.G. Lovell, "Heights and Weights of Primary School Children in St. Christopher-Nevis-Anguilla, West Indies," *WIJTMH* 68 (1965), 278–9; K.W. King, et al., "Food Patterns from Dietary Surveys in Rural Haiti," *JADA* 53 (1968), 114–18; David Lowenthal, "The Population of Barbados," *SES* 6 (1957), 462; W.E. McCulloch, "Thirty Five Years Experience of Colonial Nutrition," *WIMJ* (1958), 203–4; Jacques M. May and Donna L. McLellan, *The Ecology of Malnutrition in the Caribbean* (New York, 1973), 328 and passim; Hazel E. Munsell, "Ascorbic Acid Content of Fruits of Puerto Rico with Data on Miscellaneous Products," *Food Research* 10 (1945), 42–51. See also Fougere, Beghin, and King, "L'Ariboflavinose en Haiti," 95–107; Fernandez et al., "Nutrition Survey," 1650; and Benjamin Stanley Platt, *Nutrition in the British West Indies* (London, 1946) 2, 9–10, 19, and passim.

56 Parry, "Plantation and Provision Ground," 19.

Chapter 6. Malnutrition: Morbidity and Mortality

1 John Williamson, *Medical and Miscellaneous Observations Relative to the West India Islands*, 2 vols. (Edinburgh, 1817), 1:248.

2 Charles Wagley, "Plantation America: A Cultural Sphere," in *Caribbean Studies: A Symposium*, ed. Vera Rubin (Seattle, 1960), 12.

3 Richard B. Sheridan, "The Crisis of Slave Subsistence in the British West Indies During and After the American Revolution," *WMQ* 33 (1976), 615–41; David Lowenthal, "The Population of Barbados," *SES* 6 (1957), 445–501; Berta Cabanillas de Rodriguez, *Origens de los hábitos alimenticios del pueblo de Puerto Rico* (Madrid, 1955),

275–290; Nelson Keith and Novella Keith, "The Evolution of Social Classes in Jamaica," *Plantation Society in the Americas* 1 (1979), 100; Sidney Mintz, "Labor and Sugar in Puerto Rico and in Jamaica 1800–1850," in *Comparative Studies in Sociology and History* 1 (1959), 275; James Stephen, *The Slavery of the British West India Colonies Delineated* . . . , 2 vols. (London, 1824–30), 1:95–6 and passim; Robert Collins, *Practical Rules for the Management and Medical Treatment of Negro Slaves in the Sugar Colonies* (London, 1811), 99; Bryan Edwards, *The History, Civil and Commercial of the British Colonies in the West Indies*, 3 vols. (London, 1807) 2:161–2.

4   John D. Kirschmann (ed.), *Nutrition Almanac* (New York, 1979), 15; Henrik Dam and Ebbe Søndengaard, "Fat-Soluble Vitamins," in *Nutrition*, eds. George H. Beaton and Earle Willard McHenry, 3 vols., (New York, 1964), 2:11–15.

5   Hans Sloane, *A Voyage to the Islands Madera, Barbados . . . and Jamaica*, 2 vols. (London, 1707) 1: 132; Maturin M. Ballou, *History of Cuba; or, Notes of a Traveller in the Tropics* . . . (Boston, 1854), 57; Collins, *Practical Rules*, 287; Henri Dumont, "Antropologia y patologia comparada de los negros esclavos," *Revista bimestre Cubana* 11 (1916), 88.

6   William Hillary, *Observations on the Changes of the Air and the Concomitant Epidemical Diseases, in the Island of Barbados*, 2d ed. (London, 1807), 297–304.

7   James Grainger, *An Essay on the More Common West-India Diseases* (London, 1764), 60; Thomas Dancer, *The Medical Assistant or Jamaica Practice of Physic* . . . (Kingston, 1809), 242. However, the apparent absence of widespread keratomalacia suggests that the vitamin A deficiency was probably mostly of a seasonal nature.

8   Kirschmann (ed.), *Nutrition Almanac*, 15.

9   John Huxham, *An Essay on Fevers* . . . , 2d ed. (London, 1750), 259; Francisco Eujenio Moscoso Puello, *Apuntes para la historia de la medicina de la isla de Santo Domingo* (Santo Domingo, 1977), 39; P.M. Ashburn, *The Ranks of Death* (New York, 1947), 137.

10 As one author has noted, "A most interesting aspect of the development of clinical knowledge about vitamin C is that the knowledge seems to be highly forgettable" (Mark D. Altschule, *Nutritional Factors in General Medicine* [Springfield, Ill., 1978], 130). American Indians knew of the relationship between fresh fruits and green vegetables and scurvy prior to the discovery of America. Many mariners reaching the hemisphere during the fifteenth and sixteenth centuries also knew. James Lind, a British naval surgeon, published *A Treatise on Scurvy* during the middle of the eighteenth century, which showed how the disease could be both treated and prevented with fresh fruits, while Captain James Cook demonstrated it in his around-the-world voyage of 1772 to 1775. Nonetheless, American Revolutionary soldiers suffered extensively from the disease, as did British troops during the Crimean War and "even in World War I [British troops] had more scurvy than gunshot casualties." See also Sir Stanley Davidson, et al., *Human Nutrition and Dietetics*, 6th ed. (London, 1975), 328–9.

11 Hazel Munsell, "Ascorbic Acid Content of Fruits of Puerto Rico with Data on Miscellaneous Products," *Food Research* 10 (1945), 50; Jacques M. May and Donna L. McLellan, *The Ecology of Malnutrition in the Caribbean* (New York, 1973), 333–4, 227.

12 B.S. Platt, *Nutrition in the British West Indies* (London, 1946), 3–4; May and McLellan, *Malnutrition in the Caribbean*, 328; Nelson A. Fernandez, et al., "Nutrition Survey of Two Rural Puerto Rican Areas Before and After a Community Improvement," *AJCN* 22 (1969), 1650. One says "probably explicable" because of the tendency of blacks to appear iron deficient (see Chapter 3), which cautions that some of the difference in anemia frequency between "black" Barbadians and "brown" Puerto Ricans may be genetic.

13 Conrado Asenjo, Oro de Boroquen Segundo, and Hilda Garcia de la Noceda, "Thiamin Content of Tropical Foods," *Food Research* 13 (1948), 94; Lowenthal, "Population of Barbados," 462.

14   M.T. Ashcroft, I.C. Buchanan, and H.G. Lovell, "Heights and Weights of Primary School Children in St. Christopher-Nevis-Anguilla, West Indies," *WIJTMH* 68 (1965), 278-9; Lowenthal, "Population of Barbados," 462; Fernandez, et al., "Nutrition Survey," 1650; Platt, *Nutrition in the British West Indies*, 5; Epaminondas Quintana, "El problema dietetico del Caribe," *America indigena* 2 (1942), 25-8; For comparative purposes, during the years 1975 to 1977 in Barbados the average amount of calcium available to the individual was 82 percent of the RDA, in Cuba 80 percent, in the Dominican Republic 51 percent, in Haiti 43 percent, in Jamaica 71 percent, and in the United States 120 percent (*FAO Production Yearbook, vol. 33, 1979* [Rome, 1980]).

15   May and McLellan, *Malnutrition in the Caribbean*, 335. I hasten to acknowledge that teeth and bone ailments can also be symptomatic of other deficiencies, and that calcium deficiency is often just one factor in the problem. In the case of rickets, for example, vitamin D deficiency is usually thought to be the chief cause, with vitamin D essential for the absorption of calcium. This certainly was the major cause of rickets among slaves and blacks of the postbellum period in the United States (Kenneth F. Kiple and Virginia H. King, *Another Dimension to the Black Diaspora: Diet, Disease and Racism* [New York, 1981], 104-6 and passim). However, Geoffrey Taylor, (Letter: "Osteomalacia and Calcium Deficiency," *BMJ* 1:6015 [1976], 960) discovered a high rate of rickets in children in the Punjab where there was plenty of sunshine, and hence vitamin D, but very little calcium in the diet. For rickets in the Caribbean see Colin George Miller and Winston Chutkan, "Vitamin-D Deficiency Rickets in Jamaican Children," *ADC* 51 (1976), 214-18.

16   [John Stewart] *An Account of Jamaica* (London, 1808), 268; Williamson, *Medical and Miscellaneous Observations* 1:56-65; Collins, *Practical Rules*, 313-14. A high frequency of dental caries and other disorders of the teeth was discovered by Robert S. Corruccine et al. in their study of the "Osteology of a slave burial population from Barbados, West Indies," *AJPA* 59 (1982), 443-59.

17   Edward Long, *The History of Jamaica*, 2 vols. (London, 1874) 2:551, 548; Williamson, *Medical and Miscellaneous Observations* 1:73; Edwards, *History of the West Indies* 2: 160. See also Richard Henry Dana, *To Cuba and Back; A Vacation Voyage* (Carbondale, Ill., 1966) 58. Interestingly the same phenomenon was observed among Louisiana sugar slaves. See, for example, Thomas B. Thorpe, "The Sugar Region of Louisiana," in *Travels in the Old South*, 2 vols., ed. Eugene L. Schwaab (Lexington, Ky., 1973), 2:512.

18   Robert Dirks, "Resource Fluctuations and Competitive Transformations in West Indian Slave Societies," in *Extinction and Survival in Human Populations*, eds. Charles D. Laughlin Jr. and Ivan A. Brady (New York, 1978), 141-2; William Beckford, *A Descriptive Account of . . . Jamaica*, 2 vols. (London, 1790), 2:13; Long, *History of Jamaica* 2:551; Dana, *Cuba*, 58.

19   Claude Levy, "Slavery and the Emancipation Movement in Barbados, 1650-1833," *JNH* 55 (1970) 6; Frank Wesley Pitman, "Slavery on the British West India Plantations in the Eighteenth Century," *JNH* 2 (1926), 632. Kirschmann (ed.), *Nutrition Almanac*, 149-50; Altschule, *Nutritional Factors in General Medicine*, 104-6.

20   Orlando Patterson, *The Sociology of Slavery* (London, 1967), 265; George Roberts, *The Population of Jamaica* (Cambridge, Eng., 1957), 225.

21   Gwendolyn Midlo Hall, *Social Control in Slave Plantation Societies; A Comparison of St. Domingue and Cuba* (Baltimore, 1971), 20-3, 60; see also Secretaria del Gobierno Superior Civil de la Isla de Cuba (1846), "Espediente sobre las causas que influyen en el . . . suicidio de los esclavos. . ." AHN, Ultramar, Leg. 3550.

22   Conrado F. Asenjo, Hilda Garcia de la Noceda, and Patricia Serrano, "Riboflavin Content of Tropical Foods," *Food Research* 11 (1946), 137-41; Ivan D. Begin, W. Fougere, and K.W. King, "L'ariboflavinose en Haiti," *Archivos Latinamericanos de nutrición* 17 (1967) 95; K.W. King, et al, "Food Patterns from Dietary Surveys in Rural

Haiti," *JADA* 53 (1968), 118; Lowenthal, "Population of Barbados," 462: Platt, *Nutrition in the British West Indies*, 5.

23   Davidson, et al., *Human Nutrition and Dietetics*, 170.

24   Ibid.

25   Kirschmann (ed.), *Nutrition Almanac*, 18.

26   Margaret S. Chaney and Margaret L. Ross, *Nutrition*, 8th ed. (Boston, 1971), 267.

27   Tryptophan is the second limiting amino acid in corn protein and consequently undersupplied by corn. Hans R. Rosenberg, "Amino Acid Supplementation of Foods and Feeds," in *Protein and Amino Acid Nutrition*, ed. Anthony A. Albanese (New York, 1959), 405. Beef therefore (for slaves on a beef-corn core) would have been the slaves' only important source.

28   Coluther Gopalan and K.S. Jaya Rao, "Pellagra and Amino Acid Imbalance," *Vitamins and Hormones* 33 (1975), 516; Kamala Krishnaswamy and Coluther Gopalan, "Effect of Isoleucine on Skin and Electroencephalogram in Pellagra," *Lancet* 2 (Nov. 27, 1971), 1167; Constance Kies and Hazel M. Fox, "Interrelationships of Leucine and Lycine, Tryptophan and Niacin as they Influence Protein Value of Cereal Grains for Humans," *Cereal Chemistry* 49 (1972), 223–31.

29   For the symptoms and behavior of pellagra, see Daphne A. Roe, *A Plague of Corn: The Social History of Pellagra* (Ithaca, N.Y. 1973); Elizabeth W. Etheridge, *The Butterfly Caste: A Social History of Pellagra in the South* (Westport, Conn., 1972); Paul S. Carley, "History of Pellagra in the United States," *The Urologic and Cutaneous Review* 49 (1945), 291–303.

30   For pellagra in the antebellum south see Kenneth F. Kiple and Virginia H. Kiple, "Black Tongue and Black Men: Pellagra in the Antebellum South," *Journal of Southern History* 43 (1977), 411–28; or Kiple and King, *Another Dimension*, 123–32. For *Reports on Pellagra in the West Indies*, see those of Louis W. Sambon (London, 1917), 59 and passim.

31   Joseph Goldberger, *Goldberger on Pellagra*, ed. Milton Terris (Baton Rouge, La., 1964), 373.

32   George P. Paul, *Report on Ankylostomiasis Infection Survey of Barbados* (New York, 1917), 18; Henry Harold Scott, *A History of Tropical Medicine*, 2 vols. (London, 1939), 2:913; Julian Herman Lewis, *The Biology of the Negro* (Chicago,, 1942), 263; Platt, *Nutrition in the British West Indies*, passim; Sambon, *Reports* 19–34 and passim.

33   J.F. Siler ("Medical Notes on Barbados, British West Indies. Part 2. Pellagra in Barbados," RAC, IHB, series 435, Barbados, Box 43, Folder 260) found the death rate from pellagra in St. Michael's parish to be 480 per hundred thousand for the period January 1911 to August 1913; see also Aristides A. Moll, *Aesulapius in Latin America* (Philadelphia, 1944), 505; Scott, *History of Tropical Medicine* 2: 930; Conrado Asenjo et al., "Niacin Content of Tropical Foods," *Journal of Food Science* 15 (1950), 465; May and McLellan, *Malnutrition in the Caribbean*, 179. One might have expected the disease to have plagued Cuba as well; however, both Guiteras, who published the first work in Cuba on the disease in 1909, and Dr. Horacio Abascal believe that the disease was absent from the island. See Horacio Abascal, *Reseña histórica y sinonimia de la frambuesa y de la pelagra* (Havana, 1955). On the other hand, it was reported that subclinical pellagra was "quite prevalent" on the island during the late 1950s and it is doubtful that pellagra could have been a problem in the 1950s without having been one as well during the nineteenth century ("Nutritional Status of Cuban Children," *Nutrition Reviews* [Sept. 1958], 272).

34   James Bovell, "Observations on the Climate of Barbados, and its Influence on Disease. . . ," *BAJMPS* 4 (1848), 113–14.

35   J.B.S. Jackson, "Diseases of the Island of Barbados," *The Boston Medical and Surgical Journal* 76 (1867), 446; Charles Wilcocks and P.C.E. Manson-Bahr, *Manson's Tropical Diseases*, 17th ed. (Baltimore, 1974), 778.

36   Editor, "On the Erysipelas as it appeared in Kingston in 1826," *The Jamaica Physical Journal* 2–3 (1835), 305–7; Scott, *History of Tropical Medicine* 2:915–17.

37   Collins, *Practical Rules*, 229; E.R. Stitt, "Our Disease Inheritance From Slavery," *U.S. Medical Bulletin* 29 (1928), 807.

38   James Thomson, *A Treatise on the Diseases of Negroes as they Occur in the Island of Jamaica; with Observations on the Country Remedies* (Jamaica, 1820), 34; Collins, *Practical Rules* 203, 229; Nevin S. Scrimshaw, Carl E. Taylor, and John E. Gordon, *Interactions of Nutrition and Infection* (Geneva, 1968), 64–5; Iancu Gontzea, *Nutrition and Anti-Infectious Defence*, 2d ed. (Basel, 1974), 43.

39   R.K. Chandra and P.M. Newberne, *Nutrition, Immunity, and Infection: Mechanisms of Interactions* (New York, 1977), 42; Gontzea, *Nutrition and Anti-Infectious Defence*, 22; Jerome S. Handler, " An Archaeological Investigation of the Domestic Life of Plantation Slaves in Barbados," *Journal of the Barbados Museum and Historical Society* 34 (1974), 72.

40   Miguel Angel Gonzalez Prendes, *Historia de la lepra en Cuba* (Havana, 1963), 17; Manuel Moreno Fraginals, "Africa in Cuba; A Quantitative Analysis of the African Populations in the Island of Cuba," in *Comparative Perspectives on Slavery in New World Plantation Societies*, eds. Vera Rubin and Arthur Tuden (New York, 1977), 200.

41   See Dirks, "Resource Fluctuations," 143, and his forthcoming study, *Black Saturnalia*.

42   For nineteenth-century descriptions of this disease, which has virtually disappeared today, see Samuel Kennedy Jennings, *A Compendium of Medical Science, or Fifty Years' Experience in the Art of Healing . . .* (Tuskaloosa, Ala., 1847), 424; Alfred M. Folger, *The Family Physician; Being a Domestic Medical Work* (Spartanburg, S.C., 1845), 121; W.H. Coffin, *The Art of Medicine Simplified, or a Treatise on the Nature and Cure of Diseases, For the Use of Families and Travelers* (Wellsburg, Va., 1853), 98. For vitamin A as a factor in ergotism, consult Edward Mellanby, *Nutrition and Disease: The Interaction of Clinical and Experimental Work* (Edinburgh, 1934), 23–5.

43   Tropical sprue is a disease apparently caused by multiple vitamin deficiencies. However it may not have affected the slaves for it seems to be peculiarly a disease of whites, has not been seen in tropical Africa, and has only attacked the Spanish islands of the Caribbean, which are racially mixed. Wilcocks and Manson-Bahr, *Manson's Tropical Diseases*, 755–60; George W. Hunter, William W. Frye, and J. Clyde Swartzwelder, *A Manual of Tropical Medicine*, 4th ed. (Philadelphia, 1966), 603–5.

44   D. Juan Hava, "Comunicación dirigida a la academia sobre una epidemia de beriberi," *Academia de ciencias medical, físicas y naturales de la Habana, Anales* 2 (1865), 158–61. The victims were also all male, which conforms to beriberi's behavior, as the adult variety is most virulent in men and there is evidence to indicate that hard physical labor is a precipitating factor. See Thomas T. Mackie, George W. Hunter, and C. Brooke Worth, *A Manual of Tropical Medicine*, 2d ed. (Philadelphia, 1954), 570. Whether there is any racial predisposition to the illness remains an open question. See, Scott's allegation, in his *History of Tropical Medicine* 2: 864–5, that blacks seem to suffer more from the illness than Europeans. Certainly blacks seem to have suffered severely from it in Africa. See, for example, Great Britain, Economic Advisory Council, Committee on Nutrition in the Colonial Empire, *Nutrition in the Colonial Empire*, 2 parts (London, 1939) 2:39,40.

45   J. Minteguiaga, "Lettre sur le beriberi," *Gazette Médicale de Paris* 45 (1874), 35.

46   August Hirsch, *Handbook of Geographical and Historical Pathology*, 2 vols. (London, 1883), 2:276.

47   For subclinical beriberi, see Oscar Felsenfeld, *Synopsis of Clinical Tropical Medicine* (St. Louis, 1965), 319–20.

48   Manuel Quevado y Baez, *Historia de la medicina y cirugía de Puerto Rico*, 2 vols. (Santurce, 1946–49), 2:394–5. Among the first to identify beriberi as well as pellagra

in Puerto Rico were Rockefeller investigators of hookworm disease. See, for example, Robert W. Hegman, "Porto Rico as a Field for the Study and Investigation of Tropical Diseases," unpublished paper, and B.K. Ashford, "Health in Puerto Rico with Special Reference to Nutrition," unpublished paper dated 1922, both in RAC, IHB, 2d series, 243 Puerto Rico, Box 39, Folder 130.

49 G.M. Findlay, "The first recognized epidemic of yellow fever," *TRSTMH* 35 (1941), 143–4; Hirsch, *Handbook* 2:576; Henry Rose Carter, *Yellow Fever: An Epidemiological and Historical Study of its Place of Origin*, eds. Laura A. Carter and Wade Hampton Frost (Baltimore, 1931), 184–6; Robert Parsons, "History of Haitian Medicine," *Annals of Medical History* 1 (1929), 308–9. See also Dirks' forthcoming study, *Black Saturnalia*, and Moll, *Aesulapius in Latin America*, 501. For beriberi in the British Islands in this century, see Great Britain, *Nutrition in the Colonial Empire* 2:79–105. For Jamaica specifically, see J.F. Siler, "Medical Notes on Jamaica, British West Indies," part 1, 16. RAC, IHB, Series 2, 437 Jamaica, Box 43, Folder 261.

50 Mackie, Hunter, and Worth, *Manual of Tropical Medicine*, 570.

51 Davidson, et al., *Human Nutrition and Dietetics*, 337.

52 Ibid., 338; Wilcocks and Manson-Bahr, *Manson's Tropical Diseases*, 767–8.

53 Wilcocks and Manson-Bahr, *Manson's Tropical Diseases*, 768–79; Davidson, et al., *Human Nutrition and Dietetics*, 337–8.

54 James Maxwell, "Observation on the Nature and Treatment of Acute Cellular Dropsy," *Jamaica Physical Journal* 1 (1834), 364–5.

55 Long, *History of Jamaica* 2:433.

56 Sloane, *Voyage to the Islands* 1:151–2.

57 Abbé Guillaume Raynal, *A Philosophical and Political History of the Settlements and Trade of the Europeans in the East and West Indies*, 8 vols. trans. J.O. Justamond (London, 1788), 5:271. The symptoms described by Raynal are identical with those penned by a physician a century later. See P.T. Carpenter, "The Clinical Aspects of Beri-Beri," *The Journal of Tropical Medicine* 1 (1898–99), 319–21.

58 Dancer, *Medical Assistant*, 166.

59 Collins, *Practical Rules*, 85.

60 Although beriberi can and does afflict people whose principal cereal is not rice (Davidson, et al., *Human Nutrition and Dietetics*, 336).

61 Michael Craton and James Walvin, *A Jamaican Plantation: the History of Worthy Park* (Toronto, 1970), 197–8.

62 B.W. Higman, *Slave Population and Economy in Jamaica, 1807–1834* (Cambridge, Eng., 1976), 112–13, tables.

63 Jerome S. Handler and Frederick W. Lange, *Plantation Slavery in Barbados* (Cambridge, Mass., 1977), 99; J. Harry Bennett, *Bondsmen and Bishops: Slavery and Apprenticeship on the Codrington Plantations of Barbados, 1710–1838* (Berkeley, Calif., 1958), 56.

64 Roberts, *Population of Jamaica*, 175, table; Angel Jose Cowley, *Ensayo estadístico-médico de la mortalidad de la diocesis de la Habana durante el año de 1843* (Havana, 1845), table.

65 Long, *History of Jamaica* 2:433; Williamson, *Medical and Miscellaneous Observations* 1:182; Frank Wesley Pitman, *The Development of the British West Indies 1700–1763* (New Haven, 1917), 13, 386.

66 Thomas Roughley, *The Jamaica Planter's Guide* (London, 1823), 119; John Imray, "Observations on the Mal D'Estomac or Cachexia Africana, as it takes place among the Negroes of Dominica," *Edinburgh Medical and Surgical Journal* 59 (1843), 304–21; David Mason, "On Atrophia a Ventriculo (Mal d'Estomac) or Dirt-Eating," *Edinburgh Medical and Surgical Journal* 39 (1833), 289–96; Collins, *Practical Rules*, 294–341; Williamson, *Medical and Miscellaneous Observations* 1:357–8, 2:267.

67 Dancer, *Medical Assistant*, 170.

68 P. Dons, "Rechérches sur la Cachexie Africaine," *Gazette médicale de Paris*, 6 (1838),

289–95; Roughley, *Jamaica Planter's Guide*, 118–19; John Hunter, *Observations on the Diseases of the Army in Jamaica* (London, 1789), 249; Dancer, *Medical Assistant*, 174.

69 Williamson, *Medical and Miscellaneous Observations* 2:262–3.

70 Berthold Laufer, "Geophagy," *Field Museum of Natural History, Anthropology Series* (1930), 156 and passim; Dancer, *Medical Assistant*, 174.

71 Kiple and King, *Another Dimension*, 113, 119–23, 144–5. See also May and McLellan, (*Malnutrition in the Caribbean*, 328) who explain that as many as 40 percent of the females on Barbados practice pica with no loss of life.

72 C. Manning, *Report on Anchilostomiasis* (sic) *as it occurs in Barbados* (Barbados, 1909); Dancer, *Medical Assistant*, 170–4; Williamson, *Medical and Miscellaneous Observations* 1:110, 2:262–3; Collins, *Practical Rules*, 293; Hunter, *Diseases of the Army*, 249; Stewart, *Account of Jamaica*, 273.

73 Robert R. Williams, *Toward the Conquest of Beriberi* (Cambridge, Mass., 1961), 67 and passim.

74 Collins, *Practical Rules*, 295; Michel Gabriel Levacher, *Medical Guide of the Antilles*, 3d ed. (Paris, 1847), 252; Dancer, *Medical Assistant*, 172; Pedro Tomás de Córdova, *Memórias geográficas, económicas y estadísticas de la isla de Puerto Rico*, 6 vols. (San Juan, 1968) 4:204; Fray Iñigo Abbad y Lasierra, *Historia Geográfica, civil y natural de la isla de San Juan Bautista de Puerto Rico* (San Juan, 1886), 207.

75 Grace A. Goldsmith, "The B Vitamins: Thiamine, Riboflavin, Niacin," in *Nutrition: A Comprehensive Treatise*, 3 vols., eds. George H. Beaton and Earle Willard McHenry (New York, 1964–66), 2:120; Davidson, et al., *Human Nutrition and Dietetics*, 340; Hunter, Frye, and Swartzwelder, *Manual of Tropical Medicine*, 600.

76 Collins, *Practical Rules*, 294, 183; Dancer, *Medical Assistant*, 175; Thomson, *Diseases of Negroes*, 46; Alexander Barclay, *A Practical View of the Present State of Slavery in the West Indies. . . .* (London, 1828), 333.

77 Williamson, *Medical and Miscellaneous Observations* 2:262; Dancer, *Medical Assistant*, 173, 175; Thomson, *Diseases of Negroes*, 46.

78 See, for example, Dancer (*Medical Assistant*, 172), who explains that the pain in the stomach was the reason why the French named the disease the *mal d' estomac*.

79 Moscoso Puello, *Historia de la medicina*, 39.

80 Richard S. Dunn, *Sugar and Slaves: The Rise of the Planter Class in the English West Indies, 1624–1713* (Chapel Hill, N.C., 1972), 306; Hunter, *Diseases of the Army*, 194; Hillary, *Observations*, 182. R. Storrs ("The White Mans' Grave in the Eighteenth Century," *Journal of the Royal Army Medical Corps* 53 [1929], 227), however, points out that the disease was not exclusive to the Caribbean, but was a problem in Africa as well. See also Dancer (*Medical Assistant*, 103), Grainger (*Essay on . . . West-India Diseases* [London, 1764], 32–4), and Pitman ("Slavery on British West India Plantations," 642–3), who point out that "new rum" caused "endless troubles to black and white alike." For a variation on the lead poisoning thesis, see Ashburn (*Ranks of Death*, 37), who argued that the cause of the "dry belly ache" was white lead used to treat worms.

81 Scott, *History of Tropical Medicine* 2:939–49; Wilcocks and Manson-Bahr, *Manson's Tropical Diseases*, 817–18.

82 Scott, *History of Tropical Medicine* 2:949–53; Wilcocks and Manson-Bahr, *Manson's Tropical Diseases*, 819.

83 Laufer, "Geophagy," 156.

84 Mason, "On Atrophia a Ventriculo," 292. For another who felt that the soils were consumed for their mineral content, see M. Moreau de Jonnes, "Observations on the Dirt-Eaters of the West Indies," *Bulletin de la Société Médicale* (1816), or the appropriate pages of his *Histoire physique des Antilles Françaises, . . . la Martinique et les iles de la Guadeloupe* (Paris, 1822).

85 Michael Gelfand, *The Sick African* (Capetown, 1957), 355; John M. Hunter, "Geo-

phagy in Africa and in the United States: A Culture-Nutrition Hypothesis," *Geographical Review* 63 (1973), 173, 179, 182.

86 Hunter, "Geophagy in Africa and the United States," 182.

87 Mason, "On Atrophia a Ventriculo," 292. There are also other physiological as well as cultural reasons why pregnant African women consume earth. Among these are the easing of labor pains as well as minor discomforts such as irritation of the mother's womb by the hair of the fetus, or simply to put an end to the need to vomit. It is also believed that the practice will ensure the well-being of the fetus and a dark complexion after birth, according to Bengt Anell and Sture Lagercrantz, *Geophagical Customs* (Uppsala, Sweden, 1958), 74. For nineteenth-century views of the problem, see P.L. Dons, "Über die Sogenannte Africanische Cachexie, Erdessen (mal d'estomac, dirt eating, Jordäden)," *Journal for Medecin og Chirurgie* 8 (1833), 377–8, 381, translated as "Recherches sur la Cachexie Africaine," *Gazette médicale de Paris* 6 (1838), 289–95 and James Maxwell, "Pathological Inquiry into the Nature of Cachexia Africana as Generally Connected with Dirt Eating," *Jamaica Physical Journal* 2 (1835), 409. See also Imray, "Observations on the Mal d' Estomac," 306.

88 R. Hoeppli, *Parasitic Diseases in Africa and the Western Hemisphere; Early Documentation and Transmission by the Slave Trade* (Basel, 1969), 117–18.

89 Wilcocks and Manson-Bahr, *Manson's Tropical Diseases*, 259–60.

90 Scott, *History of Tropical Medicine* 2:843, 990; Mary Ellison, *The Black Experience Since 1865* (New York, 1974), 56.

91 Manning, *Report on Anchilostomiasis* (sic), 8; Philip D. Sartwell (ed.), *Maxcy-Rosenau, Preventive Medicine and Public Health*, 10th ed. (New York, 1973), 221–2; Elizabeth Barrett-Connor, "Anemia and Infection," *AJM* 52 (1972), 243; George I. Lythcott, Calvin H. Sinnette, and Donald R. Hopkins, "Pediatrics," in *Textbook of Black Related Diseases*, ed. Richard Allen Williams (New York, 1975), 178–9.

92 Robert Jackson, *A Sketch of the History and Cure of Febrile Diseases; More Particularly as they Appear in the West Indies Among the Soldiers of the British Army* (London, 1791), 122–6; Dancer, *Medical Assistant*, 171.

93 Alexander M. Tulloch, "Statistical Report on the Sickness, Mortality, and Invaliding Among the Troops in the West Indies," Table II in Great Britain, *Parliamentary Papers*, XL, 1837–1838 (*Accounts and Papers*, V [London, 1838]).

94 Wilcocks and Manson-Bahr, *Manson's Tropical Diseases*, 258–9.

95 For assurances that pica is frequently prevalent among mineral-deficient peoples who are hookworm free, consult the following: Ralph D. Reynolds, et al., "Papophagia and Iron Deficiency Anemia," *AIM* 69 (1968), 435–40; William H. Crosby, "Pica: A Compulsion Caused by Iron Deficiency," *British Journal of Haematology* 34 (1976), 341–2; Louis Keith, Eric R. Brown, and Cary Rosenberg, "Pica: The Unfinished Story; Background; Correlations with Anemia and Pregnancy," *Perspectives in Biology and Medicine* 13 (1970), 626–32; Kenneth M. Talkington, et al., "Effect of Ingestion of Starch and Some Clays on Iron Absorption," *American Journal of Obstetrics and Gynecology*, 108 (1970), 262–7; L. Heilmeyer and H.G. Harwerth, "Clinical Manifestations in Iron Deficiency," in *Iron Deficiency Pathogenesis. Clinical Aspects Therapy* (London, 1970); O. Carlander, "Aetiology of Pica," *Lancet* 277 (1959), 569; H.L. Jolly, "Advances in Paediatrics," *Practitioner*, 191 (1963), 417; R. Ber and A. Valero, "Pica and Hypochromic Anemia," *Harefuah* 61 (1961), 35; Hunter, "Geophagy in Africa and the United States," 182.

Chapter 7. Slave Demography

1 Elsa V. Goveia, *Slave Society in The British Leeward Islands at the End of the Eighteenth Century* (New Haven, 1965), 124.

2　Josiah C. Nott and George R. Gliddon, *Indigenous Races of the Earth; or, New Chapters of Ethnological Enquiry* . . . (Philadelphia, 1857), 387.

3　Alexander von Humboldt, *The Island of Cuba*, trans., J.S. Thrasher (New York, 1856), 227–8.

4　Captain General of Cuba to the Secretary de Estado . . . de Ultramar, 15 Feb. 1845, A.H.N., Ultramar, Leg. 3550; Seccion of Ultramar to the Captain General of Cuba, 6 July 1847; A.H.N., Ultramar, Leg. 4655. In the following discussion our use of the term *fertility* is generally intended to mean performance as opposed to *fecundity*, or "capacity to produce living offspring"; see the discussion by Frank Lorimer, *Culture and Human Fertility* (New York, 1969), 22, note.

5　James Grainger, *An Essay on the More Common West-India Diseases* (London, 1764), 14–15.

6　Ibid. Robert Collins, *Practical Rules for the Management and Medical Treatment of Negro Slaves in the Sugar Colonies* (London, 1811), 132. The notion "that sexual intercourse with another man than the husband and promiscuous sexual intercourse in general are seldom followed by conception" characterized the demographic thinking of the period. See R.R. Kuczynski, "British Demographers' Opinions on Fertility, 1660–1760," *Annals of Eugenics* 2 (1935), 149–50.

7　Philip D. Curtin, *The Atlantic Slave Trade: A Census* (Madison, Wisc., 1969), 92. For the assertion that the West Indies received "nearly" 50 percent of the total slaves imported from Africa, see H.S. Klein and S.L. Engerman, "The demographic study of the American slave population; with particular attention given the comparison between the United States and the British West Indies," unpublished paper presented to the International Colloquium in Historical Demography, 1975.

8　The reference of course is to the so called "Tannenbaum Thesis." For its elaboration, see Frank Tannenbaum, *Slave and Citizen: the Negro in the Americas* (New York, 1946); Stanley Elkins, *Slavery; A Problem in American Institutional and Intellectual Life* (Chicago, 1959), and Herbert S. Klein, *Slavery in the Americas: a Comparative Study of Virginia and Cuba* (Chicago, 1967). For a rebuttal, consult Marvin Harris, *Patterns of Race in the Americas* (New York, 1964); Franklin Knight, *Slave Society in Cuba During the Nineteenth Century* (Madison, Wisc., 1970); Sydney Mintz, "How the Doctrine of the Moral Personality of the Slave was Conveniently Forgotten as the Plantation Expanded. Review of Elkins, *Slavery*," *AA* 63 (1961), 579–87; Eugene D. Genovese, "Materialism and Idealism in the History of Negro Slavery in the Americas," *Journal of Social History* 1 (1968), 371–94. For a summary, see C. Vann Woodward, *American Counterpoint; Slavery and Racism in the North South Dialogue* (Boston, 1971).

9　The notion that Southern planters supported a thriving clandestine slave trade from Africa after it was legally closed in 1807 has long since been dispelled. See Warren S. Howard, *American Slavers and the Federal Law, 1837–1862* (Berkeley, Calif., 1963).

10　For evidence that this was an economically reasoned position, see Gwendolyn Midlo Hall, *Social Control in Slave Plantation Societies: A Comparison of St. Domingue and Cuba* (Baltimore, 1971), 23–6.

11　Michael Craton, "Hobbesian or Panglossian? Two Extremes of Slave Conditions in the British Caribbean 1783–1834," *WMQ* 35 (1978), 324–56.

12　W.R. Aykroyd, *Sweet Malefactor: Sugar, Slavery and Human Society* (London, 1967), passim.

13　Curtin, *Atlantic Slave Trade*, 71.

14　Richard B. Sheridan, "Africa and the Caribbean in the Atlantic Slave Trade," *AHR* 77 (1972), 29.

15　Ibid. B.W. Higman, *Slave Population and Economy in Jamaica* (London, 1976), 129; see also Michael Craton ("Jamaican Slave Mortality: Fresh Light from Worthy Park, Longville and the Tharp Estates," *JCH* 3 [1971], 17–18), who found that despite amelioration "the general slave population did not increase naturally."

16   Curtin, *Atlantic Slave Trade*, 28.

17   B.W. Higman, "The Slave Family and Household in the British West Indies, 1800–1834," *JIH* 6 (1975), 263–4.

18   Herbert S. Klein and Stanley L. Engerman, "Fertility Differentials between Slaves in the United States and the British West Indies: A Note on Lactation Practices and Their Possible Implications," *WMQ* 35 (1978), 372.

19   See, for example, Sidney Mintz, "Labor and Sugar in Puerto Rico and in Jamaica, 1800–1850," *Comparative Studies in Society and History* 1 (1959), 273–80. See also Eric Williams (*Capitalism and Slavery* [Chapel Hill, 1944], 3–29) for an earlier suggestion that the "humanness of slavery varied inversely with the rise and decline of capitalistic agriculture."

20   Mintz, "Labor and Sugar," 280.

21   Manuel Moreno Fraginals, "Africa in Cuba: A Quantitative Analysis of the African Populations in the Island of Cuba," in *Comparative Perspectives on Slavery in New World Plantation Societies*, eds. Vera Rubin and Arthur Tuden (New York, 1977), 192.

22   Jack Ericson Eblen, "On the Natural Increase of Slave Populations: The Example of the Cuban Black Population, 1775–1900," in *Race and Slavery in the Western Hemisphere: Quantitative Studies*, eds. Stanley L. Engerman and Eugene D. Genovese (Princeton, N.J., 1975), 211–47; Kenneth F. Kiple, *Blacks in Colonial Cuba 1774–1899* (Gainesville, Fla., 1976), passim.

23   Richard S. Dunn, "A Tale of Two Plantations: Slave Life at Mesopotamia in Jamaica and Mount Airy in Virginia, 1799 to 1828," *WMQ* 34 (1977), 61; Higman, *Slave Population and Economy*, 116–17.

24   Dunn, "Tale of Two Plantations," 40.

25   Sheridan, "Africa and the Caribbean," 20; Mintz, "Labor and Sugar," 273–80; Eugene D. Genovese, *The World the Slaveholders Made; Two Essays in Interpretation* (1969), passim, and "Materialism and Idealism," 371–94.

26   Daniel C. Littlefield, "Plantations, Paternalism and Profitability: Factors Affecting African Demography in the Old British Empire," *Journal of Southern History* 47 (1981), 171.

27   Robert Robertson, *A Detection of the State and Situation of the Present Sugar Planters* (London, 1732), 42–4; Gregory Matthew Lewis, *Journal of a West India Proprietor* (London, 1834), 42–4.

28   Littlefield, "Plantations, Paternalism and Profitability," 169.

29   Stanley L. Engerman, "Some Economic and Demographic Comparisons of Slavery in the United States and the British West Indies," *EHR* 29 (1976), 258–75.

30   George Dawson Flinter, *An Account of the Present State of the Island of Puerto Rico* (London, 1834), 207, 208, 218, 253; for Jamaica, see Higman, *Slave Population and Economy*, 174–5.

31   Robert W. Fogel and Stanley L. Engerman, "Recent Findings in the Study of Slave Demography and Family Structure," *SSR* 63 (1979), 570. See the entire article, pages 566–89, for a masterful summary of what has been done and what needs to be done.

32   Herbert S. Klein and Stanley L. Engerman, "Fertility Differentials," 557–74.

33   J. Trussell and R. Steckel, "The Age of Slaves at Menarche and their First Birth," *JIH* 8 (1978), 477–505. By examining the height data on female slaves the authors discovered (at least for the late antebellum period) that their adolescent growth spurt peaked at age thirteen. This in turn suggested that the onset of menarche was between fourteen and fifteen.

34   Barry Higman ("Growth in Afro-Caribbean Slave Populations," *AJPA* 50 [1979], 382) has taken a step in this direction by tentatively estimating the age of menarche at the beginning of age seventeen for Trinidad slave females. However, more data are needed and a lack of quantitative data constantly plagues students of West Indian slavery.

Much in the Islands has been destroyed by hurricanes, worms, rats, and other assorted enemies of historians. Many materials remain in private hands while Cuban sources have only recently again become accessible to many scholars. Materials in Great Britain have been the most systematically employed, those in France less so, while most in Spain still await discovery in the archives of Seville and Madrid.

35 Fogel and Engerman, "Recent Findings," 568.

36 Higman, "Growth in Afro-Caribbean Populations," 383–4; Fogel and Engerman, "Recent Findings," 576; Dunn, "Tale of Two Plantations," 62. The possible relationships between nutrition and fertility are complex and promise to be the subject of study for some time to come. For a quick overview, see Carl Mosk, "Nutrition and Fertility; a Review Essay," *Historical Methods* 14 (1981), 43–6. See also Jane Menken, James Trussell, and Susan Watkins, who have scrutinized "The Nutrition/Fertility Link: An Evaluation of the Evidence" (*JIH* 11 [1981], 425–41) and have concluded that, at least on the basis of hypotheses generated to date, there is no real link.

37 J.M. Tanner, *Growth at Adolescence* (Springfield, Ill., 1955), 83–91; Rose E. Frisch, "Demographic Implications of the Biological Determinants of Female Fecundity," *Social Biology* 22 (1975), 19–20; K. Boilen and M.W. Benzon, "The Influence of Climate and Nutrition on Age of Menarche; A Historical Review and Modern Hypothesis," *HB* 40 (1968), 69–85; C. Gopalan, "Effect of Nutrition on Pregancy and Lactation," *BWHO* 26 (1962), 203–11; C. Gopalan and A. Nadamuni Naidu, "Nutrition and Fertility," *Lancet* 2 (18 Aug., 1972), 1077–9.

38 Edward Long, *The History of Jamaica*, 2 vols. (London, 1774), 2:403; Collins, *Practical Rules*, 132; Grainger, *Essay . . . on West India Diseases*, 14–15.

39 The complaints arose from the suspicion that the women were using nursing as an excuse to avoid work. See Thomas Roughley, *The Jamaica Planter's Guide . . .* (London, 1823), 118; and James Maxwell, "Pathological Inquiry into the Nature of Cachexia Africana, As Generally Connected with Dirt-Eating," *Jamaica Physical Journal* 2 (1835), 413–14. Others feared that the women were hurting themselves physically by prolonged nursing and urged forcing the women to wean at fourteen to sixteen months (Lewis, *Journal of a West India Proprietor*, 382–406; Collins, *Practical Rules*, 146). On the other hand, in Cuba there was a law to the effect that slave mothers must nurse their children for three years. See "Reglamento de esclavos . . . que fue espedido en . . . 1842," in Jose Maria Zamora y Coronado, *Biblioteca de legislacion ultramarina*, 6 vols. (Madrid, 1844–49), 3:138. For a few modern authorities who have commented on the practice, see Lowell Joseph Ragatz, *The Fall of the Planter Class in the British Caribbean, 1763–1833* (New York, 1928), 34–5; Orlando Patterson, *The Sociology of Slavery* (London, 1967), 155–6; Humphrey E. Lamur, "Demography of Surinam Plantation Slaves in the Last Decade before Emancipation: The Case of Catharina Sophia," in *Comparative Perspectives on Slavery in New World Plantation Societies*, eds. Rubin and Tuden, 168; and Stanley Engerman, "Quantitative and Economic Analysis of West Indian Slave Societies: Research Problems," 607 in the same volume.

40 James Thomson, *A Treatise on the Diseases of Negroes as they Occur in the Island of Jamaica; with Observations on the Country Remedies* (Jamaica, 1820), 116.

41 *A Report of a Committee of the Council of Barbadoes, Appointed to Inquire into the Actual Condition of the Slaves* (London, 1824), 115; Melville J. Herskovits, *Life in a Haitian Valley* (New York, 1937), 99.

42 Anrudh K. Jain, J.C. Hsu, Ronald Freedman, and M.C. Chang, "Demographic Aspects of Lactation and Postpartum Amenorrhea," *Demography* 7:2 (1970), 255–71; The figure of seven months is the generally accepted one, yet the question is still debated. For lactation as effective for nine months, with a majority of conceptions delayed for fifteen months, see M. Bonte and H. van Balen, "Prolonged Lactation and Family Spacing in Rwanda," *Journal of Biosocial Science* 1 (1969), 97–100. For the physiological mechanics of lactation and amenorrhea, as well as the assertion that

pregnancy rates of lactating women remain low for one year and then increase rapidly, see Jeroen K. Van Ginneken, "The Impact of Prolonged Breast-feeding on Birth Intervals and on Postpartum Amenorrhea," in *Nutrition and Human Reproduction*, ed. W. Henry Mosley (New York, 1978), 179–95; See also John E. Tyson and A. Perez, "The Maintenance of Infecundity in Postpartum Women," in *Nutrition and Human Reproduction*, ed. Mosley, 11–27. Finally, consult Nanci Solien de Gonzalez ("Lactation and Pregnancy: A Hypothesis," *AA* 66 [1964], 873–7) for the observation that lactation will prevent ovulation for lengthy periods only so long as the infant is totally nursed and given no supplemental feeding.

43   Klein and Engerman, "Fertility Differentials," 358.

44   Ibid., 371.

45   W. Brass, "Introduction: Biosocial Factors in African Demography," in *The Population Factor in African Studies*, eds. R.P. Moss and R.J.A.R. Rathbone (London, 1975).

46   John C. Caldwell, "Fertility Control," in *Population Growth and Socioeconomic Change in West Africa*, ed. John C. Caldwell (New York, 1975), 64–5. See also Hillary Page, "Fertility Levels," in the same volume, 52.

47   Brass, "Biosocial Factors," 93; Pierre Cantrelle, "Mortality," in *Population Growth and Socioeconomic Change in West Africa*, ed. Caldwell, 105–8.

48   Lorimer, *Culture and Human Fertility*, 87–8.

49   This is not to say, however, that the practice of polygamy was discarded, but rather that it was simply not so widespread as in Africa because of the deformed circumstances of the plantation. Early eighteenth century reports from Barbados indicate that it was not an unusual practice there. See Robertson (*Situation of the Present Sugar Planters*, 42–4). Patterson (*Sociology of Slavery*, 107) suggests that in 1789 perhaps as many as 22 percent of Jamaica's slave women were involved in a polygamous relationship with about 10,000 "Head Negroes." An important encouragement for the continuation of polygamy late in the slavery period was the rapidly falling sex ratio in the absence of the slave trade. In Jamaica, for example, the slave sex ratio stood at 100 in 1817 and had fallen to 94.5 by 1832 (Higman, *Slave Population and Economy*, 72). In this century polygamy was (and still is) practiced in places such as Haiti and British Guiana (Guyana) where underdevelopment is the rule and West African cultural practices remain strong. Elsewhere Herskovits has argued that the sequence of mating or serial monogamy, which is the norm for many Caribbean blacks today, may well be a New World interpretation of West African polygamy (M.J. Herskovits and Francis S. Herskovits, *Trinidad Village* [New York, 1947], 295–6).

50   B.W. Higman, "African and Creole Slave Family Patterns in Trinidad," *Journal of Family History* 3 (1978), 163–80.

51   Caldwell, "Introduction," *Population Growth*, ed. Caldwell, 4.

52   Cantrelle, "Mortality," 98.

53   Brass, "Biosocial Factors," 91.

54   Page, "Fertility Levels," 29.

55   Klein and Engerman ("Fertility Differentials") have drawn this rate from numerous studies which they cite on p. 360.

56   Ibid., 361. The authors, however, state that the rate is unadjusted for infant mortality.

57   Higman, *Slave Population and Economy*, 116.

58   Ibid., 47–8.

59   See our discussion of slave infant mortality in Chapter 8.

60   Ansley Coale and Frank Lorimer, "Summary of Estimates of Fertility and Mortality," in *The Demography of Tropical Africa*, eds. William Brass et al. (Princeton, 1968), 157.

61   Ibid.

62   For other West African infant mortality rates in the 300 to 500 per 1,000 range, see Charles C. Hughes and John M. Hunter, "Disease and 'Development' in Africa,"

SSM 3 (1970), 448 and Great Britain, Economic Advisory Council, Committee on Nutrition in the Colonial Empire, *Nutrition in the Colonial Empire*, 2 parts (London, 1939) 2:33 and passim.

63   H.I. Ajaegbu and Christine E. Mann, "Human Population and The Disease Factor in the Development of Nigeria," in *The Population Factor in African Studies*, eds., Moss and Rathbone, 131; Coale and Lorimer, "Estimates of Fertility and Mortality," 157–8.

64   Aykroyd, *Sweet Malefactor*, 34–5; Goveia, *Slave Society*, 124; Frank Wesley Pitman, "Slavery on British West India Plantations in the Eighteenth Century," *JNH* 11 (1926), 643. For contemporary observers who put the infant mortality rate at upwards of 50 percent, see Robert Renny, *A History of Jamaica* (London, 1807), 207; John Hancock, "Observations on Tetanus Infantum, or Locked Jaw of Infants," *Edinburgh Medical and Surgical Journal* 35 (1831), 343; and Thomson, *Diseases of Negroes*, 120.

65   K.H. Hill, "Population Trends in Africa," in *The Population Factor in African Studies*, eds. Moss and Rathbone, 108–9.

66   Ibid., 110; Page, "Fertility Levels," 29.

67   Cantrelle, "Mortality," 107; Brass, "Biosocial Factors," 92.

68   Michael Craton and James Walvin, *A Jamaican Plantation: The History of Worthy Park 1670–1970* (Toronto, 1970), 134.

69   Patterson, *Sociology of Slavery*, 101–2.

70   Higman, *Slave Population and Economy*, 48.

71   J. Harry Bennett, *Bondsmen and Bishops: Slavery and Apprenticeship on the Codrington Plantations of Barbados, 1710–1835* (Berkeley, Calif., 1958), 56–7.

72   These records may be found at the Barbados Archives, Lazaretto, St. Michael. Other parish records were incomplete, yet what data were available suggest that only about one third of those aged ten and under of the slave children who died were infants aged one or less.

73   See, for example, Collins, *Practical Rules*, 393–4.

74   The following discussion is based on Jerome S. Handler and Robert S. Corruccini, "Plantation Slave Life in Barbados: A Physical Anthropological Analysis," *JIH* 14 (1983), 65–90. See also Robert S. Corruccini et al., "Osteology of a Slave Burial Population from Barbados, West Indies," *AJPA* 59 (1982), 443–59.

75   The following discussion is based on data taken from K.H. Uttley's studies of "Infant and Early Childhood Death Rates over the Last Hundred Years in the Negro Population of Antigua, British West Indies," *BJPSM* 14 (1960), 185–9; "The Birth, Stillbirth, Death and Fertility rates in the Colored Population of Antigua, West Indies, from 1857 to 1956." *TRSTMH* 5 (1961), 69–78.

76   Unless otherwise indicated, population data for Cuba and Puerto Rica have been taken from the appropriate pages of Isla de Cuba, "Clasificación de los habitantes . . . según el empadronamiento verificado el 14 de marzo de 1861" and Isla de Puerto Rico, "Clasificación de los habitantes por naturaleza, sexo, estado civil, y edad," in Spain, *Censo de la población de España según el recuento verificado en 25 de diciembre de 1860* (Madrid, 1863).

77   Eblen, "Natural Increase of Slave Populations," 245.

78   Uttley, "Birth, Stillbirth, Death and Fertility Rates," 69–78.

79   United States slave population data, unless otherwise indicated, have been taken from the appropriate pages in U.S. Census Office, *Statistics of the United States (including Mortality, Property, etc.) in 1860; compiled from the original returns and being the final exhibit of the Eighth Census, under the direction of the Secretary of the Interior* (Washington, 1866).

80   Grainger, *Essay on West-India Diseases*, 14–15; "Seccion de Ultramar al Gobernador Capitan General de la Isla de Cuba," 6 July, 1847, AHN Ultramar, Leg. 4655, no. 10; "Secretaria de Gobierno, Seccion de Fomento al Ministro de Estado de Ultramar," 12

August, 1855. AHN Ultramar, Leg. 3550; Manuel Moreno Fraginals, *El ingenio: el complejo economico social Cubano del azucar, 1760–1860* (Havana, 1964), 157; Hugh Thomas, *Cuba: The Pursuit of Freedom* (New York, 1971), 170; Adam Szasdi, "Apuntes sobre la esclavitud en San Juan de Puerto Rico, 1800–1808," *Anuario de estudios Americanos* 23 (1966), 27.

81   However, it should be noted that those who have studied slave demography in the United States feel that slave fertility was higher earlier in the century. On the other hand, there are those who feel slave fertility in the Islands was also high in earlier centuries. See, for example, Robert V. Wells, *The Population of the British Colonies in America Before 1776* (Princeton, N.J., 1975), 243 and Richard S. Dunn, *Sugar and Slaves; The Rise of the Planter Class in The English West Indies, 1624–1713* (Chapel Hill, N.C., 1972), 316 and note 22. But see also Richard B. Sheridan, "Mortality and the Medical Treatment of Slaves in the British West Indies," in *Race and Slavery in the Western Hemisphere: Quantitative Studies*, eds. Engerman and Genovese, 287. Sheridan has sketched out three phases of sugar slavery, cautioning that slave fertility may have been lower during the middle period. During the early phase, according to Sheridan, "planters conserved their human capital, were concerned for their food and clothing, and encouraged family life and reproduction." However, with the move to "near monoculture," planters found it "generally cheaper to buy new workers than to bear the cost of breeding and raising a slave to working age in the colony," more men than women were imported and, Sheridan argues, the result was on the one hand "a decline in the birth rate," and on the other "an increase in the death rate as 'seasoning,' epidemics, hard labor and malnutrition all took their toll." The third phase for Barbados began as lower profits and higher slave prices coupled with the abolitionist campaign against the slave trade to bring about "amelioration," which with reduced work loads and better nutrition saw slave mortality fall and fertility rise until the colony actually had a slave population growing by natural means.

82   Kenneth F. Kiple and Virginia Himmelsteib King, *Another Dimension to the Black Diaspora: Diet, Disease and Racism* (New York, 1981), 81–3, 122–3.

83   For a similar failure of amelioration to stimulate population growth see E. Van den Boogaart and P.C. Emmer, "Plantation Slavery in Surinam in the Last Decade Before Emancipation: The Case of Catharina Sophia," and Humphrey E. Lamur, "Demography of Surinam Plantation Slaves in the Last Decade Before Emancipation: The Case of Catharina Sophia," both in *Comparative Perspectives on Slavery in New World Plantation Societies*, eds. Vera Rubin and Arthur Tuden (New York, 1977), 211, 217–71.

Chapter 8. Slave Infant and Child Mortality

1   Sir Stanley Davidson et al., *Human Nutrition and Dietetics*, 6th ed. (Edinburgh, 1975), 6.

2   Matthew Gregory Lewis, *Journal of a West India Proprietor* (London, 1834).

3   Tomás de Cordova, *Memorias geográficas, económicas y estadísticas de la isla de Puerto Rico*, 6 vols. (San Juan, 1968), 4:201; Edward Long, *The History of Jamaica*, 2 vols. (London, 1774), 2:436; Jorge LeRoy y Cassa, *Mortalidad producida por el tétanos en la república de Cuba* (Havana, 1905); Ramon Piña y Peñuela, *Topografia médica de la isla de Cuba* (Havana, 1855), 91.

4   Thomas Dancer, *The Medical Assistant or Jamaica Practice of Physic . . .* (Kingston, 1809), 269.

5   Ibid., 269–71; Robert Collins, *Practical Rules for the Management and Medical Treatment of Negro Slaves, in the Sugar Colonies* (London, 1811), 139–40. For some physicians in the southern United States who pondered the problem, see L.A. Dugas, "A Lecture

Upon Tetanus," *Southern Medical and Surgical Journal* (1861), 433–44 and W.G. Ramsay, "The Physiological Differences between the European (or White Man) and the Negro," *Southern Agriculturist & Register of Rural Affairs* 12 (1839), 412.

6   Alexander M. Earle and W. Larimer Mellon, "Tetanus Neonatorum: A Report of Thirty-Two Cases," *American Journal of Tropical Medicine and Hygiene* 7 (1958), 315–16.

7   Dancer, *Medical Assistant*, 267; John Williamson, *Medical and Miscellaneous Observations Relative to the West India Islands*, 2 vols. (Edinburgh, 1817) 1:130–1.

8   T. Winterbottom, *An Account of the Native Africans in the Neighborhood of Sierra Leone*, 2 vols. (London, 1803), 2:220.

9   Charles Wilcocks and P.E.C. Manson-Bahr, *Manson's Tropical Diseases* (Baltimore, 1972), 546; Oscar Felsenfeld, *The Epidemiology of Tropical Diseases* (Springfield, Ill., 1966), 174.

10   James Thomson (*A Treatise on the Diseases of Negroes as they Occur in the Island of Jamaica; with Observations on the County Remedies* [Jamaica, 1820], 119) claimed about one quarter for Jamaica as did Bryan Edwards (*The History, Civil and Commercial of the British Colonies in the West Indies*, 3 vols. [London, 1807], 2:167). For a 20 percent rate in Cuba, see Manuel Moreno Fraginals, "Africa in Cuba: A Quantitative Analysis of the African Population in the Island of Cuba," in *Comparative Perspectives on Slavery in New World Plantation Societies*, eds. Vera Rubin and Arthur Tuden, 200; for a 50 percent rate in the British colonies, see the testimony cited by Frank Wesley Pitman in "Slavery on the British West India Plantations in the 18th Century," *JNH* 11 (1926), 643. See also John Hancock, "Observations on Tetanus Infantum, or Lockjaw of Infants," *Edinburgh Medical and Surgical Journal* 35 (1831), 343.

11   [John Stewart] *An Account of Jamaica* (London, 1808), 274–5; James Grainger, *An Essay on the more Common West-India Diseases . . .* (London, 1764), 15; William Lempriere, *Practical Observations on the Diseases of the Army in Jamaica, as they occurred between the years 1792 and 1797*, 2 vols. (London, 1799), 1:48–9; Jean Barthlelemy Danzille, *Observations sur les maladies des Negres, leurs causes, leurs traitemens, et les moyens de les prevenir*, 2d ed., 2 vols. (Paris, 1892), 2:128.

12   August Hirsch, *Handbook of Geographical and Historical Pathology*, 3 vols. (London, 1883–86), 3:605–6, 616.

13   K.H. Uttley, "The Epidemiology of Tetanus in the Negro Race over the Last Hundred Years in Antigua, the West Indies," *WIMJ* 8 (1959). Our calculations were made from data on pages 43 and 45.

14   LeRoy y Cassa, *Mortalidad producida por el tétanos*, 6 and "cuadro numero uno."

15   Uttley, "Epidemiology of Tetanus," 48; LeRoy y Cassa, *Mortalidad producida por el tétanos*, 8.

16   Obispado de la Habana, "Matrimonios, bautismos y entierros verificados durante los cinco anos . . . desde 1842 hasta 1846," in *Cuba; cuadro estadístico de la siempre fiel isla de Cuba correspondiente al año de 1846 . . .* (Havana, 1847); Angel José Crowley, *Ensayo estadístico-médico de la mortalidad de la diocesis de la Habana durante el año de 1843* (Havana, 1845).

17   William Sells, *Remarks on the Condition of the Slaves in the Island of Jamaica* (London, 1823), 20–1.

18   Barry Higman, *Slave Population and Economy in Jamaica, 1807–1834* (Cambridge, Eng., 1976), 112–13.

19   Sells, *Condition of the Slaves*, 20–1.

20   Lewis, *Journal*, 97. See, however, Michael Craton, who explains that during the first nine days of life Africans did not regard their infants as "yet fully part of the terrestrial world." Thus, in some cases deaths within the first nine days may have been the result of infanticide. (Michael Craton, "Hobbesian or Panglossian? Two Extremes of Slave Conditions in the British Caribbean, 1783–1834," *WMQ* 35 [1978], 343).

21   See, for example, Thomson, *The Diseases of Negroes*, 121.

22 Alexander Barclay, *A Practical View of the Present State of Slavery in the West Indies . . .* (London, 1828), 333. See also William Dickson (ed.) (*Mitigation of Slavery* [London, 1814], 249), who provides testimony of the "old bad system" where "one fourth of the Negro infants are carried off, in the first fortnight by the locked jaw alone."

23 See, for example, Collins, *Practical Rules,* 138–40. The same advice to prevent neonatal tetanus was being issued by physicians in the United States. See, for example, Isaac Wright, *Wright's Family Medicine* (Madisonville, Tenn., 1833).

24 Tetany was not actually unknown in the nineteenth century. See, for example, John Clarke, *Commentaries on Some of the Most Important Diseases of Children* (London, 1815). Chapter 4 is entitled "On a Peculiar Species of Convulsions in Infant Children," which describes the disease but has no notion of its cause. For the unraveling of the etiology of tetany, see Arthur L. Bloomfield, "A Bibliography of Internal Medicine: Tetany," *Stanford Medical Bulletin* 17, No. 1 (1959), 1–12. As more and more has been learned of tetany, the mortality rate has fallen sharply. However, as late as the 1950s, over one third of those afflicted died; F. Cockburn et al., "Neonatal Convulsions Associated with Primary Disturbance of Calcium, Phosphorus, and Magnesium Metabolism," *ADC* 48 (1973), 106; J.H. Keen, "Significance of Hypocalcaemia in Neonatal Convulsions," *ADC* 44 (1969), 356.

25 Stephen A. Roberts, Mervyn D. Cohen, and John O. Forfar, "Antenatal Factors Associated with Neonatal Hypocalcaemic Convulsions," *Lancet* 2 (1973), 809–11; Abraham Cantarow, "Mineral Metabolism," in *Diseases of Metabolism,* ed. Garfield G. Duncan (Philadelphia, 1952), 284; Allen W. Root and Harold E. Harrison, "Recent Advances in Calcium Metabolism," *JP* 88 (1976), 179; Patsy J.M. Watney, et al., "Maternal Factors in Neonatal Hypocalcaemia: A Study in Three Ethnic Groups," *BMJ* 2 (1971), 432–6; C.W.G. Turton, "Altered Vitamin D Metabolism in Pregnancy," *Lancet* 1:8005 (1977), 222–5.

26 D. Barltrop and T.E. Oppe, "Dietary Factors in Neonatal Calcium Homoeostasis," *Lancet* 2 (26 Dec., 1970), 1333–5; Roy M. Pitkin, "Calcium Metabolism in Pregnancy: A Review," *American Journal of Obstetrics and Gynecology* 121 (1975), 731.

27 Roberts, Cohen and Forfar, "Antenatal Factors," 811; Felsenfeld, *Epidemiology of Tropical Diseases,* 414.

28 Derrick B. Jelliffe, *Infant Nutrition in the Subtropics and Tropics,* 2d ed. (Geneva, 1968), 113.

29 M. Isabel Irwin and Eldon W. Kienholz, "A Conspectus of Research on Calcium Requirements of Man," *JN* 103 (1973), 1044; Reginald C. Tsang and William Oh, "Neonatal Hypocalcemia in Low Birth Weight Infants," *PED* 45 (1970), 773.

30 Or if the mother has hyperparathyroidism. J. Paupe et al., "Variations physiologiques de la calcemie chez la mère au moment de l'accouchement dans le cordon et chez le nouveau né," *Biology of the Neonate* 3 (1961), 357–78; Lars Bergman, "Studies on Early Neonatal Hypocalcemia," *Acta Paediatrica Scandinavica: Supplement* 248 (1974), 21; Root and Harrison, "Advances in Calcium Metabolism," 178; Garfield G. Duncan (ed.), *Diseases of Metabolism: Detailed Methods of Diagnosis and Treatment,* 3d ed. (1952), 269–70; Paul B. Beeson and Walsh McDermott, *Textbook of Medicine* (Philadelphia, 1971) 2:1854; Cantarow, "Mineral Metabolism," 27–74.

31 Heinz Goerke, "The Life and Scientific Works of Dr. John Quier, Practitioner of Physic and Surgery, Jamaica: 1738–1822," *WIMJ* 5 (1956), 25.

32 Ibid; Aaron Lechtig, et al., "Effect of Maternal Nutrition on Infant Mortality," and Joe D. Wray, "Maternal Nutrition, Breast-feeding and Infant Survival," both in *Nutrition and Human Reproduction,* ed. W. Henry Mosley (New York, 1978), 161 and 199–200.

33 John George F. Wurdemann, *Notes on Cuba, Containing an Account of Its Discovery and Early History; a Description of the Face of the Country, its Population, Resources, and Wealth; its Institutions and Manners and Customs of Its Inhabitants with Directions to*

Travelers Visiting the Island (Boston, 1844), 105; John W. Blassingame (ed.), *Slave Testimony: Two Centuries of Letters, Speeches, Interviews, and Autobiographies* (Baton Rouge, La., 1977), 259; "Hypocalcemia in Newborn Infants Fed Cows Milk," *Nutrition Reviews* 26 (1968), 299–301; Joan L. Caddell, "Magnesium in the Nutrition of the Child," *Clinical Pediatrics* 13 (1974), 264; Root and Harrison, "Advances in Calcium Metabolism," 178; Patrick C.N. Clarke, and I.J. Carre, "Hypocalcemia, Hypomagnesemic Convulsions," *JP* 70 (1967), 808; Iain McIntyre, "An Outline of Magnesium Metabolism in Health and Disease – A Review," *Journal of Chronic Disease* 16 (1963), 211–12; J.A. Davis, D.R. Harvey, and J.S. Yu, "Neonatal Fits Associated with Hypomagnesaemia," *ADC* 40 (1965), 289.

34   C.C. de Silva and N.G. Baptist, *Tropical Nutritional Disorders of Infants and Children* (Springfield, Ill., 1969) 20; Luc Paunier, "Primary Hypomagnesaemia with Secondary Hypocalcemia in an Infant," *PED* 41 (1968), 397; Mark D. Altschule, *Nutritional Factors in General Medicine* (Springfield, Ill, 1978), 45; Davis, Harvey and Yu, "Neonatal Fits Associated with Hypomagnesaemia," 289; Joan L. Caddell, "Magnesium Deprivation in Sudden Unexpected Infant Death," *Lancet* 2 (1972), 258–62.

35   Earle and Mellon, "Tetanus Neonatorum," 315–16; For an interesting example of a nineteenth-century physician who treated a child's "tetanus" with milk and to his "delight" discovered that it worked a cure, see R.H. Goldsmith, "Tetanus – Epidemic or Constitutional among Negroes," *Practitioner* 1 (1880), 22–4.

36   Arthur L. Rose and Cesare T. Lombroso, "A Study of Clinical, Pathological, and Electroencephalographic Features in 137 Full-term Babies with a Long-Term Follow-up," *PED* 45 (1970), 404–25; Keen, "Hypocalcaemia in Neonatal Convulsions," 356–61; Cockburn, et al., "Neonatal Convulsions," 104; Tsang and Oh, "Neonatal Hypocalcemia," 773–81.

37   Stewart, *Account of Jamaica*, 274–5; Sells, *Condition of the Slaves*, 20–1.

38   Thomson, *Diseases of Negroes*, 120–1; Collins, *Practical Rules*, 139–40; Dugas, "Lecture upon Tetanus," 443–4; Goerke, "Dr. John Quier," 25; Williamson, *Medical and Miscellaneous Observations*, 1:xiii; Hirsch, *Handbook*, 3:614–15.

39   See Kenneth F. Kiple and Virginia H. King, *Another Dimension to the Black Diaspora: Diet, Disease and Racism* (New York 1981), 101–6, for the argument that tetany was a major killer of slave infants in the American South.

40   This hypothesis was first put forward in Kenneth F. Kiple and Virginia H. Kiple, "Deficiency Diseases in the Caribbean," *JIH* 11 (1980), 197–215.

41   Kenneth F. Kiple and Virginia H. Kiple, "Black Tongue and Black Men: Pellagra in the Antebellum South," *Journal of Southern History* 43 (1977), 411–28.

42   DeSilva and Baptist, *Tropical Nutritional Disorders*, 114–15; Jelliffe, *Infant Nutrition*, 102, 98; Robert R. Williams, *Toward the Conquest of Beriberi* (Cambridge, Mass., 1961), 67.

43   Jelliffe, *Infant Nutrition*, 98–9; Davidson, et al., *Human Nutrition and Dietetics*, 338; Michael Latham et al., *Scope Manual on Nutrition* (Kalamazoo, Mich., 1972), 39.

44   Jelliffe, *Infant Nutrition*, 99–100.

45   Williams, *Conquest of Beriberi*, 85.

46   Ibid., 81.

47   Michael Craton and James Walvin, *A Jamaican Plantation. The History of Worthy Park* (Toronto, 1970), 134.

48   Lewis, *Journal*, passim.

49   Ibid., 97, 111.

50   Ibid., 145, 326–7.

51   Craton and Walvin, *Jamaican Plantation*, 134.

52   Antonio Carlo Napoleone Gallenga, *The Pearl of the Antilles* (London, 1873), 123–4; Johns Steven Cabot Abbott, *South and North; or Impressions Received During a Trip to Cuba and the South* (New York, 1860), 142.

53 Davidson et al., *Human Nutrition and Dietetics*, 339; J. Harry Bennett, *Bondsmen and Bishops; Slavery and Apprenticeship on the Codrington Plantations of Barbados, 1719–1838* (Berkeley, Calif., 1958), 56–7; Thomson, *Diseases of Negroes*, 127; Craton and Walvin, *Jamaica Plantation*, 197–8; Stewart, *Account of Jamaica*, 275; Sells, *Condition of the Slaves*, 20–1; Higman, *Slave Population and Economy*, 112–13. For Cuba, see "Epilepsia," as a cause of black infant mortality in Crowley, *Ensayo . . . de la mortalidad*, table, and for British Guiana see George W. Roberts, *The Population of Jamaica* (Cambridge, Eng., 1957), 175.

54 Collins, *Practical Rules*. 323–24.

55 Paul J. Honig, "Teething – Are Today's Pediatricians Using Yesterday's Notions," *JP* 87 (1975), 415–17; Editor, "Teething Myths," *BJM* 4 (1975), 604; Ronald Stanley Illingworth, *Common Symptoms of Disease in Children*, 3d ed. (Oxford, England, 1971), 186–241; Harvey Kravitz, et al., "Teething in Infancy; A Part of Normal Development," *Illinois Medical Journal* 151 (1977), 261–6.

56 Jelliffe, *Infant Nutrition*, 181, 98–100.

57 Crowley, *Ensayo . . . de la mortalidad*, table.

58 George I. Lythcott, Calvin H. Sinnette, and Donald R. Hopkins, "Pediatrics," in *Textbook of Black Related Diseases*, ed. Richard Allen Williams (New York, 1975), 165; Jelliffe, *Infant Nutrition*, 99.

59 James Maxwell, "Pathological Inquiry into the Nature of Cachexia Africana, as Generally Connected with Dirt-Eating," *Jamaica Physical Journal* 2 (1835), 413–14; Collins, *Practical Rules*, 141–6; Lewis, *Journal*, 406.

60 Luis M. Díaz Soler, *Historia de la esclavitud negra en Puerto Rico*, 2d ed. (Río Piedras, 1965), 126; Stewart, *Account of Jamaica*, 312; Lewis, *Journal*, 406; Abbott, *North and South*, 140–2.

61 James Stephen, *The Slavery of the British West India Colonies Delineated . . .* , 2 vols. (London, 1824–30), 2:307; Díaz Soler, *Historia*, 126; "Reglamento de esclavos de 1826," *BHPR* 10 (1923), 265; E.M. Shibstone, *Instructions for the Management of a Plantation in Barbadoes, And for the Treatment of Negroes, etc.* (London, 1786), 29. As late as 1939 it was determined that the diet of young children in the British Islands consisted mostly of cornmeal "pap," which was loaded with sugar (Great Britain Economic Advisory Council, Committee on Nutrition in the Colonial Empire, *Nutrition in the Colonial Empire*, 2 parts [London, 1939] 2:92).

62 See, for example, Thomas Roughley, *The Jamaica Planters' Guide* (London, 1823), 126.

63 Studies conducted on Caribbean blacks reveal, as one would expect, the same very high incidence of lactose intolerance as manifested by blacks in the United States. Frederick J. Simoons, "New Light on Ethnic Differences in Adult Lactose Intolerance," *American Journal of Digestive Diseases* 18 (1973) 598; Felicity King, "Intolerance to Lactose in Mother's Milk?" *Lancet* 2 (12, Aug., 1972), 335; G.C. Cook and F.D. Lee, "The Jejunum after Kwashiorkor," *Lancet* 2 (10, Dec., 1966), 1266; A. Stewart Truswell, "Carbohydrate and Lipid Metabolism in Protein Calorie Malnutrition," in *Protein-Calorie Malnutrition*, ed. Robert E. Olsen (New York, 1975), 120.

64 Iancu Gontzea, *Nutrition and Anti-Infectious Defence*, 2d ed. (Basel, 1974), 36; Fima Lifshitz, et al., "Carbohydrate Intolerance in Infants with Diarrhea," *JP* 79 (1971), 760–7.

65 F.C. Rodger, "Nutritional Factors and Helminthiasis," *Anais da escola de saúde pública e de medicina tropical* 1 (1967); D. Srikantia, "Vitamin A Deficiency and Blindness in Children," in *Human Nutrition: Current Issues and Controversies*, eds. T.H. Neuberger and T.H. Jukes (Lancaster, England, 1982), 185–216.

66 Jacques M. May and Donna L. McLellan, *The Ecology of Malnutrition in the Caribbean* (New York, 1973), 125–77; Arlene Fonaroff, "Differential Concepts of Protein-Calorie Malnutrition in Jamaica: An Exploratory Study of Information and Beliefs," *JTP*

14 (1968), 83; Hubert Carey Trowell, *Non-Infective Disease in Africa* (London, 1960), 331. If, for the Caribbean region, one simply speaks of malnutrition in the one-to-four age group instead of attempting to force symptoms under the rubrics of marasmus and kwashiorkor, then one researcher has estimated that malnutrition plays a significant part in at least half of the deaths in this age group. See Robert Cook, "Nutrition and Mortality under Five Years in the Caribbean Area," *JTP* (1969), 109–17.

67 See, for example, Roughley, *Jamaica Planters' Guide*, 119–20 and Maxwell, "Pathological Inquiry," 413.

68 G. Alleyne et al., *Protein-Energy Malnutrition* (London, 1977), 2–4; Latham, *Scope Manual of Nutrition*, 28; Trowell, *Non-Infective Diseases in Africa*, 332. Slave infants weaned to the low-fat diet so characteristic of the West Indies would automatically have had severe impairment of their ability to absorb the fat-soluble vitamins, which in turn would have accelerated the possibility of intercurrent infection. Then after PEM has developed, the body has difficulty absorbing fats (Robert E. Olsen [ed.], *Protein-Calorie Nutrition* [New York, 1975], 122).

69 Pitman, "Slavery on British West India Plantations," 643; Barclay, *Practical View*, 333; Thomson, *Diseases of Negroes*, 127; Moreno Fraginals, "Africa in Cuba," 200.

70 Nevin S. Scrimshaw, Carl E. Taylor, and John E. Gordon, *Interaction of Nutrition and Infection* (Geneva, 1968), 75; Phyllis Eveleth and J.M. Tanner, *Worldwide Variations in Human Growth* (Oxford, 1976), 75.

71 Pierre Cantrelle, "Mortality," in *Population Growth and Socio-Economic Change in West Africa*, ed., John C. Caldwell (New York, 1975), 108; Nanci L. Solien de Gonzalez, "Lactation and Pregnancy: A Hypothesis," *AA* 66 (1964), 873; Wray, "Maternal Nutrition," 218.

72 Williamson, *Medical and Miscellaneous Observations* 1:76; Ian Taylor and John Knowelden, *Principles of Epidemiology* (Boston, 1964), 225.

73 John H. Phillips and George E. Burch, "A Review of Cardiovascular Diseases in the White and Negro Races," *Medicine* 39 (1960), 245; K.H. Uttley, "The Epidemiology and Mortality of Whooping Cough in the Negro over the Last Hundred Years in Antigua, British West Indies," *WIMJ* 9 (1960), 91 and passim.

74 Hirsch, *Handbook* 3:34.

75 Collins, *Practical Rules*, 269.

76 Margaret E. Grisby, "Infectious Diseases," in *Textbook of Black-Related Disease*, ed. Williams, 480–1.

77 See, for example, K.H. Uttley, "The Mortality and Epidemiology of Diptheria Since 1857 in the Negro Population of Antigua, British West Indies," *WIMJ* 9 (1960), 156–63.

78 Eveleth and Tanner, *Worldwide Variations in Human Growth*, 105, table.

79 Adeboy S. Ademowore, Norman G. Courey, and James S. Kime, "Relationships of Maternal Nutrition and Weight Gain to Birthweight," *Obstetrics and Gynecology* 39 (1972), 460–4; Alfred F. Naylor and Ntinos C. Myrianthopoulos, "The Relation of Ethnic and Selected Socio-economic Factors to Human Birth-weight," *Annals of Human Genetics* 31 (1967), 71; Nehari Gebre-Medhin and Abeba Gobezie, "Dietary Intake in the Third Trimester of Pregnancy and Birth Weight of Offspring among Nonprivileged and Privileged Women," *AJCN* 29 (1976), 441–51; Lechtig et al., "Effect of Maternal Nutrition on Infant Mortality," 150 and passim; Richard L. Naeye, William Blanc, and Cheryl Paul, "Effects of Maternal Nutrition on the Fetus," *PED* 52:4 (1973), 494–503; David Rush, Hillard Davis, and Mervyn Susser, "Antecedents of Low Birthweight in Harlem, New York City," *International Journal of Epidemiology* 1 (1972), 375–87.

80 P.C. Jeans, Mary B. Smith, and Genevieve Stearns, "Incidence of Prematurity in Relation to Maternal Nutrition," *JADA* 31 (1955), 576–81; Jane Linken Schwartz and

Lawrence H. Schwartz, eds. *Vulnerable Infants: A Psychosocial Dilemma* (New York, 1977), 5; A. Frederick North and Hugh M. McDonald, "Why are Neonatal Mortality Rates Lower in Small Black Infants than in White Infants of Similar Birth Weights?" *JP* 90 (1977), 809–10; Jerry L. Weaver, "The Case of Black Infant Mortality," *Journal of Health Policy* 1 (1977), 439.

81 Altschule, *Nutritional Factors in General Medicine*, 102; J.N. Thompson, "The Role of Vitamin A in Reproduction," in *The Fat-Soluble Vitamins*, eds. H.F. DeLuca and J.W. Suttie (Madison, Wisc., 1970), 272; Marshall T. Newman, "Ecology and Nutritional Stress," in *Culture, Disease and Healing: Studies in Medical Anthropology*, ed. David Landy (New York, 1977), 322–3.

82 Lawrence Bergner and Mervyn W. Susser, "Low Birth Weight and Prenatal Nutrition: An Interpretive Review," PED 46 (1970), 946–66; Myron Winick, *Malnutrition and Brain Development* (New York, 1976), 57 and passim.

83 Evangeline Walker Andrews (ed.), *Journal of a Lady of Quality* (New Haven, Conn., 1927), 104, 106.

84 Lewis, *Journal*, 82.

85 Ibid., 320.

86 Ibid., 321.

87 Ibid., 97, 122–4.

88 Ibid., 111, 380.

89 We have, of course, been looking at the Lewis plantation during amelioration. It was during the latter part of this period, and during the first decades of freedom that black Caribbean populations began to grow. Earlier in the text I noted that a decline in neonatal tetanus was reported for Jamaica throughout the first decades of the nineteenth century. A similar decline was noted in Barbados, where shortly after the end of slavery a visitor reported the disease "diminished" on that island (John Davy, *The West Indies, Before and Since Slave Emancipation* [London, 1854], 102). In addition we saw that the death rates for neonatal tetanus on Cuba and Antigua for the late nineteenth and early twentieth centuries were quite low, relative to the fearsome rates the disease was reputed to have generated during slavery. So, to repeat, it is not unreasonable to suspect that it was not neonatal tetanus that declined, but rather neonatal tetany, as the black diet improved. Similarly, the incidence of the *mal d' estomach*, which I have argued was actually beriberi in many cases, also declined. A Jamaican resident wrote on the eve of abolition that the disease "so prevalant and fatal some years ago . . . is now scarcely heard of" (Barclay, *Practical View*, 333). For a similar decline in Barbados, see Davy, *The West Indies*, 102. It may be possible to link the decline in incidence of this disease to a very specific dietary change. For John Stewart, in his 1823 update of his original *Account of Jamaica* done in 1808, mentions that salt pork had recently become an important item in the slave diet (J[ohn] Stewart, *A View of the Past and Present State of the Island of Jamaica; with Remarks on the Moral and Physical Conditions of the Slaves, and on the Abolition of Slavery in the Colonies* [Edinburgh, 1823] 268) and the salt pork would have delivered both thiamine and fats to reduce thiamine requirements. In Barbados the new items of diet seem to have been sweet potatoes (apparently eliminating much of the island's "sore eyes" and night blindness), which along with fresh fish, pigeon peas, and other legumes would probably have delivered sufficient vitamin B, including thiamine, to eliminate serious B deficiencies while, as free men, blacks would have had considerably more access to lard, which would have improved their intake of fats. See James Bovel, "Observations on the Climate of Barbados, and its Influence on Disease. . . " BAJMPS 4 (1848), 114, 171; Claude Levy, *Emancipation, Sugar, Federalism: Barbados and the West Indies, 1833–1876* (Gainesville, Fla., 1980), 5; Davy, *The West Indies*, 123–4. On the other hand, see J.B.S. Jackson, "Diseases of the Island of Barbados," *Boston Medical and Surgical Journal* 76 (1867),

who felt corn, fish, and sweet potatoes constituted fare more meager than during slavery.

Chapter 9. Black Diseases and White Medicine

1 *The Report of the Committee of the Legislature of Dominica Appointed to Enquire into and Report on Certain Queries Relative to the Condition, Treatment, Rights and Privileges of the Negro Population of that Island* (London, 1823), 4–5.

2 Robert Collins, *Practical Rules for the Management and Medical Treatment of Negro Slaves, in the Sugar Colonies* (London, 1811), 236.

3 G.A. Alleyne, "Some Disease Patterns in West Indian Immigrants," *Medical World* 97 (1962), 22.

4 Ibid., 23–4. However, at about the same time a report on Caribbean illnesses pointed out that, while the amebas are still found regularly in stools, the dysentery itself is no longer a serious Caribbean health problem, presumably because the people are better nourished and thus better able to "live" with the parasites. See M.T. Ashcroft, "A History and General Survey of the Helminth and Protozoal Infections of the West Indies," *Annals of Tropical Medicine and Parasitology* 59 (1965), 488–9 and Iancu Gontzea, *Nutrition and Anti-Infectious Defence* (Basel, 1974), 22.

5 Nevin S. Scrimshaw, Carl E. Taylor, and John E. Gordon, *Interactions of Nutrition and Infection* (Geneva, 1968), passim; Gontzea, *Nutrition and Anti-Infectious Defence*, 20, 23–9, 35–6; Ian Taylor and John Knowelden, *Principles of Epidemiology* (Boston, 1964), 226–7; Jean Mayer, "Nutrition and Tuberculosis: Diet and Susceptibility to Tuberculosis," *PMJ* 50 (1971), 55–7; R.K. Chandra and P.M. Newberne, *Nutrition, Immunity and Infection: Mechanisms of Interactions* (New York, 1977), 57.

6 Matthew Gregory Lewis, *Journal of a West India Proprietor, 1815–1817* (London, 1929), 144; Thomas Dancer, *The Medical Assistant or Jamaica Practice of Physic . . .* (Kingston, Jamaica, 1809), 239.

7 William Hillary, *Observations on the Changes of the Air and the Concomitant Epidemical Diseases in the Island of Barbados* (London, 1759), 322–35; H. Harold Scott, "The Influence of the Slave Trade in the Spread of Tropical Disease," *TRSTMH* 37 (1943), 181. But see also M. Ferreira de Mira, *Historia da medicina Portuguesa* (Lisbon, 1947), 123; Charles Wilcocks and P.E.C. Manson-Bahr, *Manson's Tropical Diseases*, 17th ed. (Baltimore, 1974), 411; and Miguel Angel Gonzalez Prendes, *Historia de la lepra en Cuba* (Havana, 1963), 36–40.

8 John Hunter, *Observations on the Diseases of the Army of Jamaica* (London, 1788), 309.

9 [John Stewart] *An Account of Jamaica* (London, 1808), 269.

10 James Thomson, *A Treatise on the Diseases of Negroes as they Occur in the Island of Jamaica; with Observations on the Country Remedies* (Jamaica, 1820), 99; Dancer, *Medical Assistant*, 230, 232, 239; James Grainger, *An Essay on the More Common West-India Diseases . . .* (London, 1764), 53, 55; Hillary, *Observations*, 324.

11 Wilcocks and Manson-Bahr, *Manson's Tropical Diseases*, 17–19.

12 Herman Weber, "On the Affection of the Small Toes of Negroes, Called Ainhum," *Transactions of the Pathological Society of London* 18 (1867), 277–80 and 19 (1868) 448–51.

13 Benjamin Moseley, *A Treatise on Tropical Diseases*, 2d ed. (London, 1789), 28–9.

14 Gonzolo Hernández de Oviedo, *Historia general y natural de las Indias, islas y tierra firme del mar océano . . .* , 4 vols. (Madrid, 1851–55), 1:56.

15 Wilcocks and Manson-Bahr, *Manson's Tropical Diseases*, 17, 18, 788–90. The chigoe is a serious problem in parts of Africa today but it only reached that continent from the Americas in 1872.

16 Lewis, *Journal*, 215; Alfred W. Crosby, *The Columbian Exchange: Biological and Cultural Consequences of 1492* (Westport, Conn., 1972), 209.

17 Hillary, *Observations*, 227, 297–304; George Pinckard, *Notes on the West Indies, Including Observations Relative to the Creoles and Slaves of the Western Colonies, and the Indians of South America; Interspersed with Remarks upon the Seasoning or Yellow Fever of Hot Climates*, 2d ed., 2 vols. (London, 1816), 1:269.

18 George W. Hunter, William W. Frye, and J. Clyde Swartzwelder, *Manual of Tropical Medicine*, 4th ed. (Philadelphia, 1956), 717–19; Wilcocks and Manson-Bahr, *Manson's Tropical Diseases*, 1062.

19 Alexander Bryson, *Report on the Climate and Principal Diseases of the African Station . . .* (London, 1847), 256; R. Hoeppli, *Parasitic Diseases in Africa and the Western Hemisphere: Early Documentation and Transmission by the Slave Trade* (Basel, 1969), 165–6; Manuel Moreno Fraginals, "Africa in Cuba: A Quantitative Analysis of the African Population in the Island of Cuba," in *Comparative Perspectives on Slavery in New World Plantation Societies*, eds. Vera Rubin and Arthur Tuden (New York, 1977), 200.

20 Calculated from data in B.W. Higman, *Slave Population and Economy in Jamaica, 1807–1834* (Cambridge, Eng., 1976), 112–14; Jerome S. Handler, and Frederick W. Lange, *Plantation Slavery in Barbados* (Cambridge, Mass., 1977), 99, table; George W. Roberts, *The Population of Jamaica* (Cambridge, Eng., 1957), 175 and table.

21 Higman, *Slave Population and Economy*, 112–14; Michael Craton and James Walvin, *A Jamaican Plantation: The History of Worthy Park* (Toronto, 1970), 197–8.

22 K.H. Uttley, "The Mortality from Leprosy in the Negro Population of Antigua, West Indies from 1857 to 1956," *Leprosy Review* 31 (1960), 193–9; D. Angel José Crowley, *Ensayo estadístico-médico de la mortalidad de la diocesis de la Habana durante el año de 1843* (Havana, 1845), table. Of course leprosy deaths may be buried in other causes-of-death categories.

23 Gonzalez Prendes, *Historia de la lepra en Cuba*, 44–5.

24 Dancer, *Medical Assistant*, 222; Collins, *Practical Rules*, 354; Grainger, *Essay on . . . West India Diseases*. See Fray Iñigo Abbad y Lasierra (*Historia geográfica, civil y natural de la isla de San Juan Bautista de Puerto Rico* [San Juan, 1886], 208) for Puerto Rico, where the disease was called "pian."

25 Hunter, Frye, and Swartzwelder, *Manual of Tropical Medicine*, 129–35; Wilcocks and Manson-Bahr, *Manson's Tropical Diseases*, 575–7.

26 Oscar Felsenfeld, *The Epidemiology of Tropical Diseases* (Springfield, Ill., 1966), 201; Higman, *Slave Population and Economy of Jamaica*, 112–14; Roberts, *Population of Jamaica*, 175.

27 Edward Long, *The History of Jamaica*, 2 vols. (London, 1774), 2:434. However, physicians in West Africa assure us that leprosy, yaws, and other "morbid affections of the skin" were "common." See, for example, William Freeman Daniell, *Sketches of the Medical Topography and Native Diseases of the Gulf of Guinea, Western Africa* (London, 1849), 48.

28 Thus on the Newton plantation in Barbados where both leprosy and the "joint evil" were listed as causes of death, yaws was not, suggesting strongly that physicians and planters interpreted the outward signs of inner disease as leprosy in one locale and yaws in another (Handler and Lange, *Plantation Slavery in Barbados*, 99).

29 Yaws in the Spanish Islands is extremely difficult to disentangle from the general term "bubas," or "bubos" (Moreno Fraginals, "Africa in Cuba," 200). Today "bubos" generally means American leishmaniasis, a forest disease of Central and South America (Hunter, Frye, and Swartzwelder, *Manual of Tropical Medicine*, 391, 69). But others have intended bubos to mean either yaws or syphilis. Early in Spain's presence in the New World, Padre de Acosta wrote that "bubos" was a problem of health for the Spaniards and there is little doubt that he intended that the word mean syphilis, while Antonio Hernandez Morejón, in his monumental history of Spanish medicine, also calls "bubos" a venereal disease (*mal venereo*). Conversely, a modern authority reports that bubos means yaws as well as venereal syphilis, while

an observer in Puerto Rico explained that "pian," which he intended to connote yaws, was sometimes confused with "bubos," which he took to mean syphilis. See Padre José de Acosta, *Historia natural y moral de las Indias* (London, 1880), 130–213; Antonio Hernandez Morejón, *Historia bibliografica de la medicina Española*, 7 vols. (Madrid, 1842–52), 2:269; Hoeppli, *Parasitic Diseases*, 71–6; Abbad y Lasierra, *Historia*, 208. According to Dancer (*Medical Assistant*, 217), in the British Island "buboes" was a term employed to connote swellings of the glands in the groin, which quite possibly meant tropical or climatic bubo (lymphogranuloma venereum), sometimes called the "sixth veneral disease," with a high frequency among blacks (Wilcocks and Manson-Bahr, *Manson's Tropical Diseases*, 640–5). Thus, for the Spanish islands, both yaws and syphilis were called bubos, and with good reason, for they seem to be caused by the same pathogenic agent and frequently manifest similar symptoms. Moreover, because of this apparent kinship, there is a good deal of cross-immunity between the two, with the result that if a person has contracted one disease he is almost invariably immune to the other (E.H. Hudson, "Treponematosis and African Slavery," *British Journal of Venereal Disease* 40 (1964), 43–52; Thomas A. Cockburn, "The Origin of the Treponematoses," *BWHO* 24 (1961), 221–8). Therefore, since yaws was a black-related disease, slave "bubos" would not as a general rule have included syphilis, and indeed it was believed that "pure blacks" were never stricken with syphilis. (P.M. Ashburn, *The Ranks of Death: A Medical History of the Conquest of America* [New York, 1947], 32; Francisco Eujenio Moscoso Puello, *Apuntes para la historia de la medicina de la isla de Santo Domingo* [Santo Domingo, 1977], 58). Whites, by contrast, were, and their "bubos" was largely syphilis, which, during the days of slavery, was known in plantation America as a white man's disease, and it was not until yaws began to disappear that syphilis became a problem for Caribbean blacks (Kenneth F. Kiple, "The Historical Dimensions of Disease in the Plantation Economies," in *Health, Welfare and Development in Latin America and the Caribbean*, eds. C. Lloyd Brown-John, Frank C. Innes, and W.C. Suderlund [Windsor, Ontario, 1981], 60). This is not to say that there was no venereal disease among the slaves. Long (*History of Jamaica* 2:400–2 and 434–8) claimed that venereal disease was more common among the slaves of Jamaica than the blacks of Africa, while Thomson, (*Diseases of Negroes*, 48) explains that the disease in question was mostly gonorrhea, which he stated was rife among the slaves because of their "rambling life." However, because gonorrhea almost never kills, there is little in the records either to substantiate or refute these claims.

30 Robert Dirks, "Resource Fluctuations and Competitive Transformations in West Indian Slave Societies," in *Extinction and Survival in Human Populations*, eds. Charles D. Laughlin, Jr., and Ivan A. Brady (New York, 1978), 143.

31 Sir Stanley Davidson et al., *Human Nutrition and Dietetics*, 6th ed. (London, 1975), 338–9, 349.

32 "Three Hundred Years of Medicine in Jamaica," *Jamaican Nurse* 6 (1966), 18. Hillary, *Observations*, 339–52; John Brathwaite, "Odd Pages from Old Records," *Journal of the Barbados Museum and Historical Society* 18 (1950), 30; Abbé Guillaume Raynal, *A Philosophical and Political History of the Settlements and Trade of the Europeans in the East and West Indies*, 8 vols., trans. J.O. Justamond (London, 1788), 3:419–20; Dancer, *Medical Assistant*, 221–2. On the other hand, Stewart (*Account of Jamaica*, 270) claimed that "if a white man is seized with [the yaws] it is seldom that he recovers," which makes one wonder if Stewart was not confusing yaws with something else since medical authorities today assure us that peoples with darker skins suffer most from the yaws (Felsenfeld, *Epidemiology of Tropical Diseases*, 202). For leprosy, see Michael Gelfand, *The Sick African* (Capetown, 1957), 137–54.

33 A. Barclay, *A Practical View of the Present State of Slavery in the West Indies*, 2d ed. (London, 1827), 333.

34 R.R. Willcox, "Venereal Diseases," in *A World Geography of Human Diseases*, ed. G. Melvyn Howe (London, 1977), 208; Ivan Beghin, W. Fougere, and Kendall W. King, *L' Alimentation et la nutrition en Haiti* (Paris, 1970), passim.

35 Jean Barthelemy Danzille, *Observations sur les maladies des negres, leurs causes, leurs traitemens, et les moyens de les prevenir* 2d ed., 2 vols. (Paris, 1892), 1:24–5; David Turnbull, *Travels in the West, with Notices of Porto Rico and the Slave Trade* (New York, 1867), 286; J. Bovell, "Observations on the Climate of Barbadoes, and its Influence on Disease: together with Remarks on Ankeoleucitis (sic) or Barbadoes Leg," *BAJMPS* 4: (1848), 114.

36 Lewis, *Journal*, 110; Long, *History* 2:510; J. Harry Bennett, *Bondsmen and Bishops: Slavery and Apprenticeship on the Codrington Plantations of Barbados, 1710–1835* (Berkeley, 1958), 33; Bryan Edwards, *The History, Civil and Commercial, of the British Colonies in the West Indies* 4th ed., 3 vols. (London, 1807), 2:164–5.

37 Higman, *Slave Population and Economy of Jamaica*, 129; Orlando Patterson, *The Sociology of Slavery* (London, 1967), 100.

38 John D. Kirschmann (ed.), *Nutrition Almanac*, rev. ed. (New York, 1979), 8; H.H. Mitchell and Marjorie Edman, *Nutrition and Climatic Stress* (Springfield, Ill., 1951), 24–41. For what it is worth, experiments on animals put on a low-fat diet revealed the animals to have lowered resistance to both tuberculosis and pneumonia. See Gontzea, *Nutrition and Anti-Infectious Defence*, 100–4.

39 Mark D. Altschule, *Nutritional Factors in General Medicine* (Springfield, Ill., 1978), 31; Kirschmann (ed.), *Nutrition Almanac*, 8.

40 Mayer, "Nutrition and Tuberculosis," 55–7; Kirschmann (ed.), *Nutrition Almanac*, 15.

41 Stevenson Lyle Cummins, *Primitive Tuberculosis* (London, 1939), 14–22; C. St. C. Guild, *Tuberculosis in the Negro* (New York, 1935), 7; Richard Gallagher, *Diseases that Plague Modern Man: A History of Ten Communicable Diseases* (Dobbs Ferry, N.Y., 1969), 8.

42 Unless otherwise indicated, the following discussion of tuberculosis in the United States is based on Kenneth F. Kiple and Virginia H. King, *Another Dimension to the Black Diaspora, Diet, Disease and Racism* (New York, 1981), 139–46.

43 Rene Dubos, *Man Adapting* (New Haven, Conn., 1965), 175. For an excellent treatment of *The White Plague: Tuberculosis, Man and Society*, see the study by Rene and Jean Dubos (Boston, 1952).

44 By designating the disease as "scrofula," physicians did indicate that they thought they might be up against some form of tuberculosis, for "scrofulosis" or "scrofula" in nineteenth-century Europe meant bovine tuberculosis, from which more than one half of the population suffered. Felsenfeld, *Epidemiology*, 177.

45 Richard S. Dunn, *Sugar and Slaves, The Rise of the Planter Class in The English West Indies, 1624–1713* (Chapel Hill, N.C., 1972), 302; Frank Wesley Pitman, *The Development of the British West Indies, 1700–1763* (New Haven, 1917), 386–90.

46 MacFarlane Burnet and David O. White, *Natural History of Infectious Disease*, 4th ed. (Cambridge, Eng., 1972), 219; Wilcocks and Manson-Bahr, *Manson's Tropical Diseases*, 449; Hunter, Frye, and Swartzwelder, *Manual of Tropical Medicine*, 184, 198.

47 Handler and Lange, *Plantation Slavery in Barbados*, 99.

48 William Beckford, *A Descriptive Account of . . . Jamaica*, 2 vols. (London, 1790), 2:304; Stewart, *Account of Jamaica*, 268; Thomson, *Diseases of Negroes*, 74; Higman, *Slave Population and Economy in Jamaica*, 112–13; Craton and Walvin, *Jamaican Plantation*, 197–8; Roberts, *Population of Jamaica*, 175.

49 Crowley, *Ensayo*, table.

50 J.B.S. Jackson, "Diseases of the Island of Barbadoes," *British Medical and Surgical Journal* 76 (1867), 448; August Hirsch, *Handbook of Geographical and Historical Pathology*, 3 vols. (London, 1883), 2:622–3, 3:195.

51 Alpheus Hyatt Verrill, *Porto Rico, Past and Present and San Domingo of Today* (New York, 1920), 142–3; Manuel Quevado y Baez, *Historia de la medicina y cirugia de Puerto Rico* (Santurce, 1946–49), 2:653; E. Cochrane, "Tuberculosis in the Tropics," *Tropical Diseases Bulletin* (1937), 755; "Dr. Frederick L. Hoffman's Collection of Statistics . . . Havana, Cuba," RAC, IHB, Series 2, 315 Cuba, Box 30, Folder 178.

52 George P. Paul, *Report on Ankylostomiasis Infection Survey of Barbados*, (New York, 1917), 16; see also Harry H. Johnston, *The Negro in the New World* (London, 1919), 211, note 1.

53 Mayer, "Nutrition and Tuberculosis," 55–7.

54 Thomas McKeown and R.C. Record, "Reasons for the Decline of Mortality in England and Wales During the Nineteenth Century," *Population Studies* 16 (1962), 94–122; see also Thomas McKeown, *The Modern Rise of Population* (New York, 1976), 65 and passim.

55 E. Palermo, "Nutrition, Tuberculosis and Living Conditions," in *Hunger and Food*, ed. Josué de Castro (London, 1958), 109.

56 John Williamson, *Medical and Miscellaneous Observations Relative to the West India Islands*, 2 vols. (Edinburgh, 1817), 1:183, 2:112; Maturin M. Ballou, *History of Cuba; or, Notes of a Traveller in the Tropics . . .* (Boston, 1854), 275–6; James Maxwell, "Account of the Febrile and Eruptive Epidemics Prevalent in the Island of Jamaica between 1831 and 1832," *Edinburgh Medical and Surgical Journal* 52 (1839), 155.

57 Higman, *Slave Population and Economy in Jamaica*, 112–14; Crowley, *Ensayo*, table.

58 George H.T. Kimble, *Tropical Africa*, 2 vols. (New York, 1960), 2:47; William Malcolm Hailey, *An African Survey*, rev. ed. (London, 1957), 1122.

59 Gontzea, *Nutrition and Anti-Infectious Defence*, 20; Chandra and Newberne, *Nutrition, Immunity and Infection*, 42, 43.

60 Hirsch, *Handbook* 3:124; Johnston, *Negro in the New World*, 21; David Lowenthal, "The Population of Barbados," *SES* 6 (1957), 461.

61 For Santo Domingo, which was particularly hard hit during the seventeenth and eighteenth centuries, see Carlos Larrazabel Blanco, *Los negros y la esclavitud en Santo Domingo* (Santo Domingo, 1975), 183; and Moscoso Puello, *Historia de la medicina*, 63. For Jamaica, see Long, *History of Jamaica* 2:434 and for Puerto Rico, see Luis M. Díaz Soler, *Historia de la esclavitud negra en Puerto Rico* (Madrid, 1953), 83. Dunn (*Sugar and Slaves*, 302), however, indicates that smallpox, for some reason, was less of a problem in Barbados.

62 Craton and Walvin, *Jamaican Plantation*, 133; Williamson, *Medical and Miscellaneous Observations* 2:165; Maxwell, "Febrile and Eruptive Diseases," 163. For Puerto Rico, see the detailed instructions on how to vaccinate for smallpox and how to discern whether the vaccination had "taken" in the AGPR, Sanidad, 1823–62, Box 183; see also K.H. Uttley ("Smallpox Mortality in the Negro Population of Antigua, West Indies; A Historical Note," WIMJ 9 [1960], 169–171), who mentions a law for Antigua stating that no person could obtain a judgment from a civil court unless he had a smallpox vaccination.

63 Long, *History of Jamaica*, 2:434.

64 E. Wagner Stearn and Allen E. Stearn, *The Effect of Small Pox on the Destiny of the Amerindian* (Boston, 1945), 16–17; Díaz Soler, *Historia de la esclavitud*, 83; Moscoso Puello, *Historia de la medicina*, 63.

65 Ballou, *History of Cuba*, 276; Abiel Abbot, *Letters Written in the Interior of Cuba . . . 1828* (Boston, 1829), 144; For dates of some of Cuba's nineteenth-century epidemics, see Franklin Knight, *Slave Society in Cuba During the Nineteenth Century* (Madison, 1970), 54; and Hugh Thomas, *Cuba: The Pursuit of Freedom* (New York, 1971), 284. See also Esteban Montejo (*The Autobiography of a Runaway Slave*, ed. Miguel Barnet [New York, 1968], 42), who recalled smallpox very late in the slavery period. Indeed Havana lost 11,355 individuals to the disease during the years 1871 to 1900, most of it apparently arriving with the Spanish army. By contrast, during the years 1900 to

1914 the city saw only four smallpox deaths ("Dr. Frederick Hoffman's Collection of Statistics," table 30).

66 Craton and Walvin, *Jamaican Plantation*, 198; Uttley, "Smallpox Mortality," 169.

67 Larrazabel Blanco, *Los negros y la esclavitud*, 183; Berta Cabanillas de Rodriguez, *Origens de los habitos alimenticios del pueblo de Puerto Rico* (Madrid, 1955), 274–5; Moscoso Puello; *Historia de la medicina*, 63; Jose G. Rigau-Perez, "Smallpox Epidemics in Puerto Rico during the Prevaccine Era (1518–1803)," *JHM* 37 (1982), 429; Pitman, *Development of the British West Indies*, 373.

68 Ashburn, *Ranks of Death*, 32; Arthur H. Gale, *Epidemic Diseases* (Baltimore, 1960), 72.

69 K.H. Uttley, "The Mortality and Epidemiology of Typhoid Fever in the Coloured Inhabitants of Antigua, West Indies over the Last Hundred Years," *WIMJ* 9 (1960), 115; Paul, *Report on Ankylostomiasis*, 12, 13, 19; "Dr. Hoffman's Collection of Statistics," table 27; J.F. Siler, "Medical notes on Jamaica," Part 1 and "Medical notes on Barbados," Part 1 in RAC, IHB, Series 2, 437 Jamaica, Box 43, Folder 261 and 435, Barbados, Box 43, Folder 260, respectively. See also E.O. Jordan's "Impressions of Health Conditions in Jamaica," RAC, IHB, Series 2, 437 Jamaica, Box 43, Folder 261.

70 Hirsch, *Handbook* 1:592; Arie Leo Olitzki, *Enteric Fevers* (New York; 1972), 110, 111.

71 For a listing of these places see Hunter, Frye and Swartzwelder, *Manual of Tropical Medicine*, 876.

72 Nathaniel F. Pierce and Arabindo Mondal, "Clinical Features of Cholera," in *Cholera*, eds. Dhiman Barua and William Burrows (Philadelphia, 1974), 212–13; Arthur Gale, *Epidemic Diseases* (Baltimore, 1960), 66; Charles E. Rosenberg, *The Cholera Years: The United States in 1832, 1849 and 1866* (Chicago, 1962), 2–3. The above all provide clinical descriptions of cholera which are progressively less technical.

73 Jerome Handler and Frederick W. Lange, *Plantation Slavery in Barbados* (Cambridge, Mass., 1977), 70; Uttley, "Mortality and Epidemiology of Typhoid Fever," 114–16.

74 The estimates of cholera deaths during this and other epidemics are largely from Kenneth F. Kiple, "Cholera in the Caribbean," forthcoming in the *Journal of Latin American Studies*. The estimates for the first of Cuba's three epidemics are based largely on Jorge LeRoy y Cassa, *Estudios sobre la mortalidad de la Habana durante el siglo xix* (Havana, 1913), 13–14; Ramon de la Sagra, *Tablas necrologicas del colera-morbus en la ciudad de la Habana y sus arrabales* (Havana, 1833); and "Resumen general que manifesta los cadavers colericos sepultados en los cementerio de esta ciudad . . . en los diferentes poblaciones de esta isla desde el 25 de Fev. ultimo hasta el 30 de Set. inclusivo," AHN, Estado, Leg. 6374, No. 181, hereafter referred to as "Resumen General."

75 Kiple, "Cholera in the Caribbean". See also Ramon Piña y Peñuela, *Topografia médica de la isla de Cuba* (Havana, 1855), 44; José Garcia de Arboleya, *Manual de la isla de Cuba: compendio de su historia, geográfia, estadística y administracion* (Havana, 1852), 59; LeRoy y Cassa, *Mortalidad de la Habana*, 18–19; and J. Kennedy to Viscount Palmerston, Havana, Feb. 22, 1851 in Great Britain, Parliament, House of Commons, *Sessional Papers, Accounts and Papers,* vol. 56A (London, 1851), 183–212, 188, 192–3.

76 Kiple, "Cholera in the Caribbean". See also Gavin Milroy, "The Report on the Cholera in Jamaica," cited in George W. Roberts, *The Population of Jamaica* (Cambridge, Eng., 1957), 177; James Bowen Thompson, "Cholera in Jamaica," *Lancet* 1 (1851), 532; John Parkin, *Statistical Report of the Epidemic Cholera in Jamaica* (London, 1852), 1; Philip D. Curtin, *Two Jamaicas: The Role of Ideas in a Tropical Colony 1830–1865* (Cambridge, Mass., 1955), 160; Robert H. Shomburgk, *The History of Barbados* (London, 1848), 444; J.B.S. Jackson, "Diseases of the Island of Barbados," *British Medical and Surgical Journal* 76 (1867), 448; Claude Levy, *Emancipation, Sugar, and Federalism: Barbados and the West Indies, 1833–1876* (Gainesville, Fla., 1980), 115; "Cholera in Barbados," *Lancet* 2 (1854), 93; Manuel Quevado y Baez, *Historia de la medicina y cirugia de Puerto Rico*, 2 vols. (Puerto Rico, 1946–49), 1:176, 167, 173, 180, 208, 210, 295, 360; "Estado clasificativo del numero de defunciones causadas por la

epidemia del colera morbo en esta ysla," AHN, Ultramar, Leg. 5082; D.J. Jimeno Agius, "Poblacion y comercio de la isla de Puerto Rico," *BHPR* 5 (1981), 284; and Berta Cabanillas de Rodriguez, *Origens de los hábitos alimênticos del pueblo de Puerto Rico* (Madrid, 1955).

77 Ibid. "Estadistica de la epidemia del colera, llevado por distritios, barrios, rurales y hospitales desde que recrudecio el 20 de Junio hasta su delinacion favorable el 31 de Julio proximo passado," *Anales de la real academia de ciencias, médicas, fisicas y naturales de la Habana* 5 (1868–69), 163–5.

78 Calculated from "Estado clasificativo del numero de defunciones causadas por la epidemia del colera morbo" and "Año de 1854, Estado clasificativo del censo de almas de esta isla" AHN, Ultramar, Leg. 5082.

79 For the social history of cholera in different locales see R.E. McGrew, "The First Cholera Epidemic and Social History," *BHM* 34 (1960), 61–73; Rosenberg, *Cholera Years;* and Asa Briggs, "Cholera and Society in the Nineteenth Century," *Past and Present,* 19 (1961), 76–96.

80 "Estado que manifiesta los atacados del colora morbo. . ." AGPR, Sanidad, 1823–62, Caja 183.

81 F.J. Farre, "Cholera in the Bahamas," *Medical Times and Gazette* 6 (1853), 300; Ramon de la Sagra, *Cuba en 1860 o sea cuadro de sus adelantados en la poblacion, la agricultura, el comercio y las rentas publicas suplemento a la primera parte de la historia politica y natural de la isla de Cuba* (Paris, 1863), 35.

82 Norman Howard-Jones, "Cholera Therapy in the Nineteenth Century," *JHM* 27 (1972), 373 and passim; see also Frederick Eberson, "A Great Purging–Cholera or Calomel?" *Filson Club History Quarterly* 50 (1976), 28–35. For cholera treatment in the West Indies, see Adolfo de Hostos, *Ciudad Murada, Ensayo acerca del proceso de civilizacion en la ciudad española de San Juan Bautista de Puerto Rico, 1521–1898* (Havana, 1948), 456–7 and Farre, "Cholera in the Bahamas," 301.

83 Richard A. Cash, Jamiul Alam, and K.M. Toaha, "Gastric Acid Secretion in Cholera Patients," *Lancet* 2 (5 Dec., 1970), 1192; R.B. Hornick, et al., "The Broad Street Pump Revisited: Response of Volunteers to Ingested Cholera Vibrios," *Bulletin of the New York Academy of Medicine* 47 (1971), 1181–91; Eugene J. Gangarosa, "The Epidemiology of Cholera: Past and Present," *Bulletin of the New York Academy of Medicine* 47 (1971), 1148–58; Eugene J. Gangarosa and Wiley H. Mosley, "Epidemiology and Surveillance of Cholera," in *Cholera,* eds. Barua and Burrows, 381–403; Charles C.J. Carpenter, "Treatment of Cholera–Tradition and Authority versus Science, Reason and Humanity," *JHMJ* 139 (1976), 153–63; Jan Holmgren and Ann-Mari Svennerholm, "Mechanisms of Disease and Immunity in Cholera: A Review" *Journal of Infectious Disease* 136 (1977), 105 and passim; I.H. Rosenberg, et al., "Nutritional Studies in Cholera; The Influence of Nutritional Status on Susceptibility to Infection," in *Proceedings of the Cholera Research Symposium* (Washington D.C., 1965); Charles C. Carpenter, "Cholera," in *A Manual of Tropical Medicine,* 4th ed., eds. George W. Hunter, William W. Frye, and J. Clyde Swartzwelder (Philadelphia, 1966), 169.

84 Myron Winick, ed., *Hunger Disease: Studies by Jewish Physicians in the Warsaw Ghetto* (New York, 1979), 41; Ancel Keys, et al., *The Biology of Human Starvation,* 2 vols. (Minneapolis, 1950), 1:592-7; see also Hornick, et al., "Broad Street Pump," 190, who speculates that the poor, and consequently the malnourished, have poor acid secretion.

85 J. Lambotte-Legrand and C. Lambotte-Legrand, "Le pronostic de l'anémie drépanocytaire au Congo Belge: à propos de 300 cas et de 150 décès," *Annales de la Société Belge de Médecine Tropicale* 35 (1955), 53; Edward B. Attah and Mayen C. Ekere, "Death Patterns in Sickle Cell Anemia," *JAMA* 233 (1975), 890. These survival rates are based on the experience of youngsters in conditions of malnutrition and

disease similar to those of slaves in the eighteenth and nineteenth-century West Indies. However today, with higher living standards and improved health care, two-year survival is 87 percent among a sample of Jamaican children with homozygous sickle cell disease diagnosed at birth. See D.W. Rogers et al., "Early Deaths in Jamaican Children with Sickle Cell Disease," *BMJ* 1 (1978), 1515–16.

86 George I. Lythcott, Calvin H. Sinnette, and Donald R. Hopkins, "Pediatrics," in *Textbook of Black-Related Diseases*, ed. Richard Allen Williams (New York, 1975), 181.

87 William H. Bullock and Pongrac N. Jilly, "Hematology," in *Textbook of Black-Related Diseases*, ed. Williams, 269; William Weiss, "The Sickle Cell Trait in Relation to Infection," *Archives of Environmental Health* 8 (1964), 480–2.

88 See, for example, Collins, *Practical Rules*, 84–5, for a discussion of "horse beans."

89 Sanford Brown, Alan Merkow, Marvin Wiener, and Jamshid Khajezaden, "Low Birth Weight in Babies Born to Mothers with Sickle Cell Trait," *JAMA* 22:12 (1972), 1404–5; K.A. Harrison and P.A. Ibeziako, "Maternal Anaemia and Fetal Birthweight," *Journal of Obstetrics and Gynaecology of the British Commonwealth* 80 (1973), 798–804.

90 C.W. Woodruff, C. Latham, and S. McDavid, "Iron Nutrition in the Breastfed Infant," *JP* 90 (1977), 85–94; Ulla Lundstrom, Martii Siimes, and Peter R. Dallman, "At What Age Does Iron Supplementation Become Necessary in Low-birth Weight Infants?" *JP* 91 (1977), 878–83; Myron Winick, "Feeding Infants: I. How to Assess Nutritional Status," *Modern Medicine* (Nov., 1977), 67.

91 See, for example, Higman, *Slave Population and Economy in Jamaica*, 107–8 and Michael Craton, "Jamaican Slave Mortality: Fresh Light from Worthy Park, Longville and the Tharp Estates," *JCH* 3 (1971), 17.

92 B.W. Higman, "The Slave Family and Household in the British West Indies, 1800–1834," *JIH* 6 (1975), 263–4.

93 Ibid.

94 Computed from data contained in the United Nations, *Demographic Yearbook 1979* (New York, 1980) and R.R. Kuczynski, *Demographic Survey of the British Colonial Empire*, 3 vols. (London, 1953), vol. 3: *West Indian and American Territories*.

95 Data for the ensuing discussion of Antigua have been taken from K.H. Uttley, "Infant and Early Childhood Death Rates Over the Last Hundred Years in the Negro Population of Antigua, British West Indies," *BJPSM* 14 (1960), 185–9; K.H. Uttley, "The Birth, Stillbirth, Death and Fertility Rates of the Coloured Population of Antigua West Indies from 1857 to 1956," *TRSTMH* 55 (1961), 69–78.

96 T. Lynn Smith, *Fundamentals of Population Study* (Chicago, 1960), 196–7.

97 Uttley, "Birth, Stillbirth, Death and Fertility Rates," 76, 72.

98 Lester Firschein, "Population Dynamics of the Sickle-cell Trait in the Black Caribs of British Honduras, Central America," *AJHG* 13 (1961), 233–54. Interestingly, the Black Carib mothers with sickle trait had offspring who presented a normal sex ratio at birth, while mothers with normal hemoglobin produced the abnormally large number of female infants relative to males that accounted for the low sex ratio. See also Richard L. Naeye et al. ("Neonatal Mortality, the Male Disadvantage," PED 48 [1971], 902–6) for some thoughts on the reason for excessive male mortality.

99 Kenneth F. Kiple, *Blacks in Colonial Cuba, 1774–1899* (Gainesville, Fla., 1976), appendix.

100 Levy, *Emancipation, Sugar, and Federalism*, passim.

101 Roberts, *Population of Jamaica*, 257–62; David Lowenthal, *West Indian Societies* (New York, 1972), 66; Philip D. Curtin, *Two Jamaicas* (Cambridge, Eng., 1955), 160–1; Robert P. Parsons, "History of Haitian Medicine," *Annals of Medical History*, 1 (1924), 291–324.

102 Larrazabel Blanco, *Esclavitud en Santo Domingo*, 107; Lewis, *Journal*, 122 and passim.

103 Edwards, *History of the West Indies* 2:165, 66, 67. For Cuba, see Abbot, *Letters Written in Cuba*, 29, 143; William Henry Hurlberg, *Gan-Eden; or, Pictures of Cuba* (Boston,

1854), 191; Richard Henry Dana, *To Cuba and Back: a Vacation Voyage* (Carbondale, Ill., 1966), 69. For Santo Domingo, see Moscoso Puello, *Historia de la medicina*, 93–96. For Puerto Rico, consult Díaz Soler, *Historia de la esclavitud*, 157–8. For the Leeward Islands, see Elsa V. Goveia, *Slave Society in the British Leeward Islands at the End of the 18th Century* (New Haven, 1965), 195. For Barbados see Bennett, *Bondsmen and Bishops*, 40–1, and Handler and Lange, *Slavery in Barbados*, 97–100, and for confirmation of Edwards' statement for Jamaica, see R.R. Madden, *A Twelve Months' Residence in the West Indies . . .* 2 vols. (London, 1835), 1:117–18.

104   Bennett, *Bondsmen and Bishops*, 40–1; Abbot, *Letters Written in Cuba*, 29; Goveia, *Slave Society in the British Leeward Islands*, 195.

105   Curtin, *Two Jamaicas*, 160; Williamson, *Medical and Miscellaneous Observations* 2:189; Beckford, *Account of Jamaica* 2:305; Pitman, *Development of the British West Indies*, 390; Lowell Joseph Ragatz, *The Fall of the Planter Class in the British Caribbean, 1763–1833* (New York, 1928), 17; Higman, *Slave Population and Economy in Jamaica*, 130, reports that in 1833 there were some 200 authorized practitioners in Jamaica or "roughly one to every 1,500 slaves."

106   Ashburn, *Ranks of Death*, 47–8; Moscoso Puello, *Historia de la medicina*, 58; Fredrika Bremer, *Homes of the New World: Impressions of America . . .* , 2 vols. (New York, 1853), 2:413.

107   Richard Sheridan, *Sugar and Slavery: An Economic History of the British West Indies, 1623–1775* (Baltimore, 1974), 244; Thomas Roughley, *The Jamaica Planter's Guide* (London, 1823), 91, 95. In Barbados the wives of planters and overseers also seem to have played a nursing role. Bennett, *Bishops and Bondsmen*, 40–1.

108   Williamson, *Medical and Miscellaneous Observations* 2:189.

109   Díaz Soler, *Historia de la esclavitud*, 158; Roughley, *Jamaican Planter's Guide*, 91–2.

110   Roughley, *Jamaica Planter's Guide*, 96.

111   Collins, *Practical Rules*, 254.

112   Ibid., 91.

113   Lewis, *Journal*, 122, 168, 203–04.

114   Madden, *Twelve Months' Residence* 1:118.

115   Moreno Fraginals, "Africa in Cuba," 200.

116   Patterson, *Sociology of Slavery*, 104; William Dickson (ed.), *Mitigation of Slavery* (London, 1814).

117   Andre Pierre Ledru, *Viaje a la isla de Puerto Rico en el año 1797 . . .* (Rio Piedras, 1957), 125.

118   Ibid; Barclay, *Practical View*, 332. "Intemperance" among the slaves was frequently commented upon as a cause of death along with eating unripe fruits, promiscuity, and dancing too vigorously until too late in the evening. See, for example, Stewart, *Account of Jamaica*, 277. For "drunkenness" among the blacks of Cuba, see John Glanville Taylor, *The United States and Cuba: Eight Years of Change and Travel* (London, 1851), 232.

119   Collins, *Practical Rules*, 234; Lewis, *Journal*, 215–17; Moscoso Puello, *Historia de la medicina*, 46–7; Higman, *Slave Population and Economy in Jamaica*, 130.

120   Carlos Estaban Deive, *Vodu y magia en Santo Domingo* (Santo Domingo, 1975), 330. However, for another view, see Israel Castellanos, *Medicina legal y criminologia Afro-Cubanas* (Havana, 1937), 147–9 and passim. See also Handler and Lange, *Plantation Slavery in Barbados*, 101.

121   Ashburn, *Ranks of Death*, 32; Joseph Jones, "Researches on the Relations of the African Slave Trade in the West Indies and Tropical America to Yellow Fever," *Virginia Medical Monthly* 2 (1875), 19; Stearn and Stearn, *Effect of Smallpox*, 16–17; E.R. Stitt, "Our Disease Inheritance from Slavery," *U.S. Medical Bulletin* 26 (1928), 804.

122   Long, *History of Jamaica* 2:381; Erwin D. Ackerknecht, "Natural Diseases and Rational Treatment in Primitive Medicine," *BHM* 19 (1946), 467–97; Wilbert C. Jordan,

"Voodoo Medicine," in *Textbook of Black Related Diseases*, ed. Williams, 715–38; Julia Frances Morton, *Folk Remedies of the Low Country* (Miami, Fla., 1974).

123 Higman, *Slave Population and Economy in Jamaica*, 130. *The Jamaica Physical Journal* was begun for this purpose in the early 1830s, but failed after just three issues. A college for physicians in Jamaica was also created in 1832.

124 Abbot, *Letters Written in Cuba*, 36–7; William Lempriere, *Practical Observations on the Diseases of the Army in Jamaica, as they Occurred between the Years 1792 and 1797*, 2 vols. (London, 1799), 1:47–8.

125 See, for example, Patterson, *Sociology of Slavery*, 103.

126 Moscoso Puello, *Historia de la medicina*, 71–4; Díaz Soler, *Historia de la esclavitud*, 122; Craton and Walvin, *Jamaican Plantation*, 136.

127 Edwin F. Atkins, *Sixty Years in Cuba* (Cambridge, Mass., 1926), 57; For the story of Tomás Terry, see Rolando Ely, *Cuando reinaba su majestad el azucar, estudio historico-sociológico de una tragediá latinoamericana: el monocultivo en Cuba, origen y evolucion del proceso* (Buenos Aires, 1963).

Part III. Introduction

1 Charles Darwin, *The Voyage of the Beagle* (Garden City, N.Y., 1962), 458.

Chapter 10. Fevers and Race

1 Benjamin Moseley, *A Treatise on Tropical Diseases; or Military Operations; and the Climate of the West Indies* (London, 1789), 1.

2 Folke Henschen, *The History and Geography of Disease*, trans. Joan Tate (New York, 1966), 16.

3 Philip D. Curtin, "The African Diaspora," *Historical Reflections/Reflections Historiques* 6 (1979), 7.

4 LeRoy y Cassa (in Tables 3 and 3A, this chapter) has based his calculations on a population of about 4,666 for Havana, which he does not break down by race. Fernando Ortiz Fernandez (*Hampa Afro-Cubana, los negros esclavos* [Havana, 1916], 22–3) provides a population for the whole of Cuba for 1620 of about 7,000 whites and only 500 blacks. Hubert H. S. Aimes (*A History of Slavery in Cuba* [New York, 1907], 16) explains that "incomplete data" place 4,082 individuals in Havana for 1620. Aimes also indicates that, following 1620, considerably more blacks reached the island. Thus probably at least 600 of the 4,600 in Havana were black, giving them a death rate of about forty-three per thousand during the epidemic. By contrast, Havana's death rate for the entire population averaged forty-seven per thousand for the years 1811 to 1820, or a higher rate than that of blacks during the 1620 epidemic. See "Dr. Frederick L. Hoffman's Collection of Statistics. . ." for Havana, Cuba in RAC, IHB, Series 2, 315, Cuba, Box 30, Folder 178.

5 K.H. Uttley, "The Mortality of Yellow Fever in Antigua, West Indies, Since 1857," *WIMJ* 9 (1960), 185–8. See also our discussion of black yellow fever immunities in the southern United States in Kenneth F. Kiple and Virginia H. King, *Another Dimension to the Black Diaspora, Diet, Disease and Racism* (New York, 1981), 29–49.

6 Henry Rose Carter, *Yellow Fever: An Epidemiological and Historical Study of its Place of Origin*, eds. Laura Armistead Carter and Wade Hampton Frost (Baltimore, 1931), 50; John Duffy, *Sword of Pestilence: the New Orleans Yellow Fever Epidemic of 1853* (Baton Rouge, La., 1966), 10–11. For numerous variations in pathological descriptions, see John Sullivan, "Notes on the Yellow Fever, as Observed in Havana in 1870," *Medical Times and Gazette* (March, 1871), 304–7.

7 August Hirsch, *Handbook of Geographical and Historical Pathology*, 3 vols. (London, 1883), 1:316; Carter (*Yellow Fever*, 71) mentions the tendency of the English in Africa

to report yellow fever as malarial fever. See also John Hunter (*Observations on the Diseases of the Army in Jamaica* [London, 1788], 64–5), who explains that "black vomit is frequently a symptom of remittent fever."

8   In time, most caught on to the geography of the diseases (if not yellow fever's urban predilection), asserting that yellow fever only occurred "on the borders of the sea [. . . whereas] bilious remittent fever [malaria] . . . shows itself everywhere with the same force" (Charles Bisset, *Medical Essays and Observations* [Newcastle-upon-Tyne, 1766], 20); Charles Belot, *The Yellow Fever at Havana; Its Nature and its Treatment* (Savannah, Ga., 1878), 30; Andre Pierre Ledru, *Viaje a la isla de Puerto Rico en el año 1797* (Rio Piedras, 1957), 125.

9   George Pinckard, *Notes on the West Indies, Including Observations Relative to the Creoles and Slaves of the Western Colonies and the Indians of South America; Interspersed with Remarks upon the Seasoning, or Yellow Fever of Hot Climates*, 2d ed., 2 vols. (London, 1816), 2:475. Differentiating the two diseases continued to be a problem, for tropical physicians at least, until the end of the nineteenth century, especially in Africa. See, for example, W.M. Elliott, "Yellow Fever in West Africa," *Journal of Tropical Medicine* 1 (1898–99), 317–19.

10   John Davy, *The West Indies, Before and Since Slave Emancipation* (London, 1854), 85–6.

11   Hirsch, *Handbook* 1:230.

12   L. Schulyer Fonaroff, "Did Barbados Import its Malaria Epidemic," *Journal of the Barbados Museum and Historical Society* 34 (1973), 122–30; M.T. Ashcroft, I.C. Buchanan, and H.G. Lovell, "Heights and Weights of Primary School Children in St. Christopher-Nevis-Anguilla, West Indies," *WIJTMH* 68 (1965), 277; James Bovell, "Observations on the Climate of Barbados, and its Influence on Diseases. . .," *BAJMPS* 4 (1848), 115; Richard S. Dunn, *Sugar and Slaves; The Rise of the Planter Class in the English West Indies, 1624–1713* (Chapel Hill, N.C., 1972), 303; Sir Harry Johnston, *The Negro in the New World* (New York, 1969), 212, note; George P. Paul, *Report on Ankylostomiasis Infection Survey of Barbados* (New York, 1917), 13.

13   See, for example, William Hillary, *Observations on the Changes of the Air, and the Concomitant Epidemical Diseases in the Island of Barbados* (London, 1759), 125.

14   G.M. Findlay, "The First Recognized Epidemic of Yellow Fever," *TRSTMH* 35 (1941), 145–6; Dunn, *Sugar and Slaves*, 303. The *Aëdes* can also transmit filariasis, which, as we saw earlier, was another serious problem in Barbados.

15   "Three Hundred Years of Medicine in Jamaica," *Jamaican Nurse* 6 (1966), 18. For yellow fever's many synonyms, see J.A.F. Ozanan, *Histoire médicale générale*, 2d ed., 4 vols. (Paris, 1835), 3:227–28, and George Augustin, *History of Yellow Fever* (New Orleans, 1909), appendix. For a record of almost every epidemic in the Caribbean see Hirsch, *Handbook* 1:318–31.

16   Robert Jackson, *A Sketch of the History and Cure of Febrile Diseases; More Particularly as they Appear in the West Indies Among the Soldiers of the British Army* (London, 1791), 249–50; G. Pouchet, *The Plurality of the Human Race*, trans. and ed. from 2d ed. by H.J. Beavau (London, 1864), 58–9; [John Stewart] *An Account of Jamaica* (London, 1808), 26; Alexander von Humboldt, *Political Essay on the Kingdom of New Spain*, 4 vols., trans. John Black (London, 1811) 4:171–3; Belot, *Yellow Fever at Havana*, 39. See also an "Examination of the British Agent to Barbados, 1799," in John Brathwaite, "Odd Pages from Old Records," *Journal of the Barbados Museum and Historical Society* 18 (1950), 33, and "Captain General O'Donnel to the First Secretary of State," Havana, 1847 AHN, Ultramar, Leg. 3550.

17   Jorge Eduardo LeRoy y Cassa, *La primera epidemia de fiebre amarilla en la Habana, en 1649* (Havana, 1930), 43–4; Jacobo de la Pezuela y Lobo, *Historia de la isla de Cuba*, 4 vols. (Madrid, 1868–78) 2:106–8; H. Harold Scott, "The Influence of the Slave Trade in the Spread of Tropical Disease," *TRSTMH* 37 (1943), 179.

18 Sir Alan Burns, *History of the British West Indies* (London, 1954), 171. See also Sir Harry Johnston, *The Negro in the New World* (New York, 1910), 211–13, note.

19 Burns, *History*, 32.

20 Francisco Guerra, "The Influence of Disease on Race, Logistics and Colonization in the Antilles," *JTMH* 69 (1966), 27.

21 Ibid. See also John Poyer (*The History of Barbados* [London, 1808], 165–6), who complained that the garrison was so decimated that the island was left "exposed."

22 Guerra, "Influence of Disease," 27.

23 Gordon Willis Jones, "Virginians and 'Calenture,' " *Virginia Medical Monthly* 88 (1961), 390–6, 463–8; Alexandre Moreau de Jonnes, *Essai sur l'Hygiene militaire des Antilles* (Paris, 1817), 3.

24 Guerra, "Influence of Disease," 28.

25 Thomas Dancer, *A Brief History of the Late Expedition Against Fort San Juan* (Kingston, 1781), 20.

26 Hunter, *Diseases of the Army*, 57–8, 60. See pages 32–61 for a discussion of individual regiments. See also Frank Wesley Pitman (*The Development of the British West Indies, 1700–1763* [New Haven, 1917], 387–90) for an impression of terrible British troop mortality.

27 William Lempriere, *Practical Observations on the Diseases of the Army in Jamaica, as they Occurred Between the Years 1792 and 1797*, 2 vols. (London, 1799), 1:1.

28 Johnston, *Negro in the New World*, 218.

29 Dancer, *Late Expedition*, 12–13, 43.

30 Jerome S. Handler, *The Unappropriated People* (Baltimore, 1974), 110–16; Guerra, "Influence of Disease," 34.

31 See, for example, the remarks of Hunter, *Diseases of the Army*, 269–70.

32 Lowell Joseph Ragatz, *The Fall of the Planter Class in the British Caribbean, 1763–1833* (New York, 1928), 32–33, 222. On the other hand, see Roger Norman Buckley (*Slaves in Red Coats: The British West India Regiments, 1795–1815* [New Haven, 1979], 141 and passim), who argues that white colonial opposition to the establishment of black regiments was less a matter of fear than it was of economics.

33 J.H. Parry, and P.M. Sherlock, *A Short History of the West Indies*, 3d ed. (London, 1971), 172.

34 Thomas Trotter, *Medicina Nautica: an Essay on the Diseases of Seamen . . .* , 2d ed., 3 vols. (London, 1804), 1:32; For a description of the onset of the disease in Grenada, see C. Chisholm, "History of an Uncommon Epidemic Fever Observed in the Island of Grenada," *Medical Commentaries* (Edinburgh, 1794), 8:499–511 and for an account of the differential mortality it inflicted by race as well as heavy troop mortality, see Colin Chisholm, *An Essay on the Malignant Pestilential Fever . . .* (Philadelphia, 1799), 91–102 and 167ff. For other such data by race, consult Lempriere, *Practical Observations* 1:70, 98, 100.

35 Johnston, *Negro in the New World*, 218–19; Guerra, "Influence of Disease," 34. For a brief chronological history of each of the black West Indian regiments, see Buckley, *Slaves in Red Coats*, 156–7.

36 None of the following is meant to detract from the heroic efforts of the soon-to-be-free Haitians in gaining their own independence. For that story, the reader is referred to C.L.R. James, *The Black Jacobins*, 2d ed. (New York, 1963).

37 Sir William Pym, *Observations upon . . . Yellow Fever* (London, 1848), 269–70; Guerra, "Influence of Disease," 29; Robert V. Wells, *The Population of The British Colonies in America Before 1776* (Princeton, N.J., 1975), 243; David Geggus, *Slavery, War and Revolution; the British Occupation of Saint Domingue, 1793–1798* (Oxford, Eng., 1982), 363. Geggus points out, however, that yellow fever was not the "sole scourge" (365), but rather falciparum malaria may well have also taken a heavy toll.

38 Guerra, "Influence of Disease," 30.

39 Francisco Eujenio Moscoso Puello, *Apuntes para la historia de la medicina de la isla de Santo Domingo* (Santo Domingo, 1977), 31.

40 Robert Parsons, *History of Haitian Medicine* (New York, 1930), 2.

41 Moreau de Jonnes, *Essai*, 10; H. Hill, "Observations on the Mortality of Yellow Fever among the Seamen of the United States, Who With Northern Constitutions Sail to Havana, in Cuba and on the Health and Longevity of the Native Spanish Inhabitants," *Medical Repository* 10 (1807), 113–17; A.W. Brown, "Yellow Fever, Dengue and Dengue Haemorrhagic Fever," in *A World Geography of Human Diseases*, ed. G. Melvyn Howe (London, 1977), 292.

42 George Wilson Bridges, *The Annals of Jamaica*, 2 vols. (London, 1828), 2:243; Stewart, *Account of Jamaica*, 65, 77.

43 Philip D: Curtin, "Epidemiology and the Slave Trade," *PSQ* 83 (1968), 202.

44 Alexander M. Tulloch, "Statistical Report on the Sickness, Mortality, and Invaliding Among the Troops in the West Indies," in Great Britain, *Parliamentary Papers, XL, 1837–1838 (Accounts and Papers)*, V (London, 1838).

45 Ibid., 438. At Spanish Town the annual mortality from "fevers" alone for the twenty years in question was 141 per 1,000 (439–40). Unless otherwise indicated, the ensuing discussion is based on data taken from Tulloch, "Statistical Report," especially pages 434–7.

46 Hirsch, *Handbook* 1:230.

47 Ragatz, *Fall of the Planter Class*, 32.

48 George W. Roberts, *The Population of Jamaica* (Cambridge, Eng., 1957), 165; Ragatz, *Fall of the Planter Class*, 32.

49 R.M. Martin, *History of the Colonies of the British Empire in the West Indies . . .* (London, 1843), 20, cited by Roberts, *Population of Jamaica*, 172.

50 Ragatz, *Fall of the Planter Class*, 32; Roberts, *Population of Jamaica*, 166; Curtin, "Epidemiology and the Slave Trade," 204; Maureen Warner, "Africans in 19th Century Trinidad," *African Studies Association of the West Indies Bulletin* (1973), 32, 34.

51 Tulloch, "Statistical Report," 7, 12.

52 See, for example, Hillary, *Observations*, 145–6 and Belot, *Yellow Fever at Havana*, 10.

53 For Asian immigration to Cuba, see Arthur F. Corwin, *Spain and the Abolition of Slavery in Cuba 1817–1866* (Austin, Tex., 1967), 189, 191, and passim.

54 Taken from Cuban population data in Kenneth F. Kiple, *Blacks in Colonial Cuba 1774–1899* (Gainesville, Fla., 1976), appendix. For white immigration, see Duvon C. Corbitt, "Immigration in Cuba," *HAHR* 22 (1942), 280–308; Jacobo de la Pezuela y Lobo, *Diccionario geográfico, estadístico, historico de la isla de Cuba*, 4 vols. (Madrid, 1863–1866), 2:239; and B. Huber, *Aperçu Statistique de l'ile de Cuba*. (Paris, 1826), 53.

55 Belot, *Yellow Fever at Havana*, 10; Ramon Piña y Peñuela, *Topografia medica de la isla de Cuba* (Havana, 1855), 25.

56 D. Angel José Crowley, *Ensayo estadístico-médico de la mortalidad de la diocesis de la Habana durante el año de 1843* (Havana, 1845), table; Ramon de la Sagra, *Cuba en 1860 . . .* (Paris, 1863), 35, tables.

57 Richard Henry Dana, *To Cuba and Back; A Vacation Voyage* (Carbondale, Ill., 1966), 128–9; Jorge Eduardo LeRoy y Cassa, *Estudios sobre la mortalidad de la Habana durante el siglo XIX* (Havana, 1913), 26.

58 Michael T. Ashcroft, "Some Aspects of Growth and Development in Different Ethnic Groups in the Commonwealth West Indies," 281–310.

59 Havana, for example, lost 35,584 to yellow fever for the years 1854 to 1910, considerably fewer than European losses to yellow fever during their invasions of St. Domingue alone ("Dr. Frederick Hoffman's Collection of Statistics . . . for Havana, Cuba," RAC, IHB, Series 2, 315 Cuba, Box 30, Folder 178). That the disease may have become milder is suggested by the fact that during the years 1898 and 1899 the

United States Army lost about 200 men out of 1,400 yellow fever cases in Cuba, for a mortality rate of 14 percent (P.M. Ashburn, *The Ranks of Death: A Medical History of the Conquest of America* [New York, 1947], 230). By contrast, at the turn of the nineteenth century in Jamaica, "deaths from fever amounted to very nearly one half of the total cases " ("Sickness in the West Indies 100 years ago," *BJM* [1939], 1150). That yellow fever strains run a gamut from mild to malignant is well known even though the reasons remain obscure. For an excellent analysis of the complexity of yellow fever's epidemiology and ecology, see Wilbur G. Downs, "History of Epidemiological Aspects of Yellow Fever," *The Yale Journal of Biology and Medicine* 55 (1982), 179–85.

60   The efforts of Dr. Finlay are too frequently slighted or even ignored when the story of yellow fever's conquest is told. See, for example, "American Doctors Lead Victory Over Yellow Fever," *Journal of the Medical Association of Alabama* 45 (1976), 24, as opposed to Gilberto R. Ceparo, "Notes on the Evolution of Medicine in Colonial Cuba," *Journal of the Florida Medical Association* 64 (1977), 570–2. For Finlay's contribution, see Carlos Juan Finlay, *Obras Completas*, 4 tomas (Havana, 1964).

61   Jorge Eduardo LeRoy y Cassa, *Estadística de fiebre amarilla* (Habana, 1902), 15; W. Sykes, "Negro Immunity from Malaria and Yellow Fever," *BMJ* 11 (1904), 1776–7, (1905), 389–90; Joseph Franklin Siler, Milton W. Hall, and A. Parker Hitchins, *Dengue: Its History, Epidemiology . . .* (Manila, 1926), 13; Gordon Harrison, *Mosquitos, Malaria and Man* (New York, 1978), 4; Sir Rubert Boyce, "Note Upon Yellow Fever in the Black Race and its Bearing Upon the Question of the Endemicity of Yellow Fever in West Africa," *Annals of Tropical Medicine and Parasitology* 5 (1911), 103–10.

62   Great Britain, Colonial Office, *Papers Relative to the Yellow Fever in Bermuda . . . in 1853* (London, 1854), 10, 19.

63   Kiple and King, *Another Dimension*, 45–6; Pouchet, *Plurality*, 60–1.

64   Parry and Sherlock, *Short History of the West Indies*, 244; Harrison, *Mosquitos, Malaria and Man*, 163; Lancelot S. Lewis, *The West Indian in Panama: Black Labor in Panama, 1850–1914* (Washington, D.C., 1980), 25; Walter LaFeber, *The Panama Canal* (New York, 1979), 12, 14.

65   Harrison, *Mosquitoes, Malaria and Man*, 165, 167; R.R. Kuczynski, *Demographic Survey of the British Colonial Empire*, 3 vols. (London, 1953), vol. 3: *West Indian and American Territories*, 4–5; Leslie B. Rout, *The African Experience in Spanish America: 1502 to the Present Day* (Cambridge, Eng., 1976), 274.

66   Kuczynski, *Survey of the British Colonial Empire* 3:7; R.E. Ferrell et al., "The Blacks of Panama: Their Genetic Diversity as Assessed by 15 Inherited Biochemical Systems," *AJPA* 48 (1978), 269–75.

67   Quoted by Harrison, *Mosquitos, Malaria and Man*, 167.

68   Ibid., 5.

69   Sidney Mintz, "Caribbean Nationhood in Anthropological Perspective," in *Caribbean Integration*, eds. S. Lewis and T. G. Mathews (Rio Piedras, 1967), 151.

70   The population of Trinidad was about 6 times as large in 1921 as it was in 1841, that of British Guiana 3 times as large, Jamaica 2.4 times as large, and Barbados 1.3 times as large. The former two regions benefited from immigration; the latter two lost population because of it (Kuczynski, *Survey of the British Colonial Empire* 3:9).

Chapter 11. Epilogue: Diet, Disease, and Displacement

1   Sidney W. Mintz, *Caribbean Transformations* (Chicago, 1974), 80.

2   David Lowenthal, *West Indian Societies* (New York, 1972), 2.

3   James S. Ward, *Yellow Fever in Latin America: a Geographical Study* (Liverpool, 1972); Johnathan Leonard, "The 'Queen of Diseases' Strikes Back," *Harvard Magazine* 81 (1979), 20–4.

4   James Stephen, *The Slavery of the British West India Colonies Delineated*, 2 vols. (London, 1824–30), 2:372; Hector McLean, *An Enquiry into . . . the Great Mortality Among the Troops at St. Domingo* (London, 1797), 56; Maria Nugent, *Lady Nugent's Journal of Her Residence in Jamaica from 1801 to 1805*, ed. Philip Wright (Kingston, Jamaica, 1966), 122–3 and passim. See also Robert Collins (*Practical Rules for the Management and Medical Treatment of Negro Slaves in the Sugar Colonies* [London, 1811], 259) who agreed by saying that he believed the reason blacks did not die of fevers was the absence of a "fear of death."

5   James Thomson, *A Treatise on the Diseases of Negroes as they Occur in the Island of Jamaica; with Observations on the Country Remedies* (Jamaica, 1820), 81; Thomas Roughley, *The Jamaica Planter's Guide* (London, 1823), 118–19; John Williamson, *Medical and Miscellaneous Observations Relative to the West India Islands*, 2 vols. (Edinburgh, 1817), 1:x; [John Stewart] *An Account of Jamaica* (London, 1808), 370; Anthony J. Barker, *African Link: British Attitudes to the Negro in the Era of the Atlantic Slave Trade, 1550–1807* (Totowa, N.J., 1978), 41–58 and passim; Gordon Harrison, *Mosquitoes, Malaria and Man* (New York, 1978), 4.

6   John Huxham, *An Essay on Fevers. . . .* , 2d ed. (London, 1750), 18.

7   See, for example, Charles Bisset, *Medical Essays and Observations* (Newcastle-Upon-Tyne, 1766), 12.

8   Williamson, *Medical and Miscellaneous Observations* 1:248; Collins, *Practical Rules*, 200; Stewart, *Account of Jamaica*, 268; Benjamin Moseley, *A Treatise on Tropical Diseases* (London, 1789), 492–3; Bryan Edwards, *The History, Civil and Commercial, of the British Colonies in the West Indies* 4th ed, 3 vols. (London, 1807), 2:237–41 and passim; and Edward Long, *The History of Jamaica*, 2 vols. (London, 1774), 2:351–2 and passim.

9   R. Hoeppli, *Parasitic Diseases in Africa and the Western Hemisphere: Early Documentation and Transmission by the Slave Trade* (Basel, 1969), 16. The quote may be found in Frank Wesley Pitman, *The Development of the British West Indies 1700–1763* (New Haven, 1917), 82. For Puerto Rico, see Salvador Arana-Soto, *Historia de la medicina Puertoriqueña hasta 1898* (San Juan, 1974), 205–6 and his *Historia de nuestras calamidades* (San Juan, 1968), passim. See also AGPR, Sanidad, 1812–23 and 1823–62, and RSGPR, Sanidad, 1823–72.

10   See, for example, the *Jamaica Physical Journal*, which featured a few articles on race during its brief (1834–35) existence. They were on the whole moderate and remarkably free of prejudice. Illustrative is the essay by Edward Binns, "A Few Facts: Preliminary to a Philosophical Examination of Negro Intellect," 2 (1835), 249–55, which argued that the black had had as yet no chance to prove himself because of slavery in this hemisphere and food deprivation in Africa. To compare this with the racial judgments that emerged from the pens of physicians in the United States, see Kenneth F. Kiple and Virginia H. King, *Another Dimension to the Black Diaspora, Diet, Disease and Racism* (New York, 1981), 175–84 and passim.

11   Richard S. Dunn, "The Barbados Census of 1680: Profile of the Richest Colony in English America," *WMQ* 26 (1969), 7; "A Briefe Description of the Ilande of Barbados," in *Colonising Expeditions to the West Indies and Guiana, 1623–1667*, ed. Vincent T. Harlow (London, 1925), 338–9. These early figures on Barbados population are approximations only, for most were seriously exaggerated.

12   G.M. Findlay; "The First Recognized Epidemic of Yellow Fever," *TRSTMH* 35 (1941), 143–4; Richard S. Dunn, *Sugar and Slaves, the Rise of the Planter Class in the English West Indies 1624–1713* (Chapel Hill, N.C., 1972), 103; "Briefe Description," ed. Harlow, 338–9. See also David W. Galenson (*White Servitude in Colonial America: An Economic Analysis* [Cambridge, Eng., 1981], 125, table) for the decline in indentured servants bound for Barbados after 1650.

13   Dunn, *Sugar and Slaves*, 313. In Jamaica, for example, the white population reached

about 9,000 in 1677 and then fell to 7,000 plus, where it remained until the late 1730s when massive immigration began pushing the figure sharply upwards. See George Roberts, *The Population of Jamaica* (Cambridge, Eng., 1957), 33.

14 Pitman, *Development of the British West Indies*, 383–4; Lucien-Rene Abénon, "Blancs et libres de couleur dans deux paroisses de la Guadeloupe (Capesterre et Trois-Rivières), 1699–1779," *Revue Française d'Histoire d'Outre-mer* 60 (1973), 297–363; Jerome S. Handler, *The Unappropriated People* (Baltimore, 1974), 27.

15 Francisco Guerra, "Medicina colonial en Hispano America," in *Historia universal de la medicina* 7 vols., ed. Pedro Lain Entralgo et al. (Barcelona, 1971–75) 4:346; Jacobo de la Pezuela y Lobo, *Diccionario geográfico, estadístico, histórico, de la isla de Cuba*, 4 vols. (Madrid, 1863–66) 4:239; Duvon C. Corbitt, "Immigration in Cuba," *HAHR* 22 (1942), 280–308.

16 Abbé Guillaume Raynal, *A Philosophical and Political History of the Settlements and Trade of the Europeans in the East and West Indies*, 8 vols., trans. J.O. Justamond (London, 1788) 5:350–3.

17 See, for example, Lewis Rouppe, *Observations on Diseases Incidental to Seamen* (London, 1772), 61–3, 368. For reasons offered for white mortality see William Hillary, *Observations on the Changes of the Air and the Concomitant Epidemical Diseases in the Island of Barbados* (London, 1759), 145–6; George Wilson Bridges, *The Annals of Jamaica*, 2 vols. (London, 1828) 2:243; Francisco Eujenio Moscoso Puello, *Apuntes para la historia de la medicina de la isla de Santo Domingo* (Santo Domingo, 1977), 39; Sir Arthur Helps, *The Spanish Conquest of America and its Relation to the History of Slavery and to the Government of Colonies*, 4 vols. (London, 1855–1861) 3:148, 4:300.

18 Orlando Patterson, *The Sociology of Slavery: An Analysis of the Origins, Development and Structure of a Negro Slave Society in Jamaica* (London, 1967), 33–43, 39; Lowell Joseph Ragatz, *The Fall of the Planter Class in the British Caribbean, 1763–1833* (New York, 1928), 43–56; Michael Craton ("Jamaican Slavery," in *Race and Slavery in the Western Hemisphere: Quantitative Studies*, eds. Stanley L. Engerman and Eugene D. Genovese [Princeton, N.J., 1975], 262) states that "by 1790 probably no more than 10 percent of Jamaican owners lived in the Great Houses on their Estates"; see also Richard B. Sheridan, "The Wealth of Jamaica in the Eighteenth Century," *EHR* 18 (1965), 304, 306–10.

19 Patterson, *Sociology of Slavery*, 39; quoted by Ragatz, *Fall of the Planter Class*, 31–32.

20 Ragatz, *Fall of the Planter Class*, 55–6.

21 Dunn, *Sugar and Slaves*, 6, 276–81, 333.

22 Richard S. Dunn, "The Social History of Early New England," *American Quarterly* 24 (1972), 675; Ragatz, *Fall of the Planter Class*, 7.

23 Todd L. Savitt, *Medicine and Slavery: The Diseases and Health Care of Blacks in Antebellum Virginia* (Urbana, Ill., 1978), 65–6. This argument was advanced in Kiple and King, *Another Dimension*, 66–7.

24 Dunn, *Sugar and Slaves*, 333. This is not to say, however, that white infants flourished in the West Indies. See, for example, Dunn, "Barbados Census of 1680," 24. See also Robert V. Wells, *The Population of the British Colonies in America before 1776* (Princeton, N.J., 1975) 243.

25 Franklin Knight, *Slave Society in Cuba During the Nineteenth Century* (Madison, Wisc., 1970), 69.

26 David Turnbull, *Travels in the West: Cuba, with Notices of Porto Rico and the Slave Trade* (London, 1840), 47–8; William Henry Hurlbert, *Gan-Eden; or, Pictures of Cuba . . .* (Boston, 1854), 141. See also Richard Henry Dana, *To Cuba and Back: A Vacation Voyage* (Carbondale, Ill., 1966), 52–6, and Antonio Carlo Napoleone Gallenga, *The Pearl of the Antilles . . .* (London, 1873), 92–5.

27 In addition there was also the important matter of their indebtedness to merchants whose interest rates ran around 18 percent, although in some cases rates of even 30

percent were levied. See Hugh Thomas, *Cuba: The Pursuit of Freedom* (New York, 1971), 271.

28 Earlier notions that there were many types of yellow fever, and that a mild malaria could develop into a raging yellow fever or vice versa were now disappearing. For some of this theory see Robert Jackson, *A Sketch of the History and Cure of Febrile Diseases; More Particularly as they Appear in the West Indies Among the Soldiers of the British Army*, 2 vols. (London, 1791), 2:13, 247, and Bisset, *Medical Essays*, 20–46.

29 Douglas Hall, "Absentee-Proprietorship in the British West Indies, to About 1850," *Jamaican Historical Review* 4 (1964), 15–34.

30 Michel S. Laguerre, "Haitian Americans," in *Ethnicity and Medical Care*, ed. Alan Harwood (Cambridge, Mass., 1981), 182–3 and passim; Arlene Fonaroff, "Differential Concepts of Protein-Calorie Malnutrition in Jamaica: An Exploratory Study of Information and Beliefs," *JTP* 14 (1968), 82–105.

31 Alex Stepick, "The New Haitian Exodus," and Frank Bovenkerk, "Caribbean Migration to the Netherlands," both in *Caribbean Review* 11:1 (1982), 18, 35.

32 Michel Chossudovsky, "Latin America and the Political Economics of Health Care," in *Health, Welfare, and Development in Latin America and the Caribbean*, eds. C. Lloyd Brown-John, Frank C. Innes, and W.C. Sunderlund (Windsor, Ontario, 1981), 99–107.

33 Ibid., 101; Nelson P. Valdes, "Health and Revolution in Cuba," *Science and Society* 35 (1971), 325–6.

34 Valdes, "Health and Revolution in Cuba," 311–35; Sally Guttmacher and Ross Danielson, "Changes in Cuban Health Care: An Argument Against Technological Pessimism," *International Journal of Health Services* 7 (1977), 383–400; Roy John et al., "Public Health Care in Cuba," *Social Policy* 1 (1971), 41–46; Virginia Olesen, "Confluence in Social Change: Cuban Women and Health Care," *Journal of Interamerican Studies and World Affairs* 17 (1975), 398–410; V. Navarro, "Health, Health Services and Health Planning in Cuba," *International Journal of Health Services* 2 (1972), 397–432.

35 R.R. Kuczynski, *Demographic Survey of the British Colonial Empire*, 3 vols. (London, 1953), 3:94, 249; Manuel Quevado y Baez, *Historia de la medicina y cirugia de Puerto Rico*, 2 vols. (Santurce, 1946–49) 2:408–9.

36 This is not to say that there was no Caribbean emigration prior to the past three decades or so. On the contrary, migration has always been an important "safety valve" for crowded islands such as Barbados, and poor countries such as Haiti. See Dawn I. Marshall, "The History of Caribbean Migrations," *Caribbean Review* 11:1 (1982), 6ff.

37 Aaron Segal, "Population Policies and Caribbean Crisis," in *Population Policies in the Caribbean*, ed. Aaron Segal (Lexington, Mass., 1975), 23.

38 Lowenthal, *West Indian Societies*, 213–49.

39 Ibid., 250–92.

40 Stepick, "New Haitian Exodus," 17.

41 Malcolm J. Proudfoot, *Population Movements in the Caribbean* (Trinidad, 1950), 37 and passim.

42 Segal (ed.), *Population Policies in the Caribbean*, 8.

43 Marshall, "History of Caribbean Migrations," 52–3. Encouraging this in the United States as far as the Caribbean is concerned are feelings of having been "stung" by the Mariel exodus from Cuba, the ongoing Haitian problem, and an ingrained North American prejudice against dark-skinned peoples.

BIBLIOGRAPHIC ESSAY

Visits to archives and libraries in Great Britain, Spain, the United States, Jamaica, Haiti, the Dominican Republic, Barbados, and Puerto Rico were vital to the researching of this book. Nonetheless, although the reader will discover numerous archival sources cited, this study rests for the most part on books and articles of both a primary and secondary nature. What follows is a sampling of that literature.

Probably the single most useful guide to a study of pre-twentieth-century epidemiological problems of the Caribbean is the *Index Catalogue of the Library of the Surgeon General's Office*, 1st Series (Washington, D.C., 1880–95). For modern medical insights into these problems, consult *Index Medicus, the Social Science Citation Index*, The National Library of Medicine's annual *Bibliography of the History of Medicine*, and the Wellcome Institute of the History of Medicine's *Current Work in the History of Medicine: An International Bibliography*.

For Africa, see Charles Tettey, "Medicine in Africa: A Bibliographic Essay," *Current Bibliography of African Affairs* (Jan. 1970), 5–18 and his *Medicine in British West Africa 1880–1956, An Annotated Bibliography* (Accra, 1975).

For the Caribbean, consult Frank Cundall, *Bibliography of the West Indies* (Kingston, 1909), S.A. Bayitch, *Latin America and the Caribbean* (Coral Gables, Fla., 1967), and especially Lambros Comitas, *The Complete Caribbeana 1900–1975: A Bibliographic Guide to Scholarly Literature* (New York, 1977).

For slavery Joseph Miller's ongoing bibliographies on *Slavery: A Comparative Teaching Bibliography* (Waltham, Mass., 1977), "Slavery, A Supplementary Teaching Bibliography," *Slavery and Abolition* 1 (1980), 199–258 are of enormous usefulness. See also John D. Smith's (comp.) *Black Slavery in the Americas: An Interdisciplinary Bibliography*, 2 vols. (Westport, Conn., 1982), which promises to be equally valuable.

René Dubos, *Man Adapting* (New Haven, 1965), F.M. Burnet and D.D. White, *Natural History of Infectious Disease*, 4th ed. (Cambridge, Eng., 1972), and Ian Taylor and John Knowelden, *Principles of Epidemiology* (Boston, 1964) all provide fine introductions to medical history, while an excellent introduction to the impact of European diseases on the Caribbean region can be found in Alfred W. Crosby, *The Columbian Exchange* (Westport, Conn., 1972). P.M. Ashburn's classic, *The Ranks of Death: A Medical History of the Conquest of America* (New York, 1947), treats both European and African diseases in the region and portions of William H. McNeill's *Plagues and Peoples* (Garden City, N.Y., 1976) are also germane to the West Indies.

Indispensible to any effort to tracing eighteenth- and nineteenth-century Caribbean diseases is August Hirsch, *Handbook of Geographical and Historical Pathology*, 3 vols. (London, 1883–86). Crucial also are H. Harold Scott, *A History of Tropical Medicine*, 2 vols. (London, 1939), Henry Rose Carter, *Yellow Fever: An Epidemiological and Historical Study of its Place of Origin*, eds. Laura A. Carter and W.H. Frost (Baltimore, 1931), which treats much more than yellow fever, Folke Henschen, *The History and Geography of Disease*, trans. Joan Tate (New York, 1966), and Edwin H. Ackerknecht, *History and Geography of the Most Important Diseases* (New York, 1965). For eighteenth- and nineteenth-century medical journals, consult Samuel H. Scudder, *Catalogue of Scientific Serials . . . 1633–1876.* For twentieth-century tropical medicine, see George W. Hunter, William W. Frye, and J. Clyde Swartzwelder, *Manual of Tropical Medicine* (Philadelphia, 1956), the many relevant essays in Paul D. Hoeprich (ed.), *Infectious Disease* (Hagerstown, Md., 1972), Oscar Felsenfeld, *The Epidemiology of Tropical Diseases* (Springfield, Ill., 1966) and Charles Wilcocks and P.C.E. Manson-Bahr, *Manson's Tropical Diseases,* 17th ed. (Baltimore, 1974).

For specifically black-related health problems, consult Richard A. Williams (ed.), *Textbook of Black Related Diseases* (New York, 1975), Julian H. Lewis, *The Biology of the Negro* (Chicago, 1942), Todd L. Savitt, *Medicine and Slavery* (Urbana, Ill., 1978), and Kenneth F. Kiple and Virginia Himmelsteib King, *Another Dimension to the Black Diaspora: Diet, Disease and Racism* (New York, 1981).

For the *Columbian Exchange* of diseases with the New World, see Crosby's important contribution. For the illnesses that Iberia had to offer, consult Joaquin Villalba, *Epidemiologia española . . .* (Madrid, 1862), J.A.F. Ozanam, *Histoire médicale générale . . . ,* 2d ed., 4 vols. (Paris, 1835), and Pedro Laín Entralgo, et al. (eds.), *Historia universal de la medicina,* 7 vols. (Barcelona, 1971–75). Less has been done on diseases the Indians were accustomed to, save the possibility of their acquaintanceship with syphilis. The places to start, however, are Sherburne F. Cook, "The Incidence and Significance of Disease among the Aztecs and Related Tribes," *HAHR* 36 (1946), 220–35, Thomas A. Cockburn, "The Evolution of Infectious Disease," *International Record of Medicine,* 172 (1959), 493–508, Henschen, *History and Geography of Disease,* and Saul Jarcho, "Some Observations on Disease in Prehistoric North America," *BHM* 38 (1964), 11–15.

For early first- and second-hand reports of the rapidly changing New World disease environment, see Bartolome de las Casas, *Historia de las Indias,* 3 vols. (Mexico, 1951), Gonzalo Fernandez de Oviedo, *Historia general y natural de las Indias, islas, y tierra firme del mar oceano. . . . ,* 4 vols. (Madrid, 1851–55), and Antonio de Herrera y Tordesillas, *Historia general de los hechos de los Castellanos en las islas y tierra firme en el mar oceano,* 17 vols. (Buenos Aires, 1945). For modern attempts to sort out these reports, consult Carter, *Yellow Fever,* Ashburn, *Ranks of Death,* McNeill, *Plagues and Peoples,* and Carl Ortwin Sauer, *The Early Spanish Main* (Berkeley, Calif., 1966).

As for the "African Exchange," the literature on disease in West Africa is vast, but not systematically drawn together as yet. A fine introduction can be found in Gerald W. Hartwig and K. David Patterson (eds.), *Disease in African History* (Durham, N.C., 1978). Nineteenth-century observations of some importance include those of William Freeman Daniell, *Sketches of the Medical Topography and Native Diseases of the Gulf of Guinea, Western Africa* (London, 1849) and T. Winterbottom, *An Account of the Native Africans in the Neighbourhood of Sierra Leone,* 2 vols. (London, 1803). An important survey of the colonial empires may be found in William Malcolm Hailey's *An African Survey* (London, 1938), while modern problems are covered in superb fashion by Charles H. Hughes and John M. Hunter, "Diseases and Development in Africa," *SSM* 3 (1970), 443–93.

The impact of African disease on Europeans in Africa was highlighted by Philip D. Curtin in his seminal study, "Epidemiology and the Slave Trade," *Political Science Quarterly* 83 (1968), 190–216. See also Kenneth G. Davies, "The Living and the Dead: White Mortality in West Africa 1684–1732," in *Race and Slavery in the Western Hemisphere: Quantitative Studies,* eds. Stanley L. Engerman and Eugene D. Genovese (Princeton, N.J., 1975), 83–99 and H.M. Feinberg, "New Data on European Mortality in West Africa: The Dutch on the Gold Coast 1719–1760," *JAfH* 15 (1974), 357–71.

The nutritional status of West Africans put into the slave trade can be gleaned from numerous sources. Tadeuz Lewicki covers *West African Food in the Middle Ages: According to Arabic Sources* (London, 1974), while Frederick J. Simoons touches on African food taboos in *Eat Not this Flesh: Food Avoidance in the Old World* (Madison, Wisc., 1961), and Michael Gelfand explains *Diet and Tradition in African Culture* (Edinburgh, 1971). Elizabeth Isichei, *A History of the Igbo People* (New York, 1976) and Oliver Davis, *West Africa before the Europeans: Archaeology and Prehistory* (London, 1967), both also contain important data on West African diets.

Famine in Africa had become an important topic of late for African historians. Jill R. Dias, "Famine and Disease in the History of Angola, 1830–1930," *JAfH* 21 (1981), 349–78, and Joseph Miller, "Disease and Famine in the Agriculturally Marginal Zones of West-Central Africa," *JAfH* 23 (1982), 17–61 are both fine examples and contain important implications for West Africa. Studies of nutrition in modern West Africa abound. Good examples include Juan Papadakis, *Crop Ecological Survey in West Africa . . .*, 2 vols. (Rome, 1966), James L. Newman, "Dietary and Nutritional Conditions," in *Contemporary Africa: Geography and Change*, eds. C. Gregory Knight and James L. Newman (Englewood Cliffs, N.J., 1976), Michael Latham, *Human Nutrition in Tropical Africa* (Rome, 1965), Derrick B. Jelliffe, *Infant Nutrition in the Subtropics and Tropics*, 2d ed. (Geneva, 1968), and Jacques M. May and Donna L. McLellan, *The Ecology of Malnutrition in the French Speaking Countries of West Africa and Madagascar* (New York, 1968).

Indispensible to tracing disease from West Africa to the New World are Ashburn, *Ranks of Death*, Carter, *Yellow Fever*, Curtin, "Epidemiology and the Slave Trade," and R. Hoeppli, *Parasitic Diseases in Africa and the Western Hemisphere: Early Documentation and Transmission by the Slave Trade* (Basel, 1969). Useful also is H. Harold Scott's, "The Influence of the Slave Trade in the Spread of Tropical Disease," *TRSTMH* 37 (1943), 169–88.

Morbidity and/or mortality in the slave trade have been treated by Herbert S. Klein, *The Middle Passage* (Princeton, N.J., 1978); Robert Louis Stein, *The French Slave Trade in the Eighteenth Century* (Madison, Wisc., 1979); Johannes Postma, "Mortality in the Dutch Slave Trade, 1675–1795," in *The Uncommon Market: Essays in the Economic History of the Atlantic Slave Trade*, eds. Henry A. Gemery and Jan S. Hogendorn (New York, 1979); Joseph C. Miller, "Mortality in the Atlantic Slave Trade: Statistical Evidence on Causality," *JIH* 11 (1981), 385–423; and Colin Palmer, *Human Cargoes; the British Slave Trade to Spanish America, 1700–1739* (Urbana, Ill., 1981).

For the heights of newly arrived Africans, which speak to questions of West African nutrition, see Barry Higman, "Growth in Afro-Caribbean Slave Population," *AJPA* 50 (1979) 373–85; Manuel Moreno Fraginals, "Africa in Cuba: A Quantitative Analysis of the African Population in the Island of Cuba," in *Comparative Perspectives on Slavery in New World Plantation Societies*, ed. Vera Rubin and Arthur Tuden (New York, 1977), 187–204; David Eltis, "Nutritional Trends in Africa and the Americas: Heights of Africans 1819–1839," *JIH* 12 (1982), 453–75; Gerald Friedman, "The Heights of Slaves in Trinidad"; and Robert W. Fogel, Stanley L. Engerman, and James Trussell, "Exploring the Uses of Data on Height," both in *Social Science History* 6 (1982), 482–515 and 401–21, respectively.

For early physicians' accounts that provide information on disease and slavery in the Islands, see Richard Ligon, *A True and Exact History of the Island of Barbados* (London, 1657); Hans Sloane, *A Voyage to the Islands, Madera, Barbados, Nieves, S. Christophers and Jamaica . . .*, 2 vols. (London, 1707); William Hillary, *Observations on the Changes of Air and the Concomitant Epidemical Diseases in the Island of Barbados* (London, 1759); and Benjamin Moseley, *A Treatise on Tropical Diseases* (London, 1789). The observations of sharp-eyed nonphysician visitors to the hemisphere in the eighteenth and early nineteenth centuries are also valuable. See, for example, Abbé Guillaume Raynal, *A Philosophical and Political History of the Settlements and Trade of the Europeans in the East and West Indies*, 8 vols., trans. J.O. Justamond (London, 1788); André Pierre Ledru, *Viaje a la isla de Puerto Rico en el año 1797* (Rio Piedras, 1957); and Alexander von Humboldt, *Political Essay on the Kingdom of New Spain*, 4 vols., trans. John Black (London, 1811).

Slave diets and diseases are treated from a planter's perspective in Edward Long, *The History of Jamaica*, 3 vols. (London, 1774); Bryan Edwards, *The History, Civil and Commercial of the British West Indies*, 5 vols. (London, 1819); and M.L.E. Moreau de Saint-Méry, *Description . . . de la partie Française de l'isle de Saint Domingue*, 2 vols. (Philadelphia, 1797–98).

Perhaps the most useful materials on slave health are contained in physicians' and planters' guides to the subject. Illustrative are Robert Collins, *Practical Rules for the Management and Medical Treatment of Negro Slaves in the Sugar Colonies* (London, 1811); James Thomson, *A Treatise on the Diseases of Negroes as they Occur in the Island of Jamaica; with Observations on the Country Remedies* (Jamaica, 1820); Thomas Dancer, *The Medical Assistant; a Jamaica Practice of Physic; Designed Chiefly for the Use of Families and Plantations* (Kingston, 1801); James Grainger, *An Essay on the More Common West India Diseases and . . . some Hints on the Management, etc. of Negroes,* 2d ed. (Edinburgh, 1802); Thomas Roughley, *The Jamaican Planter's Guide* (London, 1823); Jean Barthelemy Danzille, *Observations sur les maladies des Negres . . . ,* 2d ed., 2 vols. (Paris, 1892); and Ramon Piña y Peñuela, *Topografía médica de la isla de Cuba* (Havana, 1855). Crucial also are the few extant memoirs and diaries of planters such as John Riland, *Memoirs of a West-India Planter* (London, 1827) and M.G. Lewis, *Journal of a West India Proprietor, 1815–1817* (London, 1929).

For the epidemiological observations of military physicians, see John Hunter, *Observations on the Diseases of the Army in Jamaica* (London, 1788); Robert Jackson, *A Sketch of the History and Cure of Febrile Diseases: Most Particularly as they Appear in the West Indies Among the Soldiers of the British Army* (London, 1791); and William Lempriere, *Practical Observations on the Diseases of the Army of Jamaica . . . ,* 2 vols. (London, 1799).

For articles addressing specific slave complaints, see for example James Maxwell, "Pathological Inquiry into the Nature of Cachexia Africana, as Generally Connected with Dirteating," *Jamaica Physical Journal* 2 (1835), 409–35; David Mason's, "A Descriptive Account of . . . Yaws," and "On Atrophia a Ventriculo (mal d' estomac) or Dirt Eating," both in the *Edinburgh Medical and Surgical Journal* 35 (1831), 52–66 and 39 (1833), 289–96, respectively; and John Hancock, "Observations on Tetanus Infantum or Lock-jaw of Infants," *Edinburgh Medical and Surgical Journal* 35 (1831), 343–7.

Works taking one side or the other of the abolition controversy also contain much on slave health. An extremely perceptive discussion of slave nutrition may be found in James Stephen, *The Slavery of the British West India Colonies Delineated . . . ,* 2 vols. (London, 1824–30). Planter testimony on slave provisions may be found in William Dickson (ed.), *Mitigation of Slavery* (London, 1814) and Alexander Barclay, *A Practical View of the Present State of Slavery in the West Indies . . .* (London, 1828).

Printed sources containing statistics on black-related diseases for the slaves are scarce. Some data can be found in William Sells, *Remarks on the Condition of Slaves in the Island of Jamaica* (London, 1823) and Angél Jose Crowley, *Ensayo estadístico-médico de la mortalidad de la diocesis de la Habana durante el año de 1843* (Havana, 1845). The most important data on black and white morbidity and mortality may be found in Alexander M. Tulloch, "Statistical Report on the Sickness, Mortality, and Invaliding among the Troops in the West Indies," in Great Britain, *Parliamentary Papers* XL, 1837–38, *Accounts and Papers* V (London, 1838). K.H. Uttley's efforts to provide a statistical record of mortality from various diseases in Antigua from about 1850 to 1960 has resulted in numerous articles on the model of "The Mortality and Epidemiology of Typhoid Fever in the Coloured Inhabitants of Antigua, West Indies over the Last Hundred Years," *WIMJ* 9 (1960), 114–28. They deserve to be drawn together under a single cover, although most but not all appeared in the *West Indian Medical Journal* during the 1960s. Jorge Eduardo LeRoy y Cassa embarked on a similar effort for Cuba during the first part of this century with perhaps the most useful his *Estudios sobre la mortalidad de la Habana durante el siglo xix . . .* (Havana, 1913).

Planters' accounts and physicians' observations on slave nutrition and disease are rare for the Spanish and French islands, particularly the Spanish. Much, however, can be gleaned from eighteenth- and nineteenth-century general studies. See, for example, Fray Iñigo Abbad y Lasierra, *Historia geográfica, civil y natural de la isla de San Juan Bautista de Puerto Rico* (San Juan, 1886); M.L.E. Moreau de Saint-Méry, *Description topographique, physique, civil, politique et historique de la partie Française de l' Isle de Saint Domingue,* 2 vols.

(Philadelphia, 1797–98); M. Moreau de Jonnes, *Histoire physique des antilles Françaises, savoiri la Martinique et les isles de la Guadeloupe* (Paris, 1822); Jacobo de la Pezuela y Lobo, *Diccionario geográfico, estadístico historico, de la isla de Cuba*, 4 vols. (Madrid, 1863–66); Ramon de la Sagra, *Historia económico-política y estadística de la isla de Cuba . . .* (Havana, 1831); and Jose Antonio Saco, *Historia de la esclavitud de la raza Africana en el nuevo mundo y en especial en los paises Americo-Hispanos*, 4 vols. (Havana, 1938–40).

Travel accounts also offer a window on slave nutrition and disease and the Spanish islands, especially Cuba, were well visited during the nineteenth century. Among those with the best eye for these details were David Turnbull, *Travels in the West: Cuba with Notices of Porto Rico and the Slave Trade* (London, 1840), John George Wurdemann, *Notes on Cuba . . .* (Boston, 1944), and J.D. Flinter, *An Account of the Present State of the Island of Puerto Rico* (London, 1834). Moving into twentieth-century scholarship, the best general history of the Caribbean remains that of John Parry and P.M. Sherlock, *A Short History of the West Indies* (London, 1956). Unfortunately Parry and Sherlock neglect somewhat the Spanish islands, which Eric Williams, *From Columbus to Castro: The History of the Caribbean 1492–1969* (New York, 1970), has attempted to remedy.

Aspects of slave health and diseases in the Islands have been treated in general studies such as Noel Deerr, *The History of Sugar* (London, 1949); Richard Sheridan, *Sugar and Slavery: An Economic History of the British West Indies, 1623–1775* (Baltimore, 1974); and Ramiro Guerra y Sanchez, *Azucar y poblacion en las Antillas* (Havana, 1927).

Studies of a particular slave system that treat slave nutriments and illnesses include Carlos Larrazabel Blanco, *Los Negros y la esclavitud en Santo Domingo* (Santo Domingo, 1975); Luis Díaz Soler, *La Historia de la esclavitud Negra en Puerto Rico* (Madrid, 1953); Manuel Moreno Fraginals, *El Ingenio: el complejo economico-social Cubano del azucar 1760–1860* (Havana, 1964); Frank W. Pitman, "Slavery on British West India Plantations in the Eighteenth Century," *JNH* 11 (1926), 584–668; Richard S. Dunn, *Sugar and Slaves: The Rise of the Planter Class in the English West Indies 1624–1713* (Chapel Hill, N.C., 1972); Orlando Patterson, *The Sociology of Slavery* (London, 1967); and Barry Higman, *Slave Population and Economy in Jamaica, 1807–1834* (New York, 1976).

Excellent examinations of plantations include J. Harry Bennett, *Bondsmen and Bishops: Slavery and Apprenticeship on the Codrington Plantations of Barbados, 1710–1838* (Berkeley, Calif., 1958); Jerome S. Handler and Frederick W. Lange, *Plantation Slavery in Barbados: An Archeological and Historical Investigation* (Cambridge, Mass., 1978); and Michael Craton and James Walvin, *A Jamaican Plantation. The History of Worthy Park 1670–1970* (London, 1970).

The medical histories of individual islands generally contain little on the slaves. Important exceptions are Francisco Eujenio Moscoso Puello, *Apuntes para la historia de la medicina de la isla de Santo Domingo* (Santo Domingo, 1977); Salvador Arana-Soto, *Historia de la Medicina Puerto Riqueña hasta 1898* (San Juan, 1974) and *Historia de nuestras calamidades* (San Juan, 1968); and Manuel Quevado y Baez, *Historia de la medicina y cirugia de Puerto Rico* (Santurce, 1946). For a general overview, see Francisco Guerra, "Medicina Colonial en Hispano America," in Pedro Laín Entralgo et al. (eds.), *Historia universal de la medicina*, 7 vols. (Barcelona, 1971–75), vol. 4.

What slaves ate can be gotten at from different directions. Great Britain's *Parliamentary Papers* contain many planter testimonies as to the kinds and quantities of foods they claimed were available to the slaves. Laws such as those contained in the various slave "reglamentos" for Cuba and Puerto Rico or in the British slave codes give an idea of the ideal sought. See, for example, Elsa Goveia, "The West Indian Slave Laws of the Eighteenth Century," *Revista de ciencias sociales* 4 (1960), 75–106. Richard W. Bean, "Food Imports into the British West Indies: 1680–1845," in *Comparative Perspectives on Slavery in the New World Plantation Societies*, ed. Rubin and Tuden, has attempted to determine precisely what was available from imported sources while other essays in the Rubin and Tuden volume have examined plantation records of amounts of foods allotted. Francisco Morales Padron, "La vida cotidiana en una hacienda de esclavos," *Revista del instituto de cultura Puertoriqueña* 4 (1961) and Berta Cabanillas de Rodriguez, *El Puertoriqueño y su alimentacion a traves de su historia (siglos XVI al XIX)* (San Juan, 1973), both give accounts of slave nutriments, as from a larger perspective do Cabanillas, *Origins de los habitos alimenticos del pueblo de Puerto Rico* (Madrid, 1955) and John Parry, "Plantation and Provision Ground: An Historical Sketch of the Introduction of Food Crops in Jamaica," *Revista de Historia de America* 37 (1955), 1–20. See Richard B. Sheridan, "The Crisis of Slave Subsistence in the British West Indies during and after the American Revolution," *WMQ* 33 (1976), 615–41, for examples of how political circumstances could bring hardship to the slaves. Collins, *Practical Rules* and other physician accounts also discuss slave food allotments.

Studies of the diet and diseases of the modern Caribbean are so numerous that an attempt will be made here to list only a few examples. For a guide to nutritional analysis see Sir Stanley Davidson et al., *Human Nutrition and Dietetics* (Edinburgh, 1975). For diets earlier in this century, consult Great Britain, Economic Advisory Council, Committee on Nutrition in the Colonial Empire, *Nutrition in the Colonial Empire*, 2 parts (London, 1939), B.S. Platt, *Nutrition in the British West Indies* (London, 1946), and Epaminondas Quintana, "El problema dietetico del Caribe," *America Indigena* 2 (1942), 1–28. For modern studies, see Diva Sanjur, *Puerto Rican Food Habits* (Ithaca, N.Y., 1970), and Jaques M. May and Donna L. McLellan, *The Ecology of Malnutrition in the Caribbean* (New York, 1973).

Scott, *History of Tropical Medicine*, discusses many of the Caribbeans' health problems during this century, while Hunter, Frye, and Swartzwelder, *Manual of Tropical Medicine*, provide a listing of every disease peculiar to a Caribbean country. M.T. Ashcroft has done perhaps more than any other individual of late to highlight the health problems of the Caribbean past and present and no effort will be made here to list his numerous publications save for his very valuable, "History and general survey of the helminth and protozoal infections of the West Indies," *Annals of Tropical Medicine and Parasitology* 59 (1965), 479–93.

To answer questions about slave demography is, of course, a basic reason for biological studies of slavery. Useful for placing various islands in demographic perspective are Higman, *Slave Population and Economy in Jamaica*, and many of his other works already cited. In addition, see G.W. Roberts, *The Population of Jamaica* (Cambridge, Eng., 1957); Richard Dunn, "The Barbados Census of 1680: Profile of the Richest Colony in English America," *WMQ* 26 (1969), 3–30; my own *Blacks in Colonial Cuba 1774–1899* (Gainesville, Fla., 1976); Jack E. Eblen, "On the Natural Increase of Slave Populations: The Example of the Cuban Black Populations 1775–1900," in *Race and Slavery in the Western Hemisphere: Quantitative Studies*, eds. Stanley L. Engerman and Eugene D. Genovese (Princeton, N.J., 1974); Michael Craton, "Jamaican Slave Mortality: Fresh Light from Worthy Park, Longville and the Tharp Estates," *Journal of Caribbean History* 3 (1971), 1–27; Stanley L. Engerman, "Some Economic and Demographic Comparisons of Slavery in the United States and the British West Indies," *The Economic History Review* 29 (1976), 258–75; K.H. Uttley, "The Birth, Stillbirth, Death and Fertility Rates in the Coloured Populations of Antigua, West Indies, from 1857 to 1956," *TRSTMH* 55 (1961), 69–78; and Robert V. Wells, *The Population of the British Colonies before 1776* (Princeton, N.J., 1975). See also Robert W. Fogel and Stanley L. Engerman, "Recent Findings in the Study of Slave Demography and Family Structure," *SSR* 63 (1979), 566–89.

Medical and biological studies of slavery in the hemisphere are just beginning to appear or are still forthcoming. For the United States, see Savitt, *Medicine and Slavery*, and Kiple and King, *Another Dimension to the Black Diaspora*. For Colombia see David Lee Chandler, "Health and Slavery: A Study of Health Conditions among Negro Slaves in the Viceroyalty of New Granada and its Associated Slave Trade," Ph.D. dissertation, Tulane University, 1972. For Brazil, Donald B. Cooper's "Brazil's Long Fight Against Epidemic Disease, 1849–1917, with Special Emphasis on Yellow Fever," *BHM* 5 (1975),

672–96, represents the beginning of what promises to be a serious attempt to examine systematically the impact of disease on Brazil and its peoples. Dauril Alden and Joseph C. Miller, "The Fatal Exchange: The Origins and Dissemination of Smallpox via the Slave Trade from Angola to Brazil, Circa 1560–1830," Mary Karasch, "African Mortality and Epidemic Disease in Nineteenth-Century Rio de Janeiro," James D. Goodyear, "The Slave Trade, Public Health and Yellow Fever: The Image of Africa in Brazil," all presented papers at the 1982 American Historical Association's annual meeting, which soon will be published as articles or portions of books.

For the Caribbean, see Kenneth F. Kiple and Virginia H. Kiple, "Deficiency Diseases in the Caribbean," *JIH* 11 (1980), 197–215; Robert Dirks, "Resource Fluctuations and Competitive Transformations in West Indian Societies," in *Extinction and Survival in Human Populations*, eds. Charles D. Laughlin, Jr. and Ivan A. Brady (New York, 1978) and his forthcoming *Black Saturnalia*, and Richard B. Sheridan, "Mortality and Medical Treatment of Slaves in the British West Indies," in *Race and Slavery in the Western Hemisphere*, eds. Engerman and Genovese, along with his forthcoming study of the medical treatment of Caribbean slaves. See also Herbert S. Klein and Stanley L. Engerman, "Fertility Differentials Between Slaves in the United States and the West Indies: a Note on Lactation Practices and Their Possible Implications," *WMQ* 35 (1978), 357–73. And for an exciting method of confirming malnutrition in slave populations, see Robert S. Corruccini, Jerome S. Handler, Robert J. Mutaw, and Frederick W. Lange, "Osteology of a Slave Burial Population from Barbados, West Indies," *AJPA* 59 (1982), 443–59; and Jerome Handler and Robert S. Corruccini, "Plantation Life in Barbados: A Physical Anthropological Analysis," *JIH* 14 (1983), 65–90.

Finally for studies that have attempted to demonstrate the wide-ranging historical implications of the Caribbean's disease environment for blacks, see Kiple and King, *Another Dimension*, Francisco Guerra, "The Influence of Disease on Race, Logistics and Colonization in the Antilles," *JTMH* 69 (1966), 23–35, and Gary Puckrein, "Climate, Health and Black Labor in the English Americas," *American Studies* 13 (1979), 179–93.

INDEX

Abascal, Dr. Horacio, 225 n33
Abénon, Lucien-Rene, 180
Accra, 32
ainhum, 136
akee, 87, 100, 101
amebic dysentery, 13, 61, 62, 65, 74, 135,
   136, 242 n4
  see also dysentery; flux
amelioration of slavery, 67, 71, 77, 106,
   118–19, 133–4, 257–8 n27
Anguilla, 165
Antigua, 94, 115, 116, 117, 121, 122, 131,
   133, 137, 145, 150, 162, 163, 164, 169,
   175, 241 n89, 246 n62
Ascaris, see worms
Ashburn, P. M., 10
Asiento, 60
avocados, 81, 87

bacillary dysentery, 62, 74
  see also dysentery; flux
Bahama Islands, 46, 49, 69, 76, 106, 147,
   149, 164, 169
bananas, 66, 79
Barbados, 7, 16, 20, 41, 44, 67, 68, 69, 71–
   2, 77, 91, 94, 95, 98, 105, 106, 107,
   110, 114, 117, 118–19, 121, 132, 142,
   143, 144, 145, 146, 147, 149, 150, 153,
   164, 165, 166, 169, 170, 175, 176, 179–
   80, 181, 183, 185, 186, 191 n5, 223
   n12, 224 n14, 224 n15, 233 n49, 234
   n72, 235 n81, 241 n89, 243 n61, 255
   n70, 256 n11, 258 n36
"barbados leg," *see* filariasis
Bean, Richard, 77
beef, 77, 78, 79, 80, 81, 83, 85, 93, 218 n7,
   225 n27
beriberi
  adult, 96–103

confused with other illnesses, 98–103,
   136, 137, 139, 226 n44
etiology, 96
infantile, 125–9
and Rockefeller researchers, 226–7 n48
symptoms, 96, 97
in West Africa, 29, 31, 37
Bermuda, 69, 174
Bight of Biafra, 13, 58
Bight of Guinea, 64
bilharziasis (schistosomiasis), 13, 32, 135
Black Caribs and sickle trait, 16, 150, 249
   n98
black-related disease susceptibilities
  to *Ascaris,* 73, 217 n1
  to beriberi, 226 n44
  to cholera, 146–8
  to cold, 22, 66, 67
  to filariasis, 21, 73
  to guinea worm, 21, 73
  to hypertension, 46–7
  to iron deficiency anemia, 38–9
  to lactose intolerance, 40–3
  to leprosy, 21, 139
  to pneumonia, 13, 21–2, 143–4
  to rickets, 42–3
  to tetanus, 21
  to *Trichuris,* 73, 217 n1
  to tuberculosis, 140–4
  to typhoid, 145–6
  to yaws, 21, 139, 244 n32
blacks
  birthweight, *see* low birthweight
  bone density, 45
  calcium deficiency, 39–43, 244 n15
  elevated lead levels, 205 n24
  growth patterns, 43–5
  sex ratios at birth, 48
  vitamin A mobilization, 219 n24